Teaching Young Children in Multicultural Classrooms
Issues, Concepts, and Strategies

Third Edition

Teaching Young Children in Multicultural Classrooms
Issues, Concepts, and Strategies

Third Edition

Wilma Robles de Meléndez and Vesna Beck
Nova Southeastern University

WADSWORTH
CENGAGE Learning™

Australia • Brazil • Japan • Korea • Mexico • Singapore • Spain • United Kingdom • United States

Teaching Young Children in Multicultural Classrooms: Issues, Concepts, and Strategies, Third Edition
Wilma Robles de Meléndez and Vesna Beck

Acquistions Editor: Chris Shortt

Assistant Editor: Caitlin Cox

Editorial Assistant: Linda Stewart

Technology Project Manager: Ashley Cronin

Marketing Manager: Kara Parsons

Marketing Communications Manager:
Martha Pfeiffer

Project Manager, Editorial Production:
Samen Iqbal

Creative Director: Rob Hugel

Art Director: Maria Epes

Print Buyer: Paula Vang

Permissions Editor: Margaret Chamberlain-Gaston

Production Service: Rebecca Logan,
Newgen–Austin

Photo Researcher: Mandy Groszko

Copy Editor: Jonelle Seitz

Cover Designer: Bartay Studio

Cover Image: © Cengage Learning ECE
Photo Library

Compositor: Newgen

For product information and technology assistance, contact us at
Cengage Learning Customer & Sales Support, 1-800-354-9706.
For permission to use material from this text or product,
submit all requests online at **www.cengage.com/permissions.**
Further permissions questions can be e-mailed to
permissionrequest@cengage.com.

Library of Congress Control Number: 2008941619

Student Edition:
ISBN-13: 978-1-4283-7698-4
ISBN-10: 1-4283-7698-4

Wadsworth
10 Davis Drive
Belmont, CA 94002-3098
USA

Cengage Learning is a leading provider of customized learning solutions with office locations around the globe, including Singapore, the United Kingdom, Australia, Mexico, Brazil, and Japan. Locate your local office at **www.cengage.com/international.**

Cengage Learning products are represented in Canada by Nelson Education, Ltd.

To learn more about Wadsworth, visit **www.cengage.com/wadsworth.**
Purchase any of our products at your local college store or at our preferred online store **www.ichapters.com.**

Printed in U.S.A.
2 3 4 5 6 7 12 11 10 09

CONTENTS

CHAPTER 3 Families in Our Classrooms: Many Ways, Many Voices

CHAPTER 4 Who Is the Child? Developmental Characteristics of Young Children in a Diverse Society

PART II   **Exploring the Roots of Multicultural Education: Issues and Directions**

PART III   Into Action: Implementing a Culturally Appropriate Program for All Children

CHAPTER 7   The Classroom, Where Words Become Action

CHAPTER 8   Preparing to Bring Ideas into Action

CHAPTER 9   Activities and Resources for Multicultural Teaching: A World of Possibilities!

CHAPTER 10 **A World of Resources: Engaging Families, Friends, and the Community**

APPENDICES

PREFACE

We are as proud of being Americans as we are of our own cultural heritages. We also feel proud when we hear and see that so many people still consider our country the bastion of freedom and hope. This pride is diminished, however, whenever we witness prejudice, discrimination, and unfairness against some members of our society. Instead of engaging in philosophical and theoretical discussions about such injustices, we, as educators, need to look for practical solutions that can effectively address the challenge of living in a pluralistic society. That solution is found in education. Our belief that people can learn to see the sameness in all has led us to write this book. Envisioning empowering classrooms where our young children will find themselves and their cultures validated is the dream that sustains this work. Because we believe early childhood teachers are the cornerstone of educational success, we dedicate this work as a source of ideas that will allow them to create such classrooms for all children.

Writing this book is a personal and professional journey for us—personal because both of us came to the United States as immigrants and had the opportunity to witness firsthand the inadequacies of our educational system to provide for the needs of students from diverse backgrounds. Our professional experiences as professors of early childhood education at Nova Southeastern University guided us in selecting the content and creating the conceptual scheme of this book.

| PURPOSE OF THE BOOK

The primary purpose of the book is to serve as a text for teacher candidates who already have some theoretical background in child development and curriculum development. This includes undergraduate students who are getting ready to become early childhood educators as well as practicing teachers who want to be recertified in a new major. The book can be used as a primary text for courses in early childhood undergraduate and graduate programs.

The secondary purpose of the book is to be a resource for practicing early childhood professionals who need to learn about diversity and multiculturalism. Many components of the book, such as chapter activities and lists of children's books, are intended to assist practitioners in creating more developmentally and culturally appropriate curricula and classroom environments conducive to young children's learning.

Our book is about organizing and developing culturally responsive learning environments where diversity is celebrated and explored for young children from birth to 8 years old. As we know, this book is not the only one of its kind. Many fine publications exist that address this topic very eloquently. Some works in the current market are very specialized and more narrowly focused than our book. For example, some books address only developmentally appropriate practice, whereas others are solely about the antibiased curriculum. Although we recognize the value of the specialized approach, we wanted to create a book that is comprehensive in scope and presents diversity issues in a more complete context of our society. Diversity exists in sociological, historical, political, developmental, and instructional contexts. This book presents the multifaceted approach to diversity as it relates to the education of young children.

The selection of content and the conceptual scheme for the book came from our experiences with our very diverse undergraduate and graduate student population in south Florida. As one of the most multicultural regions in the United States, south Florida teachers mirror the area's rich demographics. Many of the early childhood teacher candidates are bilingual and come from a multitude of Latin and Caribbean countries. As future teachers, they have a special desire to facilitate tolerance and acceptance of cultural and ethnic differences among young children. The comprehensive approach of our book is also the result of our realization that many times early childhood professionals and teacher candidates who work in multicultural and diverse communities do not live in them. Because of this, they tend to practice acceptance of diversity in a very limited manner in their classrooms or other places of work. Many do not understand that multiculturalism is a very personal part of today's society that permeates all aspects of life at any time and in any place.

We believe that, whether white or "people of color," whether native-born or immigrants, early childhood educators need to have a knowledge base that promotes a more holistic understanding of diversity and the role it plays in the lives of young children and in our society. We believe that the comprehensive approach to the content we chose in our book achieves that goal.

ORGANIZATION OF THE BOOK

The book is organized in three parts. Part I deals with social foundations and theory of multicultural instruction. It contains the current historical perspectives of multiculturalism, future trends, and the social and psychological developmental influences that affect young children. Part II explores the past and current issues and directions of multicultural education. It explores the historical background and different approaches to teaching diversity. Part III provides resources in the form of guidelines and ideas for classroom implementation. Several actual multicultural instruments, curriculum plans, and classroom techniques are presented.

CONCEPTUAL DEVELOPMENT

The book balances theory and practice, which makes it suitable for the several purposes mentioned earlier. The theoretical component is necessary for several reasons. *First*, we believe it is good practice to base the recommendations and conclusions on a sound scholarly knowledge base and proven practices. *Second*, teachers need to understand the principles and theories that underlie practices related to multicultural education to know how to implement them properly. *Third*, the theoretical background provides a framework for multiculturalism that makes it fit into the larger context of teaching and learning. The practical aspect of the book is a consequence of our strong commitment to practitioners in the field of early childhood education and to the commitment of bonding theory and practice.

Four types of activities are provided throughout the book: "In Action . . . ," "Snapshots," "Focus on Classroom Practices," and "Things to Do . . . ." They are intended to provide exercises, promote discussions, and present practical ideas. Each "In Action . . ." activity is accompanied with questions and other information related to the material discussed in the body of the chapter. "Snapshots" are used to present events or excerpts from literature related to the information in the chapter. "Focus on Classroom Practices" features offer examples of activities and suggestions for classroom application of the theoretical concepts discussed in each chapter. The activities at the end of the chapter, "Things to Do . . . ," provide additional practice for individuals and groups.

The activities in these special features of the book are intended for use with both pre-service and practicing teachers. We believe that most examples can be adapted to both audiences with a little imagination.

SPECIAL FEATURES

We have also chosen Barbara, the kindergarten teacher, to go on our multicultural journey. We believe that she is a typical teacher with whom many of the readers will identify. Her joys and dilemmas are familiar. As Barbara resolves her problems throughout the book, we hope you will as well.

Each chapter also contains a reference list to provide additional sources of study. The appendices include a detailed children's literature list as well as other resources.

NEW TO THIS EDITION

Several new elements have been added to this edition. Some changes were implemented as a result of the reviewers' suggestions, and other material was added to make this edition more application oriented and more current. Additional information was added about children with special needs and second language learners. Data on demographics and other information related to the multicultural issues have been updated. Barbara's journal entries, Internet resources, and chapter summaries have been added to each chapter. In addition, the instructor's manual will have a new format, and a new website for the book is also available with important downloads.

Terminology

Discussions about multiculturalism mirror the fluid sociopolitical climate of our society. Because the terminology of the field is in a constant state of flux, in this edition, we made several changes to reflect current trends. *America* was the term we used extensively in the first edition to refer to the United States of *America*. In the second and third editions, we have substituted *United States* for *America* whenever possible to reflect our awareness that people of North, Central, and South America claim the name *American*. In our experience in dealing with people in the United States and abroad, however, it is clear that they understand who monopolizes the term. Furthermore, people of Central America prefer to refer to themselves as belonging to their country. When was the last time you heard a Mexican refer to herself as "Central American"? Similarly, South Americans most often refer to themselves as "Argentinos" and "Brazileros," not "Americanos" (del Sur). In Europe and Asia, "American" and "Americans" has always been understood to be "of the United States."

We also decided to use the official terminology of the U.S. Census Bureau when referring to the various ethnic and cultural groups. The terms *white* and *black* are used despite their social and political connotations. In some instances, the race needs to be the predominant descriptor for both. This is particularly true of the term *black*, which cannot be interchangeable with African American in every instance.

Hispanic is the most widely used term to describe the various populations of Central and South America. We have decided to continue using it in this edition, but we also added the term *Latino*. Using both allows for more flexibility and respects the preferences of the members of this vastly diverse group.

Until 2000, the term *Pacific Islanders* included all the people of the Pacific Island nations. In 2000, the Census Bureaus created a separate category for *Native Hawaiians* for people who identify themselves as "Hawaiian" or "Part Hawaiian."

The Census Bureau does not have a classification for *Non-European Americans*. The term *other* is still used for groups that classify themselves as neither white nor black. We do not agree with that terminology and continue to use the term *Non-European Americans* to refer to all those born or descending from Europeans. This group consists of Asian Americans, Hispanics, African Americans, Pacific Islanders, Native Hawaiians, Caribbean Islanders, Arabs, and Middle Easterners, as well as people of all native Indian nations and Alaskan natives.

Children's Books

Children's books have been updated in every chapter with more recent publications. Some of the classic and important older publications remain because of their timeless value. Most children's literature resources are found in the "Literacy Connections . . ."

boxes interspersed throughout each chapter. They have been enriched with selected titles from the old Children's Literature Corner, which has been eliminated from the end of each chapter. Lists of children's books have also been updated in Appendix A.

Barbara's Journal

We have included an entry from Barbara's journal in every chapter in this edition. This was done as a result of many suggestions we received from readers and reviewers. Each vignette represents a realistic situation that an early childhood professional may face in the classroom. At first glance, Barbara is an experienced teacher; however, she is on the same journey as the reader when it comes to learning about multicultural education. The situations in which Barbara finds herself are taken from experiences of our students and are realistic for many teachers of diverse groups of young children.

Chapter Summaries

Chapter summaries are another new element of this edition. They were included to provide a brief overview of the content and to allow both teachers and students to peruse the material at a quick glance. This feature was added at the request of readers and reviewers.

Internet Websites

This edition contains websites at the end of each chapter that correspond to the themes and concepts presented in the content. They are not the only technological resources available, and we encourage all readers to search for their own Internet resources.

Book Website

The Internet is an invaluable resource and research tool for most of us. We recognize that as such it needs to be linked to this book. The book companion website for this edition offers free downloads and study tools for students, including chapter quizzes, flashcards, and exercises. Among the resources for teachers are the instructor's manual, a sample syllabus, and a template for a lesson plan. We invite all readers to visit the website as part of the journey through this book. To access the website, go to www.cengage .com/education/demelendez and click on any number of links that interest you.

Professional Standards Portfolio

The Standards Portfolio remains a part of this edition. It is a very important element of the book that has received much praise from students and teachers. The portfolio provides a unique experience because of its wide use in undergraduate and graduate programs as well as state and local agencies. As in the previous edition, we used the standards of the National Association of Education for Young Children (NAEYC) as the framework for the professional portfolio because they represent the most important and comprehensive guidelines for theoretical and practical aspects of the early childhood profession. We continue to correlate the NAEYC standards with widely known Interstate New Teacher Assessment and Support Consortium (INTASC) standards to broaden the application of the portfolio. The INTASC standards are generic and appropriate for a very wide audience of professionals. The portfolio provides a special opportunity for teacher candidates and early childhood practitioners to gain valuable professional experiences through the process.

Chapters

All chapters have been revised to reflect the suggestions of the reviewers and as we thought appropriate. The specific changes in each chapter are listed here:

- Chapter 1: Updated demographic information.
- Chapter 2: Updated information about ethnicities.
- Chapter 3: Refined information about child development as it relates to the role of the family, family models, and the family's ways of socialization.
- Chapter 4: Added information about development, identity, and socialization of young children.
- Chapter 5: Revised and condensed some of the historical information and added information about equality, ESOL children, and children with special needs. New children's books were added.
- Chapter 6: Provided more detail about specific curriculum models and culturally appropriate practice (DCAP).
- Chapter 7: Added information about children with special needs and ESL children.
- Chapter 8: Content was updated with additional ideas for instructional planning, and new children's books were added.
- Chapter 9: Content was updated to include users of art and thematic teaching. New children's books were added.
- Chapter 10: Content was updated regarding family and community involvement, and new children's books were added.

Appendices

Appendix A has been updated with new children's books. Appendix B, which contains addresses and websites of organizations that deal with multiculturalism and diversity, has been updated.

Illustrations

Some new illustrations were added to broaden the diversity depicted in the book. Asian Americans, Native Americans, and others are included in the new edition. Some of the old pictures were removed at the recommendation of reviewers, and many new ones were added.

Instructor's Manual

The instructor's manual has a new format and is available in hard copy and online at www.cengage.com/education/demelendez. The purpose of the manual is to assist teachers in planning instruction based on this book. We have included what we believe are the essential elements that teachers require for planning. Each chapter is presented with purpose, objectives, key terms, and teaching strategies, as well as quizzes and further resources. A set of PowerPoint slides have been created for classroom use and are also available on the website.

| ACKNOWLEDGMENTS

No work is ever accomplished without the support of family members, colleagues, and friends. We thank our families for their love, understanding, and support of this work. Thank you for staying at our side through many long hours, lost holidays, and working weekends. We are thankful to our students who generously continue to share their experiences and inspire us to continue our work in the field of multiculturalism and diversity. Their ideas and concerns have helped shape this work.

We wish to acknowledge the support of Caitlin Cox, assistant editor at Cengage, and particularly our editor, Chris Shortt, for their guidance and patience.

We extend our appreciation to the reviewers enlisted through Cengage Learning for their constructive suggestions and encouragement: Debra Pierce, Ivy Tech Community College of Indiana; Nancy Beaver, Eastfield College; Mary Cordell, Navarro College; Jana Sanders, Texas A&M—Corpus Christi; Janet Imel, Ivy Tech Community College of Indiana; Carolyn Bush, Hazar Community & Technical College; Roseann Rembert, Community College of Vermont; Sharon Hirschy, Collin College; Karin Shumacher Dyke, University of Cincinnati; Lory Langer deRamirez, Herricks Public Schools; Marie Brand, SUNY Empire State College, Administration for Children and Families; Lisa Bauer, Wilmington College; Robin Rackley, Texas A&M—College Station; and Jeanne Barker, Tallahassee Community College.

| A FINAL WORD FROM THE AUTHORS

We chose to write about education for diversity not only because we believe in its importance to education and to the future of our country, but also for very personal reasons. Like many others, we are both "newcomers" to the United States. We both have experienced, together with our families, the tribulations and sometimes painful adjustments of starting a new life in a strange new land. Many of the experiences we wrote about in the book have personal significance. We know firsthand what it is to be different. We have also experienced diversity as U.S. residents of other countries such as the U.S. Virgin Islands, Puerto Rico, Spain, Germany, India, and the former country of Yugoslavia. Our travels have taken us to many other interesting places as well. These experiences have enriched us and given us multicultural and global perspectives that we want to share through this book with our fellow educators and other readers. Join us on our journey!

Wilma Robles de Meléndez
Vesna Beck

PART I

Foundations for Multicultural Education in Today's Early Childhood Classrooms

> We are preparing children to lead rewarding, productive lives in a world that always has been, and surely always will be, diverse.
>
> *Janet Brown McCracken (1993)*

CHAPTER 1

Facing the Reality of Diversity:
The Intricate Nature of Our Society

> He met many people along the way. He shook hands
> with black men, with yellow men and red men.
>
> *Allen Say (1994)*

CHAPTER OBJECTIVES

In this chapter, we will

- define *cultural diversity*.
- explain why our country is described as multicultural.
- discuss the implications of demographic changes in U.S. society.
- establish why early childhood teachers need to be aware of cultural diversity issues.

KEY CONCEPTS

- multicultural society
- cultural diversity
- immigration
- ethnic groups
- non-European Americans

LET'S MEET BARBARA!

Throughout this book you will get to know a kindergarten teacher named Barbara. She is a reflection of early childhood educators we have met and known over the years. Her journal is based on experiences of individuals who are involved in multicultural education of young children. In other words, Barbara is a composite of real ideas and experiences of early childhood educators. And now, let's meet Barbara.

Barbara, an experienced kindergarten teacher, decided to take a summer workshop in multicultural education in order to renew her certification. Having taught for seven years, Barbara was not honestly expecting to learn anything new. The course sounded like an easy and fun way to pick up three credits and maybe get some new handouts. Besides, she had a lot of experience with cultural diversity. She thought of Etienne, the slender boy with bright big eyes who often mumbled to himself in Creole; Lucero, the quietest girl with the loveliest smile who did not have many friends; and little Caroline, who went to live with her grandparents after her family lost their home because her father was laid off. "They all came from different cultures, but they did as well as could be expected this year," Barbara reassured herself.

The workshop proved to be full of surprises. On the way home after the last class, new ideas still whirling in her head, Barbara thought, "I never really knew enough about diversity. I could have done so much more for Etienne, Lucero, and Caroline if I had known all this last year. But it's not too late for my new class. I already know I will have six children with various ethnic backgrounds."

Barbara also remembered something important the professor said: "You will be a good teacher only if you give each of your students an equal opportunity. To do that you must adjust your teaching to include the cultural backgrounds of your students." Barbara could still vividly remember the heated discussion that followed. Both experienced and beginning teachers took offense to this statement until they began to analyze their teaching. Practically everyone in the class had a different concept of culture, and most did not consider the children's cultures in their planning. For the first time, Barbara began to suspect that she was not the kind of teacher she thought she was.

Writing in the journal she started during the workshop, Barbara entered the following: *I need to make my classroom the kind of social and cultural laboratory the professor described in the workshop. But, though I recognize the role of culture in making us who we are, I still don't know enough about the extent of its influence on children. I realize that one workshop will not make me a great multicultural teacher and that there are many things I have to do on my own. My education will start now. I want to be the best teacher for my young students no matter how diverse they are.*

THE UNITED STATES—A NATION OF CONTRASTS

Nothing in this world reflects diversity more than nature. The landscape of Earth is an intricate mix of shapes, forms, and colors, each with its own identity and spirit. They are separate and yet a piece of a whole. The land we live in probably best reflects this notion.

The landscape of the United States, a quilt woven of dramatically different terrains, is populated by people equally unique and diverse. Glancing over the entire country from the Pacific to the Atlantic, you see many different environments coexisting: warm deserts, snowcapped mountains, golden plains, green valleys, lush marshlands, sandy beaches, and bustling cities. All are different yet of one country: the United States. No less than its geography, the people who inhabit the United States illustrate diversity. Much like its eclectic landscape, people of the United States mirror the diversity of the world. In small country towns and large cities alike, you will find numerous examples of world cultures. Whether they wear a sari, attend a mosque, or speak Tagalog, Hmong, or French Creole, members of different cultures have changed the semblance of our social landscape.

Throughout history, the presence of culturally diverse groups has brought people of the United States in contact with ways different from those established by the white European groups that founded this country (Baruth & Manning, 2004). Nowhere else is this more apparent than at the community level. This is where most people recognize to what extent pluralism permeates their world. Diversity makes itself known through the fascinating contrasts that bring a new vitality to our surroundings. For example, the variety of restaurants offering American food can be found beside those that serve flavorful sushi and spicy curry dishes; the Latin beat is heard on radio stations just as often as American rock and roll; sari-clad women shop next to women in jeans; and a Vietnamese-language newspaper can be found next to those in English at the neighborhood newsstand. School grounds echo with the different languages spoken by children and adults. Community centers all over the country are filled with newly arrived immigrants trying to learn the language of their adopted homeland.

Like this Eastern European family in Chicago (circa 1925), many Europeans migrated to the United States during the early part of the twentieth century. In search of a better life, they left behind their homelands to make this country their new home. Do you find any similarities between them and today's immigrant families?

SCHOOL—THE PLACE OF DIVERSITY AND ACTION

Educators at all levels are aware that diversity exists in schools. We recognize its effects on our way of thinking, and we know its impact through the new laws and regulations that mandate changes in the schools and society at large. On a more personal level, early

Wadsworth/Cengage Learning

Through the entire history of our country, children of immigrants have learned about their new home culture through school. This group of first graders from 1928 shared many things in common, but one in particular characterized them: They were all born in different countries and spoke languages different from English. Can you imagine the challenges they faced?

childhood professionals know diversity through the joyous shouting of exotic words heard on the school playground and by witnessing the frustrations that accompany conquests of new knowledge. The account of the first day of school depicted in Snapshot 1-1 is typical of many classrooms, and today's teachers can easily relate to it.

It is a well-known fact that that the ethnographic composition of schools has changed dramatically in the last two decades. More and more schools are housing students with non-European cultural backgrounds (Hobbs & Stoops, 2002; Jarvis, 2003). A visit to a classroom, like the one described in Snapshot 1-1, in many places in the United States would show the same or a similar degree of cultural variety. The presence of non-European cultural groups varies from one geographical area to another. While Hispanics are found in greater numbers in Texas, South Florida, and California, cities such as Chicago and Seattle include large populations of Asian Indians and Vietnamese, and Alaska, Arizona, and New Mexico are home to large numbers of Native Americans. Even states such as North Dakota, Montana, Vermont, and Maine, traditionally known for being populated predominantly by European Americans, are inhabited by immigrants from other continents.

In Action . . .   What Is Diversity?

You may not be fully aware of the diversity around you. To find out if diversity is a part of your community and your life, make a list of details about other cultural groups that you have observed in your community. Find out how much you know about individuals from other cultures, their backgrounds, their ways of life, and so on.

- What roles do these individuals play in your life?
- How has their presence changed your community?
- What are some important things you learned from them?
- What do you think they know about you?

SNAPSH◉T 1-1   Teacher's Notes on the
First Day of School

Today I finally met my class. Twenty-three vivacious kids! When they handed me their list of names, I never imagined what I would find. As I talked with the children and some of their parents, I realized I have a mini–United Nations in my classroom. Seven children are from Central America (Guatemala and Nicaragua), four are Jamaican, one is Haitian, two just came from Puerto Rico, one is Bahamian, and the rest are African American, like me. I've decided to make this year their best school year. I want to be their best teacher, but I don't think it will be easy.

HOW DID WE BECOME A CULTURALLY DIVERSE SOCIETY?

Culture and diversity are terms that are part of today's educational jargon. Although this will be further explained in Chapter 2, here we will briefly explore what the terms signify. *Culture* is a very hard term to define because social scientists have not yet agreed on a single definition. Some define culture as a collection of beliefs, attitudes, habits, values, and practices that a human group uses to form a view of reality. This means that every cultural group, such as Filipinos, Koreans, and Jamaicans, for example, interprets life events (marriage, death, child rearing, and others) according to the cultural frameworks they have established. These sets of ideas are accumulated and formed over time. They represent the recognized and accepted frames of reference of a cultural group. Such frameworks are owned by every cultural group and are transmitted through generations. At the classroom level, this means that young children from different cultures view our world in very heterogeneous ways. This is especially true of children of newly arrived immigrants. This also implies that teachers may have different ways of interpreting life than the children they teach. This divergence of ideas is how you encounter diversity in the classroom. This is also what makes teaching today's young children exciting and challenging.

Like the teacher in Snapshot 1-1 who had children of six different cultural origins, many classrooms are exciting mosaics of cultural diversity. They are a natural extension of the United States, where groups of many different ethnicities and extractions have come together to form a culturally diverse, pluralistic, or **multicultural society** (Baruth & Manning, 2004; Martorella, 2001).

Cultural diversity denotes contrasts, variations, or divergences from the ways of the mainstream or majority culture. When diversity is used in reference to human beings, many elements are involved in the concept. These meanings will be explored in Chapter 2 when we focus on the connotation of the term *cultural origin* or *descent*.

Cultural diversity has not only transformed the composition of the U.S. population, but it has also enriched the character of life in the United States. The various groups have brought much knowledge about other parts of the world in forms of languages, traditions, customs, and folklore. This diversity is displayed in the classroom in countless ways: the various snacks children bring to school, the words and phrases they use, the ideas about families and social relationships they express, the special holidays they celebrate, and even the fashions they prefer. The classroom is a very polychromatic place that can be considered a microcosm of society. This polychromatic quality makes the United States exciting and special. This is also why U.S. society is described as culturally diverse. A culturally diverse society is one where different cultures exist, socially interact, and yet remain visible in their own context.

A Nation of Immigrants

The United States has traditionally been defined as a nation of immigrants. Looking at some of the historical events of the United States helps in answering how, why, and when the country acquired this multicultural personality. Nieto and Bode (2008) point out that **immigration** is an ongoing process of change and not a phenomenon of the past. In fact, it is an everyday experience as immigrants from all parts of the world make their way to our country in search of a better life for themselves and future generations.

The United States has also been described as a land where dreams for a better and more equitable life become a reality. Like the characters in Eve Bunting's book *How Many Days to America* (Houghton Mifflin, 1988), the oppressed and the dreamers of the world longing to find the land where all are equal are still arriving by the thousands. Since the days of the first settlements, this part of North America has represented the pathways to liberty, justice, and opportunity. The chronicles of U.S. history are full of vivid accounts of people who left their countries, seduced by a land where freedom and respect for the individual are among the core principles (Banks & Banks, 2006). The

---

LET'S TALK AND REFLECT... **Thinking About Diversity**

The first few pages of this chapter served to remind you of the nature of our very diverse society. Although we live among people of other cultures and ethnic origins, we seldom think in-depth about our relationship with them. As an early childhood professional, it is important to reflect and ask yourself questions in order to become cognizant of your own views regarding diversity. Working with young children includes learning and developing relationships with children and families from many different parts of the world. Ask yourself in what ways you are ready to support and work with children and families with diverse cultural and linguistic characteristics.

F**O**CUS
on Classroom Practices   │   Learning That We Are Alike and Different

---

Our present U.S. society has sometimes been described as a wonderful tossed salad. This same metaphor probably describes the children in most classrooms. As children begin to notice human diversity, it is just as important to guide them to discover how alike they are. You can begin with an activity such as paper plate self-portraits. You need a paper plate for each child, a set of cutouts of the different parts of the face, glue, and yarn for the hair and for hanging the portraits. To reflect differences among facial traits, cutouts should include a variety of facial features, such as different eye colors and different shapes of noses, mouths, and ears that resemble the traits of your students. Including face parts different from those of the children in the group can be a starter for later discussions. Distribute the materials, making sure that you have provided enough cutouts. Have children work on their portraits in pairs or in groups of four. This could be an introductory activity for a thematic unit, "Who We Are." After finishing their portraits, the children can follow up with a rhyme like the following:

Hello!
We are so alike!
(Have children face each other to point at face parts as they are named.)
Eyes I have and so do you.
I have a nose and so do you.
You and I also have a mouth that says,
"Hello, come and be my friend!"
And ears we also have.
Wow! We are so alike and how!
(Showing surprise)

You can also have them play "Simon Says." Here they would stand up as Simon asks: "Stand up if you have green eyes," ". . . if you have a long nose," and so on. You may want to include other body parts to further stress similarities. Teachers may want to share stories such as *All the Colors We Are* by Katie Kissinger (Redleaf Press, 1994) and *Black is Brown is Tan* by Arnold Adoff (Amistad, 2004).

---

journey that began with the seventeenth century Mayflower Pilgrims and still continues today helped establish the distinctive trait of this country: cultural plurality.

European immigrants settled this country in the seventeenth and eighteenth centuries. Native Americans as well as Africans and people of the Caribbean brought over as slave laborers were the other significant population groups during that time. Historically, the beginning of today's U.S. multiculturalism is found in the social interaction patterns that emerged among these groups. Because these interactions were largely based on discriminatory distinctions among people based on their race and the color of their skin, the seeds of unfairness and inequality were planted in the early days of this nation. Long years of persecution of the African Americans, the systematic eradication of the Native Americans, and later the disenfranchisement of the large numbers of Mexican Americans hampered the efforts of unification among peoples destined to share this land.

An elementary class of the 1950s resembles many of today's classrooms: More than half of these students were recent newcomers or children of first-generation immigrant parents. Is it true that history repeats itself?

The First Immigrants

The first settlers shaped the culture of this land in the early seventeenth century in unprecedented ways. In addition to many positive cultural trends, their values and social ethics defined a system of discrimination and persecution that still remains today. It first began with the early settlers' discrimination and systematic eradication of the East Coast Native American groups. This was the beginning of one of the longest, most tragic, and shameful chapters in U.S. history.

The beginning of slavery in the seventeenth century marked the start of violent persecution and segregation of African Americans that formally ended with the Emancipation Proclamation in 1864. The Civil War that ravaged the country ended slavery and preserved the union. Economic, social, and political reforms following the post–Civil War years initiated a new era in America. This age also marked the beginning of a new kind of diversity that intensified the kaleidoscope nature of this country and presented new challenges.

| In Action . . . | **Diversity in Your Life** |

Perhaps you have not yet discerned how diversity touches your life. To find out, you can do a personal inventory. You need a pad of self-stick notes, a pencil, and a piece of paper. Make five columns on the paper. Label the first four columns as *Things I Use, Wear, Eat,* and *Read.* Label the fifth column *Cultures.* Now, using the sticky notes, write names of things you consider a part of your world that come from cultures other than your own. After you have finished your cultural search, place the sticky notes in the appropriate columns. Fill in the names of the cultures from which the items originate.

- What have you learned about diversity in your life?
- What are the implications of your findings?
- Can you draw some conclusions about diversity?

FΘCUS
on Classroom Practices | Discovering Diversity

At the core of diversity is the issue of human differences. Learning to live with diversity means helping children recognize its presence in their lives. To help children discover that we all hold distinctive traits, teachers can help them create a "Me Bag." This could be a part of the activities conducted at the beginning of the school year. This activity is based on the belief that each person has unique characteristics. The Me Bag is intended to help children see differences as a typically descriptive element defining each individual. This activity starts by the teacher's preparation of his or her own Me Bag to be shared with the children. This activity helps in identifying your own diverse characteristics.

You will need one large brown bag for each child. Write the children's names on the bags and ask them to draw or paste their picture on the outside. Then, ask children to put inside the bag items, drawings, or words that are special to them. Invite children to

share their bags and have them talk about the things they selected. Lead children to identify the items that are common to everyone and those that are different. Use the following questions to engage children in a discussion of their findings.

- *What did we learn about our class? Tell me something you discovered about two of your friends.*
- *What things did we discover we have in common with our classmates? What things do we not have in common?*
- *In what ways are we all alike? Why?*
- *Tell me something that makes you special.*

Bags can be displayed and kept as an ongoing activity. Other details can be added throughout the year. Follow up by adding books to the literacy center to reinforce the characteristics of diversity found among the children in the group.

The great waves of immigration began with the Irish as early as the 1850s. Most settled in the large cities, where they later made great strides in business and politics. On the West Coast, the Chinese were arriving at the same time. Some came as economic immigrants looking for a better life, whereas many more came to join the 49ers in their quest for California's gold. By 1870, over 60,000 Chinese were living mostly in California, the West, and the Southwest (Novas & Cao, 2004). The construction of the Central Pacific Railroad, completed in 1869, was largely a Chinese achievement.

Presence of people of Hispanic descent traces back to the beginnings of the United States. During the nineteenth century, Mexicans came to build the Texas Mexican Railway. Earlier, many Mexicans worked in the gold mines in California and in the copper mines in Arizona. They were employed as general laborers and were always paid less than their white counterparts. Many of these laborers were migrants who never settled permanently in the states where they worked. Others found themselves strangers in their own land after the United States annexed Texas and California.

Ellis Island was the first glimpse of the "land of the free" for many immigrants in the beginning of the twentieth century.

The New Immigrants

By the end of the nineteenth century, the United States had entered into an unprecedented age of industrialization and progress. The newcomers inspired a new backlash of nativism that led to many discriminatory practices. These practices were based on the idea of supremacy of "whiteness" as related to the notions of purity, Americanism, and the male gender (Kivel, 2002). According to historians, much of the groundwork laid in those years still remains today. For example, in the United States, the term "American" still conjures up images of people of European ancestry. Yet, the social and demographic reality of the country shows the profile of an American today is rapidly changing due to the growing cultural diversity in our society.

The first great wave of immigrants during the twentieth century occurred between 1905 and 1915, when various economic and political events in Europe caused 10 million people to seek refuge in the United States (Novas & Cao, 2004). These were mostly economic immigrants, people who came to the United States primarily in search of a better life. These large **ethnic groups** were segments of larger societies whose members had a common origin, were of a specific race, and shared a common culture and often a common religion. Approximately 2 million Italians and 1.5 million Russians, many of them Jews avoiding persecution, came to the large cities on the East Coast. The new immigrants comprised 3 percent of the labor force. The majority of European immigrants came to the United States as common people. Settling in cities where there were jobs and where they could live with their own kind in places like little Italies, Bohemias, and Germantowns, they worked hard and struggled to make a living. Many women worked in sweatshops and earned even less than men. Most immigrants lived in slums in rundown tenements without heat and running water. Working conditions were just as deplorable. Hazardous working conditions caused many accidents in which many workers were maimed for life or even killed. Part of the new U.S. labor force consisted of children. They were largely children of the poor and of immigrant families who were not able to partake in the national prosperity experienced at the turn of the twentieth century.

In Action . . .   **Portrait of America**

This is a description of New Rochelle, a suburb of New York City, in 1906 in E. L. Doctorow's *Ragtime*. This description eerily reaches into the present, whether or not we ride the trolley.

> Teddy Roosevelt was President. The popularity customarily gathered in great numbers either out of doors for parades, public concerts, fish fries, political picnics, social outings, indoor meeting halls, vaudeville theaters, operas, or ballrooms. There seemed to be no end to entertainment that did not involve great swarms of people. Trains and steamers and trolleys moved them from one place to another. That was the style: that was the way people lived. Women were stouter then. They visited the fleet carrying white parasols. Everyone wore white in summer. There was a lot of sexual fainting. There were no Negroes. There were no immigrants.

- What can you say about this United States?
- Are some corners of our country (or our minds) that are still like this?
- Write a paragraph about your community, emulating Doctorow's style.

Source: Doctorow, 1975.

In Action . . .   **A Not Just Multicultural but Also Increasingly Multiracial Country**

Census 2000 provided a unique cultural and demographical portrait of the United States. The results showed that 3 in 10 people are members of ethnic minorities. Not only did the Census results confirm the growing multicultural character of the nation, they also exposed, for the first time, the existence of a new multiracial and multiethnic group classified as "multicultural." The responses revealed the following:

- There were 6.8 million who identified their heritage as multiracial.
- Of people who defined themselves as multiracial, 93 percent stated having two races.
- Nearly 1 million children age 5 or younger were identified as having mixed racial origins.

What are the implications for the future? Projections tell us that by 2050, 21 percent of the population will be of mixed race origins. Given this trend, the number of young children with multiracial heritage in early childhood classrooms is expected to rise dramatically. For early childhood educators, learning about the needs of children and families with multiracial heritage is essential.

Source: Kasindorf & El Nasser, 2001.

LITERACY CONNECTIONS...   Teaching Children About Immigrants

Multicultural children's literature offers a rich and lively way to explore diversity concepts. Stories addressing topics related to cultural diversity are powerful learning sources for young children. The following titles will help you explore the very important topic of immigration.

- **Anzaldua, G. (1993).** *Friends from the other side.* **San Francisco: Children's Press.**
  Based on facts, the story tells about the experiences of Prietita, a girl who helps Joaquin and his mother when they come to live in the United States.

- **Hoffman, M. (2002).** *The color of home.* **New York: Fogelman Press.**
  The story tells the experiences of first grader Hassan, an immigrant boy from Somalia, as he goes to school in the

United States for the first time. This is a powerful tale that conveys the feelings and emotions of a child who misses life in his country.

- **Pak, S. (2001).** *A place to grow.* **New York: Levine Books.**
  In this story, an inquisitive child asks her father about the reasons he left his birthplace to come to a new country. This is a good starting point for families in sharing their own stories and reasons why they came to the United States.

- **Surat, M. (1989).** *Angel child, dragon child.* **New York: Scholastic.**
  This story is about the experiences of an immigrant child from Vietnam as he begins to learn how to live in the United States.

Laws Limiting Immigration

The first national limits on immigration in the form of a quota system, imposed in 1924, were known as the National Origins Act. The quotas limited the total number of immigrants per year to 150,000. Quotas for each nationality group were 2 percent of the total members of that nationality residing in the United States according to the 1890 Census. Western Europeans were exempt from the quota system because they were perceived as more desirable in terms of their education and the skills they possessed (Parillo, 2007). The main purpose of the quota system was to preserve the original racial and ethnic composition of the United States by preventing the poor and the illiterate from the Eastern, middle, and southern European countries; Russia; and Asia from coming in and becoming a social and economic burden to U.S. society. The system gave an enormous advantage to the British, the Germans, and other Western Europeans whose ancestors were among the pioneers who settled this country.

The law was changed in 1952 with the passing of the McCarran–Walter Act that repealed the quota system and instead gave preference to skilled workers in fields that are experiencing shortages in the United States, reunification of families, and protection of the domestic labor force (Frost, 1994). This system was also biased in favor of the Western Europeans, whose immigration numbers continued to be unrestricted.

In 1965, as a result of many political changes in the world, the increasing intensity of the Cold War, Castro's rise to power, and the Vietnam War, Congress passed an immigration law that was based on a humanitarian notion of "reunification of families." The law abolished the national origins system and the major restrictions against the Asiatic countries. The Western Hemisphere was also subject for the first time to an overall annual quota of 120,000. A seven-category system was created with preference given to reunification of families and to individuals with needed talents or skills.

Many immigrants who arrived in the 1960s and the early 1970s were political dissidents, artists, intellectuals, and entrepreneurs from the Eastern European communist countries, from Asia, and from Cuba. (It should be noted that this law was applied very selectively in the 1980s, granting immigrants from the communist countries legal entry whereas opponents to the right-wing dictatorships of countries such as Guatemala and El Salvador were forced to enter illegally.) Under the kinship system, newly arrived refugees did not need to have any job skills, education, or means of support. The "reunification" law brought 10 million newcomers to this country who were closely and distantly related to earlier immigrants. The second and third generations of those originally allowed into the United States are the ones changing the makeup of U.S. society.

The second-highest numbers of people immigrated in the 1980s, when the latest waves of Asians, Latin Americans, people from the Caribbean nations, and people from the countries of the Middle East arrived in the United States. Another amendment to the immigration law, which broadened the definition of "refugee," further increased the numbers of those admitted. Between 1985 and 1994, almost 10 million people came to the United States: 2.7 million came from Mexico, 1 million from the countries in the Caribbean, 1 million from Europe, and approximately 5 million came from other parts

FIGURE 1-1 **Region of Birth of Foreign Born**

Europe	31,107,573
Asia	8,226,254
Africa	4,915,557
Oceania	881,300
Latin America	16,089,974
Northern America	829,442

Source: U.S. Census Bureau, 2000b.

of the world. The current origins of the foreign-born population of the United Stated are reflected in Figure 1-1.

Four states—California, New York, Texas, and Florida—took in most of the immigrants (Figure 1-2). The new arrivals settled in large cities where the job markets were believed to be better. Consider how your state compares in terms of percentage of noncitizens as well as what the educational implications of these demographics are for teachers of young children.

The U.S. Census Bureau projects that by the year 2050, there will be 392 million people in the United States. Projections indicate that Latinos will be the fastest growing population, rising from 9.7 percent to 22.5 percent. They are expected to sur-

FIGURE 1-2 **Noncitizens in the Four Most Populous States in the United States, 2000**

	Total Population (in millions)	Noncitizens (in millions)	Noncitizens as % of Total
United States	281.422	18.534	6.4
California	34.7	5.42	15.6
Texas	20.6	2.05	9.9
New York	18.0	2.06	11.4
Florida	15.2	1.54	10.4

Source: U.S. Census Bureau & U.S. Department of Labor, 2001.

In Action . . . **Immigrants**

Have you ever wondered why people immigrate? If you know individuals who were born in another country, ask them what brought them to the United States. If you have parents or relatives who were born in another country, interview them to find out what brought them here. Write down their answers and examine them. What did you learn?

- What attracts people to this country?
- How do you feel about the people you interviewed?
- How do you feel about your country?
- What is the history of immigrants in your family?
- How are the stories of different immigrants you interviewed the same or different?
- Would you ever consider immigrating to another country? Why or why not?

pass African Americans as the largest minority in this country by 2010. Census data estimates also indicate Asian Americans as the second largest ethnic group. It also points out the fact that the population will be characterized by larger numbers of people under the ages of 5 and 18 (U.S. Census Bureau, 2005). This fact has direct implications in the planning of services for young children and their families. In particular, it calls for attention to programs that will best reflect the diverse cultural characteristics of the young.

Immigration: Key to the Growing Cultural Diversity

The features of contemporary U.S. society have dramatically changed in recent years. A look at people in towns and cities across the country attests to that. No longer does one set of specific physical or ethnic characteristics make up a profile of a typical U.S. citizen. In fact, we have become a showcase of all possible human traits.

The findings of Census 2000 show a quickly evolving demographic picture. The population of European descent is losing its predominance due to the rapid growth of groups of non-European origin (Hobbs & Stoops, 2002). In essence, non-European Americans account for the growing cultural diversity now found in the United States. The term non-European Americans defines people with ethnic roots in continents other than Europe. Findings from the Census show that U.S. society is actually formed by six main groups of non-European Americans (see Figure 1-3). In the section that follows, some of the relevant characteristics of each of these groups will be discussed. While they represent major cultural groups, they are heterogeneous. Within each, there are very distinct groups that must also be recognized for their uniqueness and contributions to U.S. society.

How do you describe your ancestry? Which are the prevalent ancestry groups in your community?

FIGURE 1-3 **Major Ancestry Groups**

German	42,885,162
Irish	30,594,130
English	24,515,138
United States or American	20,624,093
Latin Americans*	16,086,974
Polish	8,977,444
French	8,325,509

Latin Americans were not itemized by country and were selected by region of birth.

Source: U.S. Census Bureau, 2000b.

FIGURE 1-4 **Main Cultural Groups**

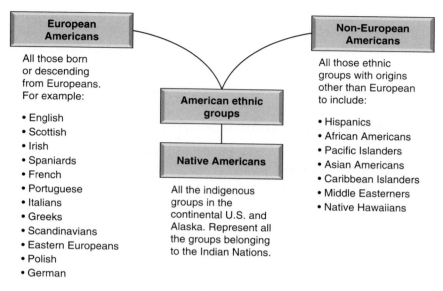

We all belong to the United States!

LET'S TALK AND REFLECT... Immigration

The United States of America, as we know it today, was and is mainly created by immigrants. At some point we all, with the exception of Native Americans, were immigrants or descendants of immigrants. Starting life over in a new and strange land is a unique experi-ence. The process is easy for some, although it takes a lifetime for others.

- How much do I know about immigration?
- What experiences have I had and what ideas do I have regarding immigration?

Asians

According to the classifications of the U.S. Census Bureau, Asian Indian, Chinese, Fili-pino, Japanese, Korean, Vietnamese, Cambodian, Hmong, Thai, and Laotian are the major groups that comprise Asian Americans (U.S. Census, 2005). There is also a cat-egory of "others" that includes much smaller numbers of people of Bangladeshi, Bur-mese, Indonesian, Pakistani, Malaysian, Nepalese, Singaporean, and Sri Lankan origin. Together, Asian Americans number approximately 12 million (Novas & Cao, 2004), which constitutes 5 percent of the U.S. population (U.S. Census, 2005). In the last two decades of the twentieth century and through the present, all the subgroups grew

---

F◯CUS
on Classroom Practices | Can We Teach Children About Immigration?

For most young children, immigration is a difficult concept to understand. Even for many who are immigrants themselves, the term will not be familiar. Others, either because of firsthand experiences or from comments by adults, might hold a negative perception of immigration. However, as we move into responsive teaching, this concept becomes a part of the ideas we want children to learn. The option here is to transform the topic into aspects more familiar to children. Brainstorming what immigration means would probably yield the following words: movement of people, moving from one country to another, coming from another part of the world, and so on. We find that *moving* is a term that young children recognize readily, and it can be used to convey concepts in relationship to immigrant children. Teachers can build a thematic unit based on the idea of moving. There are many possibilities in terms of how to develop it with your class.

One kindergarten teacher developed her ideas after her group was moved into another part of the school building. Through the story of Su Lin, a character created by the teacher, who had left behind everything she had when her family came to the United States, the class began talking about what it means to move. Asking who knew what moving was like led to an interesting conversation. The children shared how they felt and why they felt sad or happy after moving. A list titled "We can move to . . ." included items like: "a bigger house," "another bedroom," "an apartment," "our grandparents' house," "another development," "a new city," and, of course, "a different classroom." The activity led the class to prepare a big book they titled "Places We Move To."

As a culminating activity, the class decided to prepare a welcome plan for children and adults. Needless to say, with new students arriving frequently, the plan was used almost immediately.

(except for Japanese Americans) to the point that they inhabit every state and the District of Columbia (Novas & Cao, 2004). Half of the Asian American population resides in three states: California, New York, and Hawaii. New York City, Los Angeles, and Chicago have the largest concentrations of Asian Americans. Los Angeles County is the only county that has more than one million Asian Americans living in it. One of the most significant facts regarding Asian Americans is that 86 percent of them have earned a high school diploma.

The Chinese, and later other Asians, had different reasons for immigrating to the United States, which resulted in very distinct immigration experiences (Campbell, 2004). Chinese Americans began coming to California mostly for economic reasons in the first part of the nineteenth century. By the time California was annexed to the United States in 1848, the Chinese population provided basic labor on the railroads and services in laundry and cooking establishments. In the second half of the nineteenth century, the Chinese became targets of hate and oppression, which resulted in the first antiracial law, the 1882 Chinese Exclusion Act. The law encouraged white immigration from Europe and made Chinese immigration illegal.

The Chinese who came to the United States in the nineteenth century and until World War II were largely poor and illiterate people from the vast rural areas of China. The more recent immigrants from China, Hong Kong, and Taiwan are well-educated professionals and skilled blue-collar workers. Many came with their families in tow and their possessions intact. Some even had jobs waiting for them in this country. This new group of Chinese Americans has changed the nature of the Chinese communities across the country. The new Chinese Americans have entered professions and moved to the suburbs. Yet, they maintain their roots and traditions. The Japanese and Filipino immigrants first came to Hawaii to work in the sugarcane industry. Many of them eventually migrated to the West Coast of the United States and settled in states from Alaska to California. The Japanese worked hard, saved their money, and bought farms. The success of the Japanese Americans was met with suspicion and prejudice. The worst offenses against them were committed during World War II, when Japanese Americans were unfairly incarcerated and their property confiscated by the U.S. government.

In the decades following World War II, both the Japanese and Japanese Americans experienced unprecedented growth and prosperity. In the 1980s and 1990s, the formidable Japanese economy surpassed the growth rate of the U.S. economy. Efforts to compete had severe repercussions in the U.S. labor force, not the least of which were reduced salaries, loss of jobs, smaller profits, and cuts in benefits. Japan's economic prosperity contributed to the latest wave of resentment of the Japanese in this country at the close of the twentieth century (Novas & Cao, 2004).

Filipinos were not subject to the immigration restrictions in the twentieth century because the Philippines became U.S. territories in 1898. Although they were not classified as aliens, Filipinos did not have citizenship. The economic and political events in the Philippines during the last two decades of the twentieth century facilitated steady streams of Filipino immigrants to the United States. Statistics show that in the past decade, unlike in earlier times, many of the recent immigrants are white-collar professionals in the medical and health-care professions.

Asian-Indian Americans began coming in significant numbers from the subcontinent of India in the first decade of the twentieth century. In spite of persecution and exploitation during most of the twentieth century, Asian Indians managed to prosper in agriculture and related services. It was not until 1965 that significant numbers of highly educated and well-trained professionals began to enter the United States (Novas & Cao, 2004). This phenomenon is known as the "brain drain" from India. Asian Indians continue to be the highest educated group among Asian Americans. They have put their entrepreneurial skills to work in a variety of business enterprises as well as in the professional fields (Novas & Cao, 2004).

Korean Americans were subject to the same hardships as their fellow Asian immigrants. Like the Filipinos and the Chinese, they came first to the Hawaiian Islands at the turn of the twentieth century to work in the sugarcane fields. Before long, the desire for a better life lured them to the West Coast of the United States. Like other Asians, they suffered discrimination, struggled doing menial labor for minimum wages, and were ineligible for citizenship. During World War II, even though Korea was occupied by Japan, Koreans were considered Japanese citizens and were treated as enemies of the United States. In spite of that, Korean Americans fought in World War II alongside American GIs, bought war bonds, and joined the National Guard. After the Korean War, an immigration wave, mainly made up of war brides, took place. Adoptions of Korean children in the years following the Korean War also increased the numbers of this ethnic group (Novas & Cao, 2004).

Census data for 2006 shows that Asian Americans are the second-largest-growing ethnic group.

The majority of Vietnamese Americans came to this country in four waves in the aftermath of the Vietnam War. The first large wave was transported by the U.S. military in 1975 for resettlement in the United States. They were well-educated and skilled technicians from the middle and upper-middle classes of South Vietnamese society. The second wave consisted of 40,000 to 60,000 South Vietnamese who, after they could not be transported by U.S. warships and planes, started a boat evacuation themselves within the first few weeks of the communist victory (Novas & Cao, 2004). Many "boat people"

SNAPSHOT 1-2   **Early Settlers**

Once California belonged to Mexico and its land to Mexicans and a horde of tattered feverish Americans poured in. And such was their hunger for land that they took the land . . . and they guarded with guns the land they had stolen. . . . Then, with time, the squatters were no longer squatters, but owners.

Source: Steinbeck, 1975, The Grapes of Wrath

LITERACY CONNECTIONS...
Recommended Books About Japanese Americans

Immigration

- Iijima, G. (2002). *The way we do it in Japan.* New York: Albert Whitman.

- Say, A. (1993). *Grandfather's journey.* New York: Houghton Mifflin.

- Say, A. (1999). *Tea with milk.* New York: Houghton Mifflin.

Internment experience

- Mochizuki, K. (1995). *Baseball saved us.* New York: Lee and Low.

- Uchida, Y. (1996). *The bracelet.* New York: Paperstar.

never made it to the United States, having either perished or landed in other safe havens in Southeast Asia. The third wave of Vietnamese immigrants were "boat people" who continued to leave the Socialist Republic of Vietnam from 1979 into the early 1980s (Novas & Cao, 2004). Their journeys on the South Seas were also perilous and deadly. The fourth wave was comprised of Amerasian children. *Amerasian* is a term used to describe individuals born of Vietnamese mothers and U.S. service members stationed in Vietnam during the Vietnam War. In 1987, Congress passed the Amerasian Homecoming Act to facilitate the transfer of Amerasian children born between 1962 and 1977 to the United States (Novas & Cao, 2004). This allowed nearly 75,000 Amerasians and their family members to come to the United States.

Hispanics

The terms *Hispanic* and *Latino* encompass an enormous range of people and cultures of Spanish and Portuguese origin. Today, Latino is becoming more commonly used to designate this demographically growing group. From 1980 to 2000, the Hispanic (Latino) population in the United States doubled (Hobbs & Stoops, 2002). During the 1990s, the Hispanic population increased by 58 percent, or 35.3 million, making it the largest minority group, surpassing African Americans by approximately 1 million people. Latinos now represent 12.5 percent of the population. Considering that they have the highest birth rate of any ethnic or racial group in the country, they are projected to grow in the future at a much faster rate than any other group. Latinos are becoming the largest ethnic group in states such as California, Texas, New Mexico, and Florida (U.S. Census Bureau, 2004). They accounted for 40 percent of the U.S. population growth in the 1990s (Parillo, 2007).

About 5 percent of the total Hispanic population are Cuban Americans. There are, however, great social and economic differences even within this group. The early immigrants who fled Castro's regime and arrived in Florida in the 1960s represented Cuba's social, economic, and intellectual elite. They are largely responsible for making Miami an important commercial center and a "Gateway to South America." A sec-

Hispanics are currently the fastest-growing group of non-European Americans.

ond group of Cuban Americans arrived in the 1980 Mariel boatlift. More recently, the Cuban rafters who arrived on the Florida coasts constitute the newest group of immigrants from this Caribbean island.

Mexicans comprise two-thirds of the total Hispanic population. The largest concentration, of approximately 12 million, is found in California, Texas, and the Southwest. Within the total Hispanic population, more than 60 percent of the heads of household came directly from Mexico, and over 70 percent are under age 35. Many are agricultural seasonal workers or employees of service industries. Mexicans are often exploited by business owners and farmers who pay them subsistence wages and offer no employment benefits. Lack of physical borders between United States and Mexico has made it possible for this group to have a higher number of illegal aliens than all other groups combined. The seriousness of this situation has caused the question of illegal aliens to be moved to the forefront of the political agenda in the United States.

The case of Puerto Ricans is different. The Caribbean island of Puerto Rico became part of the United States in 1898. Puerto Ricans are U.S. citizens by birth and are free to live anywhere in the United States and its territories. More than one-third of Puerto Ricans live in the mainland United States. They account for 14 percent of the total Latino population of this country.

The third fastest-growing Latino group consists of those coming from the Caribbean and Central and South American countries, and this group makes up about 20 percent of the total Hispanic population in the United States. Approximately 300,000 from the Dominican Republic are estimated to have settled in New York City alone. Many Hispanics are still struggling for success. For many, language presents a major challenge: Less than 30 percent are fluent in English. Of the estimated 30 million, 70 percent live in just four states: California, Florida, New York, and Texas. Separation from their families

Puerto Ricans are American citizens with Hispano-Caribbean roots.

is also a hardship for many living in the United States. Unfamiliarity with the education and health-care systems also poses serious challenges, making it very difficult to access services. For families of young children, finding out about the available educational and family services is one the most difficult challenges to overcome.

Whether the immigration patterns from Latin America increase, decrease, or stay the same, Latino populations are projected to continue to rise in numbers as a result of the presence of the second generation. The second generation is predominantly constituted by young people—two thirds are under the age of 18—who will be citizens and products of U.S. schools (Suro & Passel, 2003). Their potential contributions to U.S. society make support to the Latino community a national priority.

Native Americans

Treat all men alike. Give them all the same law. Give them all an even chance to live and grow.

Chief Joseph (1840–1904)

Native Americans represent the indigenous inhabitants of the United States. Long before any immigrants came, many Native American nations and tribes already called this territory their homeland. Native Americans are a pluralistic society that should not be viewed as a homogeneous group. The rich history and customs of different nations and tribes are unique and should be studied and presented as individual cultures. Thus, it is difficult to collectively describe the specific family practices, ways, and traditions of Native Americans. Diversity is one of the traits that depict the Native American people on 314 reservations and trust land areas throughout the country. Yet, we could say that strong family values, respect for their elders, and a high sense of spirituality characterize Native Americans.

The end of the nineteenth century brought about the confinement of Native Americans to designated reservations, many of which were useless patches of wasteland. In addition to having to create a living in these new places, Native Americans were subjected to concerted government efforts to assimilate them into the mainstream culture. These efforts met with great resistance and caused additional clashes between the European Americans and Native Americans. Today, the violent resistance to assimilation has eased somewhat and has been replaced with a cultural revival and an adoption of some political and entrepreneurial models from the mainstream culture.

The 2000 Census showed that Native Americans and Native Alaskans increased dramatically in numbers. They represent 1 percent of the population, or 2.6 million people, a rise from 1.4 million in 1990. The doubling of the population is partly due to the increased birth rate and more accurate reporting (Hobbs & Stoops, 2002). The four states with the largest Native American populations are Oklahoma, California, Arizona, and New Mexico.

Native Americans have suffered irreparable harm by the government and by the white settlers. The damage that was done to their culture and heritage has caused many problems for the current generations. Having survived centuries of persecution and genocide, the Native Americans are working hard to reclaim their place in U.S. society.

Middle Easterners

People from the Middle East came to the United States in the late nineteenth century. Christian traders from the Ottoman Empire were probably the first to arrive in the United States in 1875 (Lynch & Hanson, 2004). Other political events led to additional migrations of Iranians, Iraqis, and Afghans. The Iranian revolution in 1978 and the Iran–Iraq war between 1980 and 1988 brought a continuous flow of Iranian immigrants to the United States. During the 1990s and following the Persian Gulf War, many Kuwaiti refugees came to the United States.

To a large extent, the immigrants from the Middle Eastern countries are concentrated in large cities. Those who arrived prior to 1980 are generally educated members of the professional class who possessed a good command of English prior to coming to this country. Those arriving in this country after 1980 seemed to have lower education levels, although most had at least a high school diploma and some knowledge of English (Lynch & Hanson, 2004). Differences exist among the various Middle

Wadsworth/Cengage Learning

Many Middle Eastern families came to our country in the early 1980s as a result of political and religious unrest in their world.

Eastern groups and, even more so, between the urban and the rural contingents of each group.

Demographically, the Arab American population in the United States increased by nearly 40 percent in the 1990s, bringing the number to 1 million (Hobbs & Stoops, 2002). The three largest Middle Eastern groups represented in the United States are the Lebanese, the Egyptians, and the Syrians. They account for approximately three-fifths of the Middle Eastern U.S. population. Most of them live in large cities, with New York City having the highest number.

Since the tragedy of September 11, Middle Eastern Americans have come under close scrutiny. Before these events, little was known about this ethnic group. Images from the media have focused negative attention on Middle Eastern Americans as a result of the war and security measures. Concerted efforts of educators and responsive individuals are needed to help change these attitudes. In a diverse and democratic society

---

LITERACY CONNECTIONS...

Children's Literature About Middle Easterners

Stories provide windows into the lives and cultures of people. The titles included in this section address topics ranging from the traditions to the folk tales of people from the Middle East. They provide young children opportunities to discuss, clarify, and learn more about this ethnic group. As a suggestion, remember to always read the story before sharing it in the classroom. Read both the text and the illustrations and research any facts that you may not be familiar with. Choose the story that best matches what the children would enjoy and are able to understand. This will help your storytelling become a dynamic and meaningful experience.

• Ghazi, S. (1996). *Ramadan*. New York: Holiday House.

• Hauff, W., & Shepard, A. (1995). *The enchanted storks: A tale of the Middle East*. Boston: Houghton Mifflin.

• Hickox, R., & Hillenbrand, W. (1999). *The golden sandal: A Middle Eastern Cinderella story*. New York: Holiday House.

• Kyuchukov, H. (2004). *My name was Hussein*. Honesdale, PA: Boyd Mills Press.

• Matz Sidhom, C., & Farnsworth, B. (2002). *The stars in my Geddoh's sky*. Morton Grove, IL: Albert Whitman & Co.

• Musch, R. (1999). *From far away*. Minneapolis, MN: Sagebrush.

• Nye, N. (1997). *Sitti's secrets*. New York: Aladdin.

• Parry, F. (1995). *The day of Ahmed's secret*. New York: Harper-Trophy.

like ours, avoiding any generalizations about an ethnic group is essential. Responding effectively to comments and remarks about Middle Easterners is necessary to prevent prejudice and stereotyping of this group.

African Americans

Historically, African Americans were the only group who did not originally come to the United States as immigrants. Removed against their will from their homeland by the unscrupulous human traffickers of colonial times, they were brought to the New World as slaves. This led to the institutionalized inhumane treatment rooted in violence and injustice, which they endured for centuries. In the post–Civil War era, this system was replaced by discrimination and racism sanctioned by legislation.

During the years following the Civil War, racial hatred produced many contradictory social initiatives that altered the fabric of U.S. society for the next hundred years. The founding of the Ku Klux Klan in 1866 for the purpose of committing atrocities against African Americans; the Black Codes enacted in 1865–1866 to disenfranchise them; and the Supreme Court decision *Plessy v. Ferguson* in 1896 that established "the separate but equal" doctrine were all designed to deny African Americans their rightful place in society.

Throughout the twentieth century, racism and discrimination kept African Americans segregated from whites in schools, factories, businesses, housing, public facilities, and services. "Jim Crow" laws, which took the form of literacy tests, "white primaries," poll taxes, and "grandfather" clauses, were all enacted to prevent African Americans from exercising their right to vote. Not being able to exercise this right prevented African Americans from participating in the greatest era of progress in U.S. history. Things did not begin to change until World War II, when the military desegregated and the landmark case of Brown v. the Board of Education in 1954 abolished school segregation (Lynch & Hanson, 2004). The late 1950s and 1960s marked the greatest years of social change in recent U.S. history. The civil rights movement became the focus of U.S. society largely as a result of the leadership of African American organizations, such as the National Association for the Advancement of Colored People (NAACP), the Urban League, and the Southern Christian Leadership Conference, as well as individuals, such as Dr. Martin Luther King Jr., Rosa Parks, Thurgood Marshall, and others. The sit-ins, freedom rides, peace demonstrations, and violence associated with African Americans attempting to gain admission to formerly all-white institutions provided the nation with a renewed look at the depth of hatred and racism. Many battles were won during those years, including the Civil Rights Act and Equal Opportunity Act of 1964 and the Voting Rights Act of 1965. The federal government poured much money into social programs intended to assist the poor and the disadvantaged during the 1960s and 1970s. These initiatives and services gave the government the right to interfere in cases of discrimination within the individual states, without which many cases involving African Americans could not be settled.

Census data indicate that there are approximately 36 million African Americans nationally, representing 12.3 percent of the total population. They are the second largest minority group after people who classified themselves other than black or white. Many are the challenges still faced by African Americans in the twenty-first century. This is partly due to the fact that societal institutions have failed to meet their needs. However, the incredible resiliency, sense of pride, and desire to improve that characterize African Americans will continue to facilitate their progress. Results from the 2008 elections in the United States marked a historical event with the election of an African American, Barack Obama, as president. His election brings about a new dimension in the social and cultural fabric of the nation and sets new expectations for the future of racial relationships in a nation defined by diversity.

Pacific Islanders

Pacific Islanders have roots in the islands and archipelagos of the vast Central and South Pacific Ocean also known as Oceania (Novas & Cao, 2004). Many are sovereign nations, and others are affiliated with the United States. Oceania is divided into three major regions: Polynesia, Micronesia, and Melanesia. Polynesia, which includes the Hawaiian Islands, is the largest. Census 2000 was the first Census that designated Native Hawaiians and other Pacific Islanders (287 islands) as a racial group distinct from Asians (Novas & Cao, 2004). Pacific Islander Americans differ from most immigrants. They did not come to the mainland United States looking for a better life. In their case, the United States came to them through extended borders propelled by the political, economic, and social winds of change.

The two Pacific Islander groups with the highest population in the United States are the Hawaiians and the Samoans. They, like many other colonized people, experienced many changes as a result of Western cultures. Samoa was occupied by the Dutch in 1722 and Christianized by the missionaries by the 1830s. Throughout the twentieth century, the United States, England, and Germany asserted power over this small nation. In 1900, Samoa was partitioned into two parts, one of which, American Samoa, still remains a U.S. territory. The majority of American Samoans came to this country for economic reasons and settled in ethnic enclaves in California. The transfer of this group was also facilitated through the transfer of navy base personnel. Samoans in the United States have been acculturated to a lesser extent than the Hawaiians, whose association with the United States has closer ties.

Hawaiians first came in touch with the Europeans through the explorer Captain James Cook in 1778. Throughout the nineteenth century, visitors from the United States, England, Germany, Spain, Portugal, and other countries influenced massive changes, not only in religious practices but also in the political and socioeconomic practices of native Hawaiian people. The Westerners had a devastating effect on the native population, largely attributed to diseases for which the natives had no immunity. Hawaiians are very proactively engaged in preserving their culture, especially in their native islands where they are in the minority.

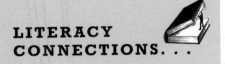

LITERACY CONNECTIONS...   Learning About African Americans

Stories have the power to bring life issues into the world of the child in ways that adults sometimes cannot. The following titles address various cultural aspects about African American traditions and family lifestyles.

- Adoff, A. (2004). *Black is brown is tan.* New York: Harper & Row.

- Anastasia, N. (2001). *I love my hair!* New York: Little Brown.

- Collier, B. (2004). *Uptown.* New York: Henry Holt.

- Hamilton, V. (1988). *In the beginning: Creation stories from around the world.* New York: Harcourt Brace Jovanovich.

- Hudson, W. (1993). *Pass it on: African-American poetry for children.* New York: Scholastic.

- Manjo, N. (1970). *The drinking gourd.* Englewood Cliffs, NJ: Harper & Row.

- Ringgold, F. (1995). *Aunt Harriet's underground railroad in the sky.* New York: Dragonfly books.

- Steptoe, J. (2001). *In daddy's arms I am tall: African Americas celebrating fathers.* New York: Lee & Low.

- Woodson, J. (2001). *The other side.* New York: Putnam.

Before 1950, few Pacific Islanders ventured into the continental United States. Today, however, demographic data indicate that over 58 percent reside in California and Hawaii (Hobbs & Stoops, 2002). Small percentages are also found in Washington, Utah, Texas, New York, and Florida.

THE UNITED STATES: A KALEIDOSCOPE OF PEOPLE

Have you ever spent time at any major U.S. airport? If you have, you probably saw a kaleidoscope of people just like the teacher in Snapshot 1-3 did when she traveled through Miami International Airport.

Similar scenarios are being played out all over the United States. Our communities, schools, and workplaces now reflect the new cultural environment. Everything we know about the demographic patterns in the United States indicates that diversity is here to stay. Even though the non-European cultural groups are playing an increasingly more dominant role, the groups of European origin will continue to be an important influence on the development of the country in the twenty-first century. Aside from both being part of the U.S. demography, the groups share another common characteristic: heterogeneity (see Figures 1-5 and 1-6).

FIGURE 1-5   **Who Are the European Americans? What Else Would You Add?**

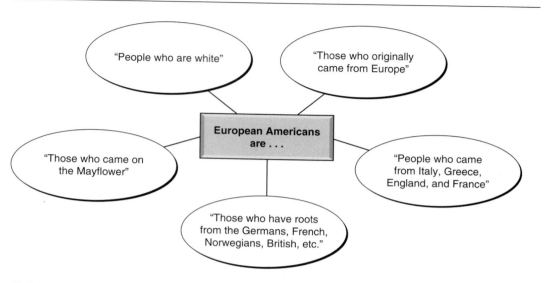

FIGURE 1-6   **Who Are the Non-European Americans?**

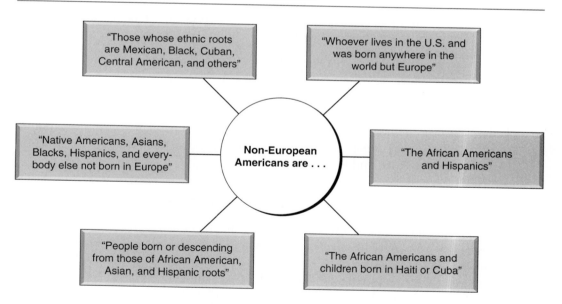

Terms are useful in identifying a specific quality or shared characteristics. Sometimes, however, a term can oversimplify the meaning or hide its magnitude. Using geographical terminology, like "Hawaiian," in connection with individual non-European American and European American cultural groups does not provide an accurate description of each group.

When a group of early childhood graduate students were informally asked to web their ideas about the terms *non-European Americans* and *European Americans*, their responses showed a wide range of ideas (Robles de Meléndez, 2006). In most cases, some cultural groups, such as the Pacific Islanders and the Middle Easterners, were not included, whereas all failed to identify the European Americans as being a diverse group in itself. What are the implications of these responses? Mainly, one: Early childhood educators must hold accurate knowledge about various cultural groups if they are to deliver developmentally appropriate programs that are sensitive and responsive to the world of today's children.

| PONDERING WHAT WE HAVE EXAMINED

A look at the demographical data from the U.S. Census 2000 provides significant details about the ethnic characteristics and immigration patterns of U.S. society at the dawn of the twenty-first century. The distinct changes indicate a transformation in the core ethnic traits of the country. These statistics show that, in 2000, one out of four Americans was of a race other than white, a significant fact that further asserts the multicultural nature of the country.

Some areas of the United States are characterized by a higher degree of non-European American population than others. For instance, cities such as Miami, Los Angeles, Chicago, New York, and El Paso stand out because of their culturally different populations. Several states across the nation, such as Arizona, Florida, California, Hawaii, and Texas, possess a higher percentage of non-European Americans.

Perhaps your state is not included among the highly demographically diverse. However, one revealing fact about current population patterns is that diversity has been brought to those areas that are traditionally not diverse. An analysis of U.S. demographics indicates that all states have a rising number of multicultural residents (Hobbs & Stoops, 2002). The conclusions are obvious: We are all faced with various degrees of diversity and we are *all* a part of it.

Cultural diversity is not a new phenomenon for the United States. Pluralism already existed at the time of this country's founding, when American society consisted of Europeans, indigenous groups of Native Americans, and Africans brought in bondage since the early seventeenth century. Learning to live together and learning to accept and recognize the sameness in all was not a simple task then or now. As in all social processes, differences in ideas and perceptions resulted in clashes. Incidents related to cultural divergences abound in the pages of U.S. history. Today, addressing cultural diversity remains a challenge for the United States that civic and professional organizations, such as the National Association for the Education of Young Children (NAEYC), Association for Supervision and Curriculum Development (ASCD), Southern Early Childhood Association (SECA), and National Council for the Social Studies (NCSS), work to overcome. There is a pressing need for early childhood educators to be aware

---

In Action . . .   **The New U.S. Society**

What are your concepts of European Americans and non-European Americans? To find out, simply web what those two terms represent to you. Web each term separately. Then, compare your webs with those in Figures 1-5 and 1-6.

- What did you find?
- Were any groups similar to or different from yours?
- Why do you think that happened?

---

of these past and present efforts in order to assist children in acquiring ways to face the challenges of our continuously growing pluralistic world.

A CALL FOR ACTION

Now more than ever, educators of young children recognize that the new complex diversity mandates programs that positively affect the learning processes and social adjustments of all school children. As an early childhood educator, providing children with developmentally and culturally appropriate practices (DCAP) is at the core of your profession (Bredekamp & Copple, 1997). Today, culture and diversity are acknowledged as elements defining program quality in all dimensions of early education. From classroom instruction to interactions with families and communities, sensitivity to and respect for the child and family's culture is intrinsic to professional practice. The NAEYC's Code of Ethical Conduct and Statement of Commitment (2005) further emphasizes the responsibilities of early educators working with culturally diverse children and families:

> Section II:
>
> *Ideals:*
>
> I-2.5. To respect the dignity and preferences of each family and to make an effort to learn about its structure, culture, language, customs, and beliefs.
> I-2.6. To respect families' childrearing values and their right to make decisions for their children.

Experiences in early childhood settings show that developmental practices are effectively guided when there is an understanding of the child in the "context of their family, culture, and society" (Bredekamp, 1995). To create responsive environments, early childhood educators cannot isolate activities from the social and cultural framework of the child. Educational designs that are based on the principles of child development recognize the undeniable influence culture has on the child (Berger, 2005).

With the increasingly changing nature of the country and world, early childhood professionals must be cognizant of the ongoing social and cultural transformations. This

SNAPSH○T 1-3   **A View of the World**

When I came to catch my flight, I never thought that I would have such a remarkable experience. The hour and a half that I had to spend because of a flight delay showed me the real face of America. Everything started when I decided to have a second cup of coffee. I went to the coffee bar in one of the concourses where they serve the best *cortadito* (espresso with milk) and *pastelitos* (guava and cheese pastries). A smiling Cuban lady served me the aromatic coffee. While sipping it, I saw an airport employee greeting a friend just returning from his hometown in Nicaragua. At the same time, several Haitians chatted while also sipping coffee. Two Colombians joined the group in front of the coffee stand. I noticed two Indian ladies, who wore the prettiest saris, chatting about their children. I finally made the line to board my flight where I heard a father call his child in very distinct Arabic. As we flew out, a thought came to my mind: My country is not just a country, it's a world in itself, a world that I see in my classroom.

Source: Rosales, 1992.

constant state of sociocultural flux affects the physical and social environments of all children. More precisely, the increased growth of the non-European American population, as demographers have predicted, is producing and will continue to produce a distinctively different social climate for children living in the twenty-first century United States.

Research has shown that the way a young child learns to view and respond to the social world depends on the cultural values held in the immediate surroundings (Jarvis, 2003; Wright & Edelman, 2004). Culture, thus, plays a crucial role in the development of the child. If the society of the twenty-first century is to be characterized by a higher degree of diversity, this unquestionably describes an environment where children will find a multiplicity of cultural values. As an early childhood educator, you must consider the following questions:

■ *Am I preparing children to live in the twenty-first century?*

■ *Am I aware that today's preschoolers, kindergartners, and primary grade students will live their adult lives in a new era very different from mine?*

■ *What am I doing about it now?*

Issues raised by these questions constitute a call for action for early childhood professionals. We need to prepare to serve children in consonance with reality. This is not only a need but a mandate if we are to teach children in genuinely developmentally appropriate ways. It is no longer satisfactory to just display pictures of groups different from the mainstream culture or to assign a week to celebrate multiculturalism, which are practices still found in many classrooms. Nor is it acceptable to decide what students should learn without regard for the new sociocultural realities.

Education is a process of guiding and preparing a child to succeed in life. Given the social reality of the future, education of the young will have to encompass the skills and knowledge children need to navigate this pluralistic world. This will include learning to live effectively and productively in a society where diversity is a major factor. The success formula for future generations will include a solid foundation in cultural knowledge of many non-European American groups. The social skills and tools to interact effectively with these groups will be an essential part of everyday life and ultimately the key to survival in the twenty-first century.

One out of three children in 2050 in the United States will be a non-European American (Hobbs & Stoops, 2002). The difference between successful and unsuccessful individuals, at that time, may be the ability to interact effectively with people of various cultures. Early childhood professionals must lay the foundation by offering all children appropriate educational programs that will enable them to become successful individuals in this multicultural environment. This is the position that describes the aspiration for early childhood practices aimed at acknowledging, respecting, and incorporating the children's cultures and diverse characteristics into daily experiences in classrooms everywhere.

James S. Banks, the leading scholar in the field of multiculturalism, defines the aim of education for diversity as a way of keeping and maintaining the spirit and the essence of the American unum (Banks, 2006; National Council for the Social Studies, 1992). This idea of the American unum, literally, "where all are one," and where everyone is equally important, is a reminder of the goals and purposes that define our country: the champion of democracy and equality for all individuals. The authors of this book also believe that the achievement and preservation of the idea of *e pluribus unum* begins with the child. Because early childhood educators play such a vital role in the development of children, the future of our society may well rest in their hands.

In Action . . .   **Becoming a Multicultural Early Childhood Educator**

Becoming a multicultural early childhood educator is a process. However, you can begin taking steps now. One step is to examine the ideas and views on multiculturalism of leading early childhood professionals. You may want to begin by reading *White Teacher* by Vivian Gussin Paley (Harvard University Press, 2001). Paley, an experienced kindergarten teacher who taught in the South and the Midwest, shared her struggles in learning how to teach culturally diverse children. As you read, you may want to reflect on your own experiences as a student and a teacher in a culturally diverse society.

In Action . . .   **Services for Children and Families**

As you answer the call for multicultural education, you may want to learn about existing programs in your community. Because its origin comes from the need to serve children with culturally diverse characteristics, you may want to contact the agencies providing services for children in your community, such as Head Start. Call for an interview with the program's coordinator and ask about its approach toward multiculturalism. A visit to a classroom could be arranged in order to get firsthand experience with the services. Your community probably has other programs for the culturally diverse child. A call to the division of Child Services at your local Department of Human Resources and Services will let you know about other programs. For example, some areas have designed programs for children of migrant families, low-income families, or for the chronically ill. Based on your interests, you may want to plan an interview with the program coordinator.

As you face this challenge, there are questions to answer: Are you ready to offer children what they need? Have you achieved a level of awareness and knowledge that enables you to design responsive programs? To answer these questions, we will continue exploring other dimensions of our social diversity in the next chapter.

CREATING YOUR STANDARDS PORTFOLIO

Documenting Your Knowledge About Multiculturalism and Diversity

As you embark on the journey of learning about multicultural education, you will have opportunities to learn about new concepts, strategies, and resources. To document your progress, we invite you to create your own portfolio. A portfolio is a way of demonstrating and documenting your knowledge and mastery of key competencies. Sample artifacts are collected over time to show how you meet expectations of teaching and working with young children and their families.

A portfolio can be created around many different elements such as a job, a hobby, volunteer work, and so on. In education, some portfolios are created around significant benchmarks, such as professional standards. For example, in Florida, students in masters of education programs are required to create a portfolio based on the Florida Accomplished Practices for Teachers. The Accomplished Practices are used as a framework for the purpose and content of the portfolio.

Similarly, we have chosen to create the portfolio around the standards of the NAEYC. We have also broadened the scope of the portfolio by correlating the NAEYC standards with the widely used standards developed by the Interstate New Teacher Assessment and Support Consortium (INTASC).

Purpose of a Professional Portfolio

A professional portfolio has many uses. It is a portrait of yourself as a current or aspiring early childhood professional and a record of your accomplishments. A portfolio can be created according to many professional guidelines that are provided by state agencies, school districts, and professional organizations. You can organize this very personal document to present yourself in the most positive light as a professional. Some of the artifacts that may be included in the portfolio are an autobiographical sketch, a résumé, your philosophy of early childhood education, and any special honors and awards, as well as evidence of mastery of professional competencies as defined by your profession. The portfolio is a creative and personal document that has many applications. The portfolio exercise also allows you to learn more about your beliefs, commitments, and skills. Creating a portfolio is an invaluable experience. We invite you to begin the process now.

Using Standards to Organize Your Portfolio

As stated previously, we have chosen for the framework of your portfolio the professional standards outlined by the NAEYC (Hyson, 2003). These guidelines address quality of professional preparation as well as effective delivery of learning experiences for young children. Five core standards describe the critical expectations and characteristics of professional early childhood educators:

1. *Promoting Child Development and Learning*
2. *Building Family and Community Relationships*
3. *Observing, Documenting, and Assessing to Support Young Children and Families*
4. *Teaching and Learning*
   a. *Connecting with Children and Families*
   b. *Using Developmentally Effective Approaches*
   c. *Understanding Content Knowledge in Early Education*
   d. *Building Meaningful Curriculum*
5. *Becoming a Professional*

The Interstate New Teacher Assessment and Support Consortium (INTASC) standards that have been correlated with the NAEYC standards describe generic principles of best teaching practices and are used in many states:

Standard 1: Content Pedagogy
Standard 2: Student Development and Learning
Standard 3: Diverse Learners
Standard 4: Instructional Strategies
Standard 5: Motivation and Management of Learning Environments
Standard 6: Communication and Technology

Standard 7: Planning
Standard 8: Assessment
Standard 9: Reflective Practice and Professional Growth
Standard 10: School–Community Involvement

Assembling Your Portfolio

Portfolios can be assembled in a variety of ways, using a three-ring binder, filing container, expandable folder, or digital folder on the Internet. No matter which method you choose, the portfolio will represent you and your accomplishments.

Begin your portfolio with an introductory section about yourself. Take your time and be selective about what you include, and make sure that you present yourself in the best light possible.

The section that addresses the NAEYC and INTASC standards will be addressed throughout this book at the end of each chapter. In each chapter, we will make the connection to a specific standard and ask you to create evidence that proves your mastery. These artifacts will become a part of the largest section of your personal portfolio.

The portfolio has many purposes. It is an excellent tool for keeping track of your professional growth and progress. Your instructor may want to see it if you are using this book in a course. We have been told on many occasions that the portfolio is extremely useful in job interviews, and many students have also used their portfolios in formal presentations and workshops. We hope that you will create an exemplary record of your work and knowledge and that it will serve you well in the future.

WHAT WE HAVE LEARNED—CHAPTER SUMMARY

In this chapter, you learned about the origins of multiculturalism in our country. The profiles and short histories of major cultural groups were presented along with some key historical events, the current demographics, and future growth patters. The concept of immigrants and processes of immigration were emphasized in order to make you aware of what many members of our society, including young children, experience. We discussed the meaning of diversity and its importance in education as well as its growing importance in the future of the United States. Being alike and being different do not need to be polarizing positions for anyone, least of all for educators of young children. Emphasizing our commonalities and expanding the understanding of others are keys to a better world that educators of young children hold as a sacred trust.

THINGS TO DO . . .

1. Discovering the cultural composition of your neighborhood and of the community of your school helps you gain a practical awareness about the people you live with. Begin by making a list of the cultures present in both environments, your neighborhood

and your school. Then, take a field trip and list all the things that reflect diversity (signs, buildings, decorations, etc.). What did you find? Highlight those cultures you feel you need to learn more about. Your school or community library is a good place to continue your search.

2. Are you aware of your own culture? To appreciate cultural diversity, you must first know your own. Get a stack of index cards. On one of the index cards, write the name of the cultural group you think you belong to. Next, find out where (geographical area) that cultural group originates and write it on another card. Use the other cards to describe the things you do that underline your being part of that cultural group. Examine your results and see what you discovered about yourself that you were not aware of before.

3. Get together with two or three colleagues and discuss your backgrounds. Identify the historical event that brought the members of your family or you to the United States. Then, create lists of social, economic, and political events that caused their or your immigration. Discuss what may have happened if they or you never left. How have your and their lives changed as a result of coming to the United States? List the positive and negative elements of the experience.

4. Take action in your classroom by examining your present curriculum for diversity. Highlight those activities and concepts that focus on pluralism.

5. This book will take you on a journey where you will find ways to develop an appropriate multicultural environment for young children. Begin a diary of your experiences. You may want to get a small notebook where you can record your thoughts and experiences. To begin your diary, enter your responses to these questions:

   ■ *What do I want for children as an individual and as a teacher?*
   ■ *How can I support the needs of children with cultural and diverse characteristics?*

6. Write a description of your community in 2050. While writing, think about what the architecture, recreation, schools, churches, and people may be like. What about language technology, transportation, and so on?

RECOMMENDED INTERNET RESOURCES

■ Articles from the Center for Immigration Studies providing historical perspectives on immigration
www.cis.org/topics/history.html

■ Links to relevant sub-topics related to historical and current immigration issues, from the Consitutional Rights Foundation
www.crf-usa.org/immigration/immigration_history.htm

■ The U.S. Census, the main source of data and information on a variety of demographic topics
www.census.gov

YOUR STANDARDS PORTFOLIO

NAEYC Standard 5: Becoming a Professional*

Begin to build your portfolio with Standard 5: Becoming a Professional. One of the critical characteristics of a professional multicultural educator is the ability to reflect on issues that concern young children, their families, and the impact of classroom practices on their lives. Reflection is a way of being introspective and examining your thoughts and opinions at a deeper level. As you reflect, you will tend to acquire additional information and in-depth knowledge. Begin a journal of reflections and record your thoughts and ideas as you explore the topics in this book. This book's components such as "In Action," "Snapshots," and "Let's Talk and Reflect . . ." will help you reflect upon and analyze key concepts. You may want to include some of your responses under Standard 9 and create artifacts that prove your mastery. Let's begin!

Creating a developmentally appropriate curriculum starts with our own reflections about what children need. Reflect on the following questions and record your answers:

- *As an early childhood educator, what do I want for young children?*
- *What do I need to know to support the needs of culturally diverse children and their families?*

REFERENCES

Banks, J. (2006). *Cultural diversity and education: Foundations, curriculum, and teaching* (5th ed.). Needham Heights, MA: Allyn & Bacon.

Banks, J., & Banks, C. M. (Eds.). (2006). *Multicultural education: Issues and perspectives* (2nd ed.). Needham Heights, MA: Allyn & Bacon.

Baruth, L., & Manning, M. L. (2004). *Multicultural education of children and adolescents* (4th ed.). Needham Heights, MA: Allyn & Bacon.

Berger, K. (2005). *The developing person through childhood and adolescence.* New York: Worth.

Bredekamp, S. (1995). *Developmentally appropriate practice in early childhood programs.* Washington, DC: National Association for the Education of Young Children.

Bredekamp, S., & Copple, C. (1997). *Developmentally appropriate practice in early childhood programs* (Rev. ed.). Washington, DC: National Association for the Education of Young Children.

Brown McCracken, J. (1993). *Valuing the primary years.* Washington, DC: National Association for the Education of Young Children.

Campbell, D. E. (2004). *Choosing democracy: A practical guide to multicultural education* (3rd ed.). Upper Saddle River, NY: Pearson.

Current Population Survey Annual Supplement. (March 2001). U.S. Bureau of the Census and U.S. Department of Labor, Bureau of Labor Statistics.

* NAEYC Standard 5 correlates with INTASC Standard 9: Reflective Practice.

Doctorow, E. L. (2007). *Ragtime*. New York: Alfred Knopf. (Original work published in 1975).

Hobbs, F., & Stoops, N. (2002). *Demographic trends in the 20th century*. (Census 2000 Special Report, Series CENSR-4.) Washington, DC: U.S. Government Printing Office.

Hyson, M. (2003). *Preparing early childhood professionals: NAEYC's standards for programs*. Washington, DC: National Association for the Education of Young Children.

Jarvis, A. (2003). *Social learning theory*. New York: RoutledgeFalmer.

Kasindorf, M., & El Nasser, H. (March 1, 2001). Impact of Census' race data debated. *USA Today*. Retrieved March 29, 2005, from http://www.usatoday.com/news/nation/census/2001-03-12-censusimpact.htm.

Kivel, P. (2002). *Uprooting racism* (Rev. ed.). Canada: New Society Publishers.

Lynch, E. W., & Hanson, M. J. (2004). *Developing cross-cultural competence: A guide for working with young children and their families*. Baltimore, MD: Paul Brookes.

Martorella, P. H. (2001). *Social studies for elementary school children*. New York: Prentice Hall.

National Association for the Education of Young Children. (2005). *Code of ethical conduct & statement of commitment: A position statement of the National Association for the Education of Young Children*. Washington, DC: Author.

National Council for the Social Studies. (1992). Guidelines for multicultural teaching. *Social Education 56*(3), 274–294.

Nieto, S., & Bode, P. (2008). *Affirming diversity: The sociopolitical context of multicultural education*. New York: Longman.

Novas, H., & Cao, L. (2004). *Everything you need to know about Asian-American History*. New York: Plume.

Parillo, V. N. (2007). *Understanding race and ethnic relations* (3rd ed.). Needham Heights, MA: Allyn & Bacon.

Robles de Meléndez, W. (2006). Activities for the graduate course *Planning the multicultural environment*. Summer. Fort Lauderdale, FL: Nova Southeastern University.

Rosales, L. (1992). *Listen to the heart: Impressions and memories of a teacher*. Unpublished manuscript.

Say, A. (1994). *Grandfather's journey*. Boston: Houghton Mifflin.

Steinbeck, J. (1975). *The Grapes of Wrath*. New York: Viking. (Original work published in 1939).

Suro, R., & Passel, J. S. (2003). The rise of the second generation: Changing patterns in Hispanic population growth. Retrieved February 22, 2005, from http://pewhispanic.org/files/reports/22.pdf.

U.S. Census Bureau. (2000a). *The Arab population: 2000* (Census 2000 brief C2KBR-23). Washington, DC: Department of Commerce.

U.S. Census Bureau. (2000b). *Profile of selected social characteristics: Census 2000 brief*. Retrieved February 15, 2005, from http://www.census.gov.

U.S. Census Bureau. (2005). *Facts for features: Asian/Pacific American Heritage Month.* Retrieved May 17, 2005, from http://www.census.gov/Press-Release/www/releases/archives/facts_for_features_special_editions/004522.html.

U.S. Census Bureau. (2008). *A new and more diverse nation by midcentury.* Retrieved August 31, 2008 from: http://www.census.gov/Press-Release/www/releases/archives/population/012496.html.

U.S. Census Bureau & U.S. Department of Labor. (2001). *Current Population Survey, March 2001 Annual Supplement.*

Wright, A., & Edelman, W. A. (2004). *Faces of hope: Children of a changing world.* New York: New World Library.

CHAPTER 2

The Nature of Culture, the Nature of People

> There is not one aspect of human life that is not touched and altered by culture.
>
> *Edward T. Hall (1990)*

CHAPTER OBJECTIVES

In this chapter, we will
- define *culture*.
- establish how culture shapes our lives.
- identify what areas of life are influenced by culture.
- describe how children reflect their culture in the classroom.

KEY CONCEPTS

- culture
- socialization
- cultural identity
- cultural diversity
- race
- stereotype
- cultural values

FROM BARBARA'S JOURNAL

Today, I brought in some apples and cut them up for my children as a snack. At 10 o'clock I asked everyone to come to my desk and take a piece. Aisha hesitated but finally approached me and said, "It's Ramadan, and my family says that you can't eat during the day." I looked at her and just patted her head. What is Ramadan? I know it's a very special time for Muslims, but I really don't know what Aisha meant. I decided to talk to one of my colleagues while the children were on break. My colleague Marisa did not know for sure what Ramadan was either, but she knew that Said, who is in her second-grade class, did not eat during school time. I decided to check out Ramadan on the Internet and find out more. I also thought that it would be a good idea to get some more information about the cultures of my other children and find out about their customs and holidays. I have planned a unit on holidays already, but I am afraid it may not include what will be relevant to them. That I must know more about the reality of the children in my group, and their cultures, is clear. It will be the only way to appropriately plan and teach.

| CULTURE, THE MAGIC WEB OF LIFE

Have you ever asked yourself why you are the way you are? Why you act the way you act? Why you believe in what you believe? Why you speak the language you speak? Why you eat what you eat? The answer is culture, a critical factor in everything we do, say, believe, and are.

The concept of culture has been a focus of discussions among social scientists, educators, philosophers, and people in general for generations. Many learned and famous people have searched hard and debated long trying to define the meaning of culture. No one seems to be able to agree on one definition. However, everybody acknowledges that we all have a culture.

Culture is a part of each individual because it is a part of every society (Geertz, 2000). No one can claim to be exempt from having a culture. This condition is inherent to human nature. Whether aware of it or not, "everybody has a culture" (Nieto & Bode, 2008). Individuals begin to assimilate culture from birth. As early childhood educators, you have probably noticed the different ways your children respond to experiences and interpret events and reality in the classroom. This may be even more evident at times

---

In Action . . .   What Is Your Idea of Culture?

Before reading any further, you should explore your ideas about culture. Take a piece of paper and fold it into three parts. Title each part as follows: *My Ideas About Culture, Formal Definitions, and Things in Common.* Fill in the first column by writing all the ideas that you believe define culture. As you read through this chapter, complete the rest of the columns. We will get back to this activity later.

LET'S TALK AND REFLECT... This Is My Culture

Our culture defines who we are and how we live. It permeates most aspects of our lives, including those that are easy to observe and those that are not. Culture can be a safe haven or a battlefield; a cherished possession or a burden.

- *What is my perception about my own culture? What are some of the aspects easily noticed? Which ones are not?*
- *How has my own culture influenced who I am?*

when your interpretations diverge from the children's interpretations. These variations are largely rooted in their individual cultural patterns.

The Need for Guideposts: What Culture Does for Human Beings

Imagine a world with no rules. Think about how it would be if there were no directions to guide our existence, no principles to tell us what is right or wrong, no frames of reference to give us clues as we confront things never encountered before. Those are the problems we would face if there were no culture.

Culture provides a framework for our lives. It is the paradigm humans use to guide their behavior, find meaning in events, interpret the past, and set aspirations. From very early in life, we learn to follow and apply the recognized guidelines of our society, sometimes without even being consciously aware of them. For a child, cultural guidelines are discovered through daily interactions with others, observing, and modeling some of the behaviors learned from families and adults. Psychologist Jerome Bruner (1990) says that when the child enters into a group, the child does so as a participant of a public process where meanings are shared. This participant status entitles the child to learn the ways of the group. Learning makes the child a member of a group. These "ways of the group" are what we call **culture.** As social human beings, we all belong to a group, and all groups have culture.

We All Have a Culture

Social scientists—sociologists, anthropologists, and psychologists—believe that culture demarcates all manners people use to interact in the context of society. Culture is needed by humans to survive in a social group. Bruner (1990) affirms that "the divide in human evolution was crossed when culture became the major factor in giving form to the minds of those living under its sway." Clearly, as humans strive for survival, the need for an organizing pattern becomes a necessity. This is what makes culture a thing shared by all social groups.

FIGURE 2-1 **Dimensions of Culture**

Through culture we . . .
SEE   PERCEIVE   INTERPRET   REPRESENT
SYMBOLIZE   VALUE   ASSIGN MEANING

There are many ways to describe and define culture. For Freire (2000), culture encompasses all that is done by people. Hernandez (2001) says that culture refers to "the complex processes of human social interaction and symbolic communication." Arvizu, Snyder, and Espinosa (cited by Hernandez, 2001) describe culture as an instrument people use as they struggle to survive in a social group. The definition used throughout this book identifies culture as the ways and manners people use to see, perceive, represent, interpret, and assign value and meaning (see Figure 2-1) to the reality they live or experience (Banks, 2007; Lynch & Hanson, 2004; Nieto & Bode, 2008).

Looking at Life Through Our Cultures

Todo es del color del cristal con que se mira. (Everything depends on the color of the glass you look through.)

Pedro Calderón de la Barca (1600–1681), *La Vida es Sueño*

Culture is a glass prism through which we look at life. Like a prism, culture has many facets. Early childhood educators need to be cognizant and aware of these various angles that help explain the behavior, reactions, and manners of children in the classroom.

Some of the key aspects of culture that contribute to understanding and responsively planning experiences for young children and their families are the following:

■ *Culture defines the accepted behaviors, roles, interpretations, and expectations of a social group.* Every social group has norms and principles that reflect agreed meanings. For example, in Nepalese society, it is accepted "to pop in and stare at the strange [Westerner] at great length, without thinking twice about it" (Murray, 1993).

■ *Culture is present in visible, tangible ways.* Culture also exists in abstract ways that are not physically perceived by the eye. For example, we see the sari dress of an Indian woman and a child's toy truck and recognize them for what they are. However, we do not know why the Indian woman is smiling or why the child is hugging the toy. These reactions are rooted in inner feelings that are not readily visible.

■ *Culture offers stable patterns to guide human behavior.* Although stable, culture is also dynamic as it constantly responds to the various influences in the surroundings, affecting changes whenever necessary. An example of this is seen in the concept of a child. Today, a child is considered an individual with unique characteristics and rights, whereas in the past, the child was not valued as a person (Roopnarine & Johnson, 2004).

■ *Culture is acquired through interactions with the environment.* The major settings where this occurs are the family and the school. One of the most evident aspects of culture acquisition is how, through interactions with parents and family members, children learn the language of their group. Cultural expectations also help children to build knowledge about their cultures. Some of the early research conducted by Mead (2000) in New Guinea revealed that the education of 6-year-old Manu children included mastering swimming and canoeing, skills usually associated with older children, because those skills are essential for survival in the Manu society. In Africa, children as young as age 5 learn to take care of younger siblings. Culture was also found to be the critical factor influencing attachment and **socialization** patterns during the early childhood years (Gardiner and Kosmitzki, 2005; Harwood, Miller, & de Lucca, 1997).

■ *We begin learning the patterns and shared meanings of the group we belong to at birth.* This knowledge increases and changes as we grow and develop, both individually and as a member of society. Think about how a 5-year-old interprets a birthday party and compare it with the reactions of a 2-year-old. Compare the ideas held about single parents in the 1950s with those of today.

■ *Culture influences different aspects of life* (Banks, 2007). Nothing escapes the power of culture. Notice, for example, how you dress yourself and how you decide what appeals to you as beautiful in contrast to what you label as not beautiful.

■ *Cultural differences also exist among people of the same culture.* Within a same group, differing lifestyles and values are not uncommon. Experiences, including personal and historical circumstances, shape people's views. For instance, ideas and practices concerning child rearing held by urban parents probably differ from the views held by parents in rural areas. Even people belonging to a same family may exhbit differences in terms of their behaviors and ideas.

■ *Culture gives people identity.* Sharing ideas, values, and practices gives humans a sense of being part of an entity. There are various factors that make people feel they are members of a group. Having a gender, age, religion, and family background are among the basic factors that provide a sense of identity. Additional traits that define someone's unique persona are derived from experiences and interactions with others within and outside one's cultural group.

Cultural Dimensions

The influence of culture is so powerful that it covers every aspect of behavior. As Hall (1990) says, "[t]here is not one aspect of life that is *not touched and altered* by culture" (emphasis added). This includes personality, how people dress themselves (including shows of emotions), the way they think, how they move, how problems are solved, how their cities are planned and laid out, how transportation systems function, and how economic and government systems are put together and function.

Hall's ideas remind us that culture can be exhibited in visible ways (that is, with our body movements, our gestures, and the physical distribution of our cities) and invisible ways (such as how we think and how we solve problems). This premise suggests

---

In Action . . .   **Exploring Culture**

One of the ways to "see" proof that we all have and respond within a cultural framework is to find two persons and ask them what they think is the right way to celebrate a wedding. Write their answers and compare them with your own.

• Were they in agreement with each other?

• Were you in agreement with them? Why?

---

another relevant feature of culture: the twofold way in which we exhibit its influences and effects. Visible to the eye are dress codes, eating patterns, and even the games played by children. Other things remain invisible to the eye, but are perceived through actions. Examples of the invisible culture may be seen in emotional reactions to events such as happy occasions or death and in ideas about how to welcome guests into one's home.

Whether visible or not, culture provides patterns to interpret life. We use them every day. Like the skin that covers our bodies and gives us our external individual identity, culture is always with us (Lynch & Hanson, 2004). As a classroom educator, you

FIGURE 2-2 **Cultural Levels in the Community and the Early Childhood Classroom**

Material Culture:
What we see, hear, and experience

- Language—accents, intonations
- Dress—colors, garments, materials, dress codes
- Food and eating—items, preparation, eating habits
- Personal decorations—jewelry, body decorations, head coverings
- Utensils and tools—cooking utensils, living utensils
- Artwork—styles, colors, use of materials, folk art
- Music—instruments, practices, sounds
- Construction—buildings, home decorations
- Household utensils

Nonmaterial Culture:
What is invisible to the eye but perceived through interactions

- Ideas
- Values
- Beliefs
- Feelings and emotions

have probably experienced times when you could easily identify the cultural patterns followed by your students; however, other times, you have probably been unable to do so. This occurs because culture presents itself in ways that are either materially or non-materially expressed (see Figure 2-2) (Gardiner & Kosmitzki, 2005; Hernandez, 2001).

Differences in values and customs are readily visible in the most familiar settings. The incident described in Snapshot 2-1 (later in this chapter) exhibits a cultural misunderstanding that could occur anywhere.

The presence of culture transcends all that we do. The material and the nonmaterial sides of culture are constantly working together. You and your children display them in the classroom through your actions and interactions. Usually, we can easily note differences in others when they are visible or, to a lesser extent, when they are not observable but perceived. Also, we can more easily observe differences in others, although we often fail to detect our own patterns of divergence. This is the result of our own culture being so embedded in us that we forget it exists. It also happens because we consider our ways the most appropriate formula for responding to the environment. To further understand how culture is seen in our classrooms, consider the findings of a kindergarten teacher who took a cultural inventory of her children. As you read Figure 2-3, Culture

FIGURE 2-3 **Culture in Action: Ways Young Children Exhibit Their Culture in the Classroom**

Verbal Skills

- Language use
  - English language learners (ELL) may show linguistic code-switching.
  - Native language is dominant.
- Oral expressions
  - Linguistic expressions
  - How they address adults
  - Use of questions
- Voice accent and inflection

Emotions

- Expressions of fears and feelings
- Expressions of love and friendship
- Reactions to stories
- Reactions to conflict (while at play, in the playground, during classroom activities)

Other Factors

- Ways of dress
- Preferred food
- Comments about family activities (special events and holidays)
- Expressing preferences
- Sharing pictures and objects from home

SNAPSH⦿T 2-1 An Indecent Practice

Ms. Allen believed that her child-care center was the best facility for young children. Every effort had been made to follow developmentally appropriate practices. Recently opened in a suburban area, the center was enthusiastically received by the parents in the community. The children seemed very happy. The staff, hand-picked by Ms. Allen, was excellent.

One morning, Ms. Allen was surprised to get a call from a very irate Mrs. Garcia, who informed her that she was moving her 4-year-old daughter to another school. Only a week before, Ms. Allen had personally registered the bright-eyed child and had a pleasant conversation with Mrs. Garcia, who then seemed very impressed by the school. Ms. Allen could not understand the reason for the parent's sudden anger or her actions.

After getting off the phone, the very puzzled Ms. Allen asked if anyone in the office was aware of an incident involving the Garcia girl. Her secretary informed her that the child's mother called the day before and complained that in her child's classroom they were doing things that were indecent, "especially for a girl." But, the secretary had been so busy this morning that she had forgotten to mention the conversation to Ms. Allen. "This can't be true," said Ms. Allen and went to see the teacher to learn more before calling back Mrs. Garcia.

Ms. Morton, the teacher, told Ms. Allen that Mrs. Garcia visited her daughter's classroom the day before and saw the children's bathrooms, which made her "very irate." Ms. Morton tried to explain that the absence of doors was a safety measure. Despite her efforts to elaborate further, Mrs. Garcia took her child and left very annoyed. "I really don't know why," Ms. Morton said. Ms. Allen thought for a moment and said, "I do, I do."

in Action, highlight the similarities between her findings and yours. Diller and Moule (2005) warn that in order to provide responsive experiences, it is essential to become aware of the children's behaviors. These provide insights about their experiences that are shaped by their cultures. Teaching that is developmentally appropriate depends on the teacher's ability to respond to the child's individual and cultural realities. Consider, for instance, the experience of the child-care center director in Snapshot 2-1. Without a doubt, the bathroom facility was designed to provide for the safety of the children in the center; however, from the parent's perspective, not having a door to provide for her daughter's privacy was a violation of her cultural principles, both at the overt and covert levels. Gaining awareness about the interplay of various cultural worlds gives the early childhood educator an opportunity to create environments sensitive to children and to their realities.

| DISCOVERING THE CULTURES OF CHILDREN

At birth, we begin to acquire the ways of those with which we live and interact. We learn about our culture and the cultures of others as we interact with people. Because every individual's environment has a culture of its own, we come in contact with many different cultural patterns. Perhaps the best place to see these differences is in the classroom. You probably have noticed already that the children you teach have unique ways. This is easier to see in the context of their interactions when they begin to share their thoughts and feelings.

To help you "see" the many cultures that characterize your children, do the following exercise. Select a story to share with the children; for instance, choose any of Verna Aardema's stories or any of the Jafta books by Hugh Lewin. If you want, present an issue for children to ponder and react to. Before sharing the story or issue, write down what is, in your opinion, the central message, point, or moral of the story. Then, share the story or the issue and ask the children to offer their interpretations. Here is where the fun part begins. As you listen to their comments, see how many different ideas are given. Compare their answers with your own. You will find that your students, despite their young age, have an exciting variety of views. Charting their comments will give you additional opportunities to learn how their answers reflect their cultures. This beginning experience will make you aware of two important facts: (1) everyone has a culture, and (2) culture influences our views.

Culture Establishes Patterns of Life

"Who are you?" said the caterpillar . . . Alice replied rather shyly, "I hardly know, sir, just at present—at least I know who I was when I got up this morning, but I think I must have been changed several times since then."
Lewis Carroll (1832–1898), Alice's Adventures in Wonderland

You probably would have answered like Alice if you found yourself in her wonderland. When Alice went down the rabbit hole, she left behind the rules and roles that gave meaning to her life, and she entered a world of unfamiliar ways. We have encountered similar experiences. For instance, how many times have you been in a place where you could not understand what others were doing or saying? Only when a familiar action is observed or expression is understood does the situation make sense.

Everything we do responds to patterns learned through and from experiences with families, individuals, and people from our own social group. In social groups, everyone tends to follow a similar frame of reference that gives meaning to life routines and experiences. This pattern gives sense and direction to our actions and behaviors, which is the essential role of culture. A system of rules, culture serves as the framework people from a group use to make decisions, see and interpret reality, and perceive one's role in the family and society.

Experiences reflect how the members of a group use their frames of reference or scripts. These frameworks are made up of the following:

- values
- beliefs
- shared meanings and interpretations
- rules

Explaining when and why the social patterns of a group were established is difficult. The origins are found in events experienced long ago by elders who, in turn, established ways and ascribed their meanings. Recognizing the need to perpetuate one's traditions, each generation has the responsibility of delivering the message from one generation to the next. How we came to learn and follow social patterns is a result of the social environment in which we were born and live.

Culture as a Main Influence in People's Lives

Underlying our behavior is a set of complex ideas that individuals in our particular group use to interpret experiences and generate actions and behaviors (Spradley & McCurdy, 2003). These are rules, values, beliefs, and principles that, when followed, provide coherence and integrity to human existence. The members of the group know each of these structures or schemes. Despite how unusual rules might look to an outsider, for its members, they are logical. In fact, when practiced, they grant a sense of identity to the collective group (Gardiner & Kosmitzki, 2005; Hernandez, 2001). Cultural schemes are used to define the behavior parameters as well as the needs and aspirations of the group. Practices are also based on the particular interpretations that the group has made of life events. For instance, this is what Milo, the character in *The Phantom Tollbooth*, discovers during his encounter with a magical child:

> Milo turned around and found himself staring at two very neatly polished brown shoes, for standing directly in front of him . . . was another boy just about his age, whose feet were easily three feet above the ground . . .
>
> "Well," said the boy, "in my family everyone is born in the air, with his head at exactly the height it's going to be when he's an adult, and then we all grow toward the ground."
>
> . . . [Milo said] "In my family we all start on the ground and grow up, and we never know how far until we actually get there." (Juster, 1961/2000)

"What a silly system," was the child's reaction to what Milo considered a logical growing style, probably the same comment you would have made had you been part of the boy's culture group.

Trying to understand the rules, beliefs, and values of other cultures while using our own values is not always effective. Each culture needs to be observed and under-

F⦶CUS
on Classroom Practices

Celebrations, One of Culture's Universal Traits

Many common elements are shared by different cultures. Perhaps one of the most characteristic is the need to celebrate. Celebrations can happen for a variety of reasons. They can also be observed in many ways, all of which are understood and shared by those who belong to the cultural group. In simple terms, celebrations are happenings that people observe because of the significance they have in their lives. Celebrations become holidays when they are observed by an entire religious group or when they hold national relevance. For early childhood teachers who want to discover more about the cultures of their students, learning how and why celebrations occur opens doors to cultural understanding. In the classroom, you may want to explore the celebrations observed by children and their families. Begin by brainstorming with children about what a celebration is. A good storybook to use is *Birthdays Around the World* by Mary Lankford and Karen Dugan (Harper-Collins, 2002). Information about the holidays and celebrations families observe can be obtained by sending home a letter with these two questions:

• What are the three most important celebrations or special days for your family?

• What are the holidays your family observes?

Take time to analyze the answers. They will give you not only a glimpse of the students' cultures but also an idea of what families consider important. With the information gathered, engage the class in creating a mural depicting the holidays and special days they celebrate. You may want to involve students in further exploration of the topic. This can even become the target of an interesting thematic unit. To help you build a thematic unit, here are some essential points that will help you focus on the cultural aspects:

What Constitutes Cultural Aspects in Holidays and Celebrations

1. Meanings: Why is it observed?
   a. religious
   b. personal
   c. national or patriotic
2. Ways in which it is observed: How is it observed? What do people do?
   a. When does it take place? (time, season, dates)
   b. What do people do? (external or physical aspects)
      • colors and symbols
      • decorations
      • traditions (such as gift-giving, food, music)
3. People involved: Who participates?
   a. adults; children
   b. all
4. Places, locations: Where do activities take place?
   a. home
   b. community
   c. school

stood from the perspective of its members. More precisely, the ideas of different cultures cannot be fully equated (Spradley & McCurdy, 2003). For example, individuality, prized in U.S. culture, is not equally valued in other cultures. Lynch and Hanson (2004) remark that in traditional Asian cultures, social orientation is focused on the collective

Native Americans have always contributed to the cultural fabric of our country.

"we" rather than on the individual. Awareness of values and visions of others contribute to our appreciation of diversity.

What we do and plan in early childhood classrooms is influenced by our cultural beliefs and values. Lewis (1991) reports how the view of responsibility varies in Japanese schools and how it influences classroom practices in nursery schools. During her study, Lewis observed how 5-year-olds were given responsibilities at an age when, in the U.S. context, the child is still guided by teachers. As their "brother's keepers," Japanese children were granted the authority to control the behavior of their peers and were held accountable for chores and tasks expected to be carried out by the group. Sanctions for activities or routines not followed emerged from the peers and not the teacher, for she was to remain a conflict-free benevolent figure.

Examples abound of differences in the interpretation of reality. Each interpretation reveals what is logical and correct in a particular culture. Knowledge of these interpretations helps the early childhood educator establish positive interactions and avoid misinterpretations. Take, for example, the extended use of baby language commonly employed by Hispanics in their communication with young children. This practice is not encouraged in the culture of the United States because the members of this group believe that adult language should be used from infancy. Another illustration pertains to visiting Native American families for the first time. Guests should ask for a place to sit, rather than assume any place is acceptable (Joe & Malach, 2004). Although special practices might differ from ours, we must always remember that they are part of what gives members of a particular culture a sense of identity.

A Sense of Identity: Being a Part of the Group

In our society, elementary school children learn far more than reading, writing, and arithmetic. Some of the mere aspects of their knowledge are never taught in a systematic way. They are acquired as part of their culture through interaction with teachers and peers.

James Spradley and David McCurdy (2003)

FIGURE 2-4 **Elements of Cultural Identity**

• ethnic or national origin	• geographical region
• family	• language
• religion	• age
• gender	• socioeconomic level
• educational background	• job or occupation

Have you ever stopped to consider what prompts you to say "I am . . ."? Are you aware of what saying what you are means? Ask a 5-year-old what she is and see how quickly she states her identity. Even if the answer is, "I am a girl," that child is establishing herself as a member of a gender group. This sense of identification reveals an awareness of a group in which the individual participates and discloses another trait of culture: a sense of identity.

Many factors determine cultural identity. These factors vary according to one's individual characteristics, experiences, and affiliations. Your identity may be influenced by gender, age, profession, ethnicity, language, and other factors. This leads us to affirm that, in fact, we all belong to many more groups than we may be aware of. Some of the elements influencing our individual identity may be any of the elements in Figure 2-4 (Banks & Banks, 2006; Gollnick & Chinn, 2005).

The interplay of a multiplicity of variables—age, family, ethnicity, religion, socioeconomic status, gender, religion, educational experiences, individual characteristics, and others—is what makes us who we are. Garza and Lipton (cited by Hernandez, 2001) state that because individuals are defined by more than just one cultural influence, "everyone is multicultural to varying degrees with [the] specific characteristics of each individual being unique."

Can you describe the cultural schema of these young Eastern European women who arrived in the United States at the turn of the twentieth century?

Wadsworth/Cengage Learning

LITERACY CONNECTIONS...

Using Children's Literature to Learn About Cultures

Learning about cultures is an exciting adventure. Today, you can obtain information about most cultural groups, which makes it easy for early childhood educators to create appropriate classroom environments where children can learn about each other's cultures. Classrooms where the children's cultures are represented also send the message that the various cultures are valued and welcome.

Sharing experiences through books is an excellent way for young children to find out about their own culture while learning to appreciate the cultures of their peers.

The following selection of books is suitable for preschoolers (ages 3–4) and kindergartners.

- Adoff, A. (1992). *Black is brown is tan.* New York: HarperTrophy. (interracial)

- Delacre, L. (1989) *Arroz con leche: Popular songs and rhymes from Latin America.* New York: Scholastic. (Latino)

- Fowler, S. (1998). *Circle of thanks.* New York: Scholastic. (Inuit)

- Grimes, N. (2002). *Danitra Brown leaves town.* New York: HarperCollins. (African American)

- Krebs, L., and Cairns, J. (2003). *We all went on a safari: A counting journey through Tanzania.* Cambridge, MA: Barefoot Books. (African)

- Lin, G. (2001). *Dim sum for everyone!* New York: Knopf. (Chinese)

- Pak, S. (2001). *Sumi's first day of school ever.* New York: Viking Books. (Korean)

- Uegaki, C. (2003). *Suki's kimono.* Toronto, Canada: Kids Can Press. (Japanese)

A MYRIAD OF CULTURAL IDENTITIES: THE ESSENCE OF CULTURAL DIVERSITY

Many factors make us who we are. A **cultural identity,** as you have seen already, is based on numerous elements, each having varying degrees of influence on a person's individuality. You have also learned that ethnic or cultural descent is not the only element that defines a cultural orientation. People might share some similar traits, like a culture of origin or religion, but they probably have values that diverge to various degrees from those of others. You as an individual represent many ideas and influences, all blended into who *you* are. They are your unique experiences and will not be like those of others. As you constructed your reality, you processed every bit of it according to your own mental schemes. If, as an early child educator, your ideas about education or about parenting differ from those of your colleagues, it is because you are the sum of your particular experiences. This is an example of diversity on a personal level.

Cultural Diversity Factors

Diversity is found in every single individual because each person is a composite of cultures. We also observe diversity in our communities. The society of the United States is one of the most complex reflections of social and cultural diversity. This comes as a result of the multitude of different nationalities and ideologies representative of the immigrant nature of this nation. Today, the term *cultural diversity* is freely used whenever we talk about the cultural spectrum found in our communities.

Often, the term **cultural diversity** is narrowly defined. Cultural diversity entails many more factors than the place of origin (where you or your parents were born or came from) or language. In the social context, cultural diversity describes the variety of social factors that, either singly or interactively, exert influence on an individual's behavior. Some of these key social factors are nationality, race, ethnicity, religion, social class, gender, exceptionalities, gender orientation, and age (see Figure 2-5). Knowledge about how diversity factors contribute to shaping the character and ways of an individual helps educators to better understand children's behaviors and learning characteristics (Banks & Banks, 2006; Copple, 2003). In the early childhood classroom, this knowledge provides the foundation for designing a sound developmentally appropriate program. How to respond to those variables in the context of your classroom is presented in the third part of this book.

Many scholars believe that concepts about diversity are socially constructed categories (Banks & Banks, 2006). In fact, these concepts are ideas or representations of physical, cultural, or social traits that individuals might possess. For instance, the social class category is very hard to define concretely, because it entails areas that are exclusive to those said to belong to it. Today, many of the attributes used to profile certain social groups are now also found across other social

Cities and towns throughout the United States reflect the multiplicity of people's ethnic roots.

Wadsworth/Cengage Learning

FIGURE 2-5 **Elements of Diversity**

Nationality	Refers to the country where the individual was born or from where his parents came.
Race/ethnicity	Defines the cultural traditions that serve to shape the individual's identity.
Religion	Refers to the religious affiliations and the freedom to exercise any faith as defined in the First Amendment of the Constitution.
Social class	Determined by income, education, occupation, lifestyles, and values typically held by a group.
Gender	Defines the behavior socially accepted and assigned to females and males, including role expectations.
Exceptionality	Defines the child who has any special needs or who is gifted.
Age	Defines the social expectations for behavior established by society for individuals of different age groups. They vary according to the individual's main cultural influence.

Understanding diversity requires an awareness of many different elements. This figure can serve as a barometer for assessing the levels of diversity in your classrooms.

In Action . . . **What Is Your Identity?**

Could you name the things that make you who you are? To find out, you need a pair of scissors, construction paper in eight different colors, and a piece of white paper. Place the white paper on a desk or table and write your name across the top. Using the colored construction papers, assign cultural elements that define cultural identity to each one. Now, reflect carefully on those factors as they pertain to your identity. Establish which one has the most impact in determining who you are. Consider the importance of the rest of the elements. As you decide their levels of impact, cut the papers in triangles proportional to the priorities they represent. Arrange the triangles in a circular form on the white paper. This is a representation of what you believe defines your identity.

• What are the reasons for your choices?

• Do this exercise with other members of your family and discuss the results.

---

groups (Banks & Banks, 2006). For this reason, we caution educators to carefully use terminology when describing children and families.

Cultural Diversity Defines the "American Way"

Today, debate still continues on the accuracy of the term *diversity* when describing people and communities in the United States. Some claim that we all are simply Americans. Others say that cultural diversity will endanger the future of the nation. These

SNAPSH⊙T 2-2 **Another Way to Define Our Cultural Identity**

Did you know that you are actually a member of many intermingling cultures? According to Vontress (1976), every individual is a member of at least five different cultures. Of these five, one is shared by all human beings; others are particular to the individual.

- *Universal:* All human beings are alike in their needs and rights.
- *Ecological:* The place where humans live on the earth determines the way they will respond and relate to their natural environment.

- *National:* Depending on the country where they were born, individuals will have characteristics that identify them (language, world views, and so on).
- *Regional:* Based on the region where humans live, they will develop area-specific cultures.
- *Racio-ethnic:* All people have distinct racial and ethnic characteristics.

Source: Adapted from Baruth & Manning, 2004.

comments usually reflect the fact that some people are still unclear about the significance of diversity.

Diversity has been the common denominator of the United States since its inception. As you saw in Chapter 1, people from many different countries came to forge the nation we feel so proud of now. Decades ago, when the founders—the poor, the idealists, and the persecuted of the world—came to this part of North America, they faced many physical, personal, and social adjustments. One of their major tasks

Even though they share a common Hispanic background, these children are diverse in their own ways. Teachers need to be aware of using only one variable when addressing children's needs.

was to adapt to their new social reality and become Americans. In this effort, newcomers laid aside their own cultures and blended into a common culture and framework. This is known as the process of acculturation. This concept is commonly described using the metaphor of the "melting pot," in which people dissolved their individual cultural identities and adopted the patterns of the mainstream culture.

Today, the concept of the United States as a "melting pot" where everyone becomes a mainstream kind of American has been challenged by the view of society as multicultural. The idea of a salad bowl is preferred over a melting pot by those affirming that it is possible for people to be productive members of American society while maintaining their own individual cultural heritage. To support this position, we find many examples derived from the stories of immigrants in communities everywhere who have integrated and adopted American lifestyles and still uphold their heritage.

Being a teacher in today's classrooms requires an understanding of the magnitude and significance of new social directions that have emerged out of the increasing presence and nature of diversity. More than ever before, professionals must understand the impact of life in a socially and culturally diverse society on early childhood practices. There is an added responsibility to meet the needs and expectations of young learners and their families. Current social realities also place demands on early childhood professionals to become more cognizant about their own cultures as well as the cultures of children they teach. This understanding is instrumental in setting an atmosphere of mutual respect for social and cultural diversity in our classrooms.

The classrooms of the United States are settings where the country's future is being forged. Preparation for the real world in our society now entails giving children the skills needed to interact with others. This has special meaning in an increasingly diverse society. As early childhood professionals strive to create the best environment for children, including and infusing the realities of society will prove to be the key elements. Teaching the whole child must include considerations of the child's cultural background.

LET'S TALK AND REFLECT... Culture and Identity

Culture plays an important part in the development of young children's identities and shapes their views of the world. Various environments also play essential roles in that process.

- How does the social and cultural environment of the community influence the children's concept of "self"?

- What messages are sent in the classroom regarding the differences in gender and exceptionalities? How do they influence children's emerging sense of self and sense of others?

| TALKING ABOUT RACE AND ETHNICITY

Probably no two concepts are more misunderstood than race and ethnicity. Both tend to be included in discussions about culture. The important issues are the relevance they have to culture and the meaning of each term.

Ethnic groups share common histories, customs, values, lifestyles, religions, and languages. In the United States, some ethnic groups have preserved their identities, whereas others have been integrated into the mainstream culture or have merged with other racial and ethnic groups. The particular preoccupation with race in the United States makes it even more difficult to define ethnic groups in absolute terms. For example, Asian Americans can have several different religions, be of different races and lifestyles, and hold totally different values.

The same is true of race. **Race** is a term used to describe the physical characteristics of a large group of people with somewhat similar genetic history (Campbell, 2004). The definition of race as defined by genetic characteristics was important in the European-dominated United States from its inception. Today, the definition of race has become more of a sociopolitical category than a biological phenomenon. The danger to our democracy is not ethnic identity or race, but racism, the oppression of a group of people based on the color of their skin (Campbell, 2004). As mentioned earlier, racist concepts evolve out of personal interactions and experiences in the environment. Prevention of racist ideas needs to take place early in life. Early childhood educators have the responsibility to eradicate racism among young children by addressing inappropriate comments and behaviors in the classroom in developmentally appropriate ways that will help clarify and thus erase what may be the emergence of erroneous concepts about others.

What Is Ethnicity?

Central to the idea of culture is the concept of ethnicity. Ethnicity is defined by three factors: nationality, ancestry, and religious affiliation. A member of an ethnic group might share some or all of these characteristics with other group members (Figure 2-6). Ethnic groups are usually described as people with a common cultural tradition and a clear sense of identity. Ethnicity, thus, becomes the set of features that historically has characterized a particular subgroup in the context of a larger dominant culture (McGoldrick, 2003). At the personal level, ethnicity becomes the sense an individual has of commonality with family and others of the same group to which he or she belongs (Feinstein, cited in McGoldrick, 2003). The family plays an instrumental role in a person's acquisition and development of a sense of ethnicity, serving as the initial source and reinforcer of ethnic characterizations. The impact of ethnicity on people is such that it identifies them within the spectrum of a society. Examples of ethnic groups found in U.S. society are the Amish, African Americans, and Jews. These three groups are good examples because they represent some of the differences you may find when defining ethnicity.

SNAPSH ◉ **T** 2-3   **America, the Melting Pot**

At the turn of the century when masses of immigrants poured into this country, America was referred to as a "melting pot," a place where everyone became one. This socialization process was the ultimate goal of the immigrants from Eastern Europe, Russia, and the Asian countries. Even though many of the ethnic groups lived in their own neighborhoods and practiced their cultural rituals, it was expected that the children assimilate into American society by becoming part of the mainstream culture.

Today, the climate is much different. The "melting pot" has given way to a pluralistic society where assimilation is not necessarily viewed as a priority. Many ethnic, cultural, and religious groups preserve their languages and ways and do not want to become part of the mainstream culture.

Many immigrants, particularly in metropolitan areas, live in large self-sufficient communities that allow the members to have meaningful and productive lives without depending on the society at large. This has facilitated the retention of the "mother tongue" and resulted in a lack of English language proficiency and the perseverance of other cultural habits, behaviors, and rituals of the mainstream culture. As the minorities continue to grow to the point that they will soon comprise the majority of the country's population, we are faced with many issues. Are we becoming a fractured society? Has the *unum* (oneness) of America all but disappeared? What are the consequences as well as the current and future goals of the new society of the United States of America?

Although the Amish have all three basic elements of diversity (religion, ancestry, and nationality) and the African Americans possess two (ancestry and nationality), the Jews, affiliated through their common religious tradition, may only have one. Regardless of what element establishes the character of an ethnic group, we all belong to one.

Baruth and Manning (2004) add another interesting dimension to the concept of ethnicity: the role of self-perception and of outsiders' perceptions about the individual. They assert that ethnicity is a "dynamic and complex concept [that] refers to how members of a group *perceive themselves*, and how, in turn, *they are perceived by others*" (emphasis added).

Subjective perception can lead to very distorted views about individuals and social groups. For example, consider the child who perceives breaking apart a brand-new toy as an exploration, while the parent may interpret the action as misbehavior. Similarly, practicing hand movements with a marker on a living room wall has a different meaning to the child than to an adult. When subjective perception is applied to ethnicity, we find that we do not agree with how others see us. For example, you might see yourself as part of an ethnic group, and yet people might not consider you as part of that group.

FIGURE 2-6 **Ethnicity Is . . .**

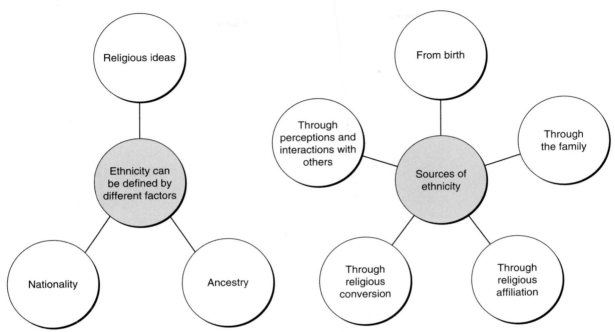

Are there any other elements or characteristics that define membership in an ethnic group?

The same can happen when people see you as part of an ethnicity that you do not perceive yourself as being a part of.

Divergences in ethnic perception commonly occur in connection with non-European American groups. Examples of this involve people from the Caribbean region as well as Hispanics. During graduate courses on multiculturalism, we have found repeatedly that non-European American students' ethnic perceptions of themselves differ from those assigned to them by the mainstream society. More specifically, a student born in Barbados was shocked to find herself defined as "black," when in her country she was not classified that way. She found that her ethnicity was being designated by the color of her skin rather than by her ethnic heritage. Similarly, it was traumatic for light-colored Hispanics to be denied the designation of "white" because of their heritage. One student commented that, for her, it was particularly disappointing to find that her color was commonly used to describe her, whereas her nationality was given a second place. One of the authors of this book remembers witnessing how a dark-skinned teacher born in Trinidad was once questioned by her colleagues when she refused to identify herself as an African American. Using solely the parameter of color, the teacher's colleagues were unable to acknowledge her Caribbean ethnicity. Similar misconceptions are common among Asian Americans, whose ethnicities are usually compounded into one

Children become aware of their differences and similarities at a very young age.

expression, "Oriental," a very abstract and misleading term.

Race: A Controversial Concept

Race has been used to establish differences that led to unfair separation of human beings in our global society. It has also been similarly used in U.S. society. The term *race* has been synonymous with color, so whenever color is the sole attribute used to define an individual, it can become a dangerous tool. Banks (2007) warns that nothing has had a more destructive effect on humankind than ideas about races. Montague affirms that it is, in fact, "man's most dangerous myth" (cited in Baruth & Manning, 2004). The term *people of color* has been coined to depict non-European groups. Some educators disagree with this terminology because of the misleading connotation given to color. We agree that *people of color* emphasizes only one irrelevant characteristic of a cultural group. We (as well as many others) prefer the more inclusive term *culturally diverse*.

Race is defined as the phenotypical characteristics that designate a group. It basically refers to the biological features common to a human group. Different from ethnicity, race describes characteristics that individuals cannot easily change . These physical characteristics are transmitted from one individual to another.

In Action . . . **Can You Define Your Ethnicity?**

Clarity about your own roots is critical when trying to understand and teach children from various cultures. To establish your ethnic affiliation, ask yourself the following questions:

• How do I define myself?

• How do I know that I belong to that group?

• How did I receive my ethnic identity?

• How do other people consider me? Are they in agreement with my view?

• What things do I do that identify me as part of that group?

SNAPSHOT 2-4   **Factors Influencing Intensity of Ethnic Feelings**

Perhaps you have wondered why all people in a group do not show the same intensity of ethnic traits. According to McGoldrick (2003), this is due to the following factors:

- *Reasons for immigration:* What they were seeking when they left their countries.
- *Length of time since immigration and the effects of generational acculturation:* How long it has been since they left and to what extent the families have become part of the mainstream.
- *Place of residence:* Whether they live or lived in an ethnic neighborhood

- *Order of migration:* Whether one person migrated alone or with the family
- *Socioeconomic status:* The upward mobility capability of the individual; education
- *Political and religious ties:* Whether the individual maintains such ties to the ethnic group
- *Language:* The languages spoken by the individual
- *Interracial marriages:* Extent of intermarriage with other ethnicities
- *Personal attitudes:* How the individual feels about his or her ethnic group

Source: McGoldrick, 2003.

The concept of race has its origins in anthropology, where it was used to describe the physical characteristics (eyes, skin color, size of head, and so on) of people (Hernandez, 2001). From this anthropological perspective, scientists identified humans according to racial groups. Today, however, even in the scientific sphere, categorizing human beings by such closed attributes is difficult. With the high incidence of interracial marriages, it becomes challenging to apply strict descriptors to define the children of diversity. Just think how you would define some of the children in your classroom who are a combination of many racial groups. Take the case of a 3-year-old living on the East Coast, whose father is Italian American and whose mother is half Asian and half African American. Racially, it would be a hard task to label the child. You would need to get a formula to determine the physical racial proportions, which, at the end, would yield no significant information about the child as an individual. Unfortunately, some people persist in using race labels. Applied as a social descriptor of people, race turns into a misleading concept. The pronounced emphasis on a physical aspect, such as color, contributes to rendering inaccurate images of people. This becomes especially evident because it ignores the social and traditional heritage embedded by culture in every individual.

There are still many implications to the meaning of race in society. Gollnick and Chinn (2005) point out the following:

■ *Race as a concept still carries a strong social meaning in our country as well as in many other societies.* This is despite the extensive movement of people from one geographical region to another and the high incidence of interracial marriages.

■ *The concept of race contributes very little to cultural understanding.* Race seldom correlates with cultural groups defined by nationality, language, or religion. The racial identity of people does not necessarily correspond to their nationality.

■ *The persistent use of racial, ethnic, and language categories in public and governmental documents provokes more confusion about the U.S. population.* The use of racial and ethnic indicators has proven to be not always effective when trying to assign individuals to a category. An individual could belong to several categories at the same time; therefore, tallying inclusive categories is difficult.

The current racial designations of the major ethnic groups are portrayed in Figure 2-7. They include whites and blacks who declared themselves to be of one race as well as the Hispanic or Latino population. The categories such as Asian, Native Hawaiian, and Pacific Islander also contain other subcategories of other ethnicities. Demographically, the United States is now considered the most racially diverse country in the world. After looking at these numbers, you may want to consider the cultural implications of the United States' racial profile.

A New Demographic Paradigm, Multicultural People

Today, the demographic profile of the United States includes a new and growing population group whose existence was acknowledged during Census 2000. For the first time, individuals were able to declare their multiracial and multiethnic heritage by selecting the "multicultural" category. Racially, these individuals are described as people born from parents with different racial and/or ethnic roots. Although interracial families have long existed, they were not officially acknowledged and recorded as a distinct group until 2000. Until then, people with mixed-race heritage were defined as "third culture" (West, 2003). Socially and demographically, the members of the "multicultural" category present a different paradigm in racial composition that describes the ever-increasing pluralistic nature of communities across the nation. Enrollment of multiracial children is already a stable trend in most schools that is projected to grow in the future (National Association of School Psychologists, 2004).

FIGURE 2-7 **Racial Profile of the Population of the United States, 2000**

White (excluding Hispanics/Latinos)	211,460,626
Hispanics or Latinos	35,305,818
Black or African American	34,758,190
American Indian and Alaska Native	2,475,956
Asian	10,242,998
Native Hawaiian and Pacific Islanders	874,414

Source: U.S. Census Bureau, 2000.

In Action . . .   **All the Colors We Are**

The story of how we get our different skin colors is given in the book *All the Colors We Are: The Story of How We Get Our Skin Color/Todos los Colores de Nuestra Piel: La Historia de por qué Tenemos Diferentes Colores de Piel,* written by Katie Kissinger (Redleaf Press, 1994). Read the following excerpt and see how she addresses this difficult concept.

> The skin color we are born with comes from our parents, ancestors, and where they lived a long time ago. Do you think your ancestors came from a very warm, sunny place or a cooler place with less sunshine? Dark skin, light skin, and skin with freckles are all caused by our ancestors, the sun, and the melanin.

What do you think about her approach? Is it developmentally appropriate?

Prejudice and Racism: The Plagues of the Past and the Present

Sadly, the world is full of old prejudices.

Doris Bergen (2003)

Any discussion about race and ethnicity must acknowledge the presence of prejudice and racism in society. Unfortunately, neither is a stranger to the United States. Sadly, U.S. history includes numerous instances in which people were victims of unfair treatment because of their differences, and many more will occur unless actions are taken to prevent unfairness.

Prejudice has caused more destruction in the world than any war and is the essence of racism and bigotry. Prejudice is based on holding negative views about others and is not supported by solid evidence. The dislikes manifested by those who are prejudiced are based on poor or inadequate knowledge.

Sometimes, those who hold prejudices are not aware of their own feelings (Kehoe, cited in Hernandez, 2001). Dislikes of others are often demonstrated through attitudes and nonverbal condemnation. Victims of prejudice have been subjected to subtle, covert disparagement, such as a condescending smile or a mocking look, which wounds and often permanently stigmatizes them. Kehoe (cited in Hernandez, 2001), in an analysis of prejudice, found key points that alert educators to its sources. Some of Kehoe's findings are included in Snapshot 2-5.

Sadly, prejudice has proven not to be a stranger in U.S. schools and classrooms. Racial slurs and hate crimes are only the more overt forms of prejudice. Statistics show that incidences of hate crimes have increased during the first decade of the twenty-first century. The subtle forms—for instance, the patronizing ways in which culturally diverse families are often treated—are as damaging and offensive as the more tangible ones.

Post–September 11 society has made many more aware of the culturally diverse nature of people. In some cases it has led to prejudice and discrimination against things and individuals unknown to us. This need for more security sometimes results in more racism and greater prejudice against the individuals and groups that are perceived as threatening. Since September 11, incidents against ethnic groups have increased to an alarming level, making the fight against intolerance imperative. Because many adults openly exhibit their feelings and convey their biased views in the presence of children, early educators need to be aware of such information being brought into the classroom. Children may repeat adults' disparaging remarks while they role-play, talk with their peers, or react to stories. Early childhood educators have a responsibility to address such incidents in appropriate and antibiased ways. This will prevent the formation and reinforcement of prejudiced behaviors.

The Classroom as a Culture of Peace

The best weapon against violence and prejudice is peace (UNESCO, 2000). Peace can be defined as a feeling of harmony and well-being. Tolerance and bias-free attitudes are avenues that lead to peace. A culture of peace begins when adults and children together share and participate in activities as equals. Peace is also found in places where violence is openly rejected and where people are free to express their views and exchange ideas.

Learning tolerance occurs through the interactions with individuals we encounter at home, in school, and in the community. These settings are major places where bias-free behaviors can be learned. For young children, the classroom can become the most powerful bias-free place where they can acquire knowledge about socially acceptable tolerant behavior. Routine activities and interactions characterized by equal treatment for all and by rejection of unfairness promote a culture of respect that leads to peace. Taking time to clarify derogatory and prejudicial comments made by children is a critical step in eradicating prejudice. Because teachers exert an influential role in the behaviors and attitudes of young children, responding and intervening appropriately in prejudice-inspired incidents is essential. As a teacher with this goal, you can do the following:

- Be sure that comments made in the classroom regarding actions of people from diverse backgrounds do not convey criticism.
- Be aware of many different messages your own body language communicates to young children. Remember, they can read you!
- Remember to respond to children's actions clearly and within the context of their actions, and make sure that children understand your responses.
- Acknowledge children's bias-free and tolerant behaviors in real context and through vicarious experiences, such as reading of multicultural books and shared children's stories.

As multiculturalists and early educators, the need to prepare children to successfully live in and embrace a culture of peace is a priority. The hope and seed for peace and successful life in a diverse society is found in every classroom.

LITERACY CONNECTIONS. . . Suggested References for Building a Culture of Peace and Tolerance

You may want to review some of the following titles that provide ideas and strategies for supporting tolerance and peace in early childhood classrooms.

- Arnow, J. (1995). *Teaching peace: How to raise children to live in harmony: Without fear, without prejudice, without violence.* New York: Perigee Books.

- Bullard, S. (1997). *Teaching tolerance.* New York: Main Street Books.

- Derman-Sparks, L., & the A.B.C. Task Force. (1989). *The anti-bias curriculum: Tools for empowering children.* Washington, DC: National Association for the Education of Young Children.

- Lalli, J. (1996). *Make someone smile: And 40 more ways to be a peaceful person.* Minneapolis, MN: Free Spirit.

- Parr, T. (2004). *The peace book.* New York: Megan Tingley.*

- Radunsky, V. (2003). *What does peace feel like?* New York: Atheneum.*

*Children's books recommended for ages 3–6

SNAPSHOT 2-5   **Facts About Prejudice**

- Individual differences in temperament cannot be attributed to race.
- Prejudice and stereotypes are learned, not innate. They are learned in the family and in school without conscious intent.
- Generally, individuals do not realize how prejudiced they are.
- Those prejudiced against one ethnic group are likely to be prejudiced against others.
- Individuals who are not directly competing with minority group members tend to be less prejudiced toward them.

- As a group's character becomes more distinctive, a consensus develops regarding stereotypes associated with that group.
- Stereotypes resist change. However, social and economic conditions, especially of the kind that modify relations among groups, can alter stereotypes.
- Prejudice is a predictor of discriminatory behavior.
- There is considerable agreement within a society about specific stereotypes assigned to particular groups.

Source: Kehoe, cited in Hernandez, 2001.

Stereotypes

One of the most damaging ways prejudice is expressed is in the form of stereotypes. A **stereotype** is an oversimplified, generalized image describing all individuals in a group as having the same characteristics in appearance, behaviors, and beliefs. Although there may be a germ of truth in a stereotype, the image usually represents "a gross distortion, or an exaggeration of the truth, and has offensive, dehumanizing implications" (Council on Interracial Books for Children, in Saracho & Spodek, 1983). The effects of being stereotyped are damaging to the individual and to those who witness it. As found by Kehoe (cited in Hernandez, 2001), stereotypes are learned usually in the context of the family and, unfortunately, in schools. Actions to prevent and stop stereotyping are the responsibility of all educators, particularly during the early years because of the inherent vulnerability of young learners. Developing an antibias curriculum, like the one developed by the staff at Pacific Oaks College in California, is a good way to start (Derman-Sparks, 1989). Familiarizing young children with action-oriented multicultural activities that promote understanding and tolerance is not only recommended but essential.

Racism is a crime many often reject but refuse to stop. It continues to be a "prevailing social practice" (Derman-Sparks, 1989). Hernandez (2001) states that racism is found in those individuals exhibiting behaviors and actions that reflect (a) the conviction that physical, psychological, and intellectual characteristics are inherited and distributed differently among humans and (b) the belief of being racially superior to other racial groups. Throughout history, many individuals and groups have been victimized as a result of these tenets. The latest are among the recently arrived non-European Americans (Derman-Sparks, 1989).

As we strive to offer children an education that will empower them to become successful members of society, early childhood educators must realize that the key to *unum* is in their hands. Prejudice and racism must be eradicated for the United States to enter strong and triumphant into the new century. Old ideas about superiority of some racial and ethnic groups have poisoned the minds of many and must be abandoned. As an early childhood educator, remember that change begins with the child. The battles to eliminate prejudice and racism are to be won in your classrooms, and you as teachers are the champions we look to.

Overcoming Unfairness and Discrimination: Legislative Landmarks

Today's society still faces the challenge of overcoming discriminatory practices in spite of the many laws and landmark legislation that have been passed to protect the rights of all members of U.S. society. Early childhood educators need to become cognizant of many legislative mandates and laws that directly influence young children in their classrooms. Many state and federal statutes exist that not only protect young children's rights to equal educational experiences but also address the diversity of needs and characteristics of young children.

The passage of the 1960s Civil Rights Act created fertile ground for recognizing the rights of every citizen regardless of his or her characteristics and conditions. Furthermore, the Act acknowledged and reaffirmed the individual rights of culturally diverse people and gave way to additional efforts that directly impacted early childhood education. Among these laws is the historic PL 94-142 of 1975 that established the rights of individuals with disabilities to receive educational services according to their needs. This transcendental legislation impacted the social framework of the nation and began to erase the unjust and discriminatory treatment of children and adults with disabilities. The rights of individuals with disabilities were expanded further by the enactment in 1990 of PL 101-476, the Individuals with Disabilities Education Act (IDEA), and later on by the amendments passed in 1997 that defined early childhood intervention.

LITERACY CONNECTIONS...

Using Literature to Address Prejudiced Comments in the Classroom

It is not surprising to hear children make comments and statements reflective of prejudiced or stereotypical views. Most of the time, they repeat what they have heard adults say, unaware of the meaning of the words. Other times, they are repeating what they have heard in the media or on the streets. Rather than ignoring these incidents, responding to their comments and clarifying the meanings is the best way to avoid repetition. Upon hearing an inappropriate comment, use your own words to let the child know that the comment is not appropriate and that you intend to discuss the statement with the child. ("Those are words that hurt and that we don't use.") Be sure to take time to (1) clarify the comment or incident and (2) explain on the child's level why it is inappropriate. These are important steps in building understanding and in avoiding having such behaviors become a part of the child's response repertoire. For example, ask the following:

- *Why did you say this?*
- *Where did you hear such words?*
- *What made you say that?*
- *What do you think it means?*
- *How would you feel if someone were to call you such a name?*

Another way for clarifying prejudiced comments in the classroom is to use stories addressing racial and ethnic content. For preschoolers, stories with fantasy characters, like the animals in *What if the Zebras Lost Their Stripes?* are age-appropriate ways to engage them in a lively discussion about words and attitudes that hurt. You may want to try some of the suggested titles included in this section:

- Derolf, S. (1997). *The crayon box that talked.* New York: Random House.

- Polacco, P. (2001). *Mr. Lincoln's way.* New York: Philomel Books.

- Reitano, J. (1998). *What if the zebras lost their stripes?* Mahwah, NJ: Paulist Press.

All children should be appreciated for who they are.

Equity in Educational Services for All Children

Unequal programs and services available to the young have presented enduring challenges for multicultural educators. The No Child Left Behind Act, passed in 2002, addressed these critical issues (U.S. Department of Education, 2004). Although the mandate placed emphasis on individual and school accountability—a facet that has caused concern for educators regarding testing bias and developmentally and culturally appropriate approaches—it also brought to the forefront the recognition of the rights of all children to quality educational services. The law also addresses the disparities and fair services, a main issue in multicultural education. It reinforces the rights of all children, especially those in poor communities, to receive educational experiences from well-trained teachers. No Child Left Behind establishes high expectations for all, regardless of their ethnic or linguistic backgrounds. Equal treatment is based on the premise that all children have potential beyond racial background or language capability and deserve quality services.

As we move forward in the twenty-first century, we recognize that although much has been gained, much still remains to be changed for the young children and families of the increasingly culturally and linguistically diverse society of the United States.

Stability and Change: The Rhythm of Culture

All cultures have shared meanings that give direction to the group (Bowman, 2001). Your classroom is the place where children come to explore and discover how to live in their social environment. The playground is another place where children express the views of the world that they have acquired so far. We say "so far" because these views are not static. Being a dynamic process, culture evolves and changes with time. This process affects our personal perceptions and beliefs about people and environments.

Your classroom reflects cultural changes in many ways. For example, educational theories of early childhood practices evolved from being teacher-centered to being child-centered. If you had been teaching in the 1950s or 1960s, your classroom would have included more academic materials and activities. A higher number of large group

In Action . . .	**That Was Me . . . Before!**

We all have changed some of our ideas, sometimes without being aware of it. To find some of the ways in which you have been a part of this process, visit your closet! Yes, that is right. If anything represents the trends of our society, that is, of culture, it is the fashions we wear. Search through your clothes and find any outfit you stopped wearing some time ago; in fact, the older the outfit, the better. Now ask yourself why you stopped wearing it and if you think you will wear it again.

- Give yourself two reasons you "forgot" that outfit.
- Examine your own answers and discuss them with a friend.

experiences would have dominated your teaching. Children would have probably been found doing many "pencil and paper" exercises while you would have been delivering more information for them "to learn." You also would have looked different. Most likely, your school dress code would not have included sneakers and today's informal, casual clothing. Because our **cultural values** have experienced modifications, we now have a very different picture of how the early childhood classroom should look.

Change is a positive characteristic of all cultures. Through change, a group keeps itself alive. Comparing culture to the human organism, we find that in the same manner that the body affects modifications when faced with new circumstances, culture similarly adapts itself to new pressures. This capacity to adapt itself grants culture the capability to respond to reality. Actually, this mechanism of change is as active as the one in our bodies. You must remain abreast of current social transformations that take place in society, which will allow you to respond and provide for the needs of children.

Supporting Cultures in Our Classroom: Taking Action

Your classroom is a reflection of our social mosaic. The children you teach bring to the classroom the ideas and experiences that characterize the United States in the twenty-first century. One of the things the children reflect is the diversity of visions found in our communities. As they interact in their social environments—the family, the classroom, the neighborhood, and the community—they learn that not all individuals are alike. For example, they will discover that what makes some people happy might be different from their own ideas of happiness. They will notice that not all people like to wear the same kind of clothes as they do or that other people have a hair texture smoother or curlier than theirs. They will learn that they have ideas of their own and that others see the world differently. While holding their own views, children—and you as a teacher—come to discover that there are other ways to see and interpret reality. Sometimes we will agree with others' interpretations, and sometimes we will disagree. Not everyone looks at life through the same glasses!

Preparing to serve children who live in a diverse country requires much initiative and imagination. Becoming effective teachers of young children in a multicultural world begins with the following steps:

■ *Discover and clarify your own cultural viewpoints.* Begin by ascertaining your own beliefs, values, and practices. To appreciate other cultures, you must be clear about your own. The search for your roots can begin by talking to your relatives and family. Examine official records that document your and your family members' birthplaces, marriages, travels, and other significant events. Analyze your responses to the activities presented in the "In Action" sections throughout this chapter. They are intended to help you clarify ideas about your own cultural identity.

■ *Learn to be more culturally competent.* Examine the cultures represented in the community where you live and those in your school. See what cultural groups are there that you know very little about or that you would like to learn more about. One way to choose is to think about those cultures commonly found in your classroom. Remember, we are all learning more about the cultures in this country. Do not feel bad if you lack knowledge about some of them!

■ *Honestly examine the stereotypes about other groups that you have in the classroom or that you have encountered.* Do a self-inventory to find out what you know about any stereotypes associated with those groups. You may be surprised to find that they are probably based on very inconsequential and unfair facts.

■ *Read about people from other cultures.* The reference list in this book is a starting point. Check your local library, where you may also find a variety of publications about different ethnic groups.

■ *Consider the importance that principles of development have on planning and designing classroom experiences.* Along with that, learn to recognize and appreciate the influence of the family in the child's overall development. These two points will be examined in Chapters 3 and 4.

WHAT WE HAVE LEARNED—CHAPTER SUMMARY

The main topic of this chapter is culture. We defined what culture is and discussed many ways in which it shapes our behavior and our lives. Culture is the most potent single influence that makes us who we are. There are many aspects of culture. Some of the elements of culture are very visible (material) while others are very covert and deal with the emotional and thinking patterns (nonmaterial) of individuals and groups. Because one's sense of identity is very closely related to one's culture, it is important for all of us as individuals to know as much about each other's cultures as possible and to understand their influences on ourselves and on the world around us. Educators of young children are expected to learn about various cultures and their rituals in order to teach and nurture young children. Through education comes understanding and tolerance that allow us to create classrooms of peace. We are all responsible for overcoming unfairness and discrimination as well as ensuring the equity of educational services provided to all children regardless of their culture, religion, or the color of their skin.

THINGS TO DO . . .

1. Based on the discussion about culture presented in this chapter, create your own definition of *culture.*

2. Visit your community or neighborhood and make a list of its cultural elements. How many of these are visible to the eye? How many are not visible?

3. Observe two young children (ages 3–5). Identify how they exhibit their cultural heritage.

4. List the ways you share your own culture with others. Include both material and non-material items.

5. Find an early childhood textbook and review two or three chapters for stereotype language and concepts.

6. Engage a group of friends or family members in a conversation about stereotypes. Make a list of the terminology that was used. What did you learn about their level of acceptance of others?

RECOMMENDED INTERNET RESOURCES

- ■ "The ABCs of Disability Rights," from the Southern Poverty Law Center
www.tolerance.org/teach/activities/activity.jsp?ar=872

- ■ *Colorín Colorado,* a website that provides a variety of resources to support the needs of young English language learners
www.colorincolorado.org

- ■ Culture and Ethnic Groups, a portal that provides resources and information from the government about the different cultural and ethnic groups in the United States
www.usa.gov/Citizen/Topics/History_Culture.shtml

- ■ *Race, the Power of an Illusion,* a PBS series
www.pbs.org/race/000_General/000_00-Home.htm

YOUR STANDARDS PORTFOLIO

NAEYC Standard 4b: Teaching and Learning Using Developmentally Effective Approaches*

Culture is one of the factors that influence the child's development and learning processes. Teaching and responding to the child's unique needs requires a clear understanding

* NAEYC Standard 4b correlates with INTASC Standard 2: Student Development and Learning.

of the cultural and linguistic contexts in which children grow and develop. Select and complete one of the following artifacts to evidence how you meet NAEYC's Standard 4b.

■ Create a pictorial cultural profile of the community where you live or teach. Include aspects such as cultural groups, religious groups, languages used, businesses, places of interest, community celebrations, and any other details. Reflect on how these elements influence and play a role in the children's development.

■ Prepare a chart about the linguistic environment in your community. Identify languages used by people and in signage in streets; names of businesses; newspapers; media, including radio and television programs; materials at the library; and any other places. Comment on your findings and reflect on how the nature of the linguistic environment may influence children.

■ Stereotypes often can be found in the visuals, children's books, and materials used in the classroom environment. Conduct observations in at least three classrooms and look for any stereotypical content in pictures, posters, children's literature, and manipulatives. Comment on your findings and reflect on how they may influence development. Suggest alternative materials to prevent stereotypes in the classroom.

REFERENCES

Banks, J. (2007). *Multicultural education* (4th ed.). Needham Heights, MA: Allyn & Bacon.

Banks, J., & Banks, C. M. (2006). *Multicultural education: Issues and perspectives* (6th ed.). Needham Heights, MA: Allyn & Bacon.

Baruth, L. G., & Manning, M. L. (2004). *Multicultural education of children and adolescents* (4th ed.). Needham Heights, MA: Allyn & Bacon.

Bergen, D. (2003). *War and genocide: A concise history of the Holocaust.* Lanham, MD: Rowman and Littlefield.

Bowman, B. (2001). Reaching potentials of minority children through developmentally and culturally appropriate programs. In S. Bredekamp & T. Rosegrant (Eds.), *Reaching potentials: Appropriate curriculum and assessment for young children* (pp. 129–135). Washington, DC: National Association for the Education of Young Children.

Bruner, J. (1990). *Acts of meaning.* Cambridge, MA: Harvard University Press.

Campbell, D. E. (2004). *Choosing democracy: A practical guide to multicultural education* (3rd ed.). Upper Saddle River, NY: Pearson.

Carroll, L. (1987). *Alice's adventures in wonderland.* New York: Philomel Books. (Original work published in 1865.)

Copple, C. (Ed.). (2003). *A world of difference: Readings on teaching young children in a diverse society.* Washington, DC: National Association for the Education of Young Children.

Derman-Sparks, L., & the A.B.C. Task Force. (1989). *The anti-bias curriculum: Tools for empowering children.* Washington, DC: National Association for the Education of Young Children.

Diller, J., & Moule, J. (2005). *Cultural competence: A primer for educators.* Burbank, CA: Thomson Learning.

Freire, P. (2000). *Pedagogy of the oppressed.* New York: Continuum International.

Gardiner, H., & Kosmitzki, C. (2005). *Lives across cultures: Cross-cultural human development.* Boston: Allyn & Bacon.

Geertz, C. (2000). *The interpretation of cultures.* New York: Basic Books.

Gollnick, D. M., & Chinn, P. C. (2005). *Multicultural education in a pluralistic society and exploring diversity package* (7th ed.). New York: Prentice Hall.

Hall, E. T. (1990). *The silent language.* New York: Fawcett.

Harwood, R., Miller, J., & de Lucca, N. (1997). *Culture and attachment: Perceptions of the child in context.* New York: Guilford Press.

Hernandez, H. (2001). *Multicultural education: A teacher's guide to content and process.* New York: Merrill.

Joe, J., & Malach, F. (2004). Families with Native American roots. In E. Lynch & M. J. Hanson (Eds.), *Developing cross-cultural competence: A guide for working with young children and their families* (pp. 89–120). Baltimore, MD: Paul Brookes.

Juster, N. (2000). *The phantom tollbooth.* New York: Random House for Young Children. (Original work published in 1961).

Lewis, C. (1991). Nursery schools: The transition from home to school. In B. Finkelstein, A. Imamura, & J. Tobin (Eds.), *Transcending stereotypes: Discovering Japanese culture and education* (pp. 109–118). Yarmouth, ME: Intercultural Press.

Lynch, E. W., & Hanson, M. J. (2004). *Developing cross-cultural competence: A guide for working with young children and their families* (3rd ed.). Baltimore, MD: Paul Brookes.

McGoldrick, M. (2003). Ethnicity, cultural diversity, and normality. In F. Walsh (Ed.), *Normal family processes* (p. 341). New York: Guilford Press.

Mead, M. (2000). *Growing up in New Guinea.* New York: Morrow. (Original work published in 1930).

Murray, G. (1993). The inner side of experiential learning. In T. Gochenour (Ed.), *Beyond experience: The experiential approach to cross-cultural education* (Rev. ed., pp. 159–174). Yarmouth, ME: Intercultural Press.

National Association of School Psychologists. (2004). Multiracial children: Practical suggestions for parents and teachers. *NASP Communiqué* 32(7), 174. Nieto, S., & Bode, P. (2008). *Affirming diversity: The sociopolitical context of multicultural education.* Needham Heights, MA: Allyn & Bacon.

Roopnarine, J. L., & Johnson, J. E. (2004). *Approaches to early childhood education* (2nd ed.). New York: Prentice Hall.

Saracho, O., & Spodek, B. (Eds.). (1983). *Understanding the multicultural experience in early childhood education.* Washington, DC: National Association for the Education of Young Children.

Spradley, J., & McCurdy, D. (2003). *The cultural experience: Ethnography in complex society.* Chicago: Waveland Press.

UNESCO. (2000). Education for a culture of peace. Retrieved May 14, 2005, from http://www.unesco.org/education/ecp/index.htm.

U.S. Census Bureau. (2000). *Profiles of general demographic characteristics, Census 2000.* Retrieved September 4, 2008, from http://www.census.gov/prod/cen2000/dp1/2kh00.pdf.

U.S. Department of Education. (2004). *No child left behind: A toolkit for teachers.* Retrieved September 30, 2005, from http://www.ed.gov/teachers/nclbguide/nclb-teachers-toolkit.pdf.

Vontress, C. (1976). Counseling the racial minorities. In G. Belkin (Ed.), *Counseling: Direction in theory and practice* (pp. 277–290). Belmont, CA: Wadsworth.

West, M. (2003). Teaching the third culture child. In C. Copple (Ed.), *A world of difference: Readings on teaching young children in a diverse society.* Washington, DC: National Association for the Education of Young Children.

Wadsworth/Cengage Learning

CHAPTER 3

Families in Our Classrooms: Many Ways, Many Voices

> No matter the size, No matter the name.
>
> One thing in families
>
> Is always the same . . .
>
> LOVE, LOVE, LOVE!
>
> *The Kindergarten Children of Westfield School,*
> *Sacramento, California (1995)*

CHAPTER OBJECTIVES

In this chapter, we will

- define *family*.
- describe the existing variety of family structures.
- discuss the characteristics of families across cultures.
- explore the role of families in the transmission of culture.

KEY CONCEPTS

- family
- family configurations

FROM BARBARA'S JOURNAL

This year, as I get to know my children, I am also learning so much more about their families. There is a parent–teacher conference for the entire school in two weeks, and when I mentioned it to my children, I got some questions that I was not expecting: "Is it OK if Pop comes?" "Nana works on Wednesday nights, but can my big sister come?" Apparently, I have children who are being raised by a single parent and by older siblings, grandparents, foster parents, gay couples, and aunts. I am aware that nowadays the family unit comes in many shapes and colors, but I did not expect to find so many different models represented in my children's families. I am planning a thematic unit on families that will allow children to talk about their families and how they live. It is so important that they learn that it doesn't matter who is in their family because love comes in many different shapes and sizes.

FAMILIES—A CONSTANT IN OUR CHANGING SOCIETY

Call it a clan, call it a network, call it a tribe, call it a family. Whatever you call it, whoever you are, you need one.

Jane Howard (1978)

The ever-presence of change, one of the constants through time, remains the force that continues to mold life patterns in society. Fortunately, one of the few constants in the cycle of life is the family, an essential unit of society. In spite of the many changes the family has experienced, it continues to be a fundamental force in creating and perpetuating humankind. The family is still the basic channel for learning about human nature because of its essential role in transmitting culture. This notion is particularly important in multicultural early childhood education, where learning about the families of young children is the best way to discover the diversity of views that form our students.

Like Barbara, you may also have encountered a kaleidoscope of family configurations in the neighborhood, in the community, and in your classrooms. Through this chapter, we will tour the world of the family with special emphasis on those characteristics that make families alike and yet so different. As we examine the nature, the composition, and the role of families in culture, you will learn about yourself and about the children in your classroom.

WHAT IS A FAMILY?

Defining **family** is not an easy task, particularly in today's society. You probably have read and heard people say that families are no longer what they used to be, that today's families are too different and complex, and even that the family no longer exists. The reality is that families have evolved along with our society. The traditional family unit has changed so much and assumed so many different formulas that even the United Nations prefers using the plural term, *families*, to more accurately describe the current nature of this social unit (United Nations, 1994). In working with children, we come to understand that "our image of what a family is and what it should be is a powerful combination of personal experience, family forms we encounter or observe, and attitudes we hold" (Gilbert, 2007).

Diversity—The Ever-Existing Character of Families

Because of today's social changes and diverse perceptions regarding family roles, trying to find just one pattern to define and fit the family is impossible. The fact is that even though families and their roles have changed recently, they have always been diverse (Walsh, 2003). In discussing the family, Walsh (2003) reminds us of the ever-existing diversity of the family and how the landscape of today's families reflects the changing and complex nature of contemporary society. We need not travel far to state with certainty that the diversity of **family configurations** is one of the essential characteristics of families. Our classrooms present the most vivid examples of this.

Although most generally acknowledge that the concept of the traditional family has changed, it is encouraging to confirm that the family as an institution continues to exist. In fact, "the concept of the family is perhaps the most basic one in social life" (United Nations, 1994). From this general acknowledgment, it is clear that the family is important for individual and social survival. How the literature defines the family is explored in the next section.

Defining the Family: What the Literature Says

Social researchers have always considered the family an important and basic societal concept. Today, families are of such interest that they have become the focus of study across many other disciplines. Numerous ideas defining the family have been proposed over time, as researchers attempted to answer the question: "What is a family?" One idea on which they all agree is the fact that establishing only one definition is difficult. By examining what several social scientists have observed, you will get a better idea of what a family is.

According to Garbarino and Abramovitz (1992), families, "'the headquarters for human development, are the most basic and enduring of social institutions." They also express the dual perspective found in the family "as a small group of people sharing love, intimacy, and responsibility for children; and, as a social institution that serves and reflects the American macrosystem." Bronfenbrenner's (2004) theory places family at the core of influences for individuals. Based on Bronfenbrenner's ecological theory, the family is the main source of influence within the microsystem that describes the network of firsthand social experiences individuals confront across cultures. According to this theory, families are the heart of the process in which each person becomes who he

FIGURE 3-1 **Like a Filter, the Family Serves As a Mediator of Culture**

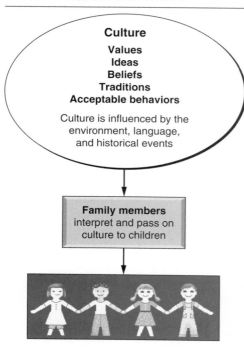

Culture

Values
Ideas
Beliefs
Traditions
Acceptable behaviors

Culture is influenced by the environment, language, and historical events

Family members
interpret and pass on culture to children

or she is. Serving as interpreters and mediators between the individual and the society, families teach individuals how to be family members and how to become members of the immediate sociocultural environs (see Figure 3-1). When we are cognizant of the incredible task of families and the powerful influence they have on children, we recognize the need to work in close collaborations with families.

Children Define the Family

In our search to gain better understanding of young children's perceptions of families, we asked some of our graduate students to ask their children to define *family*. To elicit more information, the teachers asked the children to draw their families prior to being asked the following questions: "Is this your family?" "Who is in your family?" "Can you tell me what you like best about your family?" The array of answers was fascinating, mainly because they highlighted what children perceive as meaningful about their families. They also shed light on the differences found across cultures. Their answers revealed views about family membership that included grandparents, other relatives and significant adults, and even pets.

One of the best ways to define the family is expressed by Gina and Mercer Mayer (1999) in their story *This Is My Family:*

Families come in all shapes and sizes, but they all have the same roles and functions. What are the family configurations most common in your community?

In Action . . . **Who Is in Your Family?**

As a teacher of young children, it is important to know yourself. So, before continuing, we ask you to describe your family. Consider whether your family fits the traditional or the nontraditional model. To facilitate your description, use the following prompts.

- My family is comprised of . . .
- I think my family is traditional/nontraditional because . . .
- What makes my family unique is . . .

LET'S TALK AND REFLECT. . . **Family Models**

Today's families come in many different configurations. The concept of a traditional family model is based on our personal experiences, our culture, and the environment in which we live. Ask yourself the following:

- *What is my idea of a family? What do I consider to be a family?*
- *How does my idea of family compare to the actual families in my community?*

> This is my family. Each of us is different, but we love each other a lot. I think that's what a family is all about.

As a social institution and beyond the diversity elements that may define them, families are alike in the roles, tasks, and functions they perform. Let us explore what makes our families similar.

What Are the Functions and Roles of the Family?

Society needs families essentially to prepare the young to become constructive members of society. This is accomplished through the transference of expectations, social responsibilities, and behaviors to the future generations of adults. All families share these basic social responsibilities even though cultures define the ways those functions are performed. Social researchers have defined these functions as being both basic and complex tasks. There are divergent opinions regarding the ways these specific responsibilities are carried out by families. As we describe each of them, remember that they are activities expected of *all* families, but that the way they are performed may differ as a result of each family's culture.

According to educators and sociologists, families perform several key tasks, or functions. These functions are essential to meeting and supporting the needs of family

In Action . . . **What Is a Family?**

To find out what children think about the concept of family, select a group of children, preschoolers through primary-age, and have them draw their families. Afterwards, talk with each child and let him or her describe the drawing. You may want to ask questions such as these:

- *Tell me, what is a family?*
- *Is this your family? Who is in your family?*
- *What is your family like?*
- *What do you like about your family?*

Note the similarities and differences in their responses. See whether differences are based on the children's cultural backgrounds. Look for family elements such as memberships in clubs or social groups and participation in sports or other activities. Considering all their responses and illustrations will shed some light on children's perceptions of family.

LET'S TALK AND REFLECT. . . **Early Childhood Educators and Families**

Consider the diversity of families in your community and in classrooms that you know or have visited. Think about what makes them alike and what makes them unique.

- How can you as an early childhood educator support the families of your students?
- What are the ethical responsibilities early childhood educators have toward the students' families?

members and to the family's success as a group. Some of the key functions of the family include the following (Epstein, Bishop, Ryan, Miller, & Gabor, 2002; Hildebrand, Phenice, Gray, & Hines, 2008):

- ■ *Basic needs:* All families need to have their basic needs met. These include food, shelter, and financial stability.

- ■ *Socialization tasks:* One of the key functions of the family is to socialize children by teaching them the accepted behaviors of society. This is a process that encompasses all the activities and rituals that pass on the social behaviors and ways deemed appropriate according to the family's culture and heritage. Parenting and caregiving responsibilities are central to the successful socialization of the child and family as a group. Through interactions with family members, peers, and adults, children learn the values and beliefs of their culture. Affection, sense of respect, morality, and ways to respond to others are among the behaviors learned during the early years.

- ■ *Emotional support and spirituality:* The family is also the source of emotional support for individuals. For the developing child, this critical support provides a sense of love, trust, respect, and connectedness to the family. Emotional support is also essential to building a sense of security and safety. Families also instill in their members a sense of spirituality, ideals, and beliefs, which contribute to feelings of emotional stability. Researchers have identified spirituality as an integral element that is instrumental in keeping the family together and which contributes to overcoming adversity (Walsh & Pryce, 2003).

Through time, families have played a leading role in passing on traditions to the young.

- *Economic tasks*: All families need a stable environment where necessary resources are available. Stable jobs and income allow families to be self-sufficient and to satisfy the financial needs and responsibilities.

- *Educational tasks*: The family is also responsible for providing the young with appropriate learning and schooling experiences. At home, families fulfill the task of helping children to learn important skills and responsibilities as a member of the family and of the community. Families also teach their young about cultural knowledge, including traditions, values, and beliefs. Promoting education and supporting educational goals is also a key function of the family. Views regarding education are culturally defined.

- *Crisis management tasks*: Sharing ideas about how to face challenges is an integral task of families. This includes all the skills and responses families use during emergencies and difficult situations that may arise (such as family illnesses, accidents, moving, loss of income, and death). How families respond to crises and how they engage in coping is culturally influenced.

Family Roles

Roles are another common denominator of families. Family roles describe the different behavioral patterns that families exhibit as they carry out their different family functions (Epstein, Bishop, Ryan, Miller, & Gabor, 2002). Families play four roles (Commission on Children, 1991; Epstein, Bishop, Ryan, Miller, & Gabor, 2002; Garbarino, 1992):

The family is the major facilitator of cultural ways and traditions.

1. Provide basic resources (shelter, food, clothing, health care, and financial support).
2. Provide nurturance and support to their members (establishing a warm and reassuring emotional environment in which family members find themselves being supported during crises and whenever needed).
3. Serve as role models for their younger members (offering positive social models through which children learn the ways of their group, modeling basic interactional skills, and teaching children their roles and responsibilities in a social group).
4. Transmit the values and beliefs of their cultural group (serving as vehicles for cultural and spiritual teaching and learning).

To understand the meaning of *family*, we asked a group of early childhood educators representing several ethnic groups (European American, African American, Afro-Caribbean, and Hispanic) to define the basic tasks and responsibilities of the family. As you read their answers, think about other descriptors or details that you may want to add to this list.

Families are a group of people who . . .

- Provide love and nurturance to their members
- Keep people together
- Meet the basic needs of their members
- Provide role models for their younger members
- Support each other in *all* circumstances
- Transmit values and beliefs to their members
- Teach their members to respect others
- Model problem-solving skills to their members
- Model how to live in a social group
- Transmit a sense of pride about their own cultural heritage to their members
- Establish a sense of cultural identity
- Create an invisible but strong bond among their members (Robles de Meléndez, 2006)

In Action . . .   **Define Your Family**

Considering the characteristic family tasks and roles discussed in this chapter, define your own family. Share your definition with your colleagues.

Still other elements need to be considered as we define the families of the children we teach. In the next section, we will consider the variations in family configurations.

| CULTURE AND THE FAMILY

Culture establishes meanings shared and understood by those who respond to it (Spradley & McCurdy, 2004). Because we all live and respond to the patterns of our culture, interpretations of how to perform a specific function vary. Living in a multicultural environment like the United States means that we need to realize that what one person holds as an expectation might diverge from that of another. This is the paradigm and challenge of life in a multicultural society. Working with families of different cultural backgrounds affords teachers an opportunity to experience the variety of views and interpretations of social roles and functions. Even the simplest task is viewed differently when examined cross-culturally, which punctuates that what is valued as necessary for social survival in a group becomes a task expected for families to perform. Take, for instance, the function of education, which teachers expect families to support. Although

---

SNAPSHOT 3-1   **Children's Views of the Family**

A group of early childhood teachers in Florida and Las Vegas asked their students to tell them about their families. Their findings proved very interesting. Through their responses, children ages 4–6 described the family in terms of the functions and roles they perceived. Essentially, two main roles were elicited from their responses:

1. Nurturance and a sense of a warm environment ("My family loves me." "My mommy is always with me." "Nana reads me stories.")

2. Provision of basic needs ("Daddy buys me food." "We play together." "Mi familia cocina [My family cooks]." "Grandpa bought me these [pointing toward his sneakers]." "Mom makes me potatoes.")

Although their responses are characteristic of the still-egocentric child, they reflect an early perception of what being a part of a family means.

it is true that valuing education represents a shared view among all cultures, not all cultures will expect children to acquire the same kind of knowledge. Because the concept of what is to be learned differs from culture to culture, what a young child learns by the time he or she reaches school age differs among communities. For example, children in the United States are expected to master the "Three Rs," whereas families from New Guinea believe that learning their tribal history and mastering hunting and fishing are important because these skills are related to survival (Konner, 1992). This remote example illustrates that each cultural group assigns expectations that respond to its own needs and circumstances.

A Child Is Born

Consider these comments made by future parents we interviewed: "She'll be an important person, maybe even a president!" "We want her to be a good wife and mother." "My baby will be proud of his color." "Whether it's a boy or a girl, I want our baby to be a good person." "He'll be a minister like his father." "We want our child to live in a country where there is freedom."

What we read in these parents' comments are not only their desires for a bright future for their children but also the unique ideals and expectations for the new members of their culture. The thoughts parents have about their children provide glimpses of their values and ideals, knitted by the culture they belong to. For some, the arrival of a new child brings new hope for the survival of the group; for others, it is a way to continue the family tradition; for others still, it means a new opportunity to accomplish some unrealized goals. Regardless of what expectations families have for their children-to-be, they represent the interplay of the cultural and personal characteristics of the group's members. Culture begins its profound influence on individuals through their families even from the moment of conception. Family rituals, child-rearing practices, and the structure of the family into which children are born are factors that contribute to socialization and passing on of cultural knowledge.

Family Rituals

For those who have younger siblings or children of their own, they know that the arrival of a new child entails a number of family activities. Among those activities, many represent traditional rituals that people have carried out for centuries. They are important

---

In Action . . .   Our Names

Do you know why you were given your name? Find out and see if it corresponds to any of the reasons listed in this chapter. What other reasons and motivations do you feel people have for naming a child? In what ways do these reflect their family and cultural values?

because they keep alive the essence of cultures. Some of these rituals are observed before the child is born, whereas others happen after the birth. Through time, each culture has outlined an assortment of different practices, all intended to welcome the new member.

Many family rituals begin before birth. Selecting colors and clothes for the new baby are among the many rituals that are performed across cultures. For instance, preparing a *canastillo*, a basket with all the items the new baby will need, is a traditional activity among Hispanic families. A similar practice commonly found in the United States is a baby shower, a gathering where everyone pitches in with needed items to help the family prepare to welcome the newborn. Other rituals include preserving personal items across generations. Some families keep and pass on baby clothes worn by their elders; others use the same crib their grandparents used.

Author Margy Burns Knight has collected stories of child-welcoming practices from around the world. In *Welcoming Babies*, Knight (1998) describes a series of informal and formal practices, all depicting the ways in which each society marks the arrival of its new members. Some practices involve everyone in the community, whereas others are performed by the parents and their relatives. For example, in Nigeria, some women sing after learning that the child is born, whereas in Afghanistan, a newborn's father whispers prayers into each of the baby's ears (Knight, 1998).

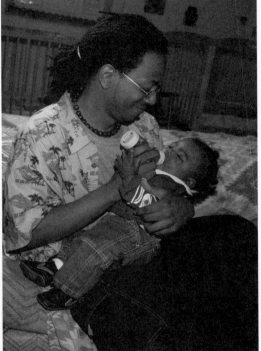

Across cultures, love and caring are essential to appropriate development. Daily routines such as feeding are special times for parents and other adults to nurture their relationships with the child.

More Than Just a Name

Perhaps one of the most interesting rituals families perform concerns choosing the name for the new baby. Selecting a name for a child not only provides identity but may also reflect cultural heritage and define the individual's roots. For example, in some Asian cultures, names are a way of honoring ancestors. Names are also a good way to note the influence of the times. During many years that we have taught and worked in children's classrooms, we have enjoyed learning from parents the reasons behind the choices of names for their offspring. Although there are always tendencies to choose fashionable names, there are several other motivations for selecting names, which are sometimes shared across cultural groups. Some of the main reasons include the following:

1. *To honor someone:*
   - An ancestor—usually grandparents' names are given to a first child, especially if the child is a boy.
   - A close relative, family member, or friend—names of uncles and aunts or the most recently deceased relatives. Honoring a special friend by naming a child after him or her is another common practice.

2. *To follow a tradition:*
   - Naming children according to their parents' names, that is, a boy with the father's name and a girl with the mother's name.
   - Having a religious authority select the most auspicious name for the child and holding a naming ceremony.
   - Choosing names that are considered acceptable to the parents' religion, such as biblical names or names that honor a religious figure or symbol.

3. *To highlight ethnic identity:*
   - Selecting names that depict ethnic origin or affiliation. Names of specific ethnic groups are sometimes used to name children (for example, *Taina* or *Ashanti*).
   - Names of local and national ethnic heroes or events of special national significance (such as *Bolivar* or *Washington*).

4. *To remember feelings or emotions:*
   - Names that depict a feeling or emotion based on the significance of the child's birth (such as *Milagros* [miracle]).
   - Name of a wonderful feeling (Joy or Aimée [the loved one]).

   Knowing the significance of names, it is important to respect and accept a child's name, regardless of how hard it might be to write or pronounce. One of the best ways to demonstrate our respect toward a family's culture is by respecting their names and avoiding the tendency to "Americanize" them.

   Following are some suggestions for dealing with names:

Cultural heritage influences the names we are given.

Wadsworth/Cengage Learning

F◯CUS
on Classroom Practices

What's in a Name?

A name is one of the best ways to show pride in our own culture and family. It is also a way to showcase who we are. For young children, names represent and exhibit their emerging sense of self-identity. Helping children to be proud of themselves is a critical developmental task. At times, children with names in their native languages can face challenges as they try to become part of the group. This is the case of the little girl in the story *My Name Is Yoon* by Helen Recorvits (Farrar, Strauss and Giroux, 2003). After sharing the story with children, teachers can use the activities shown in Figure 3-2 to help children ages 3–6 appreciate and become proud of their names.

FIGURE 3-2 **Be Proud of Your Name**

My Name is Yoon
Before Reading:
Purpose of activity:

> To have each child feel important
> To increase knowledge of the alphabet
> To increase knowledge in phonics

Each child writes his/her name on squares of paper (one letter per square). The consonants will be one color and the vowels another color. See "Karen" below:

1. Have children make their names with the letters. Each child scrambles the letters and rebuilds his or her name. Students may look at sample word cards of their names, but the goal is to build them from memory.

2. As children are sitting in small groups looking at the names in front of them, ask questions such as "Who has a name that begins like yours?" and "Whose name ends like yours?" The students can make comparisons between their names and others.

3. (Small group activity) Have children put the first letter of their name upside down in a pile in the center of the table. Each child takes a turn drawing a letter, saying the sound, and telling whose name begins with the sound of that letter.

4. Put all the letters upside down in the center of the table. Have children take turns selecting one letter at a time. If the letter belongs in their name, they keep the letter; if not, they return it to the pile. (This reinforces letter recognition and sequencing of letters for words.)

5. (For children in grades 1 and 2) Have students work in pairs (as more letters than just one student's are needed) to make two-letter words, three-letter words, four-letter words, and the longest word they can. Have them record their words on the sheet attached.

Read the Story

When you look at the cover, what do you wonder? What makes you wonder that; what evidence do you see that helps you to wonder that?

1. Everyone's name is special. What do you think of when you say your name? Draw things that will tell people about you.
2. Paste the letters of your name at the top of a large piece of paper. Find pictures or words that start the same way as your name.

My name is _____. My name is special. When I say my name, it makes me think of

_____.

My Name is Yoon

My name is _____.

My friend's name is _____.

These are the words we can make from our names:

_____

We thank Karen Burke EdD, reading specialist, who contributed this activity.

1. Always ask the family what name they prefer their child to use. Respect their choice.
2. Ask parents why they named their child that way. This will help you not only to value the child's name but also to find ways to enhance the child's self-concept.
3. If the name is difficult to pronounce, ask the parents to help with correct pronunciation. Try writing it phonetically, or you may even make an audio recording of the parent pronouncing the name.
4. If a child's name has an English translation, share it with the class. This can also become an opportunity to introduce children to a thematic unit in which they can investigate origins, meanings, and other aspects of names.
5. Some children might want to adopt a nickname. Share this with parents so that they know it is the child's desire to do so.
6. Always emphasize respect toward names. Intervene whenever a child is the target of name-calling or ridicule because of his or her name. This is both damaging and humiliating for the child.

DIVERSITY IN CHILD-REARING PRACTICES

Child rearing is an essential function and role of families. It is also an area where differences in ideas and practices are common. The child-rearing concept is closely related to the concept of the child, which does not have a shared meaning across cultural groups. Even across people of the same cultural group, it is not uncommon to find different views regarding how to raise a child. Although families in U.S. mainstream culture perceive children as young individuals whose development of independence is strongly supported and valued, it is not so among other cultural groups. In families with Latino roots, young children are believed to be totally dependent on the adults, a fact that defines the pampering and particular nurturance parents provide throughout the entire early childhood period. Contrary to families in U.S. culture, Hispanic parents "tend to be very nurturing . . . permissive and indulgent" with their children (Zuñiga, 2004). Families encourage this dependency, which gives all the family members an opportunity to create stronger bonds with the child and vice versa. Zuñiga (2004) points out that rather than pushing the child to develop early skills and independence, Hispanics "placate" their children. Independence, a highly valued behavior in U.S. mainstream culture, is not highly valued by Hispanics. A Hispanic child is often encouraged to keep a "babyish" behavior well beyond infancy and sometimes even until school age. In Hispanic culture, the need for a child to attain independence is not as relevant because, traditionally, children are brought up in a network of caring relationships defined by parents, siblings, and other family members. The family places more

Cultural traits are learned from infancy.

Wadsworth/Cengage Learning

importance on strengthening and reassuring the child's emotional ties with the family, which extends beyond the immediate family members who take care of the child. This, in turn, also affords the opportunity for the child to develop a collective orientation rather than an individualistic one. This collective orientation is also found in traditional Native American and Middle Eastern families.

Similar positions toward children are found among Asian American families. Chan (2004) reports that Asian parents consider their children until age 3 as "being relatively helpless," which helps explain the tolerant and permissive attitudes they exhibit. Emphasis on creating an emotionally supportive family environment causes attention

---

In Action . . .　Welcome to the World!

The birth of a child is a major milestone for a family and another occasion where the influence of culture is evident. Each culture acknowledges the birth of a baby in a distinct way usually learned from the elders. See how many you remember, or ask your relatives about things they do. You may be surprised to find that some of these activities have been done for generations. This type of tradition is one more piece of evidence that shows how powerful culture is.

In Action . . .   **Child Rearing**

We all have our own ideas regarding how to raise a child. These ideas are often derived from what we learned through our families. However, even within families of the same culture, we find differences regarding these practices. To find evidence of this concept, name at least five of your own beliefs about child rearing that are different from those of your family and friends. Then, examine each idea to see what makes them different.

---

to supersede development of independence in the first 3 years of life. As Asian children reach the preschool stage, Asian families prepare their children to assume responsibilities. The preschool years become a transitional stage in which children are led to achieve self-discipline (Chan, 2004). Life formalities are then emphasized and learned through the direct participation of children in adult activities.

Families are also expected to teach their younger members rules of social interaction. For example, children must learn the rules for interactions with adults and elders. The manner in which a child speaks and responds to adults will be different based on the family's culture. For example, U.S. parents tend to exhibit a more permissive attitude when children interrupt during an adult conversation. A child might literally break into a conversation, and some U.S. parents find this to be acceptable practice. This is not true of other cultures. Generally, families with Middle Eastern, Hispanic, Native American, Asian, and European roots expect their children to refrain from interrupting when adults are talking. In the same line, they also demand from their children acceptance of their decisions, for they strongly believe that authority is not to be questioned by the young. Although in a mainstream U.S. family a child tends to talk back to adults, this is considered unacceptable in the context of Middle Eastern, Hispanic, and Native American families (Joe & Malach, 2004; Sharifzadeh, 2004; Zuñiga, 2004).

Respect toward elders is another concept learned through the family. Traditionally for many cultures, the elders, whether they are relatives or not, represent a source of authority and wisdom, which, in turn, is acknowledged by exhibiting respect and honoring them (Chan, 2004; Joe & Malach, 2004). In Asian, Hispanic, and Caribbean cultures, the extended family, usually grandparents and elder family friends, commonly take direct part in child rearing. This is also a practice observed in many immigrant families, in which it is not uncommon to find grandparents assuming child-care responsibilities.

THE FAMILY STRUCTURE

One of the most evident societal transformations in today's context is the configuration of the family. As a result of family changes, values, and lifestyles, today, in addition to the traditional model headed by mother and father, several other structures have emerged. Culture, a dynamic force, continues to be an influential factor that also contributes to the changing nature of the family.

FOCUS
on Classroom Practices | A Classroom Holiday Time Line

Holidays or special celebrations are a constant in every cultural group. They are also one of the things that define the diversity of ideas and experiences of children and families in the classroom. Because holidays symbolize many of the values and beliefs of a group, they need to be acknowledged in the classroom. Recognition of the holidays other people celebrate is another way for children to become aware of diversity. Unfortunately, because many holidays have religious origins, this aspect of cultures is usually omitted in schools. However, there is nothing wrong with becoming aware of the names and times when other groups observe holidays.

One of the ways to acknowledge the different holidays observed by families is to create a time line that is developed throughout the school year. Unlike a calendar, where holidays are lost among other events, a time line can provide a linear and clear perspective of all the celebrations observed by the children's families. Displayed conspicuously, children and families can become familiar with celebrations year-round. This activity also helps children learn about the concepts of time and space.

To create your time line, you need to find out from families the holidays they observe. Gather your data and organize the holidays chronologically. If you are not familiar with some of those listed, remember to ask families about them, including the time of year they are celebrated. For the time line, you can either use a roll of manila paper (size 8 in. by 11 in.) or plain wallpaper (the size for borders is very handy). On the time line, enter the name of the holiday and, if possible, use any of its symbols or colors. Write the names of the families that observe each holiday. As holidays approach, share them with the class. Because you are acknowledging their existence and creating awareness of the holidays, simply mention the name of the holiday and any of the traditions attached to them. In this way, children will know that the family of a classmate is observing a special occasion.

Who Are the Members of a Family?

Family diversity seems to be a common denominator in today's society. No longer it is possible to identify a universal portrait of what a family looks like. Just look at the families of the children in your classroom, the families in your community, or even your own family. Diversity is likely what they all have in common. The best way to determine the family configuration is by finding out who its members are. Membership implies being an active element within the family unit. It also indicates the relationship of that member to the rest of the group, which defines the member's position within it. Today, social and family researchers agree that family membership holds a wide spectrum of possibilities. No longer are these solely defined by blood or legal relationships (Lynch & Hanson, 2004). Membership in contemporary families is often defined by the particular circumstances and even crises that the family has experienced. Early childhood teachers need an awareness of these circumstances, which may help to explain the unique family structures of their students.

The fact that our classrooms are mosaics of family configurations was proven by a group of our graduate students who examined their respective classrooms. Using a family survey instrument (see Chapter 10), they sampled both children and parents. By simply asking the adults to name the members of their families and having children draw them, these teachers made a relevant discovery. What they found disclosed an interesting mosaic of family forms. Their findings showed the following:

- Two-parent families made up 44 percent (8 percent were reconstituted or blended families by remarriage).
- Two-parent unmarried families made up 6 percent.
- Single-parent families made up 29 percent (all headed by women).
- Families headed by grandparents made up 7 percent.
- Extended families made up 14 percent.

Although these findings cannot be used to make any generalizations, they do help show that families are characterized by a diversity of configurations. Identification of the members of a family varies greatly in our society across cultures and even among our own relatives. What really matters is that, regardless of perceived family membership, a group of people can function as a unit and fulfill the roles of a family. The strong sense of "being a family" proves their validity as a social unit.

To fully understand the spectrum of dimensions of the present family, we need to examine the factors that have caused it to transform into its present state.

In Action . . .   Has Your Family Also Changed?

Early educators need to be aware of their own family characteristics. Before we continue exploring the concept of the family, you should consider how and whether your family has changed. To do so, complete the following questions. They are adapted from the characteristics that traditionally depict a family (Curran, 1983).

1. Who are the members that constitute your family?
2. Are they all related by blood or marriage?
3. Does your family provide for your economic survival?
4. Is your family your source of protection?
5. Has your family been the main source of social and cultural learning?
6. Is there a sense of mutual and shared responsibility among all your family members?

   - What did you find out? Share your findings with a colleague.
   - What are the changes, if any, that surprised you the most?
   - What implications can you derive from your findings?

When Did the Family Begin to Change?

The U.S. family began its most dramatic transformation in the second half of the twentieth century as a result of political events and economic trends. Job security became a thing of the past as early as the 1930s with the unstable economy of the Depression years. The need for higher income forced both marriage partners to seek work outside the home (Couchenour & Chrisman, 2004). The participation of women in the workforce became widespread during World War II and started a decades-long trend of U.S. women as active wage earners. This pattern also established the role of working mothers, which, in turn, drastically altered the roles and patterns of the traditional U.S. family. Today, this practice is reflected in statistics that show that, in 2004, 55 percent of women with infants were part of the workforce (U.S. Census Bureau, 2007b). The implications for early education are obvious.

Some of the societal changes observed beginning during the 1960s contributed to the transformation of the family. New lifestyles and a broader acceptance of family membership and responsibilities led to viewing the family with a different eye. These factors directly and indirectly led the family to assume new and unique configurations. With newly developed lifestyles, the family as a social organism was forced to adapt itself (Walsh, 2003). The changes being experienced by U.S. families were similarly occurring among families around the world (see Figure 3-3).

A new wave of immigrants to the United States, particularly since the 1960s, added another element that further diversified the traditional family. The variety of family patterns, as well as customs and traditions brought by different ethnic groups, further altered the old concept of family.

Family Configurations

Although most can agree that to have a family we need to have adults and, in most cases, children, we cannot so easily agree about the specific membership of a family.

FIGURE 3-3 **Factors Contributing to the Transformation of the Family: How Many Are Evident in Your Community?**

---

1. *Economic and financial situation at the national level:* The unstable economic situation forced families to become dual earners to preserve their survival. Women became workers outside the home, adding the role of wage earners to that of mothers and housewives.
2. *New lifestyles:* Traditional values and ideas about personal relationships changed. Along came an emphasis on individuality and a liberal view about family, sex, and interpersonal relationships.
3. *New wave of immigration:* A high percentage of new immigrants began coming into the country during the 1960s, a tread that continues to this date. Their new perspectives added a diverse element to the social fabric of society. With them came new ways to depict a family based on its members' cultures.

Families headed by grandparents are becoming more common in present-day society.

For some, a family consists exclusively of the parents and their offspring. For others, a family includes not only parents and children but also blood relatives and even some very special friends not related by blood or by law. While the original concepts of family membership are lost in time, each of us has inherited ideas about family membership from our own experiences as family members.

Culture Influences Family Membership

Exploring who is considered "part of the family" is an interesting way to observe the differences among cultures. For example, some Americans define their family as consisting of the mother, father, and children. In our mainstream culture, extended family members, although valued as important members, are not referred to as "family" but as "relatives" (Hanson, 2004). This view of the family, which focuses on the immediate family members or the nuclear unit, may be different from what other cultural groups acknowledge and call "my family."

According to Willis (2004), African Americans commonly describe their families as including more than just simply parents and children. With terms such as "'my family,' 'my folks,' 'my kin,' 'my people' to identify blood relatives and to denote relationships with special friends or 'cared for' individuals who are not related,'" they describe a wider concept of the family. Families with Native American roots also view the family as consisting of more than just the immediate members. Families in both these cultures are defined as including the nuclear and the extended family members (Joe & Malach, 2004). A similar position is also found among Hispanics (Zuñiga, 2004) and Italian Americans (McGoldrick, 2003), who value and regard as family the extended members as well as those with whom there might not exist a legal relationship.

Wadsworth/Cengage Learning

LET'S TALK AND REFLECT... Family Membership

Family membership is defined differently by various groups as well as by individuals. Think about the persons children talk about who provide care and who are important to them.

Are they all related by blood or legal lines? Who should, then, be considered a member of the family?

For example, in both groups, godparents, the Italian *comparaggio* and the Spanish *compadrazgo*, describe a way through which outside members, usually neighbors or close friends, become part of the family. Considered an honor, the *compadres* (godparents) assume an active role, much like that of parents, and are expected to watch over the lives of their godchildren or *ahijados*. It is not unusual to find children in the care of a godparent (*madrina* or *padrino*), especially in moments of crises.

A Diversity of Family Configurations

The various family configurations of the children in most early childhood classrooms include single-parent families, blended families, extended families, foster families, and two-parent families (see Figure 3-4). No longer is there a single model of the family. The most basic social unit has been the victim of change, much like the other spheres of society, and today's families are structured in both traditional and nontraditional forms. In fact, nontraditional families already outnumber traditional families as the result of the high divorce rate in the United States, the pregnancy rate among teenage girls, and sexual orientation patterns.

The family unit in the United States can no longer be described only in terms of the traditional model of the 1950s, in which a mother, father, and children were seen as a family unit. The family as a social unit has undergone significant changes through the past few decades. The models of the early twenty-first century can be defined in many different paradigms, all of which are present in early childhood classrooms. According to Olsen and Fuller (2003), families fall into two large categories: traditional and nontraditional (see Figure 3-4). The traditional family consists of a heterosexual couple and the biological or adopted children. This is also known as an *intact family* (Olsen & Fuller, 2003). In recent decades, the high divorce rate has produced the *blended family* model, where the children from previous marriages are assimilated into a newly formed family unit. Present statistics indicate that married-couple families represent about one-third of all families in the United States. What makes the intact and blended family models traditional is the fact that a heterosexual couple performs the traditional roles of a mother and a father.

FIGURE 3-4 **Family Models**

Traditional model	Nontraditional model
Intact family (*Two-parent heterosexual couple*) Blended family (*Stepfamily or multiple-marriage heterosexual couple*)	Single-parent family Grandparent family Foster family Sibling-headed family Gay or lesbian family

Single-Parent Families

Single-parent families have become the most common type of nontraditional family structure due to the steadily increasing divorce rate and the high incidence of teenage pregnancy. An estimated 31 percent of all children are born into single-parent families. Most of these families are headed by mothers; however, with contemporary societal views about the role of fathers, single-parent homes headed by fathers are gradually increasing. These families face the additional challenge of having one parent carry out all the family responsibilities. In spite of that, such families can also successfully meet the needs of the child and ensure a healthy family environment.

Grandparenting—A Trend in Today's Family Configurations

Today, many children live with and are in the care of relatives and grandparents. The term *kinship care* describes a family situation in which a grandparent or other extended family member is raising a child whose parents cannot (Children's Defense Fund, n.d.). Among kinship care families, recent trends show that a large number of children live with and are cared for by their grandparents. Grandparent families are growing in numbers as a consequence of various social problems in our society. An estimated 2.5 million grandparents are parenting nearly six million children (U.S. Census Bureau, 2007a). Families headed by grandparents have been a practice among some Native American groups and Latinos, but they have not been common in mainstream society (Olsen & Fuller, 2003). Immigration, teenage mothers, loss of a parent, and economic pressures are among the factors leading to an increase in grandparents raising their young grandchildren. The number of grandparent families is growing to the point that support groups are forming across the country and social reforms are taking place to assist grandparents with the upbringing of grandchildren.

Gay and Lesbian Families

One of the alternative family configurations is the gay or lesbian family. Families headed by gay men or lesbian women span the socioeconomic spectrum of society, much like heterosexual couples. It is estimated that same-sex households in the United States are increasing (Olsen & Fuller, 2003). Census data shows that, for 2004, same-sex households accounted for nearly 1 percent (U.S. Census Bureau, 2007b). Although not exact, some estimates suggests that there are "from 1 to 5 million lesbian mothers and 1 to 3 million gay fathers . . . and 6 to 14 million children of lesbian and gay parents" (Laird, 2003). Today, an increasing number of children are being raised in gay and lesbian households. Gay and lesbian parents have additional child-rearing tasks as they prepare their children for controversy and possible negative experiences associated with social opinion about their lifestyles. However, research has shown that for children in gay and lesbian families, parenting experiences are comparable to those of peers growing in heterosexual families (Clay, 2003).

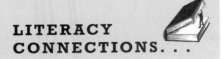

LITERACY CONNECTIONS... Recommended Readings About Grandparent Families

- De Toledo, S., & Brown, D. (1995). *Grandparents as parents: A survival guide for raising a second family.* New York: Guilford Press.

- Kornhaber, A. (1995). *Contemporary grandparenting.* Thousand Oaks, CA: Sage Press.

- Kornhaber, A. (2002). *The grandparent guide.* New York: McGraw-Hill.

- Osborne, T. (2003). *Ticklebelly Hill: Grandparents raising grandchildren.* Bloomington, IN: Authorhouse.

LITERACY CONNECTIONS... Books About Nontraditional Values

Gay and lesbian families

- Hann, L., & Nijland, S. (2002). *King & King.* New York: Tricycle.

- Valentine, J. (2004). *One dad, two dads, brown dad, blue dads.* New York: Alyson Wonderland.

- Vigna, J. (1995). *My two uncles.* New York: Albert Whitman.

Foster families

- Blomquist, G., & Blomquist, J. (1990). *Zachary's new home.* Washington, DC: Magination Press.

- Wilgocki, J., & Wright, M. (1998). *Maybe days.* Washington, DC: Magination Press.

Adopted families

- Girard, L. (1991). *Adoption is for always.* New York: Albert Whitman Publishers.

- Kirk, D. (1999). *Little Miss Spider.* New York: Scholastic.

- McCutcheon, J. (1996). *Happy adoption day.* New York: Little, Brown.

- Zisk, M. (2001). *The best single mom in the world.* New York: Albert Whitman.

Families Facing Challenges

Life situations vary and may lead some families to experience extreme stress while dealing with challenges. While well-functioning families support and nurture their children to happy and productive independence, families experiencing difficult times may not. Families of all configurations and cultures face challenges ranging from economic to social. Some families may be able to provide for the basic needs of their children while being unsuccessful in providing the emotional security necessary for healthy development. A family facing challenges is usually plagued by distrust, anxiety, and unpredictability. Adults and other family members may also exhibit low self-esteem, distrust, inability to have fun, and sometimes a sense of shame. Children of challenged families often exhibit behaviors such as anger and sadness; many are unable to experience intimacy with peers or with other adults. Unless they receive support and positive intervention that allows healthy emotional and physical development to take place, children of challenged families may face difficulties that last throughout their lifetimes (Olsen & Fuller, 2003).

Homeless Families

Life circumstances and social and economic conditions have led many individuals and their families to lose their homes. Homeless individuals are defined as those who do not own or have a permanent home. It is estimated that about 1 percent of the U.S. population may experience "a spell of homelessness at least once during a year" (Urban Institute, 2000). It is not simple to establish an ethnic profile of the homeless, for homelessness affects people across cultural and racial lines.

In recent years, communities across the country have seen an increase in the number of families with children who are homeless. There are many causes for homelessness, and among the leading reasons are poverty and the lack of affordable homes (National Coalition for the Homeless, 2007). Other reasons include domestic abuse. Frequently, the mother is the victim, forcing her to end a relationship with a spouse or other family member. Unfortunately, the homeless are often victims of discrimination and violence. Many national and local agencies advocate and provide services, including shelter, for homeless individuals and families. Federal legislation establishes the rights and provides funding for educational services to children who are homeless. Programs like Head Start provide direct services to homeless children and their families. More support and understanding of their needs is required to address the multiple issues faced by children and families who are homeless.

Immigrant Families

Immigrant families have always been present in U.S. communities. Today, with the continuous increase in immigration, the number of families of immigrants living in communities everywhere in the country has risen. Demographical statistics show that in 2005, close to 21 percent of children under age 6 living in the United States were from immigrant families (Matthews & Ewen, 2006; Matthews & Jang, 2007). The majority of these children are U.S. born with at least one parent born outside the United States. Census data show that more than half of foreign-born parents are Hispanics (7.8 million), followed by Asians and Pacific Islanders (2.5 million) (Fields, 2003).

Many are the characteristics shared by immigrant families when they come to live in the United States. Among these, it is important to highlight the fact that many arrived as intact families guided by a desire to build a future for their children. A high sense of dedication and work ethic is also noticeable among immigrant families. However, they also face several different challenges. Adjustment to life in the United States is not always an easy task. In many communities, children from immigrant families live in poverty and are less likely to benefit from child-care services. In some cases, language differences, with many lacking mastery of English, often hinders access to employment opportunities or services. Language isolation is also observed among members of families who are newcomers (Hernandez, Denton, & Macartney, 2007). Some families also face difficulties due to their immigration status. In the context of immigration law and policies, many families are faced with uncertainty about their future. Others have suffered discrimination and have been victims of racism and hate crimes. With immigration projected to continue, policy and legislation to support the needs of immigrant families and their children is a priority in the United States.

WORKING WITH DIVERSE FAMILIES: CHALLENGES AND OPPORTUNITIES

Families comprise persons who have a shared history and a shared future.

Monica McGoldrick and Betty Carter (2003)

Awareness of the broader concept of family membership is important for the early childhood educator. Knowing that a relative, whether an uncle, a cousin, or even a close family friend, shares and cares for the child as the parents do helps intervention and development of appropriate services. This sense of kinship that bonds many different family members, as well as close individuals, becomes a significant social asset for the family and for the child. This collective spiritual, emotional, and physical frame of reference becomes a resource that the child can draw upon to successfully solve problems and overcome challenges of the present and the future. From the perspective of the child, it widens the circle of people who care and participate in his or her upbringing.

Social changes have impacted all cultural groups in our country. It is important for early childhood educators to avoid stereotyping families because of their cultural orientation. Today, because of the many social circumstances faced by people, it is impossible to assert that a family will respond according to traditional cultural patterns. Because of the effects of acculturation, some families have adapted themselves to the demands of today's social reality. Another factor responsible for the changes is the economic burden

SNAPSHT 3-2

Our American Multicultural Family: Meet the El-Kollallis

Born in Cairo, Egypt, Kamellia El-Kollalli and her husband came to the United States more than two decades ago. Like many other families, they left behind the world they knew and came "in search of a dream." Arriving in Washington, DC, they soon began to see America through the eyes of the friends they made. The El-Kollallis raised two children and, like many families with dual cultures, instilled in them a sense of pride in their Egyptian and American heritage. Although believing that they and their children "are the product of the East and the West," the El-Kollallis also remember the unpleasant moments they encountered as a result of being from a different

Wadsworth/Cengage Learning

culture. Some of those most painful moments involve the discrimination their children experienced. Kamellia still remembers finding their son when he was 3 praying to God to make his "tan" disappear so that the other children would play with him. As the children grew older, they bore the burden of insensitive and ignorant remarks made not only by their peers but also by their teachers. At one point, Kamellia's son remarked that he hoped that prejudice and ignorance would not crush his sister's self-esteem and spirit. The El-Kollallis' hope is that today's multicultural education movement can bring these damaging experiences to a halt. In spite of everything, they assert that "America is the best place to be." They also believe that the schools can help society become aware of the vast cultural treasures that people from other cultures bring to our nation.

faced by some families. This has, in some cases, brought people to live with parents or to have a relative live with them in their household. Even families of recent immigrants, who usually follow their native cultural patterns, may exhibit differences. In some cases, the strains endured by recent immigration have forced some families to adopt unique family memberships (McGoldrick, 2003). Although for some immigrants these are temporary or emergency arrangements, educators need to be concerned not only with the identity of these family members but also with how and whether they are involved in meeting needs of the child.

FAMILY DIVERSITY: IMPLICATIONS FOR TEACHERS

Early childhood educators must set aside their preconceived notions about the composition, the meaning, and the role of the family to become more receptive of the varieties found among their children. Accepting that today's families are found both in traditional and nontraditional configurations enables you to objectively relate to and deal more effectively with families of the children in your classroom.

SUCCESSFUL FAMILIES

Do you ever consider what makes a family successful? Is there such a thing as a successful family? No matter what the configuration of the family, there are common characteristics that make a family "successful" (see Figure 3-5). When adopted by its members, these traits, found to be common in families across cultures, make the family function harmoniously, positively, and effectively.

Successful families have a set of identifiable values. These values are the principles that guide the decisions and the behaviors of the family members. Primary caretakers—whether grandparents, siblings, mothers, or fathers—try to model behaviors consistent with the values held by the family.

Spirituality has been identified as a key value that holds the family together, particularly during trying times; it is the "glue" that binds the family and a source of shared ideas. Spirituality stems from a family's religious affiliation or spiritual inclination. A family's spiritual sense provides guidelines that may define family lifestyles. It also

---

In Action . . .   **Extended Family**

A well-known African saying states the following:

> It takes a whole village to raise a child.

In the context of the extended family, what is the meaning of this phrase? How does it reflect the reality of today's U.S. families?

FIGURE 3-5 **Characteristics of Functional Families**

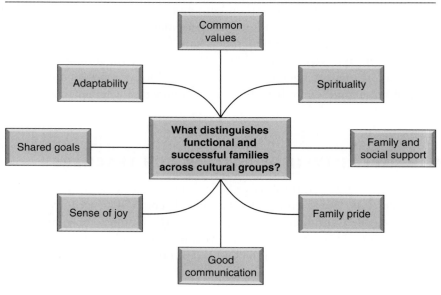

Source: Olsen & Fuller, 2003.

serves as the source for value-based behaviors such as morality, sense of respect, and responsibility toward elders and family members. African American families have been characterized by their strong spiritual bonds, as have Latino and Jewish families, whose religious ideas form the core of many of their traditions and family roles. How strongly the religion's codes will be followed is decided by each family. External elements, such as dress codes, food preparation, and food selection, can be tied to a family's religious beliefs and values. This link can be observed among many ethnic and cultural groups, such as Hindu, Middle Eastern, and Christian families.

Beyond the external aspects, family values, sense of respect, and morality may also influence factors such as the role relationships among family members, child-rearing patterns, and developmental expectations (Lynch & Hanson, 2004). Awareness of different religions and spiritual values is essential for early educators to know how to be responsive and respectful to the families of young children they serve.

Healthy families practice and believe in *family support*, which fosters growth and understanding of each other. An important part of family support is the commitment to spend time together and stay together, even during difficult times. In addition to family support, functional families demonstrate social support for others in their communities, schools, and neighborhoods. They take social responsibility for the world they live in and contribute in positive ways. Consider, for instance, the support families display toward each other during natural disasters and other emergency situations.

They also have *shared goals* to strive for. All members see themselves as key participants in achieving their aspirations. In their own ways, the members of each family collaborate to see their dreams become a reality. Good *communication skills* are essential for a well-functioning family. Members need time to learn how to express themselves as well as to listen to others. Family members that communicate well seem to have fewer problems and experience more harmony together and individually.

Adaptability and the willingness to make changes are very important in today's society. Families must be able to adapt to social, economic, and emotional pressures brought on by internal and external forces. Change in traditional roles is a good example of family adaptation. For example, taking care of the baby is no longer the exclusive job of the mother. Cooking is a shared responsibility, as is earning an income for the family.

Healthy traditional and nontraditional families show *pride* and demonstrate *loyalty*. They demonstrate their sense of pride in their success stories and in their behaviors. Family members help each other and solve problems together. They cooperate and work together as a unit when faced with adversity.

In every healthy and successful family, there must be time for *joy* and laughter. Celebrating together is one of the oldest human rituals. Successful families exhibit joyfulness, spontaneity, and enjoyment of life. Celebrations become opportunities to share a sense of happiness through interactions and in how family members respond to the needs of other members. Formal celebrations, such as birthdays, weddings, anniversaries, and cultural holidays, are times to express joy while reaffirming culture. Informal celebrations take place anytime: during mealtimes, on family outings, while playing together, and even while doing family chores. They are times when family members express their togetherness and support to each other.

Although healthy families are not guaranteed to produce well-adjusted, productive, happy children every time, it is reasonable to assume that the children from well-functioning families will do better than the children raised in families that have difficulty adjusting to challenges. The hope is that children raised in the context of a

---

LET'S TALK AND REFLECT. . . Remembering Special Family Times

Day to day experiences with family members leave indelible marks in our memory. Take time to remember any of the special times spent with your family. What stories can you share about either a happy or sad time experienced with your parents, other family members, or relatives? Think about the feelings that you experienced. How did the experience contribute to your concept of family?

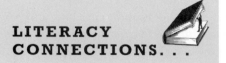

LITERACY CONNECTIONS...
Learning About Family Diversity Through Children's Literature

Many stories can help children learn and discover more about their own families. Following are a few of the many that you may want to share with children:

For younger children (ages 3–5)

- Barnwell, Y. (1998). *No mirrors in my Nana's house.* San Diego, CA: Harcourt Brace.

- Crews, D. (1991). *Bigmama's.* New York: Mulberry Books.

- Gunning, M. (2004). *A shelter in our car.* San Francisco: Children's Book Press.

- Kerley, B. (2005). *You and me together: Moms, dads, and kids around the world.* Washington, DC: National Geographic.

- Lee, J. (2002). *Bitter dumplings.* New York: Farrar, Straus & Giroux.

- Mora, P. (1997). *A birthday basket for Tia.* New York: Aladdin.

- Morris, A. (2000). *Families.* New York: Scholastic.

For primary-age children (ages 6–8)

- Galindo, M. (2001). *Icy watermelon.* Houston, Arte Publico.

- Ryland, C. (1993). *The relatives came.* New York: Aladdin.

- Woodruff, E. (1999). *The memory coat.* New York: Scholastic.

supportive family environment will go on to replicate their experiences later on in life when they form their own families.

THE FAMILY—THE MOST IMPORTANT ELEMENT IN OUR LIVES

We are all part of a family. We are who we are because of what we received and learned from our families. The family is a basic social and cultural institution and a common characteristic of people across different cultures. This sociocultural unit imparts traditions and teaches shared meanings and behaviors to the individual. We only need to look at ourselves to recognize the power embedded in a family. In general, our tastes and dislikes, our beliefs, the things we prefer to eat, and even some of the phrases we use are all grounded in what we learned from our families.

| OUR CLASSROOM, THE MIRROR OF THE CHILDREN'S FAMILIES

Your classroom is perhaps the best place to observe how relevant and powerful families are. Every time you interact with your students, you also come in contact with their families. During the early years, families play the principal role in the lives of children. When we know the members of a child's family, even the nuances and gestures exhibited by them are understood as being characteristic of certain family members. Because families perform the role of culture interpreters for the younger generations, the ways children behave also reflect the cultures they belong to.

One of the more common ways to "see" the influence of the family is in the words and phrases children use. What the family members do, say, and wear is always noticed and modeled by children. Observing children during pretend play gives teachers excellent windows into their lives and lets them know what impacts the children the most. During one of our courses, a graduate student shared the following incident she observed involving one of her prekindergartners:

> I was fascinated by what Teresita, a 4-year-old whose parents came from the Dominican Republic, did. She was playing in the housekeeping area when I started this observation. Two other girls were with her and they were all getting dressed. She opened the handbag she was playing with and went to the mirror where she started to put on some eye make-up. As I came closer, I saw her using a black marker to draw a line around her eyes. Of course, she looked as if she had been hit by someone! When I asked her what she was doing, she remarked: "*Me estoy poniendo la raya para pasear* [I am putting on the eye-liner to go out]"; I knew instantly that the idea came from her mother, a young woman who always wears noticeable eye makeup. For Teresita, getting ready to go out implied using makeup. More importantly, this example demonstrates that even at her young age, Teresita was already modeling the accepted ways of her family.

You are probably familiar with the ways young children act out the behaviors observed in their families. Take, for instance, the following example that happened in a first-grade classroom: Anthony, a vivacious 6-year-old boy of Jamaican background, was having a snack along with three other classmates, two of whom were girls. Finishing his apple, he noticed that both girls still had theirs and that the other boy at the table also had his. Extending his arm, he freely grabbed the apple from one of the girls, who loudly protested. Observing from a corner, the teacher knew that an incident was about to happen. Coming closer, she heard the following dialogue: "Give me back my apple!" said the girl. "Why? I'm a man," answered Anthony with emphasis. "I want my apple now!" replied the girl. "I told you. I'm a man and *mans* [men] eat more!" he said hitting the table with his fist. Seeing that the situation was getting heated, the teacher intervened. When asked to explain his attitude, Anthony frankly said: "My daddy gets more at home. He says *mans* need to eat more." "But you could have asked me for another

In Action . . . **Am I Like My Family?**

We learn so many things from our families that it is sometimes hard to realize the true realm of their influence. To find out how your family has influenced you, begin by finding the material things that reflect its influence. Looking around your own house, identify those things that directly or indirectly reflect the objects, items, and patterns that were found in your family's home. Consider, for instance, the colors, the kind of objects and the ways they are displayed, the way your rooms are arranged, the "messes" in your kitchen, and, of course, the food you cook. How many similarities with your family did you find? If you did not find a lot of resemblances, ask yourself why you are different from your family. You will probably discover that in the similarities, as well as in the differences, the influence of your family is a common denominator.

F☉CUS
on Classroom Practices | A Classroom Family Cookbook

One of the exciting things about cultural diversity is learning about ethnic eating habits and food patterns. Discovering what the families represented in your classroom eat is not only a source for cultural awareness but also another way to emphasize likenesses and differences among families. Because all families have a favorite dish (actually, probably several favorite dishes), a good way for children and for teachers to learn about themselves is by creating a cookbook. The classroom cookbook is basically a collection of recipes of simple favorite dishes enjoyed by families. This project provides opportunities to integrate literacy, math, and science. Using a big book format, families would be assigned a page each (or two depending on the enrollment). A picture or a drawing made by the child or any family member would illustrate the pages. To collect the recipes, teachers need to send a letter to the families explaining the purpose of the activity. Ask families for very simple recipes or those that can be made in the classroom. Possible dishes

include salads, beverages, desserts, or bread-based recipes.

As recipes are collected and added to the cookbook, test them in the classroom. Give credit to the child's family whenever a recipe is prepared. On the bulletin board, announce the dish with a sign reading: "Today's special dish is _____ contributed by the _____ family." If possible, display the recipe's ingredients early so that children can examine them. Plan to take pictures or videotape children while recipes are tested. These can be used for later discussions and to review specific aspects. Discuss the food value of the recipe and help children look for similarities and differences among the various dishes.

This is a project that could increase participation of families in the classroom. It also gives teachers another opportunity to learn about the specific families' cultures. For the children, learning what their classmates eat and the ingredients used will provide another window into how alike and different they are.

In Action . . .   **Family Aspirations?**

All families have aspirations for their new members. To explore them, conduct a survey of your own relatives and friends with children. Begin by asking your parents what aspirations they held for you. Save their comments. As you ask others, record their answers and their backgrounds (ethnicity, social level, and so on). Compare your findings and highlight the similarities and differences. Note in particular how their aspirations for their children relate to their culture.

SNAPSHOT 3-3   **Names and Surnames**

Family names, or surnames, are another relevant element that provides a person's family and cultural identity. They are also often the focus of misunderstandings, because in other cultural contexts, family names may follow a different practice. Although in the United States often a child's family name is simply that of the father with no acknowledgment of the mother's name, in other cultures, like the Hispanic, this is not the case. Even though many Hispanics have adopted the practice of using one surname, there are still many cases where you will find that a Hispanic child has more than one family name. The tradition in Hispanic countries dictates that children must carry the names of both parents as surnames.

Take, for example, the following name: Elena Rivera Cordero (child's name, father's name, mother's name). Although the child can also be called Elena Rivera, she still maintains Cordero as her other surname. This practice stems from the importance ascribed to legitimization of children during times when being a child born out of wedlock carried a stigma. From our own experience, we know that teachers often assume to know the child's name. To avoid misunderstanding, always ask the parents for the child's correct name.

SNAPSHOT 3-4   **Our Multicultural Family: Meet Aida Ramos-Cruz**

When Aida Ramos made the decision to leave her native Puerto Rico, she had only one thought: to build a better future for her and her 1-year-old child. A single parent, she came to New York almost 40 years ago with only a little knowledge of English and a firm desire to succeed. For a woman from a Spanish-speaking island, life in the United States in the 1950s and 1960s was not always easy. With limited knowledge of English, Aida never gave up, despite the many hardships she faced. Later on, after

remarrying, Aida and her husband Angel struggled to give their five children a better life in Chicago where they settled. They succeeded in keeping their cultural traditions and proudly passed them on to their children and today to their grandchildren.

Today, Aida looks back not with nostalgia but with a well-earned sense of pride. Times were difficult, but Aida agrees that there was always the knowledge that, with their desire to succeed, they would make it. And they did.

one," said the teacher. Anthony replied, "Daddy never asks. He takes it." Handing him another apple, the teacher said: "Anthony, that is at your home. Here we ask when we want to have more."

| FAMILIES—THE ESSENCE OF SOCIAL AND CULTURAL LIFE

The family serves as one of society's prime agents for cultural learning. Through day-to-day activities and interactions, families pass on to the younger generations the ideas and accepted behaviors of their cultural group. The power the family exerts covers every aspect of life. The younger the individual is, the more definitive and influential the power of the family becomes. Even before birth, we begin experiencing the influence of families, and through them, we experience the culture they belong to. Through our families, we acquire the meanings and views that make us a part of our social group.

Teaching young children presents a unique opportunity to discover their families. In every classroom in this country, we can begin not only to learn about families, but also to appreciate and value them. This is a unique opportunity to begin to understand what it means to live in and be a part of this diverse U.S. society. Because early educators are constantly trying to find more novel ways to help children, no better source and channel is found than what we have in their families. As we search for new ideas to reform our teaching in a responsive manner, the families in our classroom will be our first resource. In the next chapter, you will explore the needs of the child and see more evidence of how relevant the family is to knowing the children you teach.

WHAT WE HAVE LEARNED—CHAPTER SUMMARY

Family is the social unit most responsible for creating the child as a social, emotional, cultural, and psychological being. The learning that takes place during the formative years is most influenced by the immediate and extended family as well as by the environment. Culture and child-rearing practices, as they are transmitted through family members and encountered in the immediate environment, play major roles in the development and socialization of the child. The value system of the child is greatly affected by cultural predispositions instilled at an early age. The changes in our society have also influenced changes in the traditional family model consisting of a mother, a father, and children. Now, it is more common to encounter a variety of nontraditional configurations, such as grandparent families, gay or lesbian families, single-parent families, and foster families. Regardless of its makeup, every family needs to be the conduit of effective and positive development for each child. Given today's socioeconomic, racial, and religious pressures, this is not an easy task. In order to effectively assist in the positive development of their students, early childhood educators must have a firm grasp of the influence the family structure and culture play in the development of each child.

THINGS TO DO . . .

1. An excellent way to learn about families in a multicultural context is to find out how they see themselves. Begin by asking a sample of your own colleagues or classmates about their ideas regarding families. You may want to ask the following questions:

   ■ *How do you define family?*

   ■ *What makes your family a family?*

   ■ *What would you say makes your family special or different from others?*

   After you have collected their answers, find the things in common and the things that differ. Summarize your findings and share them with your colleagues.

2. A good way to continue learning about families is to learn about their daily routines. Routines help us to "see" the culture of the family. Begin a collection of family routines. Ask your friends, colleagues, and some of the parents of the children in your class to share some of the routines they observe during breakfast, dinner, on Saturday and Sunday, and when having visitors at their house. After collecting your data, analyze them to find trends in common, unusual patterns, and other peculiarities that characterize the families surveyed.

3. Because we all have an interest in learning more about different cultures, select one culture and do some library research about some of its family customs. Possible aspects to research are birth practices, child-rearing ideas, family tasks, funeral practices, and others. Write a paper about your findings and share it with your colleagues.

4. Using the findings from the activity in which you surveyed the family configurations in your classroom, select a minimum of five children's books reflective of those configurations. Design a classroom activity to share the books with your students.

RECOMMENDED INTERNET RESOURCES

- The Annie E. Casey Foundation (serving children and families)
  www.aecf.org/
- Center For Law And Social Policy (CLASP)
  www.clasp.org/index.php
- The Children's Defense Fund
  www.childrensdefense.org
- The National Coalition for the Homeless
  www.nationalhomeless.org/index.html
- "Resources for Child Care Providers" from the Child Care Bureau
  www.acf.hhs.gov/programs/ccb/providers/index.htm

YOUR STANDARDS PORTFOLIO

NAEYC Standard 4a: Teaching and Learning, Connecting with Children and Families*

Effective communication is central to successful collaborations between parents or families and schools. With the increased use of technology, communication between classrooms and home has been enhanced. To evidence how you meet this standard, complete the following activities:

- Create a classroom newsletter to share ideas with parents and family members.

*NAEYC Standard 4a correlates with INTASC Standard 6: Communication and Technology.

- Identify topics of interest to families with diverse backgrounds and those with children who have disabilities.

- Design a bulletin board to share ideas and information with culturally and linguistically different parents and families.

- Think about the technology available to parents and families in your community and suggest three ways to facilitate communication with parents with cultural and linguistic differences.

REFERENCES

Bronfenbrenner, U. L. (2004). *Making human beings human: Bioecological perspectives on human development.* San Francisco: Sage.

Chan, S. (2004). Families with Asian roots. In E. Lynch & M. Hanson (Eds.), *Developing cross-cultural competence: A guide for working with young children and their families* (3rd ed., pp. 251–354). Baltimore, MD: Paul Brookes.

Children's Defense Fund. (n.d.). *Kinship care resource kit for community and faith-based organizations: Helping grandparents and other relatives raising children.* Washington, DC: Author.

Clay, J. (2003). Working with lesbian and gay parents and their children. In C. Copple (Ed.), *A world of difference: Readings on teaching young children in a diverse society* (pp. 64–67). Washington, DC: National Association for the Education of Young Children.

Commission on Children. (1991). *Beyond rhetoric: A new American agenda for children and families.* Washington, DC: US Government Printing Office.

Couchenour, D., & Chrisman, K. (2004). *Families, schools, and communities: Together for young children* (2nd ed.). New York: Delmar.

Curran, D. (1983). *Traits of a healthy family.* New York: Doubleday.

Epstein, N., Bishop, D., Ryan, C., Miller, I., & Gabor, K. (2002). The McMaster model: View of healthy family functioning. In F. Walsh (Ed.), *Normal family processes* (2nd ed., pp. 581–607). New York: Guilford Press.

Fields, J. (2003). *Children's living arrangements and characteristics, March 2002.* U.S. Census Bureau. Retrieved June 28, 2008, from http://www.census.gov/prod/2003pubs/p20-547.pdf.

Garbarino, J. (1992). *Children and families in the social environment* (2nd ed.). New York: Aldine de Gruyter.

Garbarino, J., & Abramovitz, R. (1992). The family as a social system. In J. Garbarino, *Children and families in the social environment* (2nd ed., pp. 72–98). New York: Aldine de Gruyter.

Gilbert, K. (2007). Varied perspectives on the family. In *Annual Editions: The family* (p. 1). Dubuque, IA: McGraw-Hill.

Hanson, M. (2004). Families with Anglo-European Roots. In E. Lynch & M. Hanson (Eds.), *Developing cross-cultural competence: A guide for working with young children and their families* (3rd ed.). Baltimore, MD: Paul Brooke.

Hernandez, D., Denton, N., & Macartney, S. (2007). Children in immigrant families—the U.S. and 50 states: National origins, language, and early education. *Child Trends* Pub. 2007-11. Retrieved June 28, 2008, from http://www.childtrends.org/Files/Child_Trends-2007_04_01_RB_ChildrenImmigrant.pdf.

Hildebrand, V., Phenice, L., Gray, M., & Hines, R. (2008). *Knowing and serving diverse families* (3rd ed.). Upper Saddle River, NJ: Merrill.

Howard, J. (1978). *Families.* New York: Simon and Shuster.

Joe, J., & Malach, R. (2004). Families with Native American roots. In E. Lynch & M. Hanson (Eds.), *Developing cross-cultural competence: A guide for working with young children and their families* (3rd ed., pp. 127–164). Baltimore, MD: Paul Brookes.

Kindergarten Children of Westfield School. (1995). *My family, your family.* Morristown, NJ: Modern Curriculum Press.

Knight, M. (1998). *Welcoming babies.* Gardiner, ME: Tilbury House.

Konner, M. (1992). *Childhood: A multicultural view.* New York: Little, Brown.

Laird, J. (2003). Lesbian and gay families. In F. Walsh (Ed.), *Normal family processes* (3rd ed., pp. 176–209). New York: Guilford Press.

Lynch, E., & Hanson, M. (2004). (Eds.). *Developing cross-cultural competence: A guide for working with young children and their families* (3rd ed.). Baltimore, MD: Paul Brookes.

Matthews, H., & Ewen, D. (2006). *Reaching all children? Understanding early care and education among immigrant families.* Washington, DC: Center for Law and Social Policy.

Matthews, H., & Jang, D. (2007). *The challenges of change: Learning from the child care experiences and education of immigrant families.* Washington, DC: Center for Law and Social Policy.

Mayer, G., & Mayer, M. (1999). *This is my family.* New York: Golden Books.

McGoldrick, M. (2003). Ethnicity, cultural diversity, and normality. In F. Walsh (Ed.), *Normal family processes* (3rd ed., pp. 235–259). New York: Guilford Press.

McGoldrick, M., & Carter, B. (2003). The family life cycle. In F. Walsh, (Ed.), *Normal family processes* (3rd ed., pp. 375–298). New York: Guildford Press.

National Coalition for the Homeless. (2007). *Homeless families with children.* Fact Sheet 12. Washington, DC. Author.

Olsen, G., & Fuller, M. L. (2003). *Home–school relations: Working successfully with parents and families* (2nd ed.). Boston: Pearson Education.

Robles de Meléndez, W. (2006). *Family and school collaboration* (study guide). Fort Lauderdale, FL: Nova Southeastern University.

Sharifzadeh, V. (2004). Families with Middle Eastern roots. In E. Lynch & M. Hanson (Eds.), *Developing cross-cultural competence: A guide for working with young children and their families* (pp. 441–482). Baltimore, MD: Paul Brookes.

Spradley, J., & McCurdy, D. (2004). *The cultural experience: Ethnography in complex society.* Chicago: Waveland Press.

United Nations. (1994). *International year of the family.* New York: Department of Public Information.

Urban Institute. (2000). *A new look at homelessness in America.* Washington, DC: Author. Retrieved June 30, 2008, from http://www.urban.org/url.cfm?ID=900302.

U.S. Census Bureau. (2007a). *Facts for features: Grandparents' Day 2007.* Retrieved September 3, 2007, from http://www.census.gov/Press-Release/www/releases/archives/facts_for_features_special_editions/010321.html.

U.S. Census Bureau. (2007b). *Facts for features: Mother's Day.* Retrieved September 3, 2007, from http://www.census.gov/Press-Release/www/releases/archives/facts_for_features_special_editions/009747.html.

Walsh, F. (2003). (Ed.). *Normal family processes* (3rd ed.). New York: Guilford Press.

Walsh, F., & Pryce, J. (2003). The spiritual dimension of family life. In F. Walsh (Ed.), *Normal family processes* (3rd ed., pp. 337–372). New York: Guilford Press.

Willis, W. (2004). Families with African American roots. In E. Lynch & M. Hanson (Eds.), *Developing cross-cultural competence: A guide for working with young children and their families* (3rd ed., pp. 165–209). Baltimore, MD: Paul Brookes.

Zuñiga, M. (2004). Families with Latino roots. In E. Lynch & M. Hanson (Eds.), *Developing cross-cultural competence: A guide for working with young children and their families* (3rd ed., pp. 209–250). Baltimore, MD: Paul Brookes.

CHAPTER 4

Who Is the Child? Developmental Characteristics of Young Children in a Diverse Society

> *All* children are born capable of learning.
>
> *Jean-Jacques Rousseau (1712–1778)*

CHAPTER OBJECTIVES

In this chapter, we will

- define development.
- discuss the role of culture in the child development process.
- discuss the role of the environment in the development of attitudes and behaviors of children.

KEY CONCEPTS

- child development
- attitudes
- developmentally and culturally appropriate practices (DCAP)
- socialization
- diversity
- context
- racial awareness
- prejudice

FROM BARBARA'S JOURNAL

Yesterday, while the children were working at centers, I noticed how outgoing little Larissa is. The children were all drawing and working in their journals after reading the story about little Leo from Leo, the Late Bloomer, and Larissa, the self-appointed leader, was joking and telling everyone what to do. I know that I should not compare one child to another, but I could not help but notice how different all the children are. For a moment I said to myself that they are just like other 6-year-olds. But then I started to think about how each child is so special. There is Carmen, with her soft voice and inquisitive mind; Terry, with his friendly smile who charms everyone from his wheelchair; and Lashonne, who is always so witty and imaginative. What makes these children so alike but yet so different? I believe that the way they are is definitely linked to their development and culture. They have so many things in common and yet so many things that identify each as unique with his or her own needs and experiences. This makes me realize that, as a teacher, I need to be very mindful of the roles development and culture play in making the children who they are.

LOOKING AT CHILDREN: SO ALIKE AND YET SO DIFFERENT

In all children, you will find the one.

Carmen Martínez, school teacher (1972)

Each child is different and yet the same. Although these two children are siblings, beyond gender differences, they are distinct in their own ways. In the classroom, children may share the same chronological characteristics and even cultural backgrounds. But each one will still have very clear characteristics defining him or her as an individual.

In this chapter, we will briefly review some of the key aspects of **child development** that define the shared characteristics of children as well as the reasoning behind the distinctive traits that give every child a unique identity. This is an essential step for educators moving into multicultural and developmentally appropriate teaching.

DEVELOPMENT: THE PROCESS OF BECOMING

Every time a child is born it brings with it the hope that God is not yet disappointed with man [humankind].

Rabindranath Tagore (1861–1941)

Whenever you enter a classroom of young children, you are faced with the wonder of life in its most vibrant form. Smiling faces, curious looks, and lively sounds all epitomize the energy of new existence that children personify. Each child is a separate and distinct person as well as a member of the collective of children. Preparing to offer the children the best learning environment requires a careful analysis of the characteristics that make them similar and yet individual. Of particular importance is how children develop the beliefs, **attitudes,** and ideas about others that they exhibit in the classroom. This knowledge will both promote better understanding between the teacher and the students and provide valuable information to guide the instructional practices in the classroom to foster multiculturalism. The first step to this knowledge is to explore what makes people alike: the process of development.

What Is Development?

At the moment of conception, all human beings enter into a continuous dance of change and development, which is completed at the end of our existence. The constancy of change that characterizes development is also what defines it. **Development** is an integrated and coherent process experienced by all individuals.

Because development is characteristic of all people, general principles explain how children everywhere in this world grow and develop. In the same way, specific factors define and give each child an individual character. Development is, then, a process of dual character: although one function is to establish basic and similar milestones, it also determines the way individuals acquire their unique personalities.

Many elements in the environment contribute to the positive development of the child. What elements are depicted here?

Wadsworth/Cengage Learning

According to Brazelton and Greenspan (2000), all children must have several specific needs met if they are to successfully grow and thrive:

- Ongoing positive and nurturing relationships
- Physical protection, safe environments, and regulation
- Developmentally based experiences that consider their particular needs
- Reasonable expectations and predictable structure and routines
- A stable and supportive community
- Cultural continuity across home, school, and community

Developmentally and Culturally Appropriate Practices: A Concept and Ways to Teach All Children

Supporting development and addressing the needs of each child in the classroom are inherent goals of early childhood education. They also comprise the core of the concept of **developmentally and culturally appropriate practices (DCAP)** (Bredekamp & Copple, 1997). In recent years, DCAP has become the guiding concept that defines teaching and learning practices for all young children, especially those with multicultural characteristics. The DCAP concept provides the guidelines for planning practices for young children from birth through age 8. Specifically, DCAP requires practices to be based on current knowledge about how children develop and learn (Bredekamp & Copple, 1997). Central to the DCAP concept are the following three aspects: universal developmental patterns, individual development, and social and cultural experiences (see Figure 4-1). DCAP informs decisions in all classrooms and is essential to practices in a multicultural setting.

Development consists of similar and diverse milestones. Awareness of developmental commonalities and differences provides guidelines for classroom teachers.

Universality as a Defining Character of Development

As they grow—whether in Oceania, Africa, or in the United States—children of the same ages share similar physical, socioemotional, and cognitive milestones. Reaffirming the universal character of development, Konner

FIGURE 4-1   **Key Elements of the Principle of Developmentally and Culturally Appropriate Practice (DCAP)**

Universal developmental patterns

Milestones common to all individuals and cultural groups that follow predictable timelines.

Individual development

Unique changes based on a person's biological makeup that explain and acknowledge individual variation in development (diverse abilities and cultural characteristics).

Social and cultural experiences

Culture as a dynamic force that influences and mediates development and environmental context (family interactions; location; language; social and economic status; cultural experiences; interactions with adults, caregivers, and peers) plays leading roles in shaping development.

In Action . . .   A Child's Profile

Select three children and develop a common developmental profile. Consider the ways in which they are alike physically, socioemotionally, and cognitively.

(1991) explains, ". . . infants in all cultures start out with the same biological equipment." This universality establishes the likenesses of children and of people in general.

All children experience and share the process of development in much the same way, regardless of where they live. Cross-cultural research has shown that the stages of physical growth do not vary, although the tempo may vary by race, genetic inheritance, or the physical circumstances in which a child is raised. For example, for all children, everywhere, there are shared developmental events: baby teeth erupt before the permanent ones, infants' arms exhibit more control than the legs, fetal cartilage is replaced by bone following the same progression, and children have a need to feel they are part of their peer group (Berk, 2006; Konner, 1991; McDevitt & Ormond, 2002; Paludi, 2002).

Language development is another example of developmental characteristics shared by all children. Regardless of language, the same stages in learning language are experienced. From the time the linguist Noam Chomsky first defined sets of language structures common to all languages, linguists, psycholinguists, and developmental psychologists have studied how children learn these structures (Berk, 2002). They have found that language structures emerge following the same developmental progression regardless of the child's native language. For instance, babies go through stages of random vocalizations that are slowly modified as infants emulate the sounds used by parents and other caregivers. Also, children go through a stage of overgeneralizing the rules of grammar in their native language, whether, for example, in English or Russian. An example of this phenomenon is the child's use of "foots" instead of "feet" as the plural of "foot."

The documented existence of common developmental patterns is at the core of DCAP. In early childhood education, these patterns serve as guidelines to organize teaching that is responsive to children's developmental events. For example, because of the common developmental characteristics of all 4-year-olds, teachers are able to elicit learning experiences based on the general requirements of all children of that age. Developing activities that respond to the common characteristics of all children is also a basic principle of multicultural education.

The concept of developmentally and culturally appropriate practice (DCAP) is based on the belief that all children experience common growth and development milestones while recognizing the role of culture as a factor that influences and shapes development.

Individuality: A Trait of Development

Each child is a unique individual. Even children from the same family have very distinct and particular traits that give them an individual character. Many factors contribute to the uniqueness of every child. Four of those are discussed here: biological nature, developmental experiences, home environment, and culture (see Figure 4-2). The first one concerns the biological nature of each child as related to the parents. Because of the different genetic makeup of parents, the biological passport of each child is very distinctive. Stamped at the moment of conception, each child comes into this world equipped with a personalized inherited genetic code. This code determines whether the child has light or dark skin, curly or straight hair, is tall or short, and so on.

The second factor concerns the process of development. Research confirms that the development of the child is influenced by the circumstances, culture, lifestyle, and habits of parents during the nine months before birth. Such things as the mother's emotional readiness to accept parenthood, nutritional practices (including the presence of drug use), access to and

FIGURE 4-2 **Universal Factors that Influence Development**

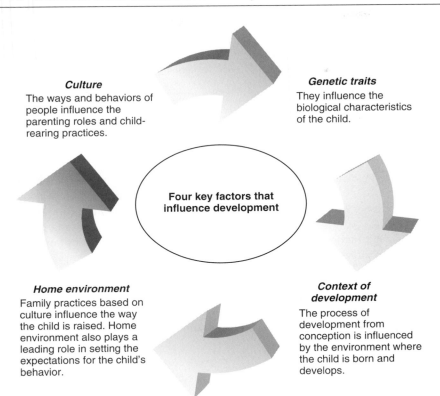

Culture
The ways and behaviors of people influence the parenting roles and child-rearing practices.

Genetic traits
They influence the biological characteristics of the child.

Four key factors that influence development

Home environment
Family practices based on culture influence the way the child is raised. Home environment also plays a leading role in setting the expectations for the child's behavior.

Context of development
The process of development from conception is influenced by the environment where the child is born and develops.

SNAPSHOT 4-1   **Nonverbal Communication as Another Descriptor of Developmental Universality**

One form of evidence of children's similarities across cultures comes from the work of the German ethnologist Irenaeus Eibl-Eibesfeldt. For more than two decades, Eibl-Eibesfeldt filmed candid instances of nonverbal communication in cultures throughout the world. He captured the behaviors of people in primitive cultures, such as the Yanomano of Brazil, the !Kung of Botswana, and the Tasaday of the Philip-pine jungles, as well as different European groups. Through his research, he was able to document similar nonverbal responses to environmental stimuli. For example, he documented similar nonverbal responses in expressing disgust at a foul odor, in hitting combined with an angry expression, and in toddlers playing with one of their mother's nipples while breastfeeding. Eibl-Eibesfeldt's evidence includes observations of similar cross-cultural reactions in adults. He further documented parents showing the same facial expressions when they interacted with an infant: broad smiles, wide-open eyes, raised eyebrows, and a bobbing up and down of the head accompanied by a high-pitched, somewhat musical vocalization.

Source: Adapted from Konner, 1991.

LET'S TALK AND REFLECT. . . **Culture and Child-Rearing Practices**

Denying children their culture is denying their identities.
Jaipaul Roopnarine and James Johnson (2005)

Culture affects child-rearing practices. Working with culturally diverse children and families allows you to experience child-rearing processes that may differ from your own. As a professional early educator, think about how accurate your knowledge is regarding the child-rearing cultural views of families in your community. How can it be improved?

---

availability of medical care, and health conditions affect the development of the unborn child. Recent evidence also demonstrates that high emotional stress levels in the mother are a risk to the child.

A third factor to consider is the home environment into which each child is born. The character of the child is determined by the family experience, the cultural ideas and values of persons close to the family (whether friends or relatives), and the neighborhood setting where the child grows up. For example, a 5-year-old boy born in a Masai village may be given the responsibility of shepherding grazing animals. Compare this responsibility with what is expected of children of the same age in the United States. You can easily see how the environment sets different behavior patterns and expectations for a child.

A fourth factor is culture. Culture plays a leading role in the way the child will learn to view the world. Developmental psychologists recognize that the influence of culture is such that it even controls the developmen-

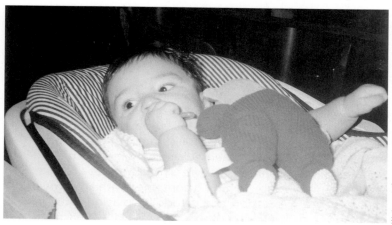

Home experiences are a major force in shaping a child's individual development.

Wadsworth/Cengage Learning

tal milestones of children (Berk, 2006; Charlesworth, 2008). For instance, for most people in the United States, "sleeping through the night" is considered an expectation for infants by the time they are four to five months old. This is not so in cultures where infants sleep with their mothers and nurse themselves without hardly interrupting the adults. Infant sleeping arrangements are also influenced by culture. While it is common in the United States to find infants sleeping in a crib and often in a separate room, co-sleeping is practiced by

Uniqueness is the most common characteristic of all children. What similarities do you observe in these four children? What individual traits are also observable among them?

people from countries around the world. For example, in Cambodia and among Central American Guatemalan Mayans, co-sleeping is a common practice believed to help in building a strong parent–child bond (Berk, 2006; Paludi, 2002). Teachers of young children are discovering daily that culture is a major contributor to the identity and individuality of each child in the classroom. As we get to know more about the children's cultures, we get to learn more about how to better address and respond to their needs.

The Shaping Force of the Environment

Where we are born and where we spend our lives growing up molds our unique identities. The experiences we had and the friends and neighbors with whom we shared our time formed the network of influences that make us who we are. As an early childhood teacher, you probably have observed how children role-play adultlike behaviors in the dramatic area. If you observe carefully, you will notice some of the social codes that

---

In Action . . .   Developmental Factors

Consider the four factors—heredity, prenatal environment, family environment, and culture—as the major contributors to each child's identity. Are there any other elements you would add? Think about yourself and describe how these four factors influenced your development as an individual.

LET'S TALK AND REFLECT. . . **The Environment as a Source of Interactions**

One of the important characteristics of environments is that they provide opportunities for people to interact with one another. Direct and indirect interactions are effective catalysts for young children to learn the social and cultural codes of their group. For most of us, those we admire or feel emotionally attached to serve as models and learning sources. Take time to think about the person or persons who exerted a significant influence on your life and from whom you learned the social rules of your community.

- Who were they?
- Were they from your family?
- Were they from your community?
- Why do you think they played such an influential role in your socialization?
- How did they influence you?

the children have already internalized. Examples include the phrases, interjections, and terms the children use in reference to bodily functions; they often are inappropriate from the teacher's frame of reference.

The role of culture and the environment is one of the central tenets of Lev Vygotsky's theory. Vygotsky's ideas are central to working with young children with cultural and diverse characteristics. His studies focused on the role that the cultural and social environment has on the child. According to Vygotsky, nurturing interactions provided by parents, family members, and adults help children to build ideas about the reality in which they live (cited in Berk, 2006). Home, parents, and the environment in which the child grows and develops provide the information and skills vital to successfully meeting the challenges of daily life. Vygotsky also recognized the use of language as a tool element that facilitates how the child makes sense of the social conventions and concepts meaningful to the family and their culture. Talking about experiences with family members and peers and listening to conversations provides the child with a valuable avenue for learning about the things important in the culture.

The ideas and concepts learned from home and family interactions become an individual's body of ideas about the behaviors and ways of the group. This knowledge, or "funds of knowledge," is "the historically accumulated and culturally developed bodies of knowledge and skills essential for household or individual functioning and well-being" (Gonzalez, Moll, & Amanti, 2005; Moll, Amanti, Neff, & Gonzalez, 1992). The concept of the "funds of knowledge" that each child possesses helps explain the influence of the environment and culture on the process of development. It also highlights the importance that culture has in shaping individual development. In the classroom, consideration of the ideas deemed relevant to the child and family's culture is essential to developing learning experiences that are reflective of DCAP.

Urie Bronfenbrenner's views regarding the role of the environment in development are of particular relevance to multicultural education. In his studies, Bronfenbrenner showed that the children in our classrooms reflect the many influences present in their environments (cited in Berk, 2006). The environment includes the family, relatives, school, and peers and the physical attributes of the home, community, and neighborhood, all of which impact the child's

Adults play a leading role in the socialization of children.

interpretation and views of life. Even within the same family, each child is impacted differently by the environment. To effectively provide appropriate and meaningful learning experiences, early childhood educators must be aware of the role the environment plays in the lives of young children.

LET'S TALK AND REFLECT. . . Media and the Socialization Process

Social learning theory postulates that interactions with people and the environment are an influential socializing force. Children learn and reflect the attitudes, behaviors, and gestures of people they interact with. They usually emulate those individuals close to them, such as parents, family members, and teachers.

Besides learning from interpersonal experiences, young children also adopt behaviors seen through the media. Media is an important element of the environment that plays a role in socialization. Statistics show that media images and messages, due to their power, capture children's attention. Take time to sample programs from local radio and television stations and identify the cultural messages they transmit to children. Think about the implications these messages have for young children in their building of self-concept and a sense of others.

- Do the media's messages contribute to children's positive sense about themselves and their culture?
- What do the messages communicate about people from other cultures?

SOCIALIZATION: LEARNING TO BE WITH OTHERS, LEARNING TO BE OURSELVES

When children come to school, they bring an array of strategies to deal with and get along with others. Most preschoolers in every culture exhibit the knowledge of ways to establish social relationships with others. Think about the smiles on their faces, the compliments they make about your clothing, or the way they get closer to you to catch your attention. All these actions show that children learn ways to gain social acceptance by others. These and other behaviors are acquired through the process of socialization.

Because we live in social groups, each culture has developed patterns and customs for regulating relationships among its members. This is known as **socialization.** Socialization is an ongoing process that assists individuals in learning to function effectively in a society. From birth, children are introduced to the cultural formulas of their group. Interactions with family members, caregivers, and adults provide examples and guide children in acquiring the responses and ways acceptable in their culture. You can imagine the extent of learning that must take place when preparing a child for an entire lifetime. From the simplest manners to attitudes about others, all is derived through the socialization process that lasts as long as we are in this world. Environments provide settings for the lifelong socialization process experienced by all of us. In the early years, the various environments the children are exposed to help them learn how to do the following:

- Interact with adults and peers
- Distinguish what is good or acceptable from what is not
- Behave in daily life situations
- Express feelings, such as happiness and sadness
- Perform basic activities, such as eating
- Respond when faced with the unknown
- Demonstrate affection, including knowing to whom to show affection
- Show interest in something
- Differentiate between likes and dislikes
- Think about and regard others

In Action . . .   Acceptable Language

Think about a time when you heard a child or adult using expressions that, in your opinion, are not acceptable language. How did you address the situation? What did you do? Share your thoughts with the class.

Cultural Socialization and the Developmental Niche

Developmental psychologists Super and Harkness (1995) proposed the idea of a developmental niche, or milieu, where children are socialized into the cultural ways of their society. Socializing forces in this setting come from adults, peers, and the environment itself. Through interactions with family members, caregivers, and the environment, cultural ideas and meanings are conveyed to the young. Each individual becomes a source for learning about the beliefs, ideas, and practices acceptable to the social and cultural setting where children grow up (Figure 4-3). The people whom the child spends time with, such as parents, relatives, and teachers, together constitute an influential element in shaping behaviors and in learning the culture. In this way, children acquire the behaviors characteristic of those in their group.

Social Learning Happens All Around Us

What are some settings where learning takes place? If your response is "everywhere," you are correct. Contexts for learning occur as the child comes in contact with the family, the neighborhood, the school, the peers, and with all those in the environment. But, which contacts are more important? As you probably know, the family plays the leading role in transmitting to the child the views, beliefs, ideas, and behaviors held and accepted by their culture. With the rise in the number of working parents, however, child-care programs have become an influential socialization force. Many children are now being exposed to the ideas and views of other adults and their peers earlier in life (see Figure 4-4).

FIGURE 4-3 **Socialization Forces**

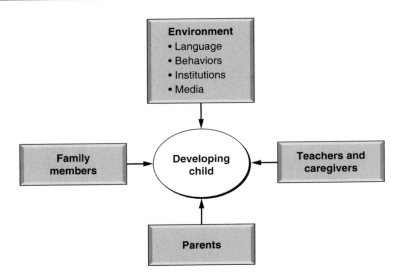

FIGURE 4-4 **Elements That Influence the Process of Cultural Socialization**

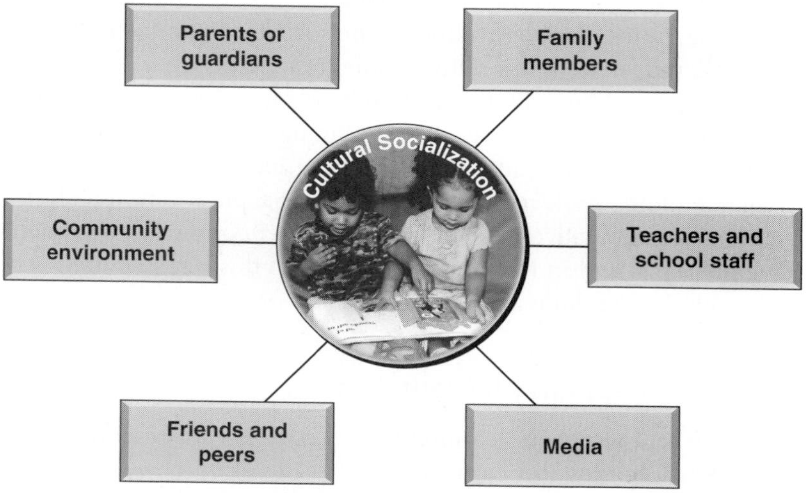

Which of these elements do you consider most influential for children? Why?

SNAPSH[O]T 4-2   The Environment in Action: Culture Influences Children's Activity Levels

The child's sociocultural environment plays an important role in forming behavior. Findings from child development research reveal that the cultural environment influences the way a person talks, smiles, and interacts with others. Being aware of the role culture plays in determining how we interact with others can help teachers understand that behaviors considered normal in some cultures would not be considered normal in their own. For instance, for Hispanics, as well as for some groups with roots in the Middle East, the use of hand gestures to emphasize what is being said is considered normal. Persons from these groups tend to be very animated when talking together. In the eyes of persons with Northern

European roots, a normal conversation among Hispanics can seem emotional and agitated, much like an argument.

Several studies have found that teachers tend to view behavior that may be culturally normal for Hispanics as disruptive or as indicators of problems. Zigler and Finn Stevenson (1993) cited one study done with Puerto Rican students. In this case, mainstream culture teachers often misinterpreted the social and emotional response styles of children of Puerto Rican origin and considered them disruptive. They also interpreted culturally acceptable interactions, such as three children talking at the same time, as signs of inattentiveness and overactivity (Bauermeister, Berrios, Acevedo, & Gordon, 1990). Using a sample of teachers, some with Puerto Rican roots and some with European American roots, the study showed differences between the ways in which Puerto Rican and European American teachers rated specific behaviors. Many behaviors of Puerto Rican children accepted by Puerto Rican teachers were considered distressing or in need of intervention by non-Hispanic teachers (Achenbach et al., cited by Zigler & Finn Stevenson, 1993). The different perceptions were probably due to the fact that the Puerto Rican teachers were aware of the normal behavioral responses in their culture. Although more research is needed in this area, teachers must be more aware of how children's cultural experiences shape their behavior. Perhaps a rule of thumb is to avoid making hasty judgments when children have a different social and cultural background from our own.

Source: Adapted from Zigler & Finn Stevenson, 1993

Along with the more traditional human socialization sources, contemporary social scientists have found that mass media has become a significant factor. Today, the media has provided a more accurate portrayal of the racial and ethnic demographics of U.S. society. Some decades ago, for example, we would never have found so many news reporters, show hosts, and artists of ethnicities other than European American. This **diversity** is also reflected among the individuals who are members of that industry. For today's young child, who typically spends a significant amount of time in front of the television and who is socialized by it, finding out that people of all ethnic and racial backgrounds can succeed sends a strong positive message about diversity. But the influence of mass media is not limited to the child. Families and parents are also influenced by ideas and behaviors broadcasted over television, the Internet, and other types of electronic communication. Many traditional culturally based child-care expectations, nutritional practices, and even parent–child interactions are being transformed by what is seen and heard through the media. The influence of the media is so powerful in today's society that it affects ways families practice child rearing. Consider the way infants are dressed, the toys they play with, and even the type of food they eat. In all of these areas, you will find that many practices and behaviors are influenced by what both the child and parents watch and hear from the media.

LET'S TALK AND REFLECT... **Culture and Socialization**

The concept of the developmental niche underlines the role of culture in the socialization process. It also points to the special elements that influence how we learn the cultural patterns of our social group. Think about the elements in your community that communicate to children the behaviors and practices that are socially and culturally acceptable. What social messages are sent?

The essential milestone of development is the building of positive self-esteem. Addressing diversity within this task is one of the primary goals of multicultural education.

Learning to See the Individual in Ourselves

"I am what I am," goes a line of a song in the movie *Popeye* that reflects the self-confidence of the main character. For children to reach that same point, at which they can proudly affirm who they are, takes a lot of effort. One of the principal goals of education for diversity is to implement practices in the classroom that contribute to the students' realization of their identities. Social identity also occurs through the experience of socialization. Erik Erikson postulated that the optimal outcome of development is the achievement of identity. Miller (2007) notes that "for Erikson, the essence of development is the formation of identity that gives coherence to one's personality." How does this happen? How does the child come to see himself or herself? According to social development theory, the perception of one's identity emerges as the individual begins to perceive oneself as a separate person. It is also gradually developed as the child constructs a sense about his or her characteristics, roles, and attributes. Recognizing one's name and responding to comments made by others are experiences that contribute to the formation of identity. Additionally, home and schooling experiences play a significant role in establishing a sense of belonging to a group.

Forming Ideas About the Self

Social development is one of the most important developmental tasks of early childhood. During the first three years of life, awareness about the self, as an individual distinct from others, emerges and grows. Comments like "I can jump high," "I am Carmen," or "I have new shoes" testify to the child's emerging concept of self. These initial descriptions focusing on specific elements of "who I am" and "what I can do" are the building blocks of the child's identity (Berk, 2002). Along with the emergence of a self-concept, self-appraisals begin to take shape. Judgments about one's worth or self-esteem are central to the positive development of self-esteem.

Early Years as the Roots of Identity

"Who am I?" is a question that many people try to answer throughout their lifetimes. This is a part of a complex search for self-identity. Psychologist Erik Erikson (1994) defined identity as "a sense of psychosocial well-being . . . a feeling of being at home in one's body, a sense of 'knowing where one is going,' and an inner assuredness of antici-

LITERACY CONNECTIONS...   Using Children's Books to Build Positive Self-Concept

During the preschool years, children begin to acquire a self-concept. Validation of one's heritage contributes to the development of a positive self-concept. Selecting and sharing age-appropriate stories about different cultural groups is an effective strategy to enhance children's sense of self and instill pride in their heritage. Stories also help young children clarify ideas and views about the behaviors of others. The following titles are suitable for helping preschoolers and kindergartners learn about childhood experiences that represent a variety of ethnic and cultural groups.

- Barnwell, Y. (1998). *No mirrors in my Nana's house.* San Diego, CA: Harcourt Brace. (African Americans)

- Best, C. (1999). *Three cheers for Catherine the Great!* London: DK Publishing. (European Americans)

- Dorros, A. (1997). *Abuela.* New York: Puffin Books. (Latinos)

- Pak, S. (2001). *Dear Juno.* New York: Viking Books. (Koreans)

- Parry, F. (1997). *The day of Ahmed's secret.* New York: HarperTrophy. (Middle-Easterners)

- Shange, N. (2004). *Ellington was not a street.* New York: Simon and Schuster. (African Americans)

- Stock, C. (1995). *Where are you going, Manyoni?* New York: HarperCollins. (Africans)

- Wing, N. (1996). *Jalapeño bagels.* New York: Atheneum. (Multiracial)

pated recognition from those who count." Although identity development is seen mainly as the task of adolescence, its beginnings are undeniably found in the early childhood years (Noguera, 2003). In the early years, experiences and interactions with adults play a leading role in the formation of who we are. How others—parents, caregivers, teachers, and peers—see us influences the evolving concept of self and, thus, contributes to the construction of our individual identity.

Early Childhood: The Beginnings of Cultural and Ethnic Identity

As discussed earlier, culture is a main element in the formation of identity. Although ethnic identity evolves through one's existence, children gain awareness of their connections to a culture and to an ethnic group early on in life. Studies show that during the preschool years, children are able to identify themselves as members of an ethnic group. What, then, seems to trigger this early sense of cultural identity? Home experiences and interactions with the family are starting places. They are, in fact, among one of the most significant forces contributing to a person's self-identification as part of a cultural group. Through the family, children are first exposed to the ways and behaviors of their group. Language is one of the most essential traits of a culture and is learned early in life. Being able to communicate opens doors to acquiring key knowledge about one's culture that will progressively grow throughout the preschool and primary years. At as young as 4 years of age, children are able to describe themselves as members of an ethnic group. Around age 8, they will be able not only to define themselves as part of a group but also to notice the traits of other cultural groups (Phinney & Rotheram, 1987).

Young children learn about culture through a variety of sources. One of the sources common to all cultures is storytelling. Through the sharing of traditional stories, family anecdotes, and individual accounts of life events, cultural values are passed on, helping to build a sense of connection to one's cultural group. Stories shared by parents and families with moral messages not only contribute to the social development of the child but also convey the cultural values of the ethnic group. Day-to-day conversations with families are another powerful avenue that influences early formation of a sense of membership in a cultural group. Proverbs and sayings, such as the *refranes* or *dichos* (sayings) in Latino culture, become cultural vehicles that introduce children to the values and beliefs of their culture. Children's folk music is another example of early cultural induction that influences the formation of identity. Over time, these cultural elements become part of the core of values and beliefs of the child's emerging identity.

Other Factors That Influence Identity Formation

Another element that influences and connects a child to his or her culture is context. **Context** is defined as an assortment of external factors and processes that combine to form a setting that makes someone feel "at home." Some of the external elements include objects, colors, flavors, dress codes, language, music, voice, and accents found in the child's cultural environment. Cultural context also consists of processes, such as acculturation; social descriptors, such as family social class and economic status; and chronological elements, such as the historical setting where a person grows up. All of them combined are a strong influence on the child's emerging sense of self. Some of the leading experiences and processes that influence the formation of an identity are the following:

- *Acculturation:* A process occurs where a mainstream (majority) culture and subordinate (minority) cultures coexist in society. The process of acculturation occurs over time when the members of the minority culture adopt some of the ways of the mainstream culture. The result is a blurring of cultural lines. For example, children of Chinese origin may adopt Western eating habits. Or, Indian girls may abandon the sari and wear jeans instead. Acculturation happens more quickly among the members of the second generations and in cross-cultural marriages.

- *Social class:* All individuals belong to a social class or group. Social class is another dimension of a person's identity. The rules and norms of a social class often define the behaviors and expectations for the individual. Membership in a social class is

LET'S TALK AND REFLECT... **About Storytelling**

Families have long used storytelling as a tool for teaching children about the experiences and struggles of their cultures. Think about the stories shared by family members that you still remember and which communicated cultural messages. What values did they communicate? What did you learn from them?

defined by the family's economic status, occupation, where the family lives, and participation in hobbies and organizations.

■ *Historical time:* Chronologically, birth ascribes characteristics and predisposes the individual to certain experiences. Current cultural trends and mores define expectations, behaviors, and beliefs that contribute to who a person is. Because each generation has its own frame of reference, children are influenced by the ideas of their time. For example, the notion of a family in the twenty-first century is vastly different from the family model of the mid-twentieth century.

DISCOVERING THAT YOU ARE NOT LIKE ME

As we discussed, socialization is a process vital for human survival. As children acquire the rules of the social game, they learn to distinguish people by their attributes. However, not all that young children learn equips them with social tools that are valid and acceptable in a society as diverse as ours. Sometimes they acquire negative and erroneous views of those whose physical characteristics and convictions are different from their own.

Although many still maintain that children are oblivious to racial differences, research shows that even very young children can notice differences and decode the existence of differences in their social contexts. Children begin to

Wadsworth/Cengage Learning

The classroom plays an influential role in helping children discover diversity and see it as part of daily reality.

discriminate the existence of differences in objects and in people as early as infancy. For instance, infants are capable of distinguishing and reacting to different facial expressions. Perception of other differences, such as race, gender, social class, and physical challenges, also occurs early in life.

Developmental theory provides the best basis for arguing that early intervention is needed if children are to accept persons different from themselves. According to the

---

F◯CUS
on Classroom Practices | A Classroom Quilt

Quilts are symbols of American tradition. Because a quilt is essentially a harmonious combination of different pieces otherwise not related, it can effectively represent the diversity found in a classroom. Creating a human quilt using your young students can help them become aware of themselves. With children as the theme and the main artists, a class quilt can be developed early in the year. This project can be used as a culminating activity for a unit on learning about themselves.

Besides helping children discover who they are, this project will allow children to experience working cooperatively, a valuable and needed skill for social survival.

1. Introduce the children to the tradition and meaning of quilts. Bring in a quilt for children to see and manipulate. If you do not own a quilt, parents or a colleague may be able to lend you one. Share any of the stories about quilts, such as *The Patchwork Quilt* by Valerie Flournoy (Dial, 1985), *Luka's Quilt* by George Guback (Greenwillow, 1994), or *The Keeping Quilt* by Patricia Polacco (Aladdin, 2001). Discuss what a quilt is and the purposes of making and having one.

2. Depending on the age and level of the children you teach, you may want to vary the materials used. However, using the simplest materials works best. (Later on,

if the interest is still there, you may move on to more elaborate constructions.) Use paper plates of different sizes and colors, which children can easily tie together with pieces of yarn.

3. Because this quilt is about the children in your classroom, each child should be represented. Give three plates to each child. On one plate, have them draw a picture of themselves, and on the other two plates, have them describe their favorite activity and their preferred story or story character.

4. After the children have completed their plates, they can begin "quilting" the pieces using yarn. Have children make a hole on each side of the plates. Holes can be made by punching a pencil through the plate or by using a paper hole punch. Working in small groups, children can "quilt" the pieces by threading yarn through the holes and tying them together. As each group finishes their piece of the quilt, discuss what it shows about the children represented. Begin by emphasizing the likenesses, and continue by noting the things that make each child unique.

5 The completed quilt can be displayed in the classroom, where it will certainly generate many interesting discussions.

LITERACY CONNECTIONS...  Books to Foster Positive Views About Diversity

Sharing stories is an effective strategy for building diversity concepts. The following books for preschoolers and kindergartners address cultural diversity and individual differences. You may want to continue adding other titles to this list.

- Fox, M. (2006). Whoever you are. New York: Voyager Books.

- Hallinan, P. (2006). *A rainbow of friends.* New York: Ideals Publications.

- Hamanaka, S. (1999). *All the colors of the Earth.* New York: HarperTrophy.

- Kates, H. (1992). *We're different, we're the same.* New York: Random House.

- Miller, J. (2001). *We all sing with the same voice.* New York: HarperTrophy.

LET'S TALK AND REFLECT... **About Gender Roles**

Gender roles are socially and culturally bound. Young children learn to distinguish gender tasks based on the behavior of adults. They also acquire gender frames of reference through messages in the media and in the environment. Images in the world at large, as well as comments from individuals, communicate gender stereotypes on a regular basis.

- Take time to watch television programs. What gender messages do they send? Are there any stereotypes? What would you propose as ways of eliminating gender stereotypes?

- Visit an early childhood classroom and note the messages about gender roles that are displayed in the materials, pictures, and posters. What do they communicate to children regarding their gender?

---

theory of differentiation postulated by Eleanor Gibson (cited in Berger, 2005), the process of discriminating the details that establish the differences in objects and in people begins in infancy. Gibson saw the infant as an active explorer engaged in discerning the attributes of the things encountered. She also pointed out that with experience, the child increases the ability to notice details (Miller, 2001). Researchers have found evidence that children perceive details such as gender, age, and color (Brown and Bigler, 2005).

F⬤CUS

on Classroom Practices

Using Prop Boxes to Promote Awareness About Diversity

Helping children to become aware of diversity is one of the major goals of early childhood education. Although many planned activities promote awareness, teachers should also take advantage of the indirect or unplanned activities happening in the classroom. Particularly relevant are the experiences that occur during free play at the learning centers. Use of prop boxes (which can be located in the dramatic center) is a good way to promote awareness of diversity. Essentially, a prop box is a thematic collection of items suitable to foster dramatic play, role-playing activities, and open exploration. To create your prop box, you need a sturdy box with a lid. The box should be easy to handle by children and of a suitable size to facilitate storage. Next, identify themes for your prop boxes that are influenced by things you have observed while talking or discussing with children and questions they have posed about any aspects of diversity.

Here are some suggested themes for prop boxes and some sample props you may want to include:

1. Cooking and eating ethnic foods
   - Typical ethnic utensils, such as a wok, a *caldero* or pot, chopsticks, a cloth coffee colander or *colador,* a small barbecue grill, Indian metal serving trays, Asian and European teapots and cups, typical Amerindian serving dishes (made from clay or gourds), place mats, and so on
   - Empty boxes and cans of ethnic food; empty containers of seasonings; plastic or laminated pictures of typical ethnic vegetables and fruits
2. Hair styling and makeup place
   - Empty bottles of hair products; typical ethnic hair pins and barrettes; ribbons, veils, scarves, and other ethnic hair ornaments; combs, brushes, hair rollers, a hairdryer, and a curling iron (without the electric cords); ethnic dolls with different hair textures or wigs and a wig stand; pictures of different ethnic hairstyles
   - Eyeliners, kohl pencils, blush, and any other ethnic makeup items
   - Earrings, necklaces, bracelets, and so on
3. Holiday decoration place
   A series of boxes for the holidays typically observed by children as well as other ethnic celebrations. Items to include are the following:
   - Typical holiday home decorations
   - Songs and music
   - Typical symbols
   - Holiday greeting cards
   - Empty boxes of typical foods
   - Stories
   Sample themes for holiday boxes are the following:
   - Birthdays
   - Wedding celebrations in different cultures
   - December celebrations: Kwanzaa, Christmas, Hanukkah
   - January gift-giving traditions such as the Three Kings (Spain and Latin America) and Befana (Italy)
   - Children's Day in Korea and Japan
4. Clothes for special occasions; the sewing and dressing place
   - Fabric scraps (of different textures, colors, and prints)
   - Pictures of clothing typically worn by people of different ethnicities in the community and in other American communities

- Pictures of clothing worn during special occasions
- Fabric glue (to be used instead of needles)
- A variety of sewing notions to include ribbons, yarn of different colors, buttons, sequins, and so on
- Accessories such as veils, scarves, gloves, shawls, and hats

5. Ethnic music and dancing
   - Typical musical instruments
   - Pictures of musical instruments
   - Recordings of different vocal and instrumental ethnic music
   - Pictures and videos of folkloric dance

Perception of Gender Differences

Scientists say that gender awareness occurs early and is shown through the verbal labels children use. Beginning at age 2, children show knowledge of their own sex. Using external indicators such as dress, activities, and toy preference, children can identify the gender of themselves and others. Assignment of gender roles is a function of culture; therefore, children learn to differentiate gender roles through the process of socialization. Each culture determines the tasks and the behavioral expectations for males and females. For instance, you may have observed that male Eastern Europeans often greet each other with a double kiss or walk arm in arm with male friends. These practices are not acceptable for males in other groups, such as U.S., Muslim, or Hispanic cultures. Like many other behaviors, what is socially established by gender is learned by participation in the culture. It follows, then, that young children become cognizant of gender role behaviors early in life.

Working with young children gives you a good opportunity to "see" how they are progressing in their development of gender roles. You have probably observed that although 3-year-old children use terms that describe gender awareness, in reality they do not yet fully understand what "boy" or "girl" really means. Still depending on external clues (physical and societal), they have not yet developed

During childhood, classroom interactions contribute to helping children develop a concept of gender-based behaviors.

Wadsworth/Cengage Learning

gender consistency: the concept that their gender will remain the same. Perhaps you have also noticed that between ages 4 and 5, children are more likely to express and use gender stereotypes as they play (Shapiro, 1994). What this reveals is that preschool children are in the process of establishing their concept of gender roles. This knowledge becomes more precise over time through increased informal social experiences. In fact, some developmental psychologists believe that clarity about one's own gender does not appear until age 7 or 8.

The early childhood years are an important phase for creating awareness of gender equality. Laura Shapiro (1994) maintains that once children have achieved a sense of their own gender, "the powerful stereotypes that guided them don't just disappear . . . images of the aggressive male and the nurturing female are with us for the rest of our lives." This statement suggests that waiting until children are more mature to address gender equality may not be as effective as dealing with it at the developmentally appropriate time.

Classroom experiences play a leading role in helping children form their concepts of gender roles. A classroom climate characterized by equal relations and opportunities for boys and girls contributes to a sense of equality. When teachers organize their classrooms to provide experiences that invite social interactions among both boys and girls, boundaries created by gender are lessened (Thorne, 1993). More attention is required to what the classroom offers and "says" to the child. Equally important are the behaviors of professionals that children use as models. Specific attention should be given to the kinds of play occurring in the classroom. Teachers must take time to observe the gender role behaviors, labels, and activities children exhibit as they play. Derman-Sparks (1989) recommends that after an analysis of our observations, we should reorganize the classroom learning areas to reflect a more balanced view of gender roles and to encourage "more cross-gender play choices." Changes should affect the entire curriculum. Literature about gender equity should be incorporated regularly into the curriculum. A list of recommended child appropriate titles appears in this chapter on page 144.

In Action . . .   Gender Roles

The following is a conversation between two 5-year-old preschoolers that took place in the classroom housekeeping area:

"Guess what? The baby is dirty," Yani said, pinching his nose to indicate that the doll smelled bad. "Yani, you better change his diaper. You are the daddy and my daddy does that at home," Yani's playmate Sarah explained. Upset, Yani moved away from the doll. "I'm not doing that. That's girl's work and I'm a boy. I don't want to play anymore," he added, leaving the play area abruptly.

• Do you think an intervention is needed? Why or why not?

• What stereotypes are depicted here?

• What actions would you take to clarify gender stereotypes?

Counteracting Gender Stereotypes in the Classroom

1. Begin by examining your own gender stereotypes and be determined to avoid them. Remember that second to parents and family, teachers are the children's most influential models.

2. Provide opportunities for appropriate development of gender identity. Include materials that will help children form correct ideas about their anatomy and that will help them understand sex differences. Inform parents of the reasons for using materials (such as dolls, books, and puzzles) and vocabulary that are anatomically correct. Extend it to the home by providing parents with suggestions about what terms to avoid because of the confusion they create in the child.

3. Learn about the gender roles that are assigned in the children's cultures. Be responsive to them by including opportunities for children to see that some people may hold different views.

4. Encourage participation across genders in activities traditionally assigned to either gender. For example, encourage boys to play in the housekeeping area and girls in the block area.

5. Select more children's stories about roles across gender lines and include biographies of people whose accomplishments were not restricted by gender biases.

6. Take a proactive stance and intervene whenever children express stereotypical labels.

Source: American Association of University Women, 2008; Derman-Sparks, 1989; Streitmatter, 1994.

Awareness of Physical Differences

One of the common areas covered in the early childhood curriculum includes the ability to recognize and discriminate details (such as color, form, and shape). Because we live in a world of forms and colors, learning to notice these characteristics is an important way of discovering what surrounds us. This same ability enables the child to see that not all people share the same physical characteristics. Preschool children are able to discern differences such as color of skin, color of eyes and hair, texture of hair, shape of the lips and nose, and other physical differences, including disabilities. Three-year-olds often reveal their awareness of these traits through their questions and comments (Katz & Kofkin, 1997; Miller, 2007). Although the timing of young children's development of awareness of specific racial and ethnic characteristics during the first three years of life is not yet clearly established, it can be argued that it derives as part of the intensive process of cognitive construction that takes place during the first 36 months of their social life. However, research does indicate that awareness of differences as representative of race or ethnicity is developed through the influence of the family and the social environment (Banks, 1992; Bigler & Averhart, 2003; Katz & Kofkin, 1997; Robles de

SNAPSHOT 4-3   Influence of Parents in the Perception of Gender Roles

Research about gender awareness and roles in children has shown that parents have a leading influence. Summarizing research findings, Anselmo and Franz (1995) found that there are at least three major ways in which parents influence children's perception of gender roles:

- Interaction with girls is characterized by being more proactive than with boys. Research shows that mothers show a significantly higher level of protection toward girls than toward boys. Mothers tend to stay closer to girls than to boys. For example, when children fall, girls are comforted while boys are guided "to dust themselves off and get back into action."

- Parents reward boys and girls differently. There is a difference in the kind of behavior that gets rewarded by parents. For instance, boys are encouraged and rewarded when they exhibit more active exploratory behaviors. Girls are rewarded for their social responsiveness.

- Parents tend to choose gender-related toys. Girls are encouraged to play with dolls and replicas of housekeeping items, whereas boys are guided toward traditional male toys such as cars and trucks.

Source: Adapted from Anselmo & Franz, 1995.

LITERACY CONNECTIONS...   Recommended Books About Gender Equity

Following are some selected titles addressing multiculturalism and gender topics suitable for young children ages 4–6:

- Hazen, B. (1992). *Mommy's office*. New York: Atheneum.

- Hoffman, G. (1991). *Amazing Grace*. New York: Dial Books.

- Howe, J. (1996). *Pinky and Rex and the bully*. New York: Atheneum.

- Klein, N. (1973). *Girls can be anything*. New York: Dutton.

- Low, A. (1999). *Mommy's briefcase*. New York: Scholastic.

- Luen, N. (1999). *Nessa's fish*. New York: Econo-Clad Books.

- Martin, B., & Sampson, M. (2001). *Little granny quarterback*. Honesdale, PA: Boyds Mills.

- Quinlan, P. (1987). *My daddy takes care of me*. New York: Annick Press.

- Zolotow, C. (1985). *William's doll*. New York: HarperTrophy.

Meléndez, 2000). The ideas and attitudes of the child's culture shape the notions that the child will express.

Racial Awareness

The problem of the twentieth century is the problem of the color-line.

W. E. B. Du Bois (1868–1963)

Race is a very misleading concept. So is color when we use it to try to characterize human beings. However, because society still uses race to describe people, children learn this concept through the process of socialization. Most of what the literature says about racial preferences in children comes from studies done primarily with African American children (Derman-Sparks, 1989; Kendall, 1999). However limited, their findings are relevant for the early childhood educator.

Many believe that race is a concept incomprehensible to children. Interactions and observations of young children, however, reveal that they do perceive racial differences from very early in life. As early as infancy, children perceive multisensorial racial signals such as accent, physical characteristics, and hair texture. By the time they enter preschool at age 3 or 4, children already have a sense of racial attributes (Katz, 2003; Sheets & Hollins, 1999). This knowledge is confirmed through their comments when retelling stories and describing story characters, people, or images in books and the media.

Studies have revealed the existence of an early awareness of one's own color. In studies by Spencer and Cross (cited in Banks, 1992), African American children showed a preference for materials (such as dolls and pictures) and people with European features. One of the interesting points regarding children's awareness of color stems from the research done by Spencer, which confirmed that children were not only aware of their own race but also could "read" how others perceived African Americans as well as whites. Discussing Spencer's findings, Banks (1992) points out that the following was established:

> Young African American children are able to distinguish their personal identity from their group, can have a high self-esteem and yet express a white bias, and that the expression of white bias results from a cognitive process that enables young children *to accurately perceive the norms and attitudes toward whites and blacks in American society* [emphasis added].

Racial awareness has also been linked to the color preferences exhibited by children. Observations of young children across social and cultural groups reveal a color bias when it comes to choosing between white and black. This bias is more of a symbolic nature, which highlights the influence of social experiences in ascribing meaning to the colors white and black. Interestingly, this behavior has been found to be common among children not only in the United States but also in other countries. The existence of a color bias, found among children as young as age 3 (Duckitt, Wall, & Pokroy, 1999; May & May, 1981), refutes the idea that children are "color-blind."

Studies on the perception of color describe the role and significance of social experiences in children's racial preferences. Using messages from their environment— family, classroom, community, and media—children will exhibit color preferences that, in turn, define their inclination toward racial groups. Without interventions, color bias may be a factor in the formation of racial **prejudice.** Research on color bias also proves that when children are exposed to a bias-free environment, color bias can be effectively reduced (Duckitt, Wall, & Pokroy, 1999). This finding has clear implications for early childhood educators, pointing to the need for including classroom strategies that address color preferences. An example of a developmentally appropriate strategy is the antibias approach (Derman-Sparks, 1989), which is centered on creating experiences and an environment that convey a sense of equity and respect for diversity. Suggestions about classroom activities that foster positive views about racial differences are described in the next Focus on Classroom Practices section.

Louise Derman-Sparks (1989), in an examination of research about biases and prejudice, found that the formation of racist views "damages White children intellectually and psychologically." The implications are clear: all young children are affected. Individual research of the effects of racism conducted by Bernard Kutner, Kenneth Clark, and Alice Miel (cited in Derman-Sparks, 1989) demonstrated the following two main negative consequences for European American children:

1. It affected the reasoning ability of children and misled their perception of reality and thus of judgment (Kutner).
2. Children were taught to hide their own feelings toward people of other races, which encouraged the moral hypocrisy of maintaining prejudices while giving lip service to the concept of equality (Clark, Miel).

Evidence from research and from daily life strongly confirms that contrary to what some adults still want to believe, children do see color and racial differences (Kendall, 1999). Copying the behavior of those they consider their models, whether parents, relatives, or neighbors, children learn to negatively discriminate against others who are not like them. By the time they enter middle childhood, most children hold racial perceptions as truths. Timely action from early childhood teachers becomes the best antidote against perpetuation of misleading interpretations and concepts.

Developing a Concept of Ourselves as Part of an Ethnic Group

Self-perception of one's own race develops with the onset of the awareness of other racial groups. For children with non-European American backgrounds, their perception of being different from others arises early. The sources of their perceptions are many. Here we will consider three of them: parents and family, peers and other adults, and the environment.

F⦶CUS
on Classroom Practices

Fostering Positive Ideas About Racial Differences

- At all times, provide equal opportunities to all children to work and participate in activities. As a practice, include children from diverse backgrounds in all activities (for example, classroom helpers, leaders during play, and cooperative activities). Your behavior will communicate to children that each one is a valuable member of the group.

- Use an inclusive approach to experiences. Encourage children to work with peers with different racial characteristics. Plan cooperative learning experiences where children can work and interact together.

- Create a visual environment that exhibits diversity and equality. Display positive images of different racial groups. Provide pictures, posters, and media images that include a variety of racial groups.

- Facilitate play with materials representing diversity. Play, a learning tool for children, provides opportunities to reenact situations and pretend with materials that characterize different racial groups. Include a variety of dolls representative of racial groups in the play areas. Clothing and other articles as-sociated with different ethnic groups should be also included in the pretend play area.

- Select and share stories with characters of different racial groups. Story characters can provide powerful sources about individuals with different ethnic and racial characteristics.

- Present images and stories that portray the good deeds of people from diverse ethnic and racial groups. Display posters with images representing individuals with diverse ethnic characteristics engaged in a variety of activities, including jobs and professions. This will help children see that contributions come from all people.

- When describing people with racial and ethnic characteristics, use accurate terms. If derogatory terms are heard or used by children, take time to clarify why these are not acceptable.

- Talk with children and listen to their comments about racial differences. Always take time to discuss their observations and provide explanations. You are key in dispelling prejudicial ideas.

The first one to examine is the influence of the child's parents and family. Family members' own pride about their racial or ethnic identity will build a similar perception in the child. The family will also provide a model for dealing with negative comments about the child's race or ethnic group. A positive and solid self-concept is likely to be developed by children who, nurtured by their families, see their racial or ethnic identity as equally valid as any other. When children find their classrooms, in addition to their families, supportive of their racial identities, they will grow confident and able to overcome most challenges.

| In Action . . . | **Are Children Aware of Color or Race?** |

The following incident happened in a classroom of 3-year-olds. The group was mainly Hispanic. As you read, consider the implications of what the children said.

M., a fair-skinned Hispanic girl, was playing in the dolls area when two other Hispanic girls joined her. One of the girls, L., had darker skin.

M. stood up and said in a commanding voice, *"Vete, tu eres fea!"* (Go, you are ugly!). Soon a discussion began between the two children. When M. was asked why she wanted L. to leave, she answered: *"Es negra, es fea."* (She is dark, she's ugly.)

- Is the child aware of color?

- What are the implications of this incident?

- What would you do if you were their teacher?

The second force that shapes how we feel about our racial and ethnic identity is how others see us and what others say about us. Children are most likely to be deeply damaged for life by racial slurs and negative comments made by their peers. Research has indicated that the origins of negative comments are found in the views and ideas of the children's parents and community. Instances where children replicate the words and behaviors of their parents are many. A graduate student who teaches kindergarten told one of the authors of this book of an incident that portrays this. The student, an African American, was teaching in a predominantly white community when one of her 5-year-olds told her that she was nice but that she was "the wrong color." Feeling shocked, she asked the child why he thought she was the wrong color, and the boy answered that his father had told him so. Obviously, there is no such thing as the "right" or "wrong" color.

Unfortunately, episodes like this one occur in everyday life. The lesson we can learn from this is clear. Early childhood educators can counter such harmful perceptions by providing positive opportunities for children to learn about diversity issues. Although parental influences are very strong, teachers are also instrumental in reducing prejudice by providing opportunities to view and exercise equality in the classroom.

What the environment "says" is the third force that influences how we feel about ourselves. Messages in the environment play a powerful role in building a concept of one's racial characteristics. The media and the environment have often fostered negative views of certain racial groups. Cases abound of African American children asking why they are black or why they cannot have straight hair. On several occasions, one of the authors had 4- and 5-year-olds of Latin descent with Amerindian features question why their eyes were not clear like those of the dolls they play with. When asked why they preferred clear eyes, they simply said "Son más bonitos" (They are prettier). Along the same lines, 3-year-old African Americans told one of the authors that they wanted to have blond hair like hers instead of their own dark hair. Educators need to be particularly attentive to subtle messages that might convey a negative attitude toward a child's race or ethnic group. Formation of positive ideas about oneself is an important outcome of early childhood.

What are the physical characteristics children most frequently notice? Children tend to perceive the following:

- Hair texture
- Skin color
- Color and shape of eyes
- Tone of voice
- Height
- Weight
- Orthopedic impairments
- Neurological impairments (particularly when they affect movement)

SNAPSHOT 4-4   Working Toward Prejudice Reduction

According to Allport (cited in Banks, 1992), prejudice can be reduced when interracial situations are characterized by the following:

- The situations are cooperative rather than competitive.
- During the situation, each individual feels of equal status to others.
- All individuals share similar goals.
- The contact has the approval of parents, teachers, and other authority figures.

There are obvious implications for developmental teaching in Allport's suggestions. These four characteristics of positive interracial contact situations indicate ways to plan and organize activities for young children that also respect the developmental principles. Essentially, what Allport recommends is the provision of more cooperative experiences where children will be racially intermixed and will find that participation has the endorsement and support of relevant adult figures. Cooperative activities must also be extended to include experiences with children and adults from diverse cultural groups. Learning to participate and work in a group is a necessary skill children must acquire because it serves as the basis of social life. When they form groups, teachers need to incorporate children with different characteristics regarding race, ethnic origin, gender, and so on. However, for these suggestions to be effective, they must become standard practice.

Source: Adapted from Banks, 1992.

Some of these characteristics are the same ones commonly used as a basis for negative comments and racial slurs. However, when these are presented as unique because of a person's heritage, children learn to accept the characteristics as part of who they are.

Young English Language Learners: Recognizing Language Diversity

Many classrooms across the United States house children whose native language is different from English. For many children and parents, knowing a language other than English has not been traditionally seen as an asset but rather as an obstacle. On many occasions, speaking a different language has resulted in discrimination. While children learn and acquire proficiency in the English language, they can also be made aware of the advantages of having or preserving the language of their own culture (Gonzalez, Yakey, & Minaya-Rowe, 2006). Because language is a crucial cultural element, making children aware of its value and significance is important. In the classroom, whether you have children who speak a different language or not, you can create awareness about the value of other languages. If you are teaching children of different language backgrounds, acknowledgment of their languages is a requirement. Here are some suggested activities:

- If teaching children who speak a language different from English, make a commitment to use their language(s) throughout the classroom. If all children in the class speak English as a first language, select a target language to be used in the classroom as activities permit.

- On the classroom door, include a welcome poster in both English and in another language. This will serve not only to warmly greet children but to communicate to them that their language or languages are welcome.

- As a routine, label classroom items in both English and another language.

- Learn phrases, songs, or greeting words in other languages.

- Have classroom charts written in two languages.

- Include books in other languages and bilingual books in the library corner. Many popular stories are now available in bilingual and multilingual editions, which help in exposing children to languages spoken by peers or persons in their community or in other communities. Choose stories with bilingual content or ones that include words in other languages such as Arthur Dorros's *Isla* (Dutton, 1999), Pat Mora's *The Rainbow Tulip* (Viking, 1999), and Lulu Delacre's *Arroz con Leche* (Scholastic, 1992), which include words and phrases in Spanish. French is used in Jonathan London's *The Sugaring-off Party* (Dutton, 2006).

- Learn the numbers in a different language.

- Invite family members or any other persons who speak a different language to teach a simple poem or song to the class.

- Have children who speak another language serve as tutors for the class in learning the numbers or the letters of the alphabet in that language.
- Bring foreign newspapers to the class. Have children browse through them at the library and writing center.
- Learn to pronounce the titles of favorite story characters in another language.
- Listen to vocal music in other languages.
- Have someone translate the children's names into another language.

SNAPSHOT 4-5   Memories Stay with Us

What our teachers, classmates, and people in the neighborhood told us in our childhood is part of the baggage we carry with us through life. This is what Kathryn Noori (1995) found through the stories written by her college students, all prospective teachers. We chose two of them to share with you. Both stories concern African American students and reveal how the negative and positive attitudes of others can influence our lives.

The first story tells about the influence that teachers can have on the self-esteem of a child:

I was always one of the African American students enrolled in the public school system [in New Mexico]. Not only was I aware of my "blackness," I was also reminded of it every time a fellow classmate or the teacher made a racist comment. I expected it from my classmates, more or less, but from my teacher—never. The remarks were often cruel and intended to make me feel like a second-class citizen (or, so I thought). For example, in first grade, my teacher asked me to sing, "Eenie, meenie, miny, moe, catch a nigger by the toe." When I wanted to try out for the debate team in fifth grade, my teacher told me that people of color usually do best in athletics.

In contrast, the following story presents the positive influence that teachers may have on a child:

Mrs. Gage, my second-grade teacher, was the person that inspired me to join the teaching profession. Mrs. Gage took a child with low self-esteem and boosted her to the sky. She was a Caucasian teacher who treated everyone equally. She didn't let your skin color determine her expectations and perceptions of you.

Because of Mrs. Gage's kindness and caring, I have decided to become a teacher, a teacher who will encourage all students regardless of their gender, religion, race, or background to be the very best they can be.

Source: Noori, 1995.

Children's Perceptions of Disabilities

Acceptance and integration of people with disabilities was mandated with the approval of Public Law 94-142 in 1975. The Individuals with Disabilities Act of 1990 reaffirmed the rights of the exceptional. As a result, children are more frequently exposed to people with different kinds of disabilities. This has increased the need to help children develop positive attitudes toward people with disabilities, a segment of the population contributing to diversity. As with racial awareness, children begin as early as age 3 to notice the physical disabilities of others. Because children are constant explorers, it is logical to find them asking and wondering about the physical differences they see. These questions provide an opportunity to guide children to accept disabilities as another characteristic some people have. When trying to fight biases concerning disabilities, teachers need to act promptly when labeling or rejection is observed among children. This early response will stop misinterpretations and behaviors from becoming permanent.

Children with special needs benefit from a positive and accepting classroom environment.

Opportunities must be provided for children to clarify their perceptions and feelings about children with disabilities. Barry Friedman and Sharon Maneki (1995) successfully developed an experience designed to create awareness about people with disabilities. They targeted blindness as the disability for their project because Maneki is a nonsighted educator. They selected a group of third graders to whom they taught the Braille alphabet. Maneki not only demonstrated how to write messages in Braille, but she also introduced the children to the special qualities of

Teachers and parents should encourage children to believe everything is possible.

people with blindness. The experience helped children clarify their ideas and become more tolerant of people who are blind.

Building awareness about people with disabilities is an important experience that contributes to promoting acceptance of individual diversity. Many times this can happen by using stories that involve characters with special needs. Stories such as Jane Cowen-Fletcher's *Mama Zooms* (Scholastic, 1993), Patricia McMahon's *Listen for the Bus: David's Story* (Boyds Mills, 1995), Meg Girnis's *1, 2, 3 For You and Me* (Albert Whitman, 2001), and Virginia Fleming's *Be Good to Eddie Lee* (Putnam, 1997) are among those with plots that provide accurate representations of people with special needs. These books are also good avenues for sharing experiences and talking about disabilities, which, in turn, clarifies ideas and counteracts prejudice.

KNOWING THE CHILD

Early educators have long known that quality services for children depend upon our knowledge of children. The same principle applies to constructing a program that will effectively guide children to appreciate social diversity. Your knowledge about the children you teach is the basis for your decisions. The further you move into multicultural education, the more you will need to know about the children in your classroom and community. Can you say that you already know them?

WHAT WE HAVE LEARNED—CHAPTER SUMMARY

In this chapter, we explored the influence of culture on the process of child development. Successful multicultural teaching that meets the needs of young children can only happen when the early educator considers the developmental characteristics of young learners. Responsive teaching follows the principles of developmentally and culturally appropriate practices (DCAP). The process of development is an experience common to all children. While all children follow predictable developmental changes, there are other influences that impact each child. Culture is one of the factors that accounts for the diversity observed in each child. One of the most evident influences of culture is on child-rearing practices, as each group may hold different views about the right way to raise a child. Family experiences and the environment are the driving forces from which children learn the acceptable social behaviors of their culture. Ethnic identity develops during the early years and continues to form during the primary years. Family and classroom experiences are central to forming a sense of identity. They are also instrumental in preparing the child to see differences as part of social life.

THINGS TO DO . . .

1. Knowledge about what makes children uniquely individual is basic for an early childhood educator. Select three children from diverse families and begin learning about their individual characteristics. Examine the data about physical traits, their families,

and the elements of diversity (religion, ethnicity, language, social class, exceptionality, and gender) that characterize them.

Child's name: _____ Age: _____

Physical Home/Family Diversity Factors:

2. The media is a powerful instrument for disseminating ideas about people. Observe any program designed for children for an hour during one week and determine what messages are presented about gender, ethnic groups, and the disabled. As part of your observation, include the commercials presented. Write a report about your findings. If you feel that changes are needed, propose them and explain your choices.

3. Considering the developmental needs of the children in your class, design two experiences targeting differences that will help children build a positive view of diversity.

RECOMMENDED INTERNET RESOURCES

- Child development information from PBS
  www.pbs.org/parents/childdevelopment/

- Information about English language learners from the Center for Applied Linguistics
  www.cal.org/topics/ell/

- Suggestions for inclusive communities from PBS
  www.pbs.org/parents/inclusivecommunities/

YOUR STANDARDS PORTFOLIO

NAEYC Standard 4b: Teaching and Learning: Using Developmentally Effective Approaches*

Teaching and learning practices are central to supporting child development. They are also influential in the process of building ideas about oneself as an individual and as a member of a cultural group. Classroom experiences convey important messages that influence the child's self-concept. During the early childhood years, responses from adults along with visuals, materials, and books support the children in building their "cultural" selves.

- Interview an early childhood teacher and find out about practices followed to support young children with diverse backgrounds.

- Observe in an early childhood classroom and identify the gender messages presented through the materials and visuals. What did you find? What would you improve?

- Prepare an inventory of learning materials that contribute to and support positive ethnic identity.

* NAEYC Standard 4b correlates with INTASC Standard 3: Working with Diverse Learners.

REFERENCES

American Association of University Women. (2008). *Where the girls are. The facts about gender equity in education.* Washington, DC: Author.

Anselmo, S., & Franz, W. (1995). *Early childhood development: Prenatal through age eight* (2nd ed.). Englewood Cliffs, NJ: Merrill.

Banks, J. (1992). Reducing prejudice in children: Guidelines from research. *Social Studies and the Young Learner 5*(2), 3–5.

Bauermeister, J., Berrios, V., Acevedo, L., & Gordon, M. (1990). Some issues and instruments for the assessment of attention deficit hyperactivity disorder in Puerto Rican children. *Journal of Clinical Psychology 19*, 9–16.

Berger, K. (2005). *The developing person through childhood and adolescence* (7th ed.).New York: Worth.

Berk, L. (2002). *Infants and children: Prenatal through middle childhood* (4th ed.). Boston: Allyn & Bacon.

Berk, L. (2006). *Infants and children: Prenatal through middle childhood* (5th ed.). Boston: Allyn & Bacon.

Bigler, R., & Averhart, C. (2003). Race and the workforce: Occupational status, aspirations, and stereotyping among African American children. *Developmental Psychology, 39*(3), 572–580.

Brazelton, T., & Greenspan, S. (2000). *The irreducible needs of children: What every child must have to grow, learn, and flourish.* Cambridge, MA: Perseus.

Bredekamp, S., & Copple, C. (1997). *Developmentally appropriate practice in early childhood programs* (Rev. ed.). Washington, DC: National Association for the Education of Young Children.

Brown, C., & Bigler, E. (2005). Children's perception of discrimination: A developmental model. *Child Development 76*(3), 533–553.

Charlesworth, R. (2008). *Understanding child development* (7th ed.). New York: Delmar.

Derman-Sparks, L., & the A.B.C. Task Force. (1989). *Anti-bias curriculum: Tools for empowering young children.* Washington, DC: National Association for the Education of Young Children.

Duckitt, J., Wall, C., & Pokroy, B. (1999). Color bias and racial preference in white South African preschool children. *The Journal of Genetic Psychology, 160*(2), 143–154.

Erikson, E. (1994). *Identity: Youth and crisis.* New York: W. W. Norton & Company.

Friedman, B., & Maneki, S. (1995). Teaching children with sight about Braille. *Childhood Education, 71*(3), 137.

Gonzalez, V., Yakey, T., & Minaya-Rowe, L. (2006). *English-as-a-second-language (ESL) teaching and learning: Pre-K–12 classroom applications for students' academic achievement and development.* Boston: Allyn & Bacon.

Gonzalez, N., Moll, L., & Amanti, C. (2005). *Funds of knowledge: Theorizing practices in households and classrooms.* Mahwah, NJ: Erlbaum.

Katz, P. A. (2003). Racists or tolerant multiculturalists? How do they begin? *American Psychologist, 58*(11), 897–909.

Katz, P. A., & Kofkin, J. A. (1997). Race, gender, and young children. In S. S. Luthar, J. A. Burack, D. Cicchetti, & J. R. Weisz (Eds.), *Developmental Psychopathology* (pp. 51–74). NY: Cambridge Press.

Kendall, F. (1999). *Diversity in the classroom: A multicultural approach to the education of young children.* New York: Teachers College Press.

Konner, M. (1991). *Childhood: A multicultural view.* Boston: Little, Brown.

May, J., & May, J. G. (1981). Effects of age on color preference for black and white infants and children. *Perceptual and Motor Skills, 52,* 255–261.

McDevitt, T., & Ormond, J. (2002). *Child development and education.* Upper Saddle River, NJ: Merrill/Prentice Hall.

Miller, P. (2001). *Theories of developmental psychology.* New York: Worth.

Miller, S. (2007). 3–4: me and you. *Scholastic Parent and Child, 15*(4), 60.

Moll, L., Amanti, C., Neff, D., & Gonzalez, N. (1992). Funds of knowledge for teaching: Using a qualitative approach to connect homes and classrooms. *Theory Into Practice, 31*(2), 132–141.

Noguera, P. (2003). How racial identity affects school performance. *Harvard Education Letter.* Retrieved May 3, 2005, from http://www.edletter.org/past/issues/2003-ma/noguera.shtml.

Noori, K. (1995). Understanding others through stories. *Childhood Education, 71*(3), 134–136.

Paludi, M. (2002). *Human development in multicultural contexts: A book of readings.* Upper Saddle River, NJ: Prentice Hall.

Phinney, J., & Rotheram, M. (1987). Children's ethnic socialization: Themes and implications. In J. Phinney & M. Rotheram, (Eds.), *Children's ethnic socialization: Pluralism and development* (pp. 274–292). San Francisco: Sage.

Robles de Meléndez, W. (July 2000). Creating the multicultural environment. Paper presented at the annual conference of the Florida Department of Education, Tampa, FL.

Shapiro, L. (1994). Guns and dolls. In L. Nunn & C. Boyatzis (Eds.), *Child growth and development 94/95* (pp. 140–143). Guilford, CT: Dushkin.

Sheets, R., & Hollins, E. (1999). *Racial and ethnic identity in school practices: Aspects of human development.* Mahwah, NJ: Lawrence Erlbaum.

Streitmatter, J. (1994). *Toward gender equity in the classroom: Everyday teachers' beliefs and practices.* Albany, NY: State University of New York Press.

Super, C. M., & Harkness, S. (1995). *Parents' cultural belief systems: The origins, expressions, and consequences.* New York: Guilford Press.

Thorne, B. (1993). *Gender play: Girls and boys in school.* New Brunswick, NJ: Rutgers University Press.

Zigler, E., & Finn Stevenson, M. (1993). *Children in a changing world: Development and social issues* (2nd ed.). Pacific Grove, CA: Brooks/Cole.

PART II

Exploring the Roots of Multicultural Education: Issues and Directions

> Recognizing that equality and equity are not the same thing, multicultural education attempts to offer all students an equitable educational opportunity, while at the same time encouraging students to critique society in the interest of social justice.
>
> *National Association of Multicultural Education (2003)*

Wadsworth/Cengage Learning

CHAPTER 5

Everything Started When . . .
Tracing the Beginnings of Multicultural Education

> But could I be heard by this great nation, I would call to mind the sublime and glorious truths with which, at its birth, it saluted a listening world . . . Put away your race prejudice. Banish the idea that one class must rule over another. Recognize . . . that the rights of the humblest citizen are as worthy of protection as are those of the highest, and . . . your Republic will stand and flourish forever.
>
> *Frederick Douglass (1818–1895)*

CHAPTER OBJECTIVES

In this chapter, we will

- discuss the historical evolution of multicultural education.
- examine some of the factors that prompted the emergence of multiculturalism in education.
- consider how the civil rights movement influenced education reform.
- discuss the contributions of some of the individuals who pioneered multiculturalism in U.S. education.

KEY CONCEPTS

- equality
- equity
- multicultural education
- civil rights movement
- educational reform

FROM BARBARA'S JOURNAL

Every day has been such an eye-opener that has helped me to reaffirm that that we are all products of our own cultures. One of my goals is to help my students become proud of who they are. Until now, I thought that I could just teach them. I realize now that I've ignored the children's realities because I was too busy teaching the only way I knew how. By doing that I managed to ignore their worlds in my classroom.

This morning when I asked one of my colleagues about teaching multiculturally, she gave me a curriculum guide from a publisher. However, that's not what I need. I want to see how other people teach about diversity; I need to have choices. I need to go back to the library. But first, I'll go to see my friends, Dennis and Belen. They said they will tell me how and why multicultural education started. Maybe this will answer some of my questions.

| SETTING THE STAGE: WE BELIEVE IN CHILDREN

Perhaps one of the traits that best defines early childhood educators is the fact that they are people with strong beliefs. First, they believe in children; second, they believe they can make a difference in the lives of children. They also believe in the special talents and potential for success every child brings to the classroom. Early childhood teachers are also dreamers. They dream all children will develop and flourish to give our society a hope for a future of continued social and national progress. Such people who dream and believe in children are committed to equality as their fundamental ideal. Early childhood teachers also realize that equality is still not fully evident in many young children's programs and services. Although considerable progress has been achieved, much still remains to be done, not only in our legislatures but also in our communities and in our classrooms. Early childhood teachers believe that some of the most important victories for equal rights are won in young children's classrooms.

Understanding humankind's quest for equality will help early childhood teachers gain a better appreciation for the efforts of multicultural educators. In this chapter, we will take you through time and acquaint you with some key events that have shaped the paradigm of multicultural education: equality.

The future is dependent on the ability of today's children to successfully face tomorrow's challenges. Education is the tool society provides to accomplish that mission. All efforts to guarantee and support equality and equity in education are an investment in our survival as a strong, advanced society. Implementing an effective multicultural education system will facilitate the successful management of the diverse environment in which we live. Quality multicultural education for all children must become one of the mandates of democracy as the United States enters the new century.

SNAPSH📷T 5-1   Equality: A Long-Term Quest

More than a thousand years ago in Greece, Protagoras, the first known professional teacher, stated that all human beings, if offered adequate learning opportunities, were capable of learning (Smith & Smith, 1994). This early Greek educator also asserted that *all* individuals had the capability to "gain excellence" (Smith & Smith, 1994). Today, more than 1,500 years later, those who support equality in education in the United States share that same belief. Commitment to equality is also a core principle of those who advocate multicultural education. Like Protagoras, the multiculturalists believe that all children, regardless of their ethnicity, exceptionality, social class, or any other characteristic, have the right to the optimum educational environment for developing to their fullest potential.

The future of a diverse society begins with children.

IN SEARCH OF EDUCATIONAL EQUALITY

. . . [I]nequality of rights has been the cause of all disturbances, insurrections, and civil wars that ever happened.

> Thomas Payne (1737–1809)

The emergence of multicultural education in the United States began with a belief in **equality.** Equality in the educational context implies providing opportunities that

Equitable opportunities for all children to access educational services are among the key goals of multicultural education.

enable all individuals to build their own futures. It also implies the availability of educational services to all individuals regardless of their social background. This ideal is one upon which U.S. public education was built. Since the beginnings of education in the United States, Americans have believed that universal education is a way to get ahead in society. However, events have shown that this ideal has not always been attainable. Educational opportunities in the United States have been and continue to be plagued with discrimination against those who, because of their social status, gender, race, or ethnicity, differ from mainstream U.S. culture. Just looking at some of our communities provides evidence that children are not being equally served. In cities and towns across our nation, hundreds of dilapidated buildings house thousands of families with children. Examples abound in the violent inner-city neighborhoods where children fear for their safety and often have to defend their lives. Lacking essential services, including access to recreational areas and appropriately equipped and staffed classrooms, many children struggle every day.

Full access to equal school opportunities has been a mandate since the 1954 landmark ruling in *Brown v. Board of Education* affirmed that segregated schools do not provide equal opportunity. Since then, equality in education has been a zealously pursued goal. Today, and in the midst of an increasingly diverse society, it serves as the justification behind the reform movement for multicultural education.

| LOOKING BACK THROUGH TIME

Perhaps you have wondered how long U.S. education has focused on multiculturalism. You may have asked yourself why some educators still do not adhere to its principles. The answers to these and other similar questions may lie in another important dimension of multicultural education: its chronology. As a strategy, multicultural education is a fairly recent movement, even though children of many nationalities and social characteristics have sat together in classrooms all over the country for more than two centuries.

However, in the past, recognition of their characteristics, needs, and requirements in an effort to appropriately serve them was seldom a part of the educational agenda. The U.S. education system was founded on the idea of **equity,** where all would become one, *e pluribus unum.* But it was also rooted in the idea that all individuals would shed their cultures of origin and blend in to become "Americans." Today, we know that people can maintain their individual cultures while becoming proud members of society and upholding the principles of U.S. democracy. This new vision of pluralism is much closer to the basic principles of democracy that comprise the ideological foundations of this country.

| A TIME LINE FOR MULTICULTURAL EDUCATION

The struggle for educational equality through the ages has been and continues to be zealously embraced by many. It has also been the goal of many pacesetters in the field of early childhood education. In this section, we will journey through time and find out how multiculturalism and the concept of equality affected the education system in our society.

In Action . . .   Equity in Education

Kenneth Howe, in an article on equal educational opportunity and multiculturalism, establishes three relevant issues that are embedded in any interpretation of equality of educational opportunities. As you read them, think about the implications they have for the education of young children.

1. Availability of desirable opportunities and the freedom to select them

2. Educational opportunities that enable the individual to succeed in life

3. Having responsible adults who will guarantee children access to equal educational opportunities

   - Which of these three issues, in your opinion, is most important?

   - In what ways are these issues related to what early childhood teachers do in the classrooms?

   - As an early childhood professional, do you feel that children are provided with equal opportunities? Explain.

Source: Howe, 1992.

Early Efforts Toward Equality in Education

As you recall from Chapter 2, **multicultural education** is based on establishing educational equality for all children. The concept of valuing the individual and respecting human diversity has evolved slowly over the years. Equality of educational opportunity may be a recent goal, but the notion of universal education has its roots in the distant past.

Pioneers of Equality for Children

The quest for equity and recognition of children's rights has been a long one. The voices of people who fought for children's rights have been resonating for centuries. They are testimony to the undeniable value of the youngest members of our society.

To learn about the evolution of multicultural education, let us look back at a few pioneers who raised their voices in the past in support of educational equity. Believing in their cause, these leaders fought for the welfare of the children of their times, often risking their own lives and personal safety. You will see how, despite the differences in time that separate them, these advocates of multicultural education parallel those of today because of the following traits:

- Awareness of inequality in educational opportunities or services
- Recognition of unfair treatment based on gender, social class, or ethnic origin
- Proactive attitudes that led them to take action to resolve or modify the existing unfair conditions

Contributions of Pioneers of Early Childhood Education

The roots of educational equality are deeply grounded in the past. We will briefly look at the work of selected leaders who defended the rights of children to receive educational services and contributed to establishing the importance of the early childhood years. Among those, we find John Amos Comenius (1592–1670), known as the father of modern education. He is best known as an educational reformer who strongly advocated for the rights of all people to be educated.

Jean-Jacques Rousseau (1712–1778), a philosopher and a political thinker, became best known for his works *The Social Contract* and *Emile*, in which he called for reforms in education and politics. His ideas about the need to provide appropriate education for

---

| In Action . . . | **Checking Our Personal Knowledge About Multicultural Education** |

- When did you first hear about multicultural education?
- Do you recall any instances in which your teachers adapted the curriculum to examine perspectives other than those of the majority?

the child and his recognition of the inherent rights of people served as an inspiration to bring about changes in education in his times and today. Rousseau's ideas constitute the fundamental postulates of the multicultural education movement.

Johann Pestalozzi, better known for the pedagogical method that bears his name, based his ideas on the essential principle that "all people, including the poor, could and should learn" (cited in Smith & Smith, 1994). Pestalozzi is credited with translating Rousseau's ideas into practice, devoting his life to education of the poor.

Maria Montessori's life's work on behalf of poor children and those with diverse characteristics was and continues to be inspirational. The first Italian woman to become a physician, Dr. Maria Montessori opened a school in 1907 in one of Rome's poorest neighborhoods. A firm believer in social justice, it was at the school where she implemented her teaching ideas that addressed the educational needs of disadvantaged and underprivileged children in new and creative ways. Her method, known as the Montessori Method, evidenced that it was possible to provide quality educational experiences to children with special needs. Anchored in developmental practices, her teaching approach offered hope to an otherwise forgotten population. Today, the Montessori Method is still widely used in education of young children.

FOCUS
on Classroom Practices | Introducing Children to the Concept of Inequality

An important step in teaching with a multicultural perspective is helping children develop an awareness of inequality. This is a topic that many times has been avoided in younger children's classrooms. Many consider inequality a concept that eludes the young child. However, because circumstances in the classroom and in the community demonstrate inequality, children are already exposed to it. Waiting until a child enters the upper grades to bring attention to this reality is not wise. Developmental research shows that it is during the early childhood years when the foundations for moral decisions are established. For this reason, it is important to incorporate experiences into the classroom curriculum to allow young children to gain a gradual awareness of their reality.

Teachers can use daily events to help children develop an awareness of inequality.

Whether in the classroom or in the community, opportunities for designing such experiences abound.

Suggestions for Designing Curricular Content on Inequality

1. Substitute the term "inequality" for the concept of "what is unfair" when, for instance, a child is not allowed to play or served a smaller portion for no reason that the child can identify. This is something most young children understand early in life and can relate to.

2. Identify the areas in which the child is likely to experience situations of unfairness. This will define your content. You will find examples in events and places familiar to the child. For example, consider the following contexts and possible scenarios:

- *At home:* Many chores are assigned to one family member whereas others do little or nothing; children leave their rooms disorganized and parents have to clean them up; one family member gets to choose all the TV programs; a child forgets to refill the pet's water dish, which is already dry.

- *In the neighborhood:* A group of children make fun of an older man because of the way he walks; people refuse to say hello to the new neighbors because they are African American; people in the neighborhood want to close a shelter for the homeless; on a bus, people take the seats assigned for the elderly and disabled, who then have to stand.

- *In the classroom:* A child refuses to let another child play with a set of manipulatives; girls in the housekeeping area send boys away; boys in the block center do not allow girls to play; some children refuse to wait their turn in the lunchroom; some children refuse to play with a child because she "speaks funny"; a child hides another child's pair of eyeglasses; children make fun of a family member because of the way she dresses; some children use racial epithets.

- *On television:* Consider the kind of programs children watch. Make an effort to watch them as well. This will alert you to programs whose content is likely to impact the class. If you find children are talking about a special show or program, or if the parents bring it to your attention, plan to discuss it. Discussion about a specific show or program should only take place with the whole class if the majority of children show a reaction to it.

3. Make a list of those situations that could happen more frequently. Target those first. Periodically plan weekly activities to deal with the target situations. However, remember that when a situation happens, it must be dealt with immediately. Having the children's attention and interest is essential for exploration.

4. Aside from your planned activities, make use of teachable moments. Nothing proves more effective than the moment when we are trying to discover the "whys" behind an event.

5. Select appropriate literature. Using the list of areas and topics you chose in Step 2, find related literature. Today, a wide variety of titles are available for initiating discussions on practically every topic.

6. Plan concrete, child-appropriate activities. Because unfairness is an abstract concept, design experiences in ways children can relate to them literally. Remember to consider that children learn through their senses and use a variety of ways to present and foster interest in the topic.

7. Use puppets or dolls to introduce difficult topics, particularly when they involve a child in your class (Derman-Sparks, 1989). Persona dolls are used to represent characters with specific ethnic or cultural characteristics, disabilities, or other diversity traits. They help in conveying to children specific life experiences related to diversity. Also, dolls can be used to discuss topics children may have seen on television that require clarification.

8. Become a perceptive observer. If you have good observational skills, you will see the curriculum sprouting all around you. Observe particularly what children do and say and the gestures they make during free-choice play. Listen to what they tell you while discussing a story. These comments will let you know how children react among themselves and what levels of awareness they exhibit.

LITERACY CONNECTIONS. . .

Learning About Equality
Through Children's Books

- Coles, R. (2004). *The story of Ruby Bridges.* New York: Scholastic.

- Hopkinson, D. (2003). *Sweet Clara and the Freedom Quilt.* New York: Knopf.

- Hopkinson, D. (2005). *Under the quilt of night.* New York: Atheneum.

- Ringgold, F. (2003). *If a bus could talk: The story of Rosa Parks.* New York: Simon and Schuster.

- Sisulu, E. (1999). *The day Gogo went to vote.* New York: Little, Brown.

People of the Americas Blaze the Trail Toward Equality

The names of those who fought for equality are many. Their work has become a prototype and an inspiration for all those who continue the task today. Among those to be remembered, we find men and women of both humble and noble origins. One common thread links them: their pursuit of equality and freedom for all.

There are many examples of the accomplishments made by advocates of equality in education from different parts of the Americas. Among the more illustrious names are Rafael Cordero, Sarah Winnemucca, Booker T. Washington, Jane Addams, and Miles Cary. They all honored the cause of multiculturalism and diversity and embodied the struggles of ethnic minorities in the United States. They are considered pioneers of early childhood education during its beginnings in the United States. Figure 5-1 highlights some of their contributions.

Wadsworth/Cengage Learning

Classroom interactions are an influential experience in becoming aware about diversity.

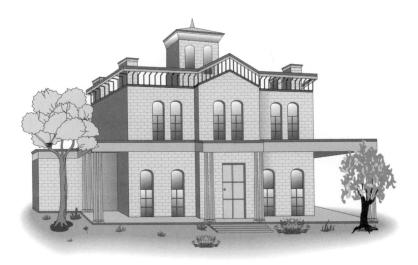

Jane Addams' Hull House was a landmark institution that provided educational opportunities to the underprivileged.

FIGURE 5-1 **Pioneers and Leaders for Educational Equality**

Maestro Cordero's School for the Poor

Primary education, as we know it today, was a privilege of few during the nineteenth century. Illiteracy was rampant, especially among the poor, all over the world. In the nineteenth century, Rafael Cordero, the son of former slaves and a cigar maker by trade, opened a school where, beyond social class lines, he taught children of the poor and the rich on Luna Street in San Juan, Puerto Rico (Gómez Tejera & Cruz López, 1970). In his spare time, the humble "Maestro Cordero" helped the children learn to read and write, turning his tobacco workshop into a school. At the time that he opened his school, there was no official elementary education in the then–Spanish-ruled island of Puerto Rico. Education was offered by private teachers who left out the children of the poor and the children of the blacks. Aware of their need, Cordero began offering classes in 1810, three decades before the Spanish government officially instituted elementary education (Tovar, 1973). Hundreds of children learned to read and write with Maestro Cordero, who never charged for his lessons. Today he is remembered as the pioneer of elementary education for the humble in Puerto Rico.

Sarah Winnemucca, a Champion for the Rights of Native Americans

The daughter of a Paiute chief, Sarah Winnemucca left an invaluable legacy of tenacity and faith in the education of Native American children (Zanjani, 2004). A writer and founder of the first school for Native Americans, she was described by her friend Elizabeth Peabody as the "Indian Joan of Arc." Early in life, Sarah learned about prejudice and discrimination. Her great desire to learn led her to enroll in a convent school in California. Because of opposition by white parents, she had to leave and move back to Nevada, where she worked as a domestic. Spending most of her salary on books, Sarah taught herself and became, years later, a translator and a spokesperson for the Paiutes (Zanjani, 2004). Later, she became a school assistant and, during her travels, met Elizabeth Peabody, a leader in kindergarten education. The friendship influenced Winnemucca to organize a school for the Paiute children.

Booker T. Washington, a New Beginning for African Americans

The education of African Americans was given a start with the abolition of slavery in the United States. Determined to become a productive part of U.S. society and to build a future, African Americans embraced education with great eagerness. The government formally undertook education for African Americans as part of the Reconstruction efforts after the Civil War. Under the auspices of the federal government, thousands of teachers arrived in the South, a result of the 51 voluntary Freedmen's Aid Societies that were formed (Smith & Smith, 1994). A distinctive attitude toward learning to read and write characterized the former slaves who attended these schools (Watkins & Kelley, 2001). Few were too young, and none too old, to learn. This desire became the force that drove African Americans to give their strongest support to the schooling movement. In the latter part of the nineteenth century, higher education would also become a reality, when many schools and colleges were opened for the now free African Americans.

Booker T. Washington is one example of the African Americans' eagerness to learn. Historical accounts show that he learned he was a free person when "a Union officer appeared on his owner's porch and read the Emancipation Proclamation" (Smith & Smith, 1994). This marked the beginning of a courageous and historic life for young Booker T. In 1872, Washington started his formal education at the Hampton Normal and Agricultural Institute. Overcoming humiliations and despite hard work and disappointments, he never lost hope and became a brilliant teacher. Today, Booker T. Washington is remembered as the founder of the prestigious Tuskegee University in Alabama.

Mary McLeod Bethune's Legacy

Mary McLeod Bethune was a pioneer in establishing educational opportunities for young African Americans in Florida. With no formal school for black children in Daytona, she campaigned and called upon the generosity of people. In 1904, she opened the Daytona Normal and Industrial Institute for Girls with five students, aged 8–12 (Zrinyi Long, 2004). In the beginning years, students and teachers raised funds by selling ice cream and sweet potato pies. Mary's hard work and the support of many prominent Americans, such as John D. Rockefeller and James Gamble of Procter & Gamble, made her dream possible. Years later, her school, then a college, joined the Cookman Institute, becoming the now-prestigious Bethune-Cookman University.

Hull House, the Work of Jane Addams

The founder of Hull House, Jane Addams, was born to a well-off Chicago family. Through her travels, she became aware of the needs of the poor and witnessed the efforts of some dedicated individuals to alleviate their problems. In 1889, she moved into a rented house on Halsted Street, in one of Chicago's poorest areas, opening it as a center for services for the poor. Before long, the Hull House became a haven for many immigrants in the Chicago area (Caravantes, 2004). Among Jane's first projects was a kindergarten that, in less than a month, had 24 children in attendance with many more on the waiting list. Addams dedicated her entire life to social justice, struggling to provide opportunities to families and children of the poor. Her philanthropic work was extended to serve people and children throughout the world, and her efforts were recognized when she was awarded the Nobel Peace Prize in 1931 (Caravantes, 2004). Today, the Hull House Association still serves needy children and adults in the Chicago area.

Miles Cary and the Poston School at the Relocation Camps

During the 1940s, another educator made a difference in the lives of others. Miles A. Cary organized educational services for thousands of Japanese American children in relocation camps. The magnitude of his accomplishment must be measured in the context of one of the most shameful periods of U.S. history. The relocation camps were an injustice committed during World War II against one of our country's ethnic groups, the Japanese Americans. At the time of the Japanese attack on Pearl Harbor, on December 7, 1941, there was a significant Japanese American minority population living in the United States. Many of the members of this group had been born in the United States and had ancestors who had been citizens of this country for generations. Despite this fact, and fearing another attack and anti-American activities from the Japanese immigrants, the government decided to confine this group to mass detention camps.

Camps were established to house nearly 6 million Japanese Americans, including more than 33,000 children. This experience forever marked the lives of those children who came to live behind barbed wire. In the midst of these unfortunate circumstances, educator Miles A. Cary became a voice that spoke against the unfair relocation of Japanese Americans. Cary, who believed relocation was an immoral act, accepted responsibility for organizing educational services in the Poston Relocation Center that housed more than 4,000 Japanese Americans (Smith & Smith, 1994). At Poston, the school designed by Cary became a spiritual oasis for hundreds of students who lived there. Today, many still remember that going to school at Poston was the best part of the years they spent behind the fences.

A Legacy of the Past

It is said that the past holds undeniable truths. The past also allows us to better focus the lens through which we look at life. Before continuing our search for the genesis of multicultural education, it is important to assess what we have learned from the past.

■ Awareness of inequality has existed since ancient times. Education for the poor and gender equity have been two areas of early awareness.

■ Despite the awareness, actions by society to correct inequality have been delayed or never taken.

LITERACY CONNECTIONS. . .

Learning About the Men and Women Who Fought Inequality

Children can increase their awareness of inequality when they learn how it affects real people in the context of daily life. Because literature has a special appeal for children, the use of biographical literature and historical fiction is particularly effective. One of the benefits of biographies is that they help children build a sense of the different kinds of inequalities real people have experienced. When concretely presented (such as by using artifacts or in role-playing), historical fiction is a "true voyage into time." A list of suggested titles is included here. Ask the school librarian and check your local library for additional and recent titles.

- Bains, R. (2005). *Harriet Tubman: The road to freedom*. New York: Troll.

- Carrick, C. (1989). *Stay away from Simon!* New York: Clarion.

- de Kay, J. (2001). *Meet Martin Luther King, Jr.* New York: Random House.

- Delacorte-Taylor, M. (1998). *The gold Cadillac*. New York: Dial Books.

- Flores, C. N. (2006). *Our house on Huece*. Lubbock, TX: Texas Tech University Press.

- Greenfield, E. (1995). *Rosa Parks*. New York: Crowell.

- Krull, K. (2003). *Harvesting hope: The story of Cesar Chavez*. New York: Harcourt.

- Levine, J. (2002). *Henry's freedom box*. New York: Scholastic.

- Martin, M. (2003). *Deaf child crossing*. New York: Aladdin.

- Monjo, F. (1999). *The drinking gourd*. New York: Harper & Row.

- Rockwell, A. (2002). *Only passing through: The story of Sojourner Truth*. New York: Dragonfly Books.

- ■ Both men and women played active roles in exposing and disclosing the existing inequities.
- ■ Realization of unfairness in various aspects of life (such as gender and social class) established the beginnings of the concept of diversity.
- ■ Of the many cries for equality, only a few resulted in concrete deeds. Often, only a few benefited from the change. However, the changes served to strengthen the desire for fair service for all.

SNAPSH⬤T 5-5   Impressions

George Takei was 4 years old when he learned that his family could no longer live as free people. The following are his impressions of the moment when he and his family were forced to leave for an internment camp.

> Then a terrible war had broken out, and my father's whole world was blown away. All people of Japanese ancestry in America were to be immediately removed to internment camps, leaving everything behind. So much was irretrievably lost. The business— abandoned. The rented house on Garnett Street—hurriedly vacated. The car sold for the best offer, five dollars—better to get something than leave it behind. But the new refrigerator got no offer. It nearly killed Mama to have to abandon it to the vultures. Everything other than what we were allowed to carry—all abandoned. All memories now. All fleeting as the sand blowing past the window. All gone.

Source: Takei, 1994.

LET'S TALK AND REFLECT . . .   Lessons from the Past for Today

As you have seen, quality education for all children has been the goal of many educators and concerned individuals from many walks of life. Their efforts contributed to legitimizing the movement for multicultural and diversity education.

Today, many individuals continue to advocate for equal educational opportunities for children. With your colleagues or classmates, find out about individuals who support multicultural efforts in your community. After learning about the efforts and deeds of so many, think about the efforts that still need to be made to achieve the dream of equity and equality.

| THE ROAD TO MULTICULTURAL EDUCATION

Considering the impact education has on the life of a young child, teachers know that to provide a developmentally appropriate environment, the nature and needs of the child must be reflected in the program. Today, diversity is a major element to be considered when designing programs for the young; however, this was not always so. According to multicultural scholars, multicultural education is a phenomenon of the 1960s. As pointed out earlier, little or no effort was made until then to accommodate the needs and particularities of children with diverse backgrounds. Various factors are responsible for this delayed awareness:

Collaboration of teachers and families in culturally diverse settings enhances opportunities and promotes positive outcomes for children.

- Slavery was abolished in 1865 after Abraham Lincoln issued the Emancipation Proclamation, but history shows that acceptance and entry of free African Americans into society was a slow and painful process. Numerous accounts tell of unjust and unfair acts committed against former slaves through the decades following the Emancipation Proclamation.

- During the late nineteenth and early twentieth centuries, while the United States was coping with the new societal role of African Americans, waves of immigrants were pouring into this country. The demographic changes caused by the immigrant population presented new challenges. The fact that many new immigrants belonged to ethnic and racial groups different from those of the first settlers set in motion a new period of discrimination.

- Court rulings lent legal validity to segregation and affirmed differences among people based on race. Among these rulings were the Supreme Court's 1883 declaration that the Civil Rights Act of 1875 was unconstitutional and the Court's approval of "separate but equal" facilities in *Plessy v. Ferguson* (1896).

- Policies that accented the differences between specific ethnic groups and the majority were still enforced. Examples include the policy that led to the incarceration of Japanese Americans at the start of World War II and the reaction against Mexican immigrants that led to "Operation Wetback" in the 1950s.

Struggle for Equality and Civil Rights

African Americans found the legal and social obstacles present in the United States unbearable. Their frustrated hopes and a feeling of powerlessness nurtured the spirit that ignited and sustained the **civil rights movement** of the 1960s. Two events in the 1950s

SNAPSH◉T 5-6   Plessy v. Ferguson (1896)

Justice Harlan expressed his disagreement with a decision that sanctioned the practice of assigning separate seats in public places based on race in an eloquent letter. According to the court ruling, the separate assignment did not imply that blacks or any other ethnic minorities were to be seen as not equal to whites.

. . . In respect of civil rights, common to all citizens, the Constitution of the United States does not, I think, permit any public authority to know the race of those entitled to be protected in the enjoyment of such rights . . . In

the view of the Constitution, in the eye of the law, there is in this country no superior, dominant, ruling class of citizens. There is no caste here. Our Constitution is color-blind, it neither knows nor tolerates classes among citizens. In respect of civil rights, all citizens are equal before the law.

In my opinion, the judgment rendered this day will, in time, prove to be quite as pernicious as the decision made in the Dred Scott Case.

Source: Plessy v. Ferguson (1896), in J. Kromkowski, 1994.

Wadsworth/Cengage Learning

Landmark civil rights legislation made it possible for all children to have access to more equitable quality educational opportunities.

fueled the beginning of this struggle for equality. The first was the landmark Supreme Court decision of *Brown v. Board of Education of Topeka, Kansas,* in 1954, which ruled that segregated schools did not provide equal opportunities. The Brown decision reversed the view the Court had taken in *Plessy v. Ferguson;* "separate but equal" facilities were now considered unconstitutional. This decision marked the end of legal segregation in U.S. schools and initiated equalization of education services. It also established the beginning of multiculturalization of our schools. The desegregation of schools that followed the 1954 Brown decision was enforced throughout the 1960s, largely as a result of the work and determination of the leaders of the civil rights movement.

The second event was the Rosa Parks incident, which took place on December 1, 1955, in Montgomery, Alabama. Mrs. Parks' refusal to move from a seat designated for "white" people, even though a white man was left standing, led to her arrest and trial for breaking the law (Turner-Sadler, 2006). The result was the famous Montgomery bus boycott, in which the entire black community rose to her defense and refused to ride the public transportation system. After 381 days of boycott, the city capitulated, ending the practice of segregation in public transportation and allowing blacks the freedom to sit anywhere they wanted on buses. The incident sparked the unification of African Americans across the South and marked the official beginning of the civil rights movement. The Rosa Parks incident brought prominence to a young minister, Dr. Martin Luther King Jr., who had similar aspirations for equality (Turner-Sadler, 2006). When the boycott of the buses was called, Dr. King became the spokesperson for the newly formed Montgomery movement. Addressing the community, he spoke about unity and nonviolence, which set the tone for the boycott.

The inability of many mainstream Americans to accept the decision to desegregate and their efforts to set back the fight for equality served to unite the African Americans in the greatest struggle for freedom and equality known to this country. Civil rights became a major issue in national elections. Civil rights issues were also vigorously pursued by many black-led activist organizations. Among the most prominent were the National Association for the Advancement of Colored People (NAACP), formed in 1909 by W. E. B. Du Bois and a small group of African Americans and white supporters, and the Congress on Racial Equality, founded in 1942. The social measures and programs accomplished during the civil rights movement in the 1960s were numerous. They contributed to establishing services and initiatives for people across racial lines. Yet, the fight for equality continues. Ensuring that the constitutional rights of all are protected and guaranteed to people regardless of their origin, race, or religious affiliation is still at the forefront of the agenda of national and state advocacy groups, especially those representing children and families from ethnic minorities.

Legacy of the Civil Rights Movement

I have a dream that my four little children will one day live in a nation where they will not be judged by the color of their skin but by the content of their character.

Dr. Martin Luther King Jr. (1929–1968)

A major social force of the 1960s, the civil rights movement survived tragedies, humiliations, and injustices to win many major battles fought for the dignity of the individual. Among these were battles for registration of black voters, desegregation of public facilities and private businesses, and desegregation in schools. The progress made in the area of equality in recent years can be traced to victories won by the supporters of the civil rights movement who continue their work today.

SNAPSH●T 5-7   What Started *Brown v. Board of Education?*

To many, the events that led to the landmark 1954 decision have faded. Briefly, let us recall the incident that initiated this historic lawsuit.

During the 1940s, the unfair and unequal conditions of schools for African Americans had become obvious. During this time, the National Association for the Advancement of Colored People (NAACP) had brought the issue to local and national attention. It was in 1947 when Esther Brown, a white woman, became concerned about the state of schools for African Americans in South Park, outside of Kansas City (Kelley & Lewis, 2000). Initially, Ms. Brown tried to persuade the school board to improve the grade schools but failed. She then consulted about the situation with an attorney from Topeka, Elisha Scott, who found that there were legal grounds in the issue. According to Kansas law, segregation was permitted in school districts larger than South Park (Kelley & Lewis, 2000).

Determined to fight for what was right and equal for black children, African American parent and assistant pastor Oliver Brown, along with the parents and children of South Park, boycotted the schools in the fall of 1950. The rest is history. With the support of the black community, Oliver Brown moved the case forward, achieving one of the major victories in the struggle for social justice.

Source: Kelley & Lewis, 2000.

In Action . . .   The Impact of a Court Ruling

Here is James Fanner's description of the impact that *Brown v. Board of Education* had upon the civil rights movement. While you read it, imagine how civil rights activists felt at the time. Think about how the effects of the decision relate to multicultural education.

> The Brown decision set in motion boundless energies, spawned by the promise of Jeffersonian egalitarianism but penned up by the delay of fulfilling that promise. From Little Rock to Oxford, Mississippi, and throughout the South, children and youth of irrepressible and heroic dimensions rose and the barriers came down. There were other foci in the equality drive of the 1950s and 1960s. There were boycotts and freedom rides; sit-ins at lunch counters; voter registration drives; lynchings and killings; and admission of black students to all-white universities. Dr. Martin Luther King, who with his charismatic appeal succeeded in mobilizing as much as one-fourth of the entire black population, as well as millions of whites, led marches for across-the-board desegregation and for universal dignity of man. One of the most successful civil rights demonstrations was the march on Washington in 1963, which was conducted in support of the decision that segregation of educational facilities by race was unconstitutional.

Source: Turner-Sadler, 2006.

THE BIRTH OF MULTICULTURAL EDUCATION

Educators attribute the contemporary beginnings of multicultural education to the events and the social climate of the 1960s. According to Gollnick and Chinn (2006), interest in ethnic studies was brought to attention in the 1960s and early 1970s. Major sociopolitical events such as the assassinations of John F. Kennedy, Martin Luther King Jr., and Robert Kennedy; the "hippie movement"; the anti–

Educational equity is one of the central goals of multicultural education.

Vietnam War movement; the changes in social values; and the new drug culture created a climate of unprecedented change in U.S. society. In this atmosphere of uncertainty and flux, multicultural education got its start.

Equal Services for All Children

The issue of inequality, central to many social and political movements of the 1960s, gave way to initiatives such as the War on Poverty of 1964. During this time, people realized that children of minorities were at a disadvantage compared with children of U.S. mainstream culture. Although this view of minorities led to misconceptions about the "culturally deprived," it acknowledged the existence of different cultural backgrounds. Concerted efforts made to bring people out of their "disadvantages" gave way to a number of important social and educational programs. Through these efforts, the government affirmed its interest in children. As a way to equalize opportunities for all, educators such as Jerome Brunner and Edward Zigler advocated the development of programs to serve the children of the poor and those of culturally different backgrounds.

Efforts Toward Equal Services for Children

By the safeguard of health and the protection of childhood we further contribute to that equality of opportunity which is the unique basis of American civilization.

President Herbert Hoover (1929), Excerpt from the Announcement of the White House Conference on Children

---

In Action . . .   **Early Experiences with Other Cultures**

Can you recall the topics about other cultures you studied during kindergarten and primary school? What was their focus?

The spirit of the 1960s was the perfect breeding medium for social reform. Thousands of people across the country, representing all ethnic and cultural minorities, joined hands with African Americans to bring inequality to a stop. The constancy of their efforts for achieving equality was the force that rang the bell for action for children. With the understanding that children of the poor (who at the same time represented the ethnic minorities) would do better if offered additional educational services, the greatest revolution for young children began to unfold. Because people believed that early intervention was a way to ameliorate differences in social experiences, the public and the government took a decisive interest in young children (Dahlberg, Moss, & Pence, 2006). Developing out of the War on Poverty and the civil rights movement, the government's focus turned to the improvement of services for children living in poverty. It was estimated that 40 million children were living in poverty in the United States, the wealthiest country in the world (Dahlberg, Moss, & Pence, 2006). Recognizing that children from socially and economically disadvantaged environments were entering school less equipped for success, many initiatives were undertaken to serve the culturally diverse child. Targeting those from low socioeconomic communities across the nation, the government began focusing its efforts on children from various ethnic minorities. Although many programs were designed during the 1960s to meet their needs, Head Start stands out as a leading effort to provide comprehensive services and education to young children.

A "Head Start" for U.S. Children

Project Head Start began during the summer of 1965. At the time, approximately 2,500 Child Development Centers were established to serve more than 550,000 children across the nation (Osborn, 1998). The program was designed to provide learning experiences for children entering first grade in the fall of 1965 and who had not experienced kindergarten or preschool. Centers opened their doors to children in urban areas, on Indian reservations, and in places as far as Guam, Puerto Rico, and the Virgin Islands.

Head Start also proved that, to serve children, educators needed to involve the community and parents as partners. The experiences during the days and weeks of that memorable summer session in 1965 marked the first substantial efforts to reduce inequality. The program was a first effort to directly empower citizens by involving them in the educational decision-making process. Head Start programs opened and blos-

---

F◯CUS
on Classroom Practices | Goals of the Head Start Program

Seven goals guided the foundation of the Head Start Program in 1965. Today, they still describe the mission of the nation's largest early childhood program. Head Start aspires to do the following:

1. Improve the child's physical health and physical abilities.

2. Help the emotional and social development of the child by encouraging self-confidence, spontaneity, curiosity, and self-discipline.

3. Improve the child's mental processes and skills, with particular attention to conceptual and verbal skills.

4. Establish patterns and expectations of success for the child that will create a climate of confidence for future learning efforts.

5. Enhance the child's capacity to relate positively to family members and others, while at the same time strengthening the family's ability to relate positively to the child and his or her problems.

6. Develop in the child and his or her family a responsible attitude toward society, and encourage society to work with the poor in solving their problems.

7. Increase the sense of dignity and self-worth within the child and his or her family.

Source: Zigler & Valentine, 1997.

---

somed thanks to responsive communities everywhere. Knowing that this was an opportunity for their children to have a better education, people gave their full support to the project.

The need for parents and teachers to work as partners was realized through the concept of the child development center. Different from the classroom, the child development center affirmed the roles of parents and the community in a child's education. According to Osborn (1998), "in concept it [the child development center] represents drawing together all the resources—family, community, and professionals—which can contribute to the child's total development." Designed as a comprehensive program for preschool children, Head Start was founded on the belief that a child's success was not to be defined only by intellectual growth but, rather, by a holistic perspective of the individual child. Consideration of the integral development of young children has since been the driving force behind Head Start services. Following this holistic view, interventions were planned to include a variety of direct and preventive services. Today, interventions take place through the following:

■ *Developmental services:* Individualized developmental education services are offered.

■ *Health services:* Comprehensive medical, dental, and mental health services are offered. Preventive health is among its objectives.

■ *Nutrition services:* Since its beginning, Head Start has emphasized the need for children to be well fed. Balanced meals (breakfast, snack, and lunch) are served family style, in what has become another trademark of this program. A strong nutrition program complements the meal services.

■ *Family services:* A full range of social services is offered. Their purpose is to promote the best conditions for an improved quality of family life. A well-planned parenting skills empowerment program is also part of the services. In the program, parents and families refine and acquire knowledge to enhance their child–parent relationships and interactions.

Currently, Head Start serves more than 900,000 children (infants to preschoolers), representing almost 40 percent of those eligible (Head Start Bureau, 2005). Of its enrollment, 67 percent are ethnic minorities, with African Americans and Hispanics as the largest groups (see Figure 5-2). Today, Head Start continues to be the optimum "head start" for thousands of children. Head Start is the longest-lasting program stemming from the 1964 War on Poverty.

FIGURE 5-2 **Head Start Program: Enrollment and Ethnic Distribution, 2004**

Distribution of Age Groups in Head Start and Early Head Start Programs

Age Groups	%
Five-year-olds and older	5%
Four-year-olds and older	52%
Three-year-olds	34%
Under three years of age	9%
Total enrollment for 2004	905,851

Demographical Information: Racial and Ethnic Composition of Head Start Enrollment

Racial and Ethnic Group	%
American Indian/Alaska Native	3.1%
Hispanic	31.2%
Black	31.1%
White	26.9%
Asian	1.8%
Hawaiian/Pacific Islander	0.9%
Multiracial/Other	5.0%

Source: U.S. Department of Health and Human Services, 2005.

The inclusion of children with special needs in Head Start programs recognizes their rights to services and education, one of the outcomes of federal legislation initiated by PL 94-192.

Head Start and Children with Special Needs   Since 1972, Head Start has served children with special needs. Today, at least 10 percent of its enrollment must be allocated to children with disabilities (Head Start Bureau, 2004). Constant training and in-service activities prepare the staff of Head Start programs to offer quality services to children with disabilities. A full range of support services is offered to meet the needs of the child with disabilities. Determination of appropriate placement and services follows the IDEA guidelines for preschoolers. The goal is to provide developmentally appropriate experiences in the least restrictive environment that will best promote the child's development.

Early Head Start, Services for the Very Young   During the 1990s, Head Start extended its services to infants and toddlers. This initiative intended to prove that intervention begins at birth, something that most early educators have advocated for years. In 1994, Congress approved Early Head Start, a new program that provides services to infants, toddlers, and pregnant women. Based on research findings, the program acknowledges the value of early intervention and provides services to low-income families and young children during the prenatal and infant–toddler years. The program also offers support to pregnant women by providing parenting education classes.

Services for Young Children with Disabilities

All children, including those with exceptionalities, have a right to quality educational experiences and services. Exceptionalities are one of the aspects of diversity found across society and ethnic lines (Paasha, Gorrill, & Strom, 2003). Yet, it is one that has been

The Head Start program was created to provide equitable and quality services to young children.

In Action . . .   **Learning More About the Head Start Program**

To appreciate the relevancy of the Head Start program, try the following:

- Interview someone who experienced Head Start during its beginning years. Ask about the kinds of activities and materials used and, especially, about the nature of the children enrolled.
- Visit your local Head Start office and find out about its services. Identify the populations being served.
- Visit a Head Start classroom. Compare its program with other early childhood services.
- Search the Internet and read about the origins of the program and its successes.

---

acknowledged only in recent decades. Before the 1970s, views about exceptionalities translated into discriminatory practices that resulted in children being placed in isolated classrooms or special institutions. Responding to a Congressional disposition, in 1972 the Head Start Program allocated 10 percent of its enrollment to children with special needs. With the passing of legislation in the 1970s, services to these children were formally initiated. The Education for All Handicapped Children Act of 1975, or PL 94-142, established the rights of young children with disabilities and exceptionalities to receive free education and services in a least restrictive environment. The law opened the door for children with special needs to participate in regular or mainstream classrooms.

During the 1980s, services for young preschoolers with special needs were mandated by the passing of PL 99-457. This legislation established the creation of the Federal Preschool Program and mandated states to offer services for infants and toddlers and their families. Furthermore, the law established the right to services of children with exceptionalities ages 3–5. Dispositions also included the development of an individual family service plan (IFSP) to better address the needs of both the child and the family.

Early Head Start provides developmentally appropriate learning experiences to infants and toddlers that support development during the very critical early years.

Further steps toward equity were taken by the passing of the Americans with Disabilities Act of 1990. This important legislation established the rights of young children to receive experiences in settings and environments especially designed with accommodations that meet their needs (Paasha, Gorrill, & Strom, 2003). This legislation also acknowledged the children's rights to be included in regular classrooms. Thus, the concept of "inclusion" was created. This practice brought about the need for better-trained early childhood educators who are able to respond to children with special needs and deliver to them the quality experiences fundamental to equitable education. Although advocacy for the exceptional child continues, today, in classrooms around the country, young children with special needs share experiences and learn along with their less challenged peers. Together, they form a community that exemplifies the social diversity of our society.

LET'S TALK AND REFLECT . . . Serving Young Children with Special Needs

Working with children with special needs requires the efforts of families, schools, and agencies. Talk with early childhood teachers and find out about current services available for young children in your community. How many of these services include parents and families?

LET'S TALK AND REFLECT... Linguistic Diversity in Your Community

- Do you speak a language other than English?
- What are the repercussions for children in your community who do not speak English?
- What is your personal view of people who live in the United States who do not learn to speak English?

Becoming aware of language diversity in your community is a step toward understanding the multicultural reality of children. Take time to answer the following and to share your thoughts with colleagues or classmates: What languages other than English do the children in your community speak?

Linguistic Diversity: Another Descriptor of Multiculturalism

Language is one of the aspects that define diversity. It is also one of the fundamental tools of cultural acquisition and a part of a child's cultural identity. Whether Spanish, Arabic, Russian, Creole, or French, some of the many languages spoken throughout U.S. communities, languages evidence the ever-increasing diversity of U.S. society (see Figure 5-3).

FIGURE 5-3 **Non-English Languages Spoken at Home by Region, 2000.**

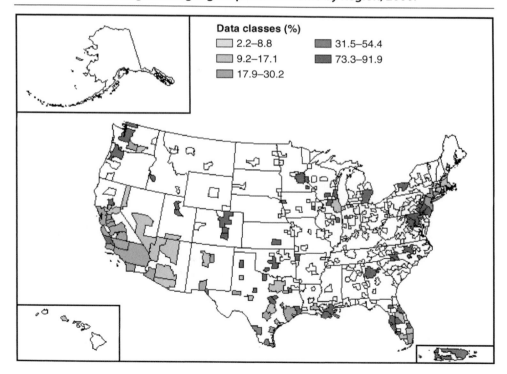

Source: U.S. Census Bureau, 2000.

FIGURE 5-4 **Non-English Speaking Home and Difficulty Speaking English**

	1995	2003
Children ages 5 to 17 who speak a language other than English at home	14%	19%
Children ages 5 to 17 who speak a language other than English at home and have difficulty speaking English	5%	5%

Source: Federal Interagency Forum on Child and Family Statistics, 2004.

Supporting the Needs of Children with Linguistic Differences

Linguistic diversity is one of the most visible and fastest growing distinguishing characteristics in our society. Many households in the United States speak languages other than English (Figure 5-4). This phenomenon is reflected in classrooms across the country. Statistics show that in many school districts, children speak as many as 40 different languages. Nationally, enrollment of English language learners (ELLs) showed a growth of almost 57 percent in grades Pre-K–12 (National Clearinghouse for English Language Acquisition and Language Instruction Educational Program [NCELA], 2006). While over 76 percent of ELLs speak Spanish, there is a wide variety of languages other than English in classrooms across the United States (National Council of Teachers of English, 2006). (See Figure 5-5.)

"Who is the English language learner?" is a question asked by many. Typically, ELL children are "students whose first language is not English and who are in the process of learning English" (NCELA, 2008). Many of them are not born in the United States, although Census data show that demographically, the majority of English language learners are U.S. born.

FIGURE 5-5 **Home Languages of ELL Students in U.S. Classrooms (2001–2002)**

Language	Percentage (%)
Spanish	76.9
Vietnamese	2.4
Hmong	1.8
Korean	1.2
Arabic	1.1
Haitian-Creole	1.1

Source: Hopstock & Stephenson, 2003.

For decades, second language learning has been a debatable issue. Policies and teaching practices in the past were created from the perspective of deficiency. Children with other languages were perceived as lacking until they acquired English language skills. No value was placed on the retention of the children's native languages. The result of these policies was that many children grew up thinking that it was an embarrassment to speak a language other than English. Parents and families wanting to carve a future in U.S. society thought that it was best for their children to give up their home language and become "Americans" as soon as possible. The result was the erosion of native languages, many of which disappeared and many more of which are still at risk of vanishing forever.

Due to the efforts of families, educators, language scholars, multicultural research-ers, and concerned leaders, the legislation was changed to acknowledge the importance of the home language. The need to support the child's cultural heritage while acquir-ing English language skills has been recognized as an important aspect of the child's development. Research in second language development has revealed the following in particular (Garcia, 2005; Tabors, 1997):

■ Language acquisition and development is best facilitated during the early years. Al-though the ability to acquire a new language remains, during early childhood chil-dren tend to acquire languages in a more native-like way.

■ Young children are capable of learning more than one language. Becoming bilin-gual is a task that brings valuable developmental benefits to the child.

■ Second language learning happens most effectively in familiar, natural contexts.

■ The first language scaffolds and contributes to the acquisition of a second language, in this case, English.

■ There are ample developmental gains (cognitive, social, and emotional) for the young child through the acquisition of another language.

■ Learning another language fosters understanding of more than one cultural reality, a necessary characteristic in a multicultural society.

■ Knowing another language fosters empathy and tolerance by facilitating an under-standing of the values and frames of reference of others.

■ Maintaining the home language contributes to the family's sense of connection. It facilitates communication with family members and links children to gaining an understanding of their family's heritage.

Supporting young ELLs while preserving their home languages is considered to-day the appropriate educational practice that adheres to DCAP principles. It is also a critical element in classrooms serving multicultural children. Careful planning must occur to assist each child who is learning English while facilitating the preservation of the first language. With the national emphasis on reading and literacy development, it is particularly important to consider the selection of materials, strategies, and assessment practices to use with young ELLs. Keeping in mind that the environment is one of the elements that promotes language learning, creating a classroom atmosphere that both supports learning English and respects and values the child's first language is essential. Expectations set by the No Child Left Behind legislation, which projects that, by 2014, all children will be proficient in reading by grade 3, imply the need to provide experiences that will match the needs of the young second language learner. When selecting strategies, educators should be mindful of the children's needs and learning styles as well as appropriate practices. Necessary accommodations must be made to meet the development needs of ELL children.

What works best with young ELLs depends on the needs, experiences, and characteristics of the children. Some suggested practices include the following:

- *Environment*: Preparing the classroom for language acquisition and preservation of first languages includes selecting literacy materials in both English and the first languages of the children, such as the following:
  - Age-appropriate children's books
  - Printed materials such as newspapers, flyers, and others that can be used and displayed
  - Posters, signs, and labels of materials
  - Music, both instrumental and vocal, that is representative of diverse cultures and of the first languages of the children and English
  - Child-appropriate software
  - Manipulatives and realia to support concept formation
  - Language usage; use of both languages by adults and children
- *Experiences*: Planning is based on the language needs and acquisition ability of each child. The process begins by assessing the children to identify their level of language proficiency. Relevant and meaningful activities are planned with expectations set at levels that children can meet. Best practices in early childhood and second language learning point out that meaningful classroom experiences connecting the child to his or her reality are central to successful learning. Planning needs to be soundly anchored to what is relevant to the child and purposely designed to build language skills. Use of thematic units helps ELL children to connect with their own cultural and language experiences, facilitating acquisition of new concepts and language. The content also needs to uphold expectations appropriate to the age group that reflect the standards while challenging the child to learn. Selection of appropriate teaching strategies and incorporation of necessary modifications to lessons and materials to facilitate learning are also critical.
- *Assessment*: Continuous observation and use of alternative assessment practices are necessary to document progress. Use of standardized instruments must be carefully decided upon to avoid any testing bias that may unfairly depict the child's performance level.
- *Collaboration with families*: Maintaining open communication and interaction with the child's parents and families is vital. This is particularly important for the

preservation of the first language as the second language is learned. Providing materials, giving suggestions, responding to questions about language learning, and asking families to share materials and favorite stories that can be incorporated into classroom experiences set a positive tone and build a strong relationship between the home and the classroom. Suggestions to help preserve the first language may include activities such as encouraging family members to read and share stories with their children, to take time to sing songs meaningful to their culture, and to talk to their children in the first language.

- *Teacher's knowledge:* Two types of knowledge are necessary:
  - *Knowledge about practices of second language acquisition.* Having knowledge regarding the acquisition of a second language and first language preservation practices is essential. Because this is an area where many studies are being conducted, keep up with current research and use the findings for developing your own ideas about the role of the educator in first and second language learning.
  - *Cultural ideas.* Language is a vital cultural element and a learning tool. For that reason, the early educator must understand the role that language plays in the life of a child.

THE ROAD IS FINALLY LAID

As public interest in diversity issues increased during the 1970s and 1980s, educators began to realize that efforts alone were not sufficient to effect true **educational reform.** Baruth and Manning (2008) note that the negative attitudes of teachers also influenced the effectiveness of the multiethnic education approach. In time, the scope of multicultural education gave way to a broader view of cultures and encompassed the total school and classroom environments. This inclusive perspective was reinforced by the passing in 1975 of PL 94-142, the Education for All Handicapped Act, which recognized the rights to equal education for children with disabilities. The Individuals with Disabilities Education Act (IDEA) of 1990 reaffirmed the commitment to serve the exceptional.

Today, more than ever, early childhood educators recognize their responsibilities toward children. A desire to reach all the children we teach has become clear to many more educators. Although we feel optimistic about the future, there is still much to be done. We count on those of you who believe in unity and equality to bring equitable and fair education to all children, who will help us build a strong and prosperous nation.

MOVING AHEAD

The history of efforts toward the multiculturalism of U.S. education and, particularly, of early childhood education, continues to unfold every day. Although much has been accomplished, many areas still require reform as our society grows more diverse. Many chapters remain to be written. Which one will you begin?

Supporting Home Languages

Helping children preserve their home languages can happen as they acquire proficiency in English language and become bilingual. A child-responsive second language environment exemplifies the following principles:

General characteristics

- Follows developmental practices. Teachers have a solid knowledge about language acquisition and second language development. Decisions are based on developmental information about the child and families.
- Exhibits knowledge of various cultural and ethnic characteristics. Practices demonstrate accurate knowledge and respect toward children's ethnic and cultural groups.
- Encourages participation of and collaboration with parents and families. Integrates parents as members of the classroom. Recognizes their expertise and knowledge.
- Is emotionally supportive and respectful. Supports children's self-concept by acknowledging their cultural knowledge (views children as experts in their own cultures).
- Validates children's cultures by observing and integrating customs and traditions.
- Is cognitively challenging. Plans and provides relevant child-appropriate learning experiences. Experiences are connected and aligned to age-appropriate learning expectations (performance standards, learning outcomes).

Literacy and second language practices

- Is print-rich. Integrates first languages in classroom and centers (such as with signage and labeling). Includes literacy materials in first languages and English.
- Has a rich oral and listening environment. Encourages and engages children in conversations (with peers, teacher, assistants, and staff).
- Supports use of first languages to communicate while English is acquired.
- Celebrates and acknowledges success.
- Provides listening experiences and materials.
- Is multisensorial and concrete. Includes artifacts representative of children's cultures. Displays and integrates visuals, objects, and other culturally authentic materials throughout the centers.

WHAT WE HAVE LEARNED—CHAPTER SUMMARY

Multicultural education has a rich history. In this chapter, we learned about the contributions of many educators, philosophers, and activists, such as Maestro Cordero, Sarah Winnemucca, Rosa Parks, Johann Pestalozzi, Booker T. Washington, and others. We also learned that the struggles for educational equality, equity, and access have been a part of human history for hundreds of years. The multicultural education movement had its major impetus in the 1960s in the midst of political and social turmoil in our country. It was during this time that the civil rights movement facilitated major educational reforms and provided opportunities for equal education for the "disadvantaged." One of the major programs created during that time was Head Start, which, to this day, remains the most effective and the longest-running early childhood education program in the country. The passing of the Education for All Handicapped Children Act, PL 94-142, in 1975 established the rights to education for children with special needs. Additional support for children with special needs was sanctioned by the Americans with Disabilities Act of 1990. Today, educators are also focused on providing special services for the needs of children with linguistic differences. This chapter makes us aware of how much has been accomplished in the field of early childhood education and how much still needs to be done.

THINGS TO DO . . .

1. What are the main components of the multicultural education movement? Select three that you think are the most relevant.

2. Choose one of the advocates of equality from the individuals mentioned in this chapter. Do some library research to find at least two other characteristics that highlight his or her contributions.

3. *Equality* is a very difficult concept to define. To gain some insight of how people see it, ask five people to define it. But first, write down your own definition. Begin your interviews and make sure to jot down the responses. Examine the responses to find the similarities and differences. Then, redefine *equality* to reflect what you learned. Share your findings with a classmate or colleague.

4. Equality is the catalyst for developing multicultural education. Do you think your school provides equal opportunities to all children? What areas do you think still require improvement? Explain.

5. It has been said that multicultural education is not fully supported by educators. Some have argued that this is a problem. What is your position on this argument?

RECOMMENDED INTERNET RESOURCES

- Anti-Defamation League
  www.adl.org/default.htm
- Early Head Start National Resource Center
  www.ehsnrc.org
- National Association for Multicultural Education
  www.nameorg.org
- National Head Start Association
  www.nhsa.org

YOUR STANDARDS PORTFOLIO

NAEYC 4c: Teaching and Learning: Understanding Content Knowledge in Early Education*

Organizing and designing classroom experiences is one of the most challenging tasks in education. To engage children in learning about new ideas, begin by creating experiences that are meaningful and relevant to each one. Conveying content in a developmentally and culturally appropriate way calls for early childhood educators to base selection of materials and resources on knowledge about the needs and characteristics of young children. To demonstrate how you meet this important standard, complete the following activities:

- Review a curricular guide used at a local center and identify ways to adapt the content to make it interesting to children from culturally diverse backgrounds.

- Observe in an early childhood classroom with diverse learners. Based on your observations, develop a thematic unit on a topic of interest for the children.

- Create a list of materials appropriate to teach literacy concepts for children who are English Language Learners and children with disabilities.

REFERENCES

Baruth, L., & Manning, M. L. (2008). *Multicultural education of children and adolescents* (5th ed.). Boston: Allyn & Bacon.

Caravantes, P. (2004). *Waging peace: The story of Jane Addams.* Greensboro, NC: Reynolds.

Dahlberg, G., Moss, P., & Pence, A. (2006). *Beyond quality in early education and care: Postmodernist perspectives.* New York: RoutledgeFalmer.

Derman-Sparks, L., & the A.B.C. Task Force. (1989). *Anti-bias curriculum: Tools for empowering young children.* Washington, DC: National Association for the Education of Young Children.

Federal Interagency Forum on Child and Family Statistics. (2004). *America's Children in Brief: Key National Indicators of Well-Being: 2004.* Author. Retrieved August 24, 2008, from http://www.childstats.gov/pdf/ac2004/ac_04.pdf.

Garcia, E. (2005). *Teaching and learning in two languages: Bilingualism and schooling in the United States.* New York: Teachers College Press.

Gollnick, D., & Chinn, P. (2006). *Multicultural education in a pluralistic society* (7th ed.). New York: Prentice Hall.

Gómez Tejera, C., & Cruz López, D. (1970). *La escuela Puertorriqueña* [The Puerto Rican school]. Sharon, CT: Troutman.

---

* NAEYC Standard 4c correlates with INTASC Standard 1: Subject Matter.

Head Start Bureau. (2004). Statement of purpose. Head Start Act, Section 636. Washington, DC: U.S. Department of Health and Human Services.

Head Start Bureau. (2005). *Head Start facts.* Washington, DC: U.S. Department of Health and Human Services.

Hopstock, P., and Stephenson, T. (2003). *Descriptive study of services to LEP students and LEP students with disabilities.* Washington, DC: NCELA, p. 11.

Howe, K. (1992). Liberal democracy, equal educational opportunity, and the challenge of multiculturalism. *American Educational Research Journal 29,* 455–470.

Kelley, R. D. G., & Lewis, E. (2000). *To make our world anew: A history of African Americans.* New York: Oxford University Press.

Kromkowski, J. (1994). (Ed.). *Race and ethnic relations 94/95.* Guilford, CT: Dushkin.

National Association of Multicultural Education. (2003). Definition of multicultural education. Retrieved on September 3, 2008, from http://www.nameorg.org/resolutions/definition.html.

National Clearinghouse for English Language Acquisition and Language Instruction Educational Programs (NCELA). (2006). *NCELA FAQ: How many school-aged English language learners (ELLs) are there in the U.S.?* Retrieved September 5, 2008, from http://www.ncela.gwu.edu/expert/faq/01leps.html.

National Council of Teachers of English. (2006). Position paper on the role of English teachers in educating English language learners. Urbana, IL: Author. Retrieved July 10, 2008, from http://www.ncte.org/about/over/positions/category/div/124545.htm.

Osborn, K. (1998). *Project Head Start: An assessment.* In K. Paciorek & J. Munro (Eds.), *Sources: Notable selections in early childhood education* (Article 12.2). Guilford, CT: Dushkin.

Paasha, C. L., Gorrill, L., & Strom, B. (2003). *Children with special needs in early childhood settings.* New York: Delmar Cengage Learning.

Smith, L. G., & Smith, J. (1994). *Lives in education: A narrative of people and ideas* (2nd ed.). New York: St. Martin's Press.

Tabors, P. (1997). *One child, two languages: A guide for preschool educators of children learning English as a second language.* Baltimore, MD: Paul Brookes.

Takei, G. (1994). *To the stars: The autobiography of George Takei.* New York: Pocket Books.

Tovar, R. F. (1973). *Chronological history of Puerto Rico.* New York: Plus Ultra Educational Publishers.

Turner-Sadler, J. (2006). *African American History: An introduction.* New York: Peter Lang.

U.S. Census Bureau. (2000). American FactFinder. Retrieved July 8, 2005, from http://www.factfinder.census.gov/servlet/ThematicMapFramesetsrvlet?_bm=y&MapEvent=dir.

U.S. Census Bureau. (2003). *Language use and English-speaking ability 2000* (Figure 4). Retrieved September 7, 2008, from http://www.census.gov/prod/2003pubs/c2kbr-29.pdf.

U.S. Department of Health and Human Services. (2005). *Head Start Fact Sheet.* Retrieved July 9, 2005, from http://www.acf.hhs.gov/programs/hsb/research/2005.htm.

Watkins, W. H., & Kelley, R. D. G. (2001). *The white architects of black education: Ideology and power in America, 1865–1954.* New York: Teachers College Press.

Zanjani, S. (2004). *Sarah Winnemucca.* Lincoln, NB: University of Nebraska Press.

Zrinyi Long, N. A. (2004). *The life and legacy of Mary McLeod Bethune.* Cocoa, FL: Florida Historical Society.

CHAPTER 6

Approaches to Multicultural Education: Ways and Designs for Classroom Implementation

> Multicultural education is a vision of what education can be, should be, and must be for all students.
>
> *Hilda Hernandez (2001)*

CHAPTER OBJECTIVES

In this chapter, we will

- define the curriculum process in multicultural education.
- examine selected approaches and models for multicultural education.
- establish the applicability of multicultural approaches in the early childhood context.

KEY CONCEPTS

- approach
- model
- curriculum
- cultural contributions
- antibias

FROM BARBARA'S JOURNAL

After I finished my student teaching, I thought that I would remember all the things I learned in my methods courses. Well, it's not that simple. Most of the time I have been preoccupied with getting to know the children, the school, the curriculum, the parents, and my colleagues. Now that things have settled down a bit, I find there is a lot of room for creativity and my contributions to the curriculum. I made up my mind to put my personal stamp on my teaching. I have observed my friend Kim's class and attended a couple of professional development workshops and conference sessions about multicultural topics. I learned that there are actual models for implementation that have been created by some of the best-known professionals in the field. Talking with my friends and reading about teaching strategies has helped me to see that there are many ways to create exciting learning experiences. I am going to apply some of their ideas in the lessons and thematic units that I am planning for the children. Creativity is my strong point, but now I realize that it's not enough. Instruction needs to be effective, appropriate, and, most importantly, culturally meaningful for my children. That's what I want to accomplish.

| TIME FOR DECISIONS

This chapter begins with the assumption that you have made a decision to bring multicultural education into your classroom. Congratulations! Now, it is time to make important decisions.

Having looked at some of the ideas that describe the origins of multicultural education, now you can search for ways to translate the ideas into practice. Hopefully, by now you realize the importance of multiculturalism and are determined to make multicultural education benefit your young students. These resolutions are part of the first phase, "exploring and thinking," that is experienced by teachers when moving toward acceptance of multicultural education. The next two phases, "making choices" and "activating ideas," are related to implementation and practices (Figure 6-1).

| WHY ENGAGE IN EDUCATIONAL REFORM?

What you are about to begin can best be defined as educational reform in action. Teachers throughout the United States already know or have heard that multicultural education is one of today's educational priorities. Many of them experience diversity daily in their own classrooms as a result of cultural diversification in communities across this country. Consequently, conscientious teachers of the young have come to recognize the opportunities found in teaching culturally diverse children. They are aware that providing developmentally appropriate responsive educational programs now requires a different method of delivery. This constitutes educational reform.

FIGURE 6-1 **Phases of Multicultural Education**

Moving into Multicultural Teaching	
Phase I:	*Exploring and thinking*
	Inquiring about the need and the supporting rationale. Reflecting upon your findings. Formulating a personal conviction. Establishing why multicultural education is considered important (both for the child and personally).
Phase II:	*Making choices*
	Selecting and deciding on the ways to design the program. Exploring the available models, approaches, practices, and materials. Reconfirming the decision to teach multiculturally.
Phase III:	*Activating ideas*
	Implementing the program. Constantly revising to redirect the efforts.

| GETTING TO WORK

The transition from believing in multicultural education to putting it into practice should be a simple process. However, many early childhood educators find themselves facing barriers. In recent years, whenever teachers were asked about major obstacles to translating multicultural education into practice, the responses have been the same: "What does it look like?" and "How can I do it?" Reflected in these questions are two major issues. The first question reveals the problem of finding a design or pattern to follow as a practical model. The second presents a dual issue: (1) the nature and feasibility of the model and (2) how it matches the individual characteristics of the learners. There is always a need for guidelines when dealing with innovation. The absence of both model and guidelines has often accounted for the inertia found among teachers. Lack of adequate knowledge is also a reason given by teachers when they are asked why multicultural education has not yet become a part of their school's curricula.

When teachers are empowered, the desire to effect change is heightened and their willingness to engage in change increases. This book is intended to empower you to transform those desires and aspirations into reality by providing you with the following:

1. Assistance in making a decision to teach in a multicultural way
2. Relevant knowledge that will help you implement a multicultural program

In this effort, we adhere to the principles drawn from Paulo Freire's ideas. Central to his concept of *critical pedagogy* lies the importance of knowledge and the power it offers to those who possess it (Freire, 2000). Education in Freirean ideology is an instrument capable of eroding social inequalities by providing students with knowledge. In his view, effective and meaningful experiences take place when teachers recognize the role of the students' realities and cultures in shaping their identities. He also views

Good planning and effective teaching go hand in hand.

learning as a dialogue where teachers engage students in exploring and critically discussing ideas and situations (Leystina, 2004; Merret, 2000). Well-informed teachers, within the context of Freire's thesis, can become effective participants and serve as leaders of the multicultural education movement.

In this chapter, we will examine some of the existing models and approaches of leading multiculturalists. Part III of this book is designed to answer the question, *How can I teach multiculturally?*

| EXPLORING APPROACHES AND MODELS

The terms *approach* and *model* are often used interchangeably in education. Essentially, they indicate what a teacher does to orient, organize, and deliver the curriculum.

Establishing Definitions

An **approach** is a set of guidelines that defines an overall method used to attain a specific purpose. An approach dictates ways to present, develop, and select topics for classroom instruction. In the context of multicultural education, an approach describes techniques and practices for dealing with diversity issues. Whole language and collaborative learning are two examples of instructional approaches.

A **model** is a conceptual framework of sequential stages and processes designed to meet a specific purpose or to complete a process. Models can be structured or fluid. A structured model's procedures and ways to implement them are specified and must be followed. On the other hand, fluid models allow for modification as required by the target population. They are often named after or attributed to leading authorities in a special field or discipline. Bank Street (Goffin, 2001) and High/Scope (Schweinhart & Weikart, 1997) are examples of models.

There are many ways to define *curriculum*. For Gordon and Browne (2007), **curriculum** includes practically all "that happens" at school. Williams (1999) notes that the term *curriculum* can have many different meanings. For some educators, curriculum is established by their school districts, whereas others consider it to be what they construct based on their experience and knowledge about children. However, Williams adds that most educators of children from birth to age 8 see the curriculum as centered

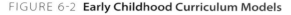

FIGURE 6-2 **Early Childhood Curriculum Models**

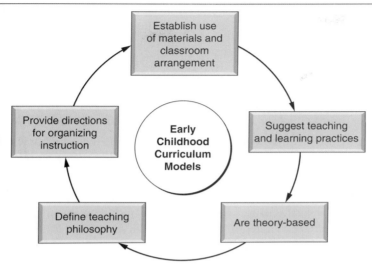

and emerging from the whole child. This idea is in agreement with the essential parameters of developmental appropriateness and is relevant for teachers examining ways to bring multiculturalism into the early childhood classroom. We believe that the multicultural curriculum is what emerges after a careful analysis of the needs, individual and family characteristics, and interests of the child and also of the particular cultural and societal needs of the community. In this process, teachers are instrumental in creating a culturally responsive curriculum.

Like templates, curriculum models include directions for implementing educational programs (Figure 6-2). A curriculum also provides ways to organize the educational environment. Evans (quoted in Goffin, 2001) explains that a curriculum model also "refers to a conceptual framework for decision making about educational priorities, administrative policies, instructional methods, and evaluation criteria."

Key Characteristics of Appropriate Early Childhood Multicultural Curriculum

A variety of models and implementation plans have been proposed since the beginnings of multicultural education in the 1960s. The central tenet in all of them is that awareness and building knowledge about the many cultures in our society promotes the understanding necessary for optimizing personal interactions. The teacher decides which model to select. As you examine the approaches and models presented in this chapter, take notes on their characteristics and ways in which they align with the children's learning experiences. More importantly, start pondering how the approaches and models described here would respond to the needs of the children in your community or those you teach. Remember that providing a quality program is only possible when you consider the cultural reality of the children you teach as well as their needs. To help you reaffirm your decision to begin teaching multiculturally, bear in mind that this is a way to support the children's developmental needs. An appropriate early childhood multicultural curriculum recognizes the following:

- Experiences during the early years contribute to shaping and influencing one's attitudes and ways to interpret reality.

- Opportunities for children to learn about themselves and about their own ways and heritages are essential for supporting positive social and emotional development.

- Classroom interactions with peers and adults with diverse characteristics prepare children to perceive differences as part of social reality and contribute to building an appreciation of others and their cultures.

- Responsive curricular experiences engage the child in meaningful learning about cultures and diversity issues. Exploration of real-life events and behaviors, such as occurrences of racism and other unfair practices, help children to recognize and talk about them and take action.

- Challenging and meaningful experiences for children promote knowledge about their own culture and those of their peers and environment.

Guidelines for Examining Models

Selecting what you like is not always an easy task. As you read through this section, you will begin to make choices about the models you prefer. Be sure to acquaint yourself with all of them before making your choice. Remember that engaging in successful educational reform requires much reflection. The list of guidelines in Figure 6-3 will assist you in examining the different multicultural models.

FIGURE 6-3 **Guidelines for the Evaluation of Teaching Models**

Name of model: _____

Age/grade level I teach: _____

 A. Main tenets of the model
  1. What are the basic assumptions and theories about the nature of multicultural education on which the model is based?
  2. What are the emphases?
  3. Check for developmentally and culturally appropriate practices (DCAP)
   a. Are the tenets consistent with the DAP criteria?
   b. Are the beliefs consistent with research and theory regarding:
    (1) children's social and emotional development?
    (2) children's intellectual development?

B. Goals of the model
   1. What are the expected outcomes?
   2. What kind of materials, if any, are needed?
   3. DCAP check
      a. Are the activities adequate for the age level of the children I teach?
      b. Are the activities consistent with child development principles?

C. Personal opinion
   1. Do I agree with the model's tenets?
   Yes, I agree because _____
   _____
   _____
   _____

   No, I do not agree because _____
   _____
   _____
   _____

   2. As an early childhood educator, do I agree with the goals and practices of the model?
   3. Do I believe I can implement the model in my classroom? (If the answer is no, why not?)

| MODELS OF MULTICULTURAL EDUCATION

Models of multicultural education are of two types: those developed through an analysis of existing experiences derived from classroom practices and those that are based on specific approaches or theories. For example, Banks (1994) and Sleeter and Grant (1994) developed their implementation models through the analysis of existing practices. The Starting Small model from the Southern Poverty Law Center and Gussin-Paley (1997) is another example that emerged from successful practices exhibited by teachers in selected classrooms across the United States. These models provide frameworks and recommendations for practice. Among the theory-based models are those of Derman-Sparks (1989), Kendall (1996), and Derman-Sparks and Ramsey (2006).

Proposed models for the implementation of multicultural education all have in common the fact that they evolved out of the efforts begun in the 1960s. They also share the belief that persistence in the use of a mainstream-centric curriculum does not facilitate the attainment of the *e pluribus unum* ("out of the many, one") ideal, which, according to Banks (1994), is the ultimate goal of education in the United States. Banks also says that insistence on following current mainstream-centric curricula is detrimental not only to children of diverse backgrounds but also to mainstream children. In his opinion, mainstream-centric curriculum is negative for mainstream students because it provides

Classroom experiences offer a variety of opportunities to explore diversity. Carefully selected and developmentally appropriate materials can engage the child in learning about his or her own cultural characteristics and those of peers.

. . . a misleading conception of their relationship with other racial and ethnic groups, and denies them the opportunity to benefit from the knowledge, perspectives, and frames of reference that can be gained from studying and experiencing other cultures and groups. A mainstream-centric curriculum also denies children . . . the opportunity to view their culture from the perspectives of other cultures and groups.

Recognizing that infusion of multiculturalism in education is essential for all children, educators such as Banks, Sleeter, Grant, Kendall, and Derman-Sparks have designed different educational models. Each of these educators has analyzed existing practices, giving an account of the process. They also propose models most consistent with their beliefs.

Although none of these educators, with the exception of Kendall, Derman-Sparks, and Derman-Sparks and Ramsey, focus their ideas specifically on early childhood education, their observations provide practitioners with relevant information on multicultural teaching practices. While other frameworks have been proposed by educators and social researchers, for the purposes of this chapter, we will limit our inquiry to the models of authors already mentioned. These models provide more opportunities for teaching young children and are also basic and open frameworks that allow teachers to add their own elements or build their own frameworks. If at any point you feel that the curricular ideas proposed in a model do not fit into your philosophy of early childhood education, review its main tenets for suggestions and ideas for designing your own multicultural curriculum. One way for teachers to teach responsively is by designing their own teaching models. We hope this discussion will assist you in building models based on the realities of the children in your classrooms.

Banks's Levels of Integration of Multicultural Content

James Banks, one of the leaders in multicultural education in the United States, has studied the evolution of multiculturalism since its beginnings. For Banks (2006), multicultural education is an idea and a process based on the premise that all students, despite their backgrounds, should have equal educational opportunities. That premise sustains the need to review and transform the curriculum to incorporate cultural diversity elements.

FIGURE 6-4 **Banks's Levels of Integration**

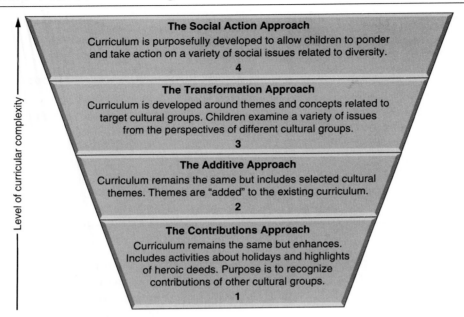

Source: Adapted from Banks, 2006.

A witness to evolution of multiculturalism in schools, Banks describes the various approaches in multicultural education used during the past three decades. The common link in all these approaches is curricular change. Change, in Banks's view, happens as ethnic and multicultural content is integrated into the existing curriculum, with integration taking place at varying levels. Banks proposes four levels of multicultural curricular integration. These levels are of ascending value, relating to both degree of complexity and degree of commitment to multicultural education (Figure 6-4). In the next section, you will find a description of each of these levels with applications to the early childhood classroom.

Level 1—The Contributions Approach

Level 1 in Banks's typology is described as the Contributions Approach. At this level, topics about ethnic groups are added to the regular curriculum (2006). Occasionally, ethnic contributions are also presented through a selection of holidays and ethnic elements such as food and music. Banks warns that these insertions add to the existing curriculum but do not alter the already existing curricular goals and objectives. Including ethnic names and objects has basically the effect of "filling in" rather than promoting knowledge about the social reality in a diverse society (Figure 6-5).

Level 1 can be seen as a beginning effort to integrate multicultural concepts into the curriculum. This level requires limited knowledge about the material that is added.

FIGURE 6-5 **Examples of Ethnic Content in Level 1**

Topics teachers include when using the contributions approach may include the following:

Heroes
- Eugenio M. de Hostos
- Benito Juárez
- Martin Luther King, Jr.
- Pocahontas

Artifacts
- food (eating tamales)
- dances (dancing a Venezuelan *joropo*)
- crafts (making an *ojo de Dios*)
- musical instruments (playing the ukulele)

Holidays
- October: Hispanic heritage month
- January: Chinese New Year
- February: Black history month
- May: Cinco de Mayo

Because these topics are presented as brief snapshots, relevant aspects of specific cultures are often not the focus. Actually, if teachers are not careful in their selection and presentation of the topics, concepts may be displayed in stereotypical ways. Although well intentioned, this practice communicates misleading information to the child. An example of commonly shown stereotypes is the use of "gauchos" to depict Argentineans or portraying calypso dancers as representative of all the people in the Caribbean. One of our students told us that her second-grade class doubted her Japanese heritage because she did not wear a kimono. These examples are but a few of the many instances in which children's ideas are influenced by their exposure to stereotypes either present in the media or learned from interactions with peers and adults.

We have a responsibility to remember the power that teachers exert over children. Information presented in class often remains with students through a lifetime. If cultural contributions are not carefully selected, students are likely to derive little from these experiences. An important point regarding the Level 1 approach is that it serves as an initial step for many early educators who decide to infuse perspectives of diversity into their curriculum. Such efforts deserve to be acknowledged and commended because the teachers are demonstrating a commitment to change classroom experiences. Providing teachers with support and opportunities for learning more about how to integrate ethnic topics into the curriculum is crucial at this point. This can help teachers continue the process of curricular change.

Level 2—The Additive Approach

The Additive Approach, or Level 2, is based on the addition "of content, concepts, themes, and perspectives to the curriculum without changing its basic structures, purposes, and characteristics" (Banks, 2006). In this approach, teachers select an ethnic topic and plan activities around it. In Banks's opinion, this second level implies a first step toward the transformation of the curriculum. Success of this approach depends on how the teacher organizes the presentation of the concepts in accordance with the developmental characteristics of the children. Examples of how this level could be practiced in the early childhood classroom appear in Figure 6-6.

FIGURE 6-6 **Working with the Additive Approach**

Applying the Additive Approach in the Classroom (4- to 5-year-olds)

Main theme: Things we like to eat at home and at school
Concept: Food
Integration: Social studies, science, math, literacy

Topics to explore:

1. Foods we like
2. Food we eat for breakfast
3. Food we eat at school
4. Food children eat in Japan and Mexico*

Literacy
Objectives: Learning new words, learning food words, learning words in other languages, comparing and contrasting, sequencing, retelling

Books to share and discuss with children:

1. Carle, E. (1970). *Pancakes, pancakes.*
2. Brown, M. (1947). *Stone soup.*
3. Brandenburg, A. (1976). *Corn is maize: The gift of the Indians.**
4. Hitte, K. (1970). *Mexican soup.**
5. Morris, A. (1989). *Bread, bread, bread.**
6. Baer, E. (1995). *This the way we eat our lunch: A book about children around the world.**

Social studies activities
Objectives: Identifying eating patterns, investigating the eating schedule in other countries, discussing how fruits and vegetables get to the grocery store, locating places where our food comes from, mapping

1. Preparing charts describing what children prefer for breakfast, dinner
2. Making a graph to show the class favorite fruits, vegetables, and so on
3. Taking a field trip to an ethnic grocery store to identify what they have*
4. Preparing a cooperative map to show the places/countries where our preferred food items come from
5. Learning the names of favorite dishes in another language*
6. Discussing the eating schedules in other countries*

(continued)

FIGURE 6-6 **(continued)**

Science/cooking experiences

Objectives: Observing changes in food (when mashed, ground, cooked), tasting, comparing flavors, identifying vegetables and fruits with similar colors

1. Making applesauce
2. Making Mexican quesadillas (cheese-filled tortillas)*
3. Making an Asian vegetable salad*
4. Tasting different types of cheeses
5. Comparing different types of breads (flat or unleavened, sweet, salty, crusty, and so on)*
6. Preparing a cooperative vegetable soup with vegetables from different countries (for instance, root vegetables, pumpkin, white sweet potatoes, plantains)*

Art experiences

Objectives: Using art to represent one's ideas, using common house items to create art, working cooperatively

1. Preparing a picture menu
2. Making "food mobiles"
3. Preparing a cooperative mural about food children eat in the United States, Japan, and Mexico*

Indicates insertion of ethnic content.

Level 3—The Transformation Approach

The third level, the Transformation Approach, represents a phase of substantial changes. At this level, teachers reconstruct the curriculum on the assumption that the content should address targeted situations involving social justice areas that children may be able to relate and explore. Content based on the Transformation Approach is designed to enable students to examine the issues from a variety of perspectives. As students look at a problem from a variety of angles, they gain an enhanced concept of the reality or of the time being studied. For example, while exploring how to reorganize the classroom, children can be led to consider how to facilitate access for peers that may have physical disabilities. Another example is presented in Figure 6-7.

Banks (2006) recommends that teachers applying the Transformation Approach remember that the key lies in the presentation of logically infused "perspectives, frames of reference, and content from various groups." He warns against adding topics to the already existing curriculum and recommends fusing the new with concepts already familiar to children. For the early childhood teacher, this means selecting materials that will not only respond to the developmental levels and interests of children but also be pertinent to the child. In this type of approach, considering the surrounding reality of the child is crucial to making the curriculum valid and culturally responsive. The term *responsive* is used because children are not only discovering their cultural identities but

FIGURE 6-7 **Transformation Approach—Let's Talk About Ornaments**

A kindergarten teacher who uses the Level-3 approach would make the following changes in the curriculum:

Theme: Things we wear and use

Topic: We all use personal ornaments

Concepts:

1. People are alike and different in many ways
2. People wear different objects
3. Personal ornaments have special meaning for people

Skills:

1. Looking for details
2. Observing and classifying
3. Identifying things that are alike and different

Goals:

1. To understand that most people use and wear personal ornaments (watches, bracelets, hair pins, scarves, necklaces, and so on)
2. To become aware of the different ornaments (earrings, Hindu dots [bindi], rings, African kente, and so on) that people in our community use
3. To realize that people with different cultural roots prefer different ornaments
4. To understand that ornaments have special meanings for people
5. To comment on the different occasions people use ornaments (weddings, birthdays, holidays, and so on)

Learning centers:

1. Housekeeping area: A variety of clothing reflective of what people in the community wear; an assortment of clothing and accessories used by the target cultural groups.
2. Art/manipulatives: A variety of materials to create ornaments and crafts, including beads, coconut shells, dry leaves and flowers, and so on. Have materials used for women's makeup (for example, kohl pencils, blush, and so on). Do the makeup on paper plate faces for different occasions.
3. Math/science: Estimate how many pieces of coconut are needed to make a necklace. Taste raw coconut and coconut flakes to compare their taste.
4. Movement: Listen to music typically used during special occasions (weddings, birthdays, and so on). Respond to the music by creating steps. Learn a typical dance.

(continued)

FIGURE 6-7 **(continued)**

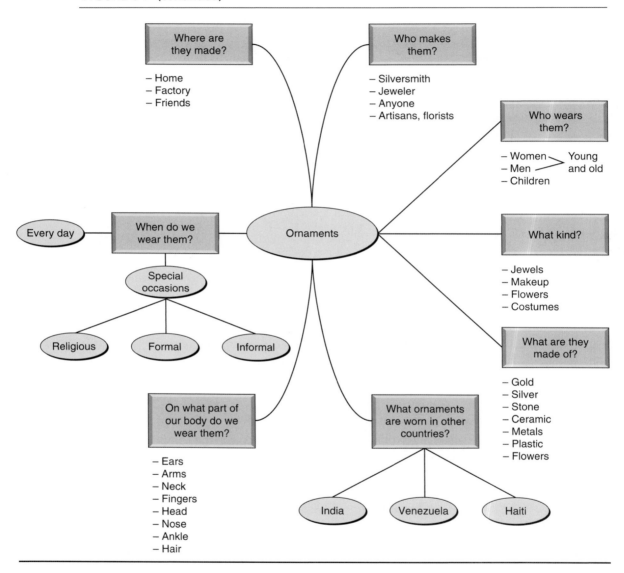

are also provided with opportunities to explore and learn about those of their peers. Teachers working with Level 3 know that it requires constant planning and a great deal of flexibility to accommodate necessary changes. The flexibility gives teachers an opportunity to offer a pool of socially significant experiences for young children.

F⭕CUS
on Classroom Practices

| Using Thematic Teaching to
Create the Level 3 Curriculum

Translating ideas into action is sometimes a hard thing to do. When some of our students began exploring how to apply the Transformation Approach, they felt overwhelmed by the task. As we talked with them, we discovered that they were trying to transform their entire program at once. We suggested that they start small by changing one small portion of the curriculum first. With that advice in mind, one of our students who teaches first grade chose to focus on the movement curriculum. Using thematic teaching as her strategy, she decided to target her activities on learning games from different cultures. She began by first selecting games played by people in the children's community (mainly European American) and then added games representing Asian and Hispanic cultures. Group games, musical games, dances were selected, providing opportunities for children to employ a wide variety of skills within the framework of play.

Using references such as *The Multicultural Game Book* by Louise Orlando (Scholastic, 1999) and *Children Around the World* by Verna Wilkins (QED Publishing, 2004), our student began to compile ideas for her curriculum. The result was an appealing curriculum in which children were introduced to diversity through one of the best cultural artifacts: games. As she told us later, this initial trial with the Transformation Approach was the bridge she used to move into other areas of multiculturalism. In her words, once she "tasted" teaching in a different way, she just could not go back to her old curriculum.

Theme: It Is Playtime!

- Favorite games of our families
- Games from the African American tradition (hot butter beans; skelly; roly poly; tin can alley; hand soccer; four squares; jack rocks)
- Traditional games of European American families (hide and seek, hopscotch, tops)
- Games from the Hispanic tradition (arroz con leche; Doña Ana*)
- Games and dances from other countries
  1. Ghana: The clapping game**
  2. Zaire: Catching stars***
  3. Taiwan: Clapstick blind man's buff**
  4. China: 1, 2, 3 dragon***
  5. Haiti: Manee gogo**
  6. Jamaica: Sally water**
  7. Puerto Rico: Ambos a dos; Candela, candela
  8. Chile: Guessing game (Quién es?**)
  9. Mexico: La raspa
  10. Brazil: Bossa nova

*Delacre, L. (2002). *Rafi and Rosi: Carnival. Popular songs and rhymes from Latin America.* New York: Scholastic Books.

**Nelson, W., & Glass, B. (1992). *International playtime: Classroom games and dances from around the world.* Carthage, IL: Fearon Teachers' Aids.

***Orlando, L. (1999). *The multicultural game book: More than 70 traditional games from 30 countries.* New York: Scholastic Books.

FOCUS
on Classroom Practices | Defining a Contribution

Perhaps you have already decided to follow the Contribution Approach. However, selecting what to include is sometimes difficult. Because you want to develop a good curriculum, it is important to begin defining what constitutes a cultural contribution. This will help you select appropriate themes.

Cultural contributions are those cultural details currently defining a culture and the events or actions that either made lasting changes or that dramatically affected the culture. The following example will help you identify and select key elements for your curriculum.

When identifying cultural contributions, look for the following:

- Events of lasting effect: independence of a country; abolition of slavery (in the United States and in other parts of the world; for instance, in Puerto Rico, the abolition of slavery is officially observed on March 22)
- Discoveries and inventions: geographical discoveries, such as the discovery of the Americas or of the Pacific Ocean by the

Europeans; scientific discoveries, such as the botanical work of George Washington Carver; inventions such as the helicopter by Russian scientist Igor Sikorsky
- Foundations of leading organizations: for example, the Red Cross and the United Nations
- Heroes or people distinguished because of their contributions to society: Mahatma Gandhi, leader of the nonviolent movement that led to the independence of India; Harriet Tubman, an African American woman who risked her life for the cause of freedom; Eugenio M. de Hostos, a distinguished educator and philosopher who influenced educational practices in the Caribbean; African American poet Maya Angelou, who has been recognized as one of the most important contemporary U.S. poets and writers
- The Arts: music, dances, drama, literature and poetry, crafts, and decorative arts
- Beliefs and traditions: festivals, folklore, myths

Level 4—The Decision-Making and Social Action Approach

The Social Action Approach is the highest level in Banks's typology and "includes all the elements of the Transformation Approach but adds components that require students to make decisions and take actions related to the concept, issue, or problem they have studied in the unit" (2006). Teachers using Level 4 have two major goals, both consistent with early childhood aspirations and practices (Bredekamp, 1989). They are the following:

1. To prepare children for social criticism (provide them with the ability to examine and analyze social situations and to originate and participate in the social change process)

2. To prepare children to become decision makers (help them learn decision-making skills)

Classroom instruction based on Level 4 is characterized by intense activity rather than the passive examination of issues and events from both the past and the present. Children operating in Level 4 are asked to analyze facts and practices closely. For example, a social analysis of a topic may be presented for the purpose of examining the issue of fairness. A goal of Level 4 is to confront children with situations describing unfair events for the purpose of leading them to take action. Expected behavior includes proposals of alternative views and suggestions of corrective measures for a situation. An example of this is the case of a preschool teacher who shared with her class the story of a homeless family who had moved to their community. After the children learned that the family living in their car was expecting a baby, they decided to help. Prompted by the teacher on how to help, the class suggested collecting items for the baby. The result was not only a well-assorted baby basket but also clothing and other items for the family. Teaching topics related to social realities provides valuable social learning experiences for children, who will discover that they can become agents for change.

Developing a curriculum based on Level 4 requires a careful selection of issues characterized by both relevancy and developmental pertinence. Lesson plans following the Social Action Approach have the four major components shown in Figure 6-8.

FIGURE 6-8 **Teaching Components of the Social Action Approach**

1 *A decision problem or a question* (an issue or situation that requires attention)

Example: Children are posed with the problem of a child who is being rejected by others because he speaks with an accent. Because of what is happening, the child does not want to come to school. Is there anything we can do? Is it right for others to make fun of him because of his accent?

2. *An inquiry that will provide children with data related to the problem* (questioning to discover the real cause of the problem, who is affected and how are they affected, and examples of the problem)

Example: Lead children in the analysis of the situation with questions such as:
- What do we know about the boy/girl who has the problem?
- Is it wrong or bad to be different?
- What happened to make the boy/girl feel bad?
- Is he/she the only one who is different in our classroom/school?
- If he/she is rejected, who else might feel rejected, too?

3. *A value inquiry and moral analysis* (discussions, role playing, presentation of different cases with the same issue)

Example: Children will read and discuss selected readings to further illustrate that what happened was wrong and that it hurts people. For instance, they could discuss stories like *All Kinds: Who Cares about Race and Colour?* (Child's Play International, 1989) and *Crow Boy* (Yashima, 1955).

(continued)

FIGURE 6-8 **(continued)**

4. *A decision and a list of social actions to be taken* (a final determination of the case and a list of needed actions to correct the issue)

Examples:

- Working in small groups, children can prepare an action plan to avoid similar situations. Children can also create a slogan to help them reinforce their commitment to what they have decided to do. For example, declaring the classroom as a place where "Everyone is welcome because we are all the same."

- Children can be prompted to take actions using questions such as:
  - What will this class do from now on?
  - If you find that someone is making a bad comment about another child, what should you do?
  - Can we help others understand what our beliefs are? How?

Source: Adapted from Banks, 2006.

Teaching with the Decision-Making and Social Action Approach provides ways to introducing children to topics that are not often studied in the classroom. While children can be introduced to topics such as social inequities, prejudice, and racism, these might be considered difficult or controversial by school colleagues and parents. Therefore, teachers who decide to teach about such issues must carefully select child-appropriate materials, experiences, and strategies, thus spending more time preparing to explore these in the classroom. Communication with families must be incorporated into the process if this approach is to be successful. A simple letter stating the topic and the purposes for studying it not only helps clarify them for those who have doubts but also allows families to see the need for the activities.

Creating a socially responsive curriculum in Level 4 is a challenging and exciting experience. This is a level that teachers can reach after they have gained experience and confidence dealing with the multicultural content. It is advisable to try the other levels before venturing into this highest one. Remember, moving toward reform takes time.

In Action . . . **Thinking About Banks's Approaches**

After learning about the levels or approaches that Banks proposes, take time to reflect and ask yourself the following questions:

- *Which one would I choose to use with children?*
- *Which one have I already experienced?*
- *Which one seems to be most developmentally appropriate for the children whom I teach? Why?*

LITERACY CONNECTIONS. . .

Using Stories to Engage Children in the Social Action Approach (Level 4)

Stories can spark interest for myriad topics related to social action in a culturally diverse society. In this section, you will find some of our age-appropriate favorites to share with young children.

Differences and racial issues

- Fresh, D. (2002). *Think again*. New York: Cartwheel. (primary-age)

- Igus, T. (2001). *Two Mrs. Gibsons*. San Francisco: Children's Book Press. (preschoolers–kindergartners)

- Katz, K. (2007). *The colors of us*. New York: Henry Holt. (preschoolers–kindergartners)

- Monk, I. (1999). *Hope*. Minneapolis, MN: Carolrhoda. (kindergartners and primary-age)

- Seuss, Dr. (2003). *The sneetches and other stories*. New York: Random House. (Original work published in 1961).

Homelessness

- Bunting, E. (2004). *Fly away home*. New York: Clarion. (preschoolers–primary)

- DySalvo, D. (1999). *Uncle Willie and the soup kitchen*. New York: Tandem Library.

- McGovern, A. (1999). *The lady in the box*. New York: Turtle Books. (primary)

Disabilities

- Fassler, J. (1974). *Howie helps himself*. New York: Albert Whitman. (preschoolers–primary)

- Shriver, M. (2001). *What's wrong with Timmy?* New York: Little, Brown. (preschoolers–primary)

Social class and family issues

- Bartoletti, S. (2001). *The Christmas promise*. New York: Blue Sky Press/Scholastic. (preschoolers–primary)

- Loh, M. (1991). *Tucking Mommy in*. New York: Orchard Books. (preschoolers–kindergartners)

- Woodson, J. (2002). *Visiting day*. New York: Scholastic. (preschoolers–primary)

Gender

- Morrow, B. (2003). *A good night for freedom*. New York: Holiday House. (preschoolers–primary)

- Moss, M. (2001). *Brave Harriet*. New York: Silver Whistle. (preschoolers–primary)

The Sleeter and Grant Typology for Multicultural Education

The model developed by Christine Sleeter and Carl Grant is a product of their extensive and continuous research in multicultural education. Their five approaches were constructed based on their experiences as educators and social scientists along with their extensive analyses of multicultural curricula in grades K–12 (Sleeter & Grant, 1994). These approaches are structured around the social diversity issues of race, class, disability, and gender. The typology also serves as a way to observe how multicultural education has evolved since its inception. The typology offers an array of possibilities from which early childhood professionals can choose and adapt the one that best fits their needs. In Sleeter and Grant's typology, multicultural education is offered through the following approaches:

1. Teaching the exceptional and the culturally different
2. Human relations
3. Single-group studies
4. Multicultural education
5. Education that is multicultural and social reconstructionist

Approach I: Teaching the Exceptional and the Culturally Different

The first approach is a description of the programs many educators find in their districts. The essence of teaching the exceptional and the culturally different is based on the factors that make some students different from the mainstream. These factors include having a particular disability, being a part of a given social class or minority group, having a different language, or being a low-achieving female (Sleeter & Grant, 2006). These factors are also seen as areas that require actions. Actions are taken with the purpose of facilitating the child's entrance into the existing social structure of the United States. The belief here is that if children are taught according to their needs, they will be able to perform effectively. Providing the child with the necessary skills, knowledge, and language to effectively participate in society is the main goal of this approach.

Teachers following this approach adapt instruction to the students' skill levels and particular learning styles. Practices are based upon four important elements or bridges (Sleeter & Grant, 2006):

1. *Curriculum content:* This consists of challenging experiences that both engage and build necessary skills through meaningful content and relevant language.
   a. *Meaningful content:* The curriculum is designed around themes of interest to children and is related to their reality. Teachers need to have mastery of content (skills, concepts, and facts) as well as the ability to link the children's realities with what is being learned.
   b. *Language needs:* Strategies need to be carefully selected to support language learning for students with first languages other than English. Classroom activities must

connect to the children's experiences "to make the content user friendly" (Sleeter & Grant, 2006). Teachers need to be aware of second language strategies and processes to plan experiences that support the children's learning. Teachers must keep in mind that acquiring another language takes time and that it happens as children learn the content.

2. *Instructional process*: Selection and use of age-appropriate and individualized pedagogical activities is essential. Adaptations must be made to respond to the children's learning styles and modalities. Practices need to be adapted to the characteristics of individuals and groups.

3. *Program structure:* There are several program formats for children who are culturally different or exceptional, such as inclusion, pullout, self-contained classes, after-school, and gifted enrichment programs. Typically, children with language differences may be served in bilingual classrooms, pullout programs, and ESL classrooms. Most schools also have compensatory education programs that provide additional educational experiences and assistance (such as Title I, Head Start, Even Start, Early Head Start, and other readiness programs).

4. *Parent involvement*: Collaborations with parents and families of exceptional or culturally different children are essential. For such collaborations to be successful, teachers need to be aware of the cultural nuances of such relationships. Showing respect and consideration toward the parents and family members is essential for building effective alliances that benefit the children.

School programs following this approach are structured in four different ways. Sleeter and Grant state that one form is when schools keep the exceptional or culturally different child in the regular program, to which adaptations are made. A second approach is to keep the child in the same school program while offering academic support and enrichment. Pullout programs, the third way, are those in which the child spends some time away from the regular classroom receiving additional support. The fourth structure is assignment of children to an entirely different program where they remain until they have overcome their deficiencies and can be integrated into the regular

Wadsworth/Cengage Learning

Culturally appropriate materials, visuals, and literacy resources and a well-designed classroom environment are effective ways to support second language learning.

school program. (This practice is being reconsidered as a result of the movement toward inclusion.) Examples of this approach can be found in the following:

- ESOL programs
- Title I programs
- Bilingual kindergarten programs
- Self-contained special education programs
- Programs for children at risk
- Head Start and Even Start programs

Commenting about the first approach, Sleeter and Grant (2006) say that it reflects the ideas of those who perceive our society "as the land of opportunity and as a good, technological society that is constantly improving itself." For this reason, the exceptional and culturally different child needs help to enter the U.S. mainstream.

FOCUS on Classroom Practices | Selecting Early Childhood Context for the Level 4 Curriculum

Working with Banks's Level 4 requires careful preparation. It particularly requires effective selection of the issues children will explore. One of the ways to find sound and child-valid topics is to create a list of possible areas requiring social action both at the community level and at the national and international levels. To do this, you will need good observation and analytic skills. As you exercise them, you will find that there are plenty of areas to study. We have listed some suggestions to help you select themes for your classroom. When considering what topics or social issues to include, look for the following:

- Issues arising from the classroom or school interaction patterns: For example, an incident of name calling, cases of lack of acceptance of some children and adults because of their religious ideas, or reluctance to interact with adults based on their appearance.

- Issues from the community: For instance, cases of violent acts, situations of unfair practices against elderly people, loss of a recreational area, presence of homeless people.

- Issues at the national and/or international level: Possible topics are poverty, cases of unfairness because of people's status, loss of housing because of commercial expansion or construction, cases of violence against families, situations forcing people to leave their countries (immigrants and refugees), effects of epidemic diseases, and needs of communities after a natural disaster.

- Issues from the past: Examples include examining the life of African Americans during the years of slavery, emotions of Africans as they were taken away from their homeland, reactions of Native Americans as they were forced to abandon their land and lifestyles, heroic accomplishments for the cause of justice, children and the Holocaust, and the lives of immigrants.

Approach II: Human Relations

The second approach offers specific suggestions to create and organize a multicultural curriculum. Grounded on the idea of prosocial behavior, the concept of human relations evokes many ideas but essentially brings to mind the desire for positive interaction among people aside from their characteristics. Central to this approach is promoting positive feelings in children that lead them to a sense of unity, tolerance, and acceptance of social diversity within the existing framework of U.S. society. With such expectations, all children become the target. The following are the goals of this approach:

- To help students communicate with, accept, and get along with people who are different from them
- To reduce or eliminate stereotypes that students have (or might have) about people
- To help students feel good about themselves as individuals and as members of the group they belong to
- To prevent situations in which children offend others by putting them down because of their affiliations or characteristics (Sleeter & Grant, 1994)

Four basic principles define the human relations approach. First, this is a comprehensive approach, requiring infusion of its tenets throughout the entire curriculum. Sleeter and Grant recommend that this kind of program become schoolwide to avoid sending mixed messages to students. As a second principle, they recommend using a variety of teaching strategies that actively engage children. The third principle emphasizes the use of real-life and child-relevant experiences. Lastly, activities should be built around success for all children. Teachers should avoid competition and in its place should emphasize participation and involvement as end goals for classroom experiences. When using this approach in the curriculum, some of the themes could include the following:

- *We are friends*
- *We care for people*
- *Sharing with our friends*
- *I am important*
- *My family and yours*
- *We all have feelings*
- *Friends everywhere*
- *We can all play together*
- *We all live and work together in a community*
- *We are alike and we are different*

The goals and principles of human relations are consistent with the ideas of many early childhood professionals. To effectively organize a human relations curriculum, teachers need to keep in mind that the emphasis is on the development of prosocial behavior as the vehicle to promote positive interactions among all. Caution should be placed in the selection of topics in order to avoid falling into the trap of stereotypical and condescending material. For instance, in examining topics about the family, inclusive and broad views about the many different family memberships found in the classroom and community should be presented. Topics and activities must be age-appropriate and culturally sound. Teachers need to check materials constantly to verify that opportunities to develop a sense of fairness and equality are appropriately presented. In fact, use of this approach can provide relevant enabling experiences for teachers, preparing them to engage in more complex approaches to multicultural education.

Approach III: Single-Group Studies

This approach represents one of the three more complex methods of multicultural education. The term, coined by Sleeter and Grant, defines those programs in which a particular cultural group or element of diversity becomes the central focus of study. Promotion of social equality for a special group, as well as the recognition of that group, is the essence of the single-group studies approach. Advocates of this approach believe that exposing students to the realities of a specific group will result in the reduction of social stratification. Targets commonly chosen include women, ethnic groups such as Asian Americans, people with disabilities, or the working class (Sleeter & Grant, 2006). An important goal of this approach is to provide students with relevant knowledge that will encourage their willingness "to work toward social change that would benefit the identified group" (Sleeter & Grant, 2006).

When using this approach, early childhood teachers need to consider that effective teaching requires integration of subject areas. Topics taught in isolation may contribute little to the formation of ideas. Because children learn when concepts are presented in a holistic way, presentation of target topics must permeate all classroom activities. In designing curricular activities, remember that learning occurs as a result of the child's exposure to a continuum of logically interrelated experiences. Effective plan-

Interactions among children are facilitated during playtime. These experiences prepare them to learn to see each one as part of the group. They also contribute to learning how to communicate with and accept others.

Wadsworth/Cengage Learning

ning of the single-group approach resembles thematic teaching, in which children are immersed in the topic throughout the entire program. Opportunities for application are crucial in this approach, both for assessment purposes and as ways to provide the child with instances showing the actual need and importance of the concepts explored. Topics for single-group studies can be organized around investigative questions (Figure 6-9).

Classroom teaching structured around single-group studies requires careful preparation and knowledge about the chosen group. Sleeter and Grant (2006) recommend using authentic materials produced by and focused on members of the targeted group. This step is relevant if teachers want to demonstrate how people in that group perceive and feel about given events or facts. An accurate portrayal of the group's opinions and feelings will help students determine whether equality exists. These studies may also help children learn how each group interprets and views social reality. For example, children can examine the importance of knowing how to address a Hispanic adult (by his or her title rather than by the first name, if you are not a close friend). This will help them learn how social relationships are interpreted by that group.

Because of its empowering character, this approach is particularly valuable in helping children learn not only about themselves but also to begin gaining an appreciation about their own cultures. Effectively used, this approach is also valuable in helping the child develop a proactive awareness about social and cultural issues.

As with any other approach, caution should be used not only in the selection of topics but also in their treatment and presentation. Many times, in spite of the best teaching intentions, topics are presented in a trivial and stereotypical form. Taking time for good planning and reflection is the best way to infuse quality into our teaching experiences.

FIGURE 6-9 **Topics for Single-Group Studies at the Primary Level (Ages 5–8)**

- Life of homeless children
  (Who are the homeless? Who can become a homeless person? How does it feel when you do not have a home? Who helps the homeless? How can we help the homeless?)
- Learning about people with disabilities
  (What does it mean to have a disability? How do people with disabilities feel? How can we help?)
- Learning about refugees
  (Why do people leave their countries? How can we help?)
- Valuing our elders
  (Who are our elders? Why are they important to us? What can we learn from them? How can we show respect and appreciation toward our elders?)
- Learning about children in other neighborhoods
  (Where do they live? What activities do they do? What are their schools like? What games do they play? What do we have in common? In what ways are they unique?)

F⟋CUS
on Classroom Practices | Planning Activities for the Human Relations Approach

Structuring an effective human relations curriculum means that we select goals and objectives that are child-appropriate and use child-appropriate strategies. We begin by establishing target goals similar to those proposed by Sleeter and Grant. Using them as guides, we then select a number of basic concepts. Finally, in choosing a teaching strategy we opt for literature-based thematic teaching. The result, shown next, is a teaching framework easily adaptable to any age level. As you read it, think about ways to adapt it for your own classroom.

Sample Framework Using the Human Relations Approach

Goal I: To get along with people who are different from ourselves

Theme 1: We all have things that make us special

Concepts:

• Discovering ourselves: Finding that we all are special in some way

• Accepting differences in ourselves and others

• Becoming friends with all the children in our class

Goal II: To eliminate and fight against stereotypes about people

Theme 2: We are all alike and diverse

Concepts:

• Welcoming people as they are

• Clarifying our ideas about ourselves and others

• We listen and think: Learning to stop words that hurt

Goal III: To feel proud about one's identity

Theme 3: We are happy being what we are

Concepts:

• Valuing ourselves and our families

• Feeling proud of our identities: Learning who we are (ethnicity, religion, language, and so on)

• Accepting others

Goal IV: To become aware of unfairness and to take action

Theme 4: You and I can help make a better society!

Concepts:

• Working with everyone: Learning to be a good member of the classroom and school

• We can do it: Helping stop unfairness

• We can help make everyone feel accepted

Approach IV: Multicultural Education

The multicultural education approach is based on the importance and value of cultural pluralism in U.S. society. A main tenet of this approach is that the United States is like a "tossed salad" made up of distinct parts to create a wonderful new whole (Sleeter & Grant, 2006). Rather than focusing on a specific curriculum topic, multicultural edu-

FIGURE 6-10 **Parameters of the Multicultural Education Approach**

1. To promote cultural values
2. To promote human rights and respect for those who are different from oneself
3. To promote alternative life choices for people
4. To promote social justice and equality for all people
5. To promote equity in the distribution of power and income among groups

Source: Gollnick & Chinn, 2005.

cation is viewed as a comprehensive curriculum reform process affecting all aspects of schooling. Important to the organization of the curriculum are the social contextual realities and experiences pertinent to the classroom audience. This approach shares similar characteristics with Banks's Level 3. Basic to the multicultural approach are the ways in which students are led to analyze social issues involving bias, prejudice, and racism.

Gollnick and Chinn (2005) have developed goals for the multicultural education approach (Figure 6-10).

Nieto and Bode (2007) claim that effective multicultural education programs require modifications to the entire school "culture." Such changes encompass not only the materials but also the content, which should be drawn out of the cultural backgrounds of the students. Ability grouping, the behaviors and attitudes of teachers and staff, and the ways parents are involved in the school should be reviewed and changed. These changes reflect what several authors have agreed on: Multicultural education is a process of total education reform (Banks, 2006; Gollnick & Chinn, 2005; Kendall, 1996; Nieto & Bode, 2007).

Although, ideally, this is an approach for implementation at the school level, it also provides direction for the early childhood teacher. When implemented, this approach requires the following steps:

1. *Knowledge of the classroom cultural composition:* Essential to any successful activity is knowledge about the cultural identities of both the class and the community. This step requires a clear concept of the cultural setting where your teaching takes place. No responsive planning can be done without a realistic assessment of the classrooms. Elements of diversity, such as religion and gender, are also considered cultures. The following are questions to answer:

   ■ *What are the cultures or diversity found in my classroom?*
   ■ *What are the cultures or diversity found in this community?*

2. *An appraisal of the existing curriculum:* Before you begin changing your curriculum, take time to analyze what you have. In other words, do not discard everything yet! In the process of determining the "fit," you will undoubtedly remove some topics and keep others. To expedite this analysis, review your curriculum framework or the list

of topics planned for the year and check off those that correspond to the cultural and diverse characteristics reflective of children and the community. Reviewing the curricular expectations, consider the best ways to present those to children in ways that they can best relate to them.

3. *Establishing goals and selecting topics:* This step leads the teacher toward making specific curriculum decisions and creating the curriculum framework. Using the information gathered in Step 1, begin to outline your main targets or goals. Teachers following a mandated curriculum find it necessary to do some revisions to identify topics that match their targets. After your goals are established, begin to select your content, that is, the themes and topics you want to explore with the class. Instead of choosing the content for an entire year, begin by simply listing those you could develop in a month's time. Designing activities for only a month at a time proves to be easier. Remember that your activities should be age appropriate. Finally, implement the curriculum.

4. *Periodical review and assessment plan:* Taking time to review what actually happened is an important step. Having a simple assessment plan will help you identify the effective parts of the curriculum and alert you to the areas that need improvement. An assessment plan could actually consist of three simple questions:

- *How did children react to the activities/materials?*
- *Am I satisfied with the outcomes of the activities? Why?*
- *Were my goals/objectives met? How?*

Approach V: Education That Is Multicultural and Social Reconstructionist

This approach is the most complex one in the Sleeter and Grant typology. It is also the one they prefer. The name itself—education that is multicultural and social reconstructionist—indicates a higher level of sophistication. The goal of this approach is to foster a belief and a sense of social equality and cultural pluralism so that students will want to become actively engaged in achieving equality. A major expectation and a result of this approach is having students become active participants in the elimination of social oppression. In general, teachers find that this approach has many ideas in common with Banks's Level 4.

Implementation of the multicultural and social reconstructionist approach presents two important challenges:

1. A need to redesign the total educational program to reflect the needs of diverse cultural groups
2. An openness to welcome children's questions, ideas, and proposals for dealing with current social issues

Sleeter and Grant (2006) present three advantages that support their selection of the multicultural and social reconstructionist approach. These same points become teaching guidelines when developing the classroom curriculum.

1. It targets issues and problems that have a current impact on some of the students.

   Classroom application: The curriculum developed deals with existent issues or problems at the classroom level or in the community. Activities and materials directly reflect issues currently faced by children.

2. It allows students "to take an active stance," offering opportunities to present alternatives to the existing situations.

   Classroom application: Curricular topics tackle problems about unfairness. Activities are based on a participatory philosophy in which children take on the roles of active decision makers. By engaging children in a dialogue where they can express ideas and propose solutions, they have a leading voice in establishing a course of action to resolve situations of unfairness and discrimination. This approach is reflective of Freire's ideas on engaging the learner in a dialogue to critically examine situations with the goal of identifying actions to take (Freire, 2000).

3. It helps students participate and work as a group "to speak out, be heard, and effect change."

   Classroom application: Teaching activities are designed around the concept of the project approach and the group investigations strategy (Joyce, Weil, & Calhoun, 2003). Here children work as a group in cooperative activities to find ways to resolve or to confront events and situations requiring action. Activities engage children in discussions to help them work out ideas together.

The multicultural and social reconstructionist approach represents a more direct way of dealing with social issues than the other models do. Given its complexity, educators are advised to carefully reflect on the requirements for its implementation (Sleeter & Grant, 2006).

FOCUS
on Classroom Practices | The Group Investigation Model

Aimed at offering children opportunities to develop skills needed to interact in a group and to become effective group members, the group investigation model (GIM) encourages the development of a sense of social life (Joyce, Weil, & Calhoun, 2003). Using the classroom as a model of the community or larger society, children are led through active participation to learn how to be group members and interact with others. Using cooperative inquiry, children are guided to problem solve or investigate specific situations. Properly used, the GIM is an effective and practical way for not only teaching children academic concepts but also providing experiences through which they can participate in the social process. Joyce, Weil, and Calhoun further emphasize that, besides the instructional effects, GIM also has relevant nurturant outcomes. They specifically identify the following significant nurturant effects, all relevant to multicultural teaching:

- To encourage a sense of respect for the dignity of all and a commitment to pluralism
- To instill a commitment to social inquiry
- To foster a sense of independence as learners

Sharing elements with the project approach and cooperative learning, activities designed according to the GIM consist of the following phases:

Phase I: Children encounter a puzzling situation. The teacher, acting as a facilitator, describes and presents the problem to the class.

Phase II: Children are led to freely discuss and comment on the problem or situation. The teacher monitors the discussion, posing questions to help clarify any angles.

Phase III: With the help of the teacher, study areas are identified and groups are formed. Members of each group are democratically assigned tasks and roles.

Phase IV: Working in their groups, children look for resources and collect information.

Phase V: Each group takes time to examine what they have collected. Decisions are made as to what else needs to be investigated. The teacher acts as a facilitator during their meetings.

Phase VI: Children in each group present their findings. New areas of study are identified.

Using the Sleeter and Grant Typology in Early Education

The five approaches suggested by Sleeter and Grant are a collection of options early educators can also consider. Like those proposed by Banks, these approaches also vary in complexity. The following approaches are adequate ways to teach multiculturally in an early childhood context: human relations, multicultural education, and education that is multicultural and social reconstructionist. Approach I, teaching the exceptional and culturally different, is a mandate in terms of educational services required for this population. It must also be infused with true perspectives about diversity issues. The single-studies approach, despite its positive characteristics, does not represent a way to infuse the entire curriculum, which is what multicultural educators view as effective practice. Because of its characteristics (Sleeter & Grant, 2006), this approach requires careful selection of topics that will guide the child in exploring and building concepts about the reality of people with diverse characteristics. Its success also depends on good planning and knowledge about the topic. Before implementing it in the classroom, it is essential to ask oneself, "How much do I know about the topic?" If this is the approach of your choice, remember that a conscientious and appropriate selection of topics is required for its successful implementation. Good planning will avoid bringing into the classroom irrelevant issues that will contribute little or nothing to the overall goals of multicultural education activities.

About the Human Relations Approach   Despite the advantages of the human relations approach, some educators caution that the issue of the quality of the classroom experience is to be carefully considered. Unfortunately, there have been times when the classroom curriculum has been characterized by trivial and stereotypical activities. Generally, this has happened when children are presented only with situations where no inquiry into social realities takes place. It can also occur as a result of poorly selected materials that do not reflect the characteristics of local and national diversity. An effective human relations curriculum not only needs to emphasize social harmony, equality, and justice, but also must confront children with an accurate portrayal of our society.

Reflecting on Approaches IV and V   Sleeter and Grant's last two approaches, multicultural and social reconstructionist, are more complex. They offer a more direct way to bring diversity issues into young children's classrooms and employ strategies similar in nature to those found in the antibias curriculum. Approaches IV and V present good choices for teachers after they have gained experience in teaching multiculturally.

LET'S TALK AND REFLECT . . . **Selecting an Approach That Meets the Children's Needs**

Deciding what approach to use is a challenging task. The first step is to learn about the variety of choices that are available. After exploring the approaches described by both Banks and Sleeter and Grant, and, based on the realities of your community and of the children, which one would you choose? With your colleagues or classmates, comment on the reasons for your choice.

In Action . . .   **Reflecting on the Sleeter and Grant Approach**

Having examined Sleeter and Grant's five approaches to multicultural education, answer the following questions:

• Have you used any of these approaches before?

• What other choices can you use to implement multicultural education?

• Which of these five approaches do you prefer? Why?

• Which approach is most appropriate for your classroom?

Which Approach Should Teachers Select?

Which approach to select is in the hands of the teacher and depends on the characteristics of the young learners, their families, and the community. Because not all teachers are at the same level of professional development, the selected approach should complement the teacher's strengths. How confident you feel as you deliver your program is basic to the success of any intended reforms. As Sleeter and Grant recommend, teachers should begin teaching about diversity by using the human relations approach. As a first step, an appropriately designed human relations curriculum offers the teacher ample opportunity to begin gaining experience in teaching about diversity. Selecting and organizing activities, leading the child to see how alike people are, and establishing the importance of shared equality are all part of an initial level that teachers can gradually surpass as they become more experienced in dealing with multicultural issues. Accomplishments on this level provide teachers with the necessary knowledge and skills to introduce the child to the more serious issues that are targeted by Approaches III through V.

| EARLY CHILDHOOD MULTICULTURAL APPROACHES

After reviewing the generic multicultural approaches, we now take time to explore models designed for early childhood education. Three models will be discussed: the antibias approach, Kendall's model, and the Head Start Multicultural Principles framework.

The Antibias Approach

The **antibias** approach to early childhood curriculum centers on changing existing social inequalities. This approach proposes to eliminate the sources of stereotypes that lead individuals to form prejudices and cultural biases. The antibias approach is founded on the "practice of freedom" as defined by Paulo Freire. According to Freire (2000), people need to be able to face their social reality critically and propose ways to transform inequalities. Derman-Sparks (1989) asserts that this conceptual stance is "fundamental to anti-bias education." It has the potential to equip children to take action to stop injustice against themselves or others.

The antibias approach to multicultural education was developed to address diversity issues in the early childhood classroom. It is based on a belief that young children can be guided to develop positive attitudes toward social diversity. The antibias approach is grounded in cognitive theory and research on concept formation. Derman-Sparks contends that children will develop positive attitudes toward diversity and adopt a proactive stance against unfairness if the classroom offers experiences through which they can see people responding against unfair situations and accepting differences, and in which the children are encouraged to act in the same fashion.

Four central goals define the philosophy of the antibias approach; they also indicate the developmental appropriateness of the approach (see Figure 6-11). Structured within the parameters of DCAP, curriculum in the antibias approach emerges from these four main sources (Derman-Sparks, 2003):

1. *Children's cultural realities, experiences, behaviors, and interests:* Observations and information about the individual children and their comments, questions, and developmental characteristics are the starting place for developing meaningful curricular experiences.

2. *The families' interests, beliefs, and concerns for children:* Awareness about the cultural beliefs and desires that families have for their young ones is a relevant and culturally valuable source for classroom experiences. It is also a way to demonstrate respect toward the child-rearing patterns followed by families. For instance, regard for a family's eating patterns based on faith (Hebrew) or custom (Chinese) is a way to show respect.

3. *Societal events, messages, and realities that surround children:* Most learning is contextual; thus, what happens in the children's environment is a fundamental source for building a curriculum. Social and cultural realities of the time need to be brought into the classroom in developmentally appropriate ways. For instance, incorporate discussion of diversity and cultural issues shown in the media. Addressing the children's questions helps to clarify their perceptions and avoids formation of erroneous views.

4. *Teachers' knowledge, beliefs, and values:* Classroom teachers are catalysts that transform the information gathered from children's families and society into meaningful and valuable learning experiences. How the curriculum is structured is largely influenced by the teachers' ideas and beliefs about diversity. Early childhood educators must have a clear understanding of their own views regarding diversity and multiculturalism.

Teachers following this approach find themselves eliminating the color-blind or color-denial position that "assumes that differences are insignificant" (Derman-Sparks & the A.B.C. Task Force, 1989). They find themselves dealing directly with prejudice, racism, and stereotypes as they arise. As teachers deal with unfair situations, children join them, learning how to take action to correct a given circumstance. The model is

FIGURE 6-11 **Curriculum Goals of the Antibias Approach**

Every child will be able to
- construct a knowledgeable, confident self-identity.
- develop comfortable, empathetic, and just interaction with diversity.
- develop critical thinking skills.
- develop the skills for standing up for oneself and others in the face of injustice.

Source: Derman-Sparks & the A.B.C. Task Force, 1989.

intended to assist children in acquiring attitudes and behavior modeled in the context of direct confrontations.

The Derman-Sparks antibias model presents and addresses cultural diversity content with an emphasis on promoting fairness and equality. It also refrains from using a tourist-like curriculum where the child "visits" a culture and usually learns about its more exotic details. Such curricula only offer glimpses of cultures, contributing little to development of awareness and knowledge about the daily life and problems people face in other cultures. Derman-Sparks provides specific guidelines for avoiding a tourist approach to curriculum (see Figure 6-12).

Two other important differences in the antibias approach are the inclusion of components of diversity appropriate for young children and the use of a developmental framework. Perhaps the best way to characterize the antibias approach is that it is targeted at preventing the formation of misconceptions about the individual and group. The approach offers a way to help children deal with the diversity embedded in our society through activities that are based on principles of child development. For that reason, it is an excellent strategy for the early childhood classroom.

Antibias/Multicultural Education

The need to prevent prejudice and racial views during the early years has been focused by Derman-Sparks and Ramsey (2005), who proposed an antibias/multicultural education approach to diversity. Their interest stems out of the need to provide the young with experiences that will guide the development of socially acceptable attitudes and ideas toward others, and they emphasize the need to prevent the formation of racist concepts and behavior (Derman-Sparks & Ramsey, 2006). Because, developmentally, racist behaviors begin to form very early in life and are influenced by interactions with

FIGURE 6-12 **Guidelines for Avoiding a Tourist Approach to the Curriculum**

1. Connect cultural activities to individual children and their families.
2. Remember that, although cultural patterns are real and affect all members of an ethnic group, families live their culture in their own individual ways.
3. Connect cultural activities to concrete, daily life.
4. Explore cultural diversity within the principle that everyone has a culture.
5. Have cultural diversity permeate the daily life of the classroom through frequent, concrete, hands-on experiences related to young children's interests.
6. Avoid the editorial "we" when talking to children ("we" implies homogeneity).
7. Explore the similarities among people through their differences.
8. Begin with the cultural diversity among the children and staff in your classroom, and then focus on the diversity of others.

Source: Derman-Sparks & the A.B.C. Task Force, 1989.

adults and the environment, classroom experiences are central to building concepts of social equality. It is one of their goals to underline the role of purposefully designed experiences as a tool that helps children to see themselves and value people beyond racial lines.

The Head Start Multicultural Framework

As you learned earlier in the book, Head Start was established to improve the experiences and opportunities of young children with social and economic challenges. During the early part of the 1990s, Head Start proposed 10 multicultural principles as the framework for its programs. They were developed in response to the increasing ethnic and cultural diversity in our society. These principles provide guidance for program planning and delivery (see Figure 6-13) and also define performance standards for the young participants of the program.

Although developed for the Head Start program, the Multicultural Principles serve as a guide in designing all aspects of early childhood programs. They emphasize the role of culture in the lives of children and families and identify the responsibility of programs to acknowledge and integrate diversity into their practices. The principles

FIGURE 6-13 **Head Start Multicultural Principles**

1. Every individual is rooted in culture.
2. The cultural groups represented in the communities and families of each Head Start program are the primary sources for culturally relevant programming.
3. Culturally relevant and diverse programming requires learning accurate information about the cultures of different groups and discarding stereotypes.
4. Addressing cultural relevance in making curriculum choices is a necessary, developmentally appropriate practice.
5. Every individual has the right to maintain his or her own identity while acquiring the skills required for functioning in our diverse society.
6. Effective programs for children with limited English speaking ability require continued development of the primary language while the acquisition of English is facilitated.
7. Culturally relevant programming requires staff who reflect the community and families served.
8. Multicultural programming for children enables children to develop an awareness of, respect for, and appreciation of individual cultural differences. It is beneficial to all children.
9. Culturally relevant and diverse programming examines and challenges institutional and personal biases.
10. Culturally relevant and diverse programming and practices are incorporated in all components and services.

Source: Head Start Bureau, 1992.

set the goal for creating "appropriate multicultural programming that builds upon each child's culture and helps the child accept the many differences among individuals and eventually deal effectively with other cultures" (Head Start Bureau, 1992). Principle 9 describes the ethical responsibility of early childhood educators working with culturally diverse children and families. Specifically, it indicates the need to put aside biases and to examine one's views and ideas about cultural diversity (Head Start Bureau, 1992). Equally relevant is the assertion regarding the child's cultural heritage made by Principle 5, which recognizes that "Every individual has the right to maintain his or her own identity while acquiring the skills required to function in our diverse society." This statement has implications on language diversity and directly establishes the need to value not only a child's culture but also language, which is recognized in Principle 6.

In general, the principles define what should be the nature of the overall program, based on diversity and multiculturalism, and stipulate the importance of addressing the needs of all children and their families. The principles define best practices by emphasizing the importance of developing programs based on the realities of children, families, and the community. They affirm that successful multicultural experiences emerge and are related to the setting where children live. Also important is how they delineate developmental practices to effectively support the children's cultures and diverse needs. For teachers, the principles provide direction in organizing and establishing the quality of classroom experiences and interactions. They also describe the need to support first languages while children acquire English. More importantly, they task the teacher with a responsibility for creating a respectful and culturally sensitive environment that will help children be socially competent, proud of their own culture, and able to interact with others in positive ways.

Facilitating and making early experiences available to all children is an essential tenet of multicultural education.

Another Model for Early Childhood Education

Frances Kendall, an early childhood educator, sketched a model based on the framework of the developmental-interaction philosophy (the same model used by Bank Street) and the late Hilda Taba (Kendall, 1996). Kendall believes that existing racism can be overcome through education, and she aspires to help children learn to affirm their cultural differences and to respect those of other people. In her model, she bases the success and the attainment of these goals on the

FIGURE 6-14 **Kendall's Goals for Multicultural Education**

1. To teach children to respect others' cultures and values as well as their own
2. To help all children learn to function successfully in a multicultural, multiracial society
3. To develop a positive self-concept in those children who are most affected by racism—children of color*
4. To help all children experience both their differences as culturally diverse people and their similarities as human beings in positive ways
5. To encourage children to experience people of diverse cultures working together as unique parts of a whole community

The term "children of color" refers to children of origins other than European American. In this book, we have excluded this term because it emphasizes not only a misleading human element but also one that has been responsible for many painful incidents.

Source: Kendall, 1996.

teacher as the pivotal element in the process of multicultural education. She believes that "teachers are models for children; therefore, they should show respect and concern for all people" (Kendall, 1996). In Kendall's view, the focus of any multicultural program begins with enabling teachers to, first, recognize their own beliefs and, second, to learn how to implement the program. Her ideas are relevant not only to the early childhood teacher but also to those aiming to initiate schoolwide diversity programs (see Figure 6-14).

Taking a Stance on Multicultural Education for Young Children

Through this chapter we have examined the variety of models and approaches available to deliver multicultural education. Selection is never an easy task. We feel that much can be learned from the models and approaches discussed in this chapter. Our own stance regarding what is the best way to create an engaging and appropriate environment was not a simple process either. It came as a result of a careful analysis of what the literature presents (Banks & Banks, 2006; Derman-Sparks, 2003; Head Start, 1992) and through our continuous observations of teachers, children, and families in a variety of culturally diverse classrooms and communities. Their experiences are a living document and source of ideas and information on how to make learning meaningful for all. For us, the eclectic framework for teaching that is multicultural should be guided by an emphasis on providing experiences that are developmentally and culturally appropriate and intentionally planned to support learning. We also believe in teaching that is guided to promote pride in one's own heritage while recognizing that of others and that leads to the formation of a sense of social fairness and positive attitudes toward diversity (Figure 6-15).

FIGURE 6-15 **Model for Multicultural Teaching Practices in Early Childhood Education**

Families and community are active participants and collaborate in classroom activities and decision making.

Responsive teaching: based on knowledge of the child, family, and community's cultural and diverse characteristics.

Teacher as facilitator of knowledge leading children to explore, inquire, and critically examine issues related to fairness. Teacher as model for fair and equity-based practices.

Framework for multicultural teaching practices in early childhood education

Classroom environment: setting where children feel welcomed, celebrate their heritage, and recognize their individuality.

Challenging content: addresses curricular and academic expectations for all children through culturally relevant activities. Experiences allow child to build skills to successfully interact with diversity with emphasis on prejudice prevention.

Learning experiences: based on learning expectations that are developmental and culturally appropriate. Actively engage children in activities emerging from their needs and interests. Curriculum supports and meets learning needs of English-language learners and children with disabilities.

REFLECTING ON THE APPROACHES FOR MULTICULTURAL EDUCATION

Today, school districts and community-based programs acknowledge the requirement to address the needs of young children and families with culturally diverse characteristics. Yet, the search for establishing multicultural practices that appropriately respond to the young continues. The challenge of multicultural education has such dimensions that the best approach is still to be designed. In the interim, several choices are available to the early childhood educator. The ones presented in this chapter are only a few that we consider most relevant. Concerned educators have also proposed other models, and many early childhood educators have eclectically devised their own.

As you prepare yourself to become a multicultural educator of the young, it is important that you take time to reflect on the kind of classroom environment you want to create. Ask yourself the following:

1. *Why do I want to teach in a multicultural way?*
2. *How do I define multicultural education?*
3. *What are my expectations of multicultural education?*
4. *What do my students need?*
5. *What are the cultural challenges present in my community?*
6. *Would my teaching be more developmentally appropriate if I infused a multicultural perspective?*

The more time you take to reflect on your convictions regarding multiculturalism, the more certain you will become of the direction you want to take. This will help guide you in planning the multicultural program you want to establish. Of all the decisions to make in multicultural education, the hardest one is resolving to change your teaching strategies. If you have resolved to do that (and we hope you have!), other decisions regarding teaching multiculturally will come more easily.

WHAT WE HAVE LEARNED—CHAPTER SUMMARY

Multicultural education started in the 1960s. Since that time, many approaches and models have evolved through research and practice. In this chapter, we presented several major models and approaches created by the most important professionals in education and early childhood education: James Banks, Christine Sleeter and Carl Grant, and Louise Derman-Sparks. Each one has as its core the welfare of young children from diverse cultures. They share the belief that the child is the center of the educational process. All major researchers also agree that the success of every early childhood program depends on the degree to which the curriculum addresses the characteristics and needs of children with diverse backgrounds. Our intent for presenting the information in this chapter is to inform early childhood educators that goodwill and creativity in the classroom are important, but that they need to ground their teaching in proven models and approaches that will ensure the effectiveness of teaching efforts and positively affect the learning process.

THINGS TO DO . . .

1. Explain the following key concepts: *approach, model,* and *curriculum.*

2. Examine the typology of James Banks and provide examples of each of his four levels.

3. Banks's and Sleeter and Grant's typologies have common points. Examine both carefully and find the common elements.

4. Define the antibias approach. Does this model have any points in common with the other approaches? Explain.

5. After exploring the different approaches to multicultural education, which one would you select? Why?

6. Some people have argued that many of the approaches to multicultural education are not suitable for the early childhood classroom. What is your opinion? Why?

7. Thinking about the multicultural approach you chose for question 5, prepare a draft of the changes you would need to make in your classroom to implement it. After completing your draft, go back to it and find the following:

   ■ *the five major changes*

   ■ *the three hardest changes*

   ■ *the five easiest things to change*

   ■ *three initial changes*

RECOMMENDED INTERNET RESOURCES

■ ESL standards for Grades Pre-K–3 (TESOL)
www.tesol.org/s_tesol/sec_document.asp?CID=113&DID=314

■ "Instructional Models for Early Childhood Education," from the Clearinghouse on Early Education and Parenting
http://ceep.crc.uiuc.edu/eecearchive/digests/2002/golbeck02.pdf

■ "The Role of Curriculum Models in Early Childhood Education," from the Clearinghouse on Early Education and Parenting
http://ceep.crc.uiuc.edu/eecearchive/digests/2000/goffin00.html

YOUR STANDARDS PORTFOLIO

NAEYC Standard 4b: Teaching and Learning: Using Developmentally Effective Approaches*

Working with young children with cultural and diverse characteristics requires the use of a variety of strategies. Keeping in mind the different approaches discussed in this chapter, complete the following activities.

1. Write a brief description about what you think is an effective multicultural approach for the early childhood classroom.

2. Visit your library and find information about cooperative learning strategies in early childhood classrooms. Based on the information, prepare a one-page description of the benefits of cooperative learning for young children.

3. Interview the local coordinator of a local ESOL program and find out about teaching approaches that best support the needs of young ELLs. Summarize the comments and highlight the recommended approaches.

REFERENCES

Banks, J. (1994). Transforming the mainstream curriculum. *Education Leadership*, 5(8), 4–8.

Banks, J. (2006). Approaches to multicultural curriculum reform. In J. Banks & C. Banks (Eds.), *Multicultural education: Issues and perspectives* (6th ed., pp. 247–270). Needham Heights, MA: Allyn & Bacon.

Banks, J., & Banks, C. (2006). *Multicultural education: Issues and perspectives* (6th ed.). Needham Heights, MA: Allyn & Bacon.

Bredekamp, S. (Ed.). (1989). *Developmentally appropriate practice in early childhood programs serving children birth through age 8*. Washington, DC: National Association for the Education of Young Children.

Derman-Sparks, L. (2003). Developing antibias, multicultural curriculum. In C. Copple (Ed.), *A world of differences: Readings on teaching children in a diverse society* (pp. 173–178). Washington, DC: National Association for the Education of Young Children.

Derman-Sparks, L., & the A.B.C. Task Force. (1989). *Anti-bias curriculum tools for empowering young children*. Washington, DC: National Association for the Education of Young Children.

Derman-Sparks, L., & Ramsey, P. (2005). What if all the children in my class are white? *Young Children: Beyond the journal*. Retrieved September 28, 2008, from http://www.journal.naeyc.org/btj/200511/DermanSparksBTJ1105.asp.

Derman-Sparks, L., & Ramsey, P. (2006). *What if all the children in my class are white?* New York: Teachers College Press.

* NAEYC Standard 4b correlates with INTASC Standard 4: Instructional Strategies.

Freire, D. (2000). *Pedagogy of the oppressed.* New York: Continuum International Publishing.

Goffin, S. (2001). *Curriculum models and early childhood education: Appraising the relationship.* New York: Merrill.

Gollnick, D. M., & Chinn, P. C. (2005). *Multicultural education in a pluralistic society* (7th ed.). New York: Prentice Hall.

Gordon, A., & Browne, K. (2007). *Beginnings and beyond.* Clifton Park, NY: Thomson Delmar Learning.

Head Start Bureau. (1992). *Multicultural principles for Head Start programs.* Washington, DC: U.S. Department of Health and Human Services.

Hernandez, H. (2001). Multicultural Education: A teachers' guide to linking context, process and content. New York: Allyn & Bacon.

Joyce, B., Weil, M., & Calhoun, E. (2003). *Models of teaching* (7th ed.). Englewood Cliffs, NJ: Prentice Hall.

Kendall, F. (1996). *Diversity in the classroom: A multicultural approach to the education of young children.* New York: Teachers College Press.

Leystina, P. (2004). Presence of mind in the process of learning and knowing: A dialogue with Paulo Freire. *Teacher Education Quarterly, 31*(1), 17–29.

Merret, C. (2000). Teaching social justice: Reviving geography's neglected tradition. *Journal of Geography, 99*(5), 207–218.

Nieto, S., & Bode, P. (2007). *Affirming diversity: The sociopolitical context of multicultural education.* Needham Heights, MA: Allyn & Bacon.

Schweinhart, L. J., & Weikart, D. P. (1997). The High/Scope preschool curriculum comparison study through age 23. *Early Childhood Research Quarterly, 12*(2), 117–143.

Sleeter, C. E., & Grant, C. (1994). *Making choices for multicultural education* (2nd ed.). New York: Merrill.

Sleeter, C. E., & Grant, C. (2006). *Making choices for multicultural education: Five approaches to race, class, and gender* (5th ed.). New York: Wiley & Sons.

Southern Poverty Law Center & Gussin-Paley, V. (1997). *Starting small: Teaching tolerance in preschool and the early grades.* Montgomery, AL: Author.

Williams, L. (1999). *Determining the curriculum.* In C. Seefeldt (Ed.), *The early childhood curriculum* (3rd ed., pp. 1–12). New York: Teachers College Press.

PART III

Into Action: Implementing a Culturally Appropriate Program for All Children

Wadsworth/Cengage Learning

CHAPTER 7

The Classroom, Where Words Become Action

> Curriculum respects and supports individual, cultural and linguistic diversity. Curriculum supports and encourages positive relationships with children's families.
>
> *National Association for the Education of Young Children (NAEYC) and National Association of Early Childhood Specialists in State Departments of Education (NAECS/SDE) (2003)*

CHAPTER OBJECTIVES

In this chapter, we will

- describe the role of teachers as multicultural curriculum designers.
- discuss the impact of developmentally and culturally appropriate practices in the curriculum.
- define the characteristics of an early childhood multicultural educator.

KEY CONCEPTS

- needs assessment
- multicultural curriculum

FROM BARBARA'S JOURNAL

The more I learn about the things my children have experienced, the more I realize why I need to engage in multicultural education. My understanding has become stronger as I get to know them and their families. Yesterday while I drove through the community, I felt even more compelled to do things differently. The phrase on one mural I saw just got me: "Every time a child smiles, you can see the future." Do I see it? I surely can and know that there is much to do. It's not a choice anymore; children simply need to feel that each one is important, that they have so much to be proud of, and that I'm here to help them become their best.

I want to start my new year on a different note. I don't know how I will do it yet. I do know that I want my kindergartners to succeed academically. But I also want them to feel pride in who they are and learn to accept and respect others. More than that, my classroom will be the place where children will learn to enjoy this diverse world they live in. It will be a challenge but one that I welcome. So, let's see what happens.

REAFFIRMING THE DECISION TO TEACH MULTICULTURALLY

Every day in classrooms across the United States, children and teachers join in the journey of schooling. Through this experience, children begin to understand at an early age what it means to be an American. This discovery process takes place primarily in the classroom. Therefore, the instructional practices in the early years must reflect the true nature, values, and needs of our society. To accomplish this in a meaningful way, we must look for effective ways to include multiculturalism in the curriculum.

One of the undisputed facts concerning U.S. schools is that although we have growing numbers of students of increasingly diverse backgrounds, the large majority of teachers continue to be white, of European American ancestry. Some of them may not be professionally equipped to teach children who are so vastly different from them in cultural, religious, linguistic, and social class orientation (Romo, Bradfield, & Serrano, 2004). Cases of teachers who misunderstand, fear, and even ignore culturally diverse children in their classes are not uncommon. With the ethnic minorities becoming the majority of the population in the United States in the next decades, marginalizing students from various ethnic groups, religions, and cultures will have far-reaching effects on society. Social rejection has one of the most negative effects on a child because it hinders positive emotional growth and negatively impacts self-confidence. Cohesiveness with social and ethnic groups, on the other hand, promotes feelings of belonging and group pride. In light of the challenges that U.S. society faces, it is critical to create classrooms where each child feels valued and where the cultures of children are respected and welcome. Therefore, teachers of young children must be committed to building collaborative relationships with diverse groups in communities and schools to create more equitable and nurturing environments for all children. By committing themselves to multicultural teaching, early childhood educators will become advocates who are inclusive and more socially just members of society.

Moving into Teaching That is Multicultural

Making the transition to a multicultural educational program requires not only time and careful preparation, but also an examination of curricular practices. Such analysis must cover all aspects of teaching: the beliefs, the content, the activities, the materials, and the classroom environment. In this chapter, we will explore the ways teachers moving into multiculturalism need to transform their teaching.

When you make the decision to infuse the multicultural perspective into your teaching, you make a commitment to invigorate your instructional practices and provide children with learning experiences that are valid in the context of today's world. Teachers who become multicultural educators are also responsive to the particular developmental demands that children bring to the classroom. For example, young children during preschool years are very curious, so they may frequently raise issues about other people's characteristics, evidenced by, for example, the European American child who asks, "Why is she so dark?" when referring to an East Indian classmate or the child who stares and wonders why a physically challenged peer uses a wheelchair. The Asian American child may find his classmates giggling at him because of the shape of his eyes. Incidents like these are used by some professional educators as knowledge-building experiences. However, not all early childhood educators perceive these as opportunities to prepare children for increasingly complex social interactions in our multicultural world.

Keep in mind these assumptions, outlined by Hernandez (2001):

■ It is increasingly important for political, social, educational, and economic reasons to recognize that the United States is a culturally diverse society.

■ Multicultural education is for *all* students.

■ Multicultural education is synonymous with effective teaching.

■ Teaching is a cross-cultural encounter.

■ The educational system has not served students equally well.

■ Multicultural education is synonymous with educational innovation and reform.

■ Next to parents, teachers are the single most important factor in the lives of children.

■ Classroom interaction between teachers and students constitutes the major part of the educational process for most students.

Your determination should be reaffirmed by realizing that teaching multiculturally means teaching and understanding all children. In the next sections, we will examine some of the relevant steps you must take to reach that goal.

Where Do You Start?

There are many steps to teaching with a multicultural perspective. The first step is to look at yourself. You must recognize how important you are as a teacher and, even more, as a professional early childhood educator. As a professional educator, you are the best champion children have. Their hopes for a responsive education are placed on you.

Next, we will examine those qualities and characteristics that make you the key to a successful multicultural program.

TEACHERS ARE THE KEY TO SUCCESSFUL MULTICULTURAL EDUCATION

Teaching transforms lives, according to the old adage. Good teaching, as defined by leading educators and professional organizations, happens when teachers care and look for ways to reconcile the child's own needs with the aspirations of education. Some of these aspirations are grounded in the principles of developmentally and culturally appropriate practices (DCAP). Teachers of young children need to incorporate both the perspectives of diversity and DCAP into their instruction to respond to the whole child; this is the essence of a multicultural teacher. Good multicultural programs for children exist because teachers have a special commitment to children. This special sense of responsibility helps these professionals look for ways to organize their classroom environment in developmentally and culturally responsive ways. Teachers who achieve this balance are the professionals every child deserves and needs. They also model ideal ethical traits that should distinguish all early childhood educators.

Nieto and Bode (2007) consider that a true multicultural educator also believes in multiculturalism and diversity as an asset for the society at large. They believe that multicultural educators are characterized by very specific traits:

- *Thorough and strong knowledge:* Learning more about pluralism and how it is reflected in people and in our interactions

- *Honest assessment of our own biases:* Accepting that we all hold biases, sometimes very well hidden inside ourselves

- *Ability to view reality through countless perspectives:* Learning to approach reality from more than one angle

Traits of the Multicultural Early Childhood Educator

A good multicultural teacher must believe in social justice and advancement of democracy. He or she has an obligation to ensure that every child is treated fairly and has equal opportunity to develop to his or her full potential. The just and equitable treatment of children from all corners of the world strengthens our democracy and benefits all those who inhabit this country. Early childhood professionals must concentrate on transforming their perspectives about their profession, the children they teach, their role as educators and caretakers, and how their role fits into the larger social and cultural framework of the society. Early childhood professionals must enhance their knowledge of *who* they are, *who* the children are, and *who* we are as a society (nationally and globally) and embrace the need for social justice (Gallavan, cited in Romo, Bradfield, & Serrano, 2004).

Drawing upon the ideas of leading educators and the ideal traits defined by professional organizations such as the National Association for the Education of Young Children (NAEYC), the Association for Childhood Education International (ACEI), and the World Organisation for Early Childhood Education [Organisation Mondiale pour L'Education Prescolaire] (OMEP), we can now draw a profile of an early childhood multicultural educator.

Teacher collaboration is an important element of multicultural education.

An early childhood multicultural educator . . .

- has a sound knowledge about child development that he or she uses and applies in classroom teaching.
- believes that multiculturalism is an integral part of our society and that schools need to incorporate multiculturalism into their programs.
- is committed to helping the child face and understand our social diversity.
- is aware of and works to clarify his or her own ideas about diversity, biases, and beliefs, and recognizes and accepts his or her own diversity and that of children.
- holds high expectations equally for all children and helps all children to develop to their fullest.
- works and interacts in a respectful way with all families as partners and collaborators for the benefit of the child.
- is willing to try out new methods and materials to accommodate the needs of children.
- is constantly assessing his or her own teaching to guarantee its responsiveness to the children's needs.
- is constantly searching for new approaches and/or methods to improve multicultural teaching.
- creates a classroom environment where tolerance, respect, and openness to learn and understand others are its essential characteristics.

FIGURE 7-1 **Multicultural Early Childhood Teachers are Leaders**

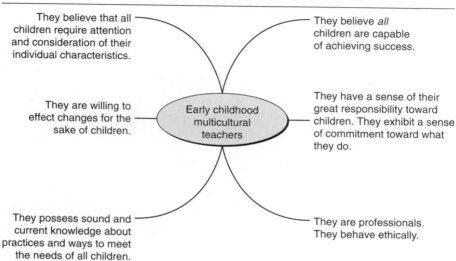

- keeps a positive, willing, and open attitude toward self and others as professionals.
- recognizes that reality is a composite of many different perspectives.

These characteristics describe a classroom leader, the teacher, who will use skills and knowledge on behalf of children. This list of attributes also reflects a composite of knowledge and values, both personal and professional, that depict an educator who is personally and professionally willing to take action and set direction (Figure 7-1).

Becoming a Good Multicultural Early Educator

You probably realize that many of the essential characteristics of multicultural educators are attributes that you already possess and that there are others you still need to achieve. Because all professionals are constantly growing and improving, you should expect to have areas where you will need further development. Learning about your own teaching strengths and weaknesses is an important step for a teacher who is moving into multicultural education. This knowledge determines the directions and the intensity of the changes you need to make.

Educators who commit to undertaking multicultural teaching often discover that they possess many more good teaching qualities than they had thought. This knowledge reassures them and acts as a catalyst for change. The change process is described in Figure 7-2. The first two steps are the focus of this chapter.

FIGURE 7-2 **Steps Toward Multicultural Teaching**

1. *Knowing ourselves as teachers.* Who am I as a teacher? Self-assessment in which teachers examine their own teaching and beliefs.
2. *Assessing our present practices.* Where do I stand now? What kind of program do I offer my students? Analysis of current curriculum to determine the content and processes used. What is the school context like? What should my teaching be like? What do my students need?
3. *Designing the program.* Which goals and objectives will I have? What approach will I use? What materials and resources do I have and need?
4. *Implementing.* When will actions take place? How can I find out about their effects?

| In Action . . . | **Reflecting on the Profile of the Early Childhood Educator** |

- Which of the characteristics of an early childhood multicultural educator mentioned here describe you?
- Which do you think are the most important ones?
- Which ones would you say are the hardest to achieve? Why?
- What other descriptors would you add to the list?

Exploring Your Learning Environment

High-quality and effective multicultural education requires sound and objective knowledge of the setting and program where you teach. The next section focuses on learning more about your classrooms, your curricula, and, in general, the school and classroom programs.

Where Do You Start?

Before any changes can effectively take place, we need to know where we stand. Imagine you have been invited to a party, and you want to buy something new to wear. Without any further information or details about the event, it would be impossible to buy clothes to suit the occasion. You might like to wear elegant evening attire, but if the activity turns out to be an outdoor picnic, you will be out of place. You might be an excellent guest, but if you do not prepare for an event, you will probably have a difficult time fitting in. The same concepts apply to curriculum change. When planning for school and classroom change, it is important to clearly understand the setting where the change will take place. A thorough knowledge of the classroom environment and the children helps the teacher set realistic expectations. Good and effective planning happens only when those involved in the planning are knowledgeable about the environment where the curriculum will be implemented. High-quality planning aimed at producing long-lasting transformations is based on sound knowledge of the children you teach. This common sense approach has been advocated by many distinguished educators. John Dewey, a pioneer of education in the United States, advocated for an active and child-based curriculum and argued that good curriculum was determined by its relationship to society (Campbell, 1995; Hickman & Alexander, 1999).

Educational directions, according to Dewey, should emerge from the people and the societal context. Consideration of the social context, he felt, provides the appropriate and essential bases on which to plan and design school activities. Dewey believed that changes cannot take place without taking into account how they relate to the child and social reality. This important point reaffirms the need to hold a thorough knowledge about our settings. To know the settings where we work means to do a reality check to discover the characteristics of that environment.

Dewey's ideas of an effective curriculum for young children bring attention to three essential elements: knowledge about the children's developmental needs, the na-

---

LITERACY CONNECTIONS...

Recommended Resources on Appropriate Practices

You may want to review or add to your professional library the following resources that will help you learn about appropriate curricular and program practices.

- Bredekamp, S., & Copple, C. (2009). *Developmentally appropriate practice in early childhood programs serving children from birth through age 8* (3rd ed.). Washington, DC: National Association for the Education of Young Children.

- Division of Early Childhood of the Council for Exceptional Children. (2007). *Promoting positive outcomes for children with disabilities: Recommendations for curriculum, assessment, and evaluation.* Missoula, MT: Author.

- Garcia, E., McLaughlin, B., Spodek, B., & Saracho, O. (Eds.). (1995). *Meeting the challenge of linguistic and cultural diversity in early childhood education.* New York: Teachers College Press.

- National Association for the Education of Young Children & National Association of *Early Childhood Specialists in State Departments of Education. (2003). Early childhood curriculum, assessment, and program evaluation.* Washington, DC: Author. Available at http://www.naeyc.org/about/positions/pdf/CAPEexpand.pdf.

ture of the family, and the reality of the community (Hickman & Alexander, 1999). Incorporating all three aspects is consistent with the aspiration of what constitutes culturally sensitive and developmentally appropriate curricular experiences in every early childhood classroom in our country.

WHY PLANNING IS SO IMPORTANT

Literature abounds with examples of well-intended innovations that never met with success. Upon close examination, many failures were due to inadequate investigation of facts in the planning phase. Deciding to teach multiculturally already places you close to the finish line. But to cross it and remain a winner requires having clear objectives and expectations. Taking time now to carefully plan and assess your setting will prove beneficial for determining present and future directions. To avoid failure, take some time to do that important reality check.

KNOWING YOUR PROGRAM

Being early childhood educators has provided us with firsthand experiences about how children learn. One very important lesson we have mastered is that learning does not happen in isolated bits and pieces. The same is true of teaching. Teaching is an important part of the growth process, complemented by familial and societal experiences. To make teaching a truly integrated intellectual and social experience, materials and the school environment must mirror the community of the children and families served (Bredekamp & Rosegrant, 2001). Therefore, examining the nature of the settings where teaching takes place is essential. The knowledge gained from this experience often

---

In Action . . .   **Learning About the Classroom**

To facilitate change, you must have thorough knowledge of what happens in the classroom. Before moving into action, you may want to assess your knowledge by answering the following questions. Your responses will help you understand where you are in terms of multicultural practices.

- In terms of diversity and multicultural education, how well do you know your community? How much do you know about the curricular programs and services available at the local schools?

- What aspects of the classroom do you feel you need to learn more about? Consider the curriculum, materials, and teaching practices.

- In your opinion, what should be the essential characteristics of a program aimed at providing multicultural experiences for young children? What is your vision of a multicultural program?

prevents disappointment. By determining the particular attributes that depict a community, the early childhood educator comes to know the needs of the stakeholders, which in turn determine the direction of required change. Other school professionals need to assess the setting as well. Ornstein and Levine (cited by Ornstein & Hunkins, 2004) suggest that to generate success, changes must be school-focused and adapted to reality.

The Needs Assessment: How to Gain a True Perspective of Your Practices

Effective learning and teaching is anchored by what is relevant for the child to learn. A well-known principle in early childhood education is to never assume that you know what the child needs or knows. In fact, this is why teachers are constantly observing and checking what children do and say in the classroom. In the multicultural early childhood environment, verifying and checking what children bring into the classroom is crucial. Time spent in assessment is as important as selecting materials and designing activities. Actually, this is what guarantees that you are taking the right developmental direction.

Teachers of young children in today's diverse classrooms need to confirm that their teaching strategies meet the needs of their students. The process requires that the teacher identify the specific areas of concern from which the educator will later develop instructional goals and expectations. This process is better described as a **needs assessment.**

In education, a needs assessment is a process that ensures we implement projects, changes, and new programs and other educational ventures that satisfy the needs of one or more constituencies. The process is structured and organized and permits us to determine the needs of the market through both formal and informal means. The process of needs assessment can take place on many different levels in early childhood education. Needs identification should provide the teacher with a three-dimensional sense of the setting by providing information regarding the community where the school is located or which it serves (if children are bused in); the school itself as an entity formed by faculty and staff; and the children and their families. Getting a feel for the setting as seen from these perspectives provides information that contributes to designing an appropriate curriculum.

Because multicultural education is a transformational process, it is essential to constantly evaluate your own practices to ascertain *what* needs to be changed and *why* it needs to be changed. This is one way to identify the status of program practices and your own strengths and challenges regarding the program in your classroom. By conducting your own assessment (see Figure 7-3) you gain a deeper understanding of your own approach and responses to young children with diverse and multicultural characteristics.

Assessing Practices From the Perspective of the Children's Experiences

The goal in the multicultural classroom is for every child to find a nurturing and appropriate environment where they are welcomed as they are. It is important in a needs assessment to collect information about children's environments and families as well

FIGURE 7-3 **Conducting a Needs Assessment: Informal Activities**

About teaching practices:

- Write down your own comments about classroom activities that support diversity. (I can support diversity by . . . .)
- Develop statements identifying the essential diverse characteristics of an early childhood classroom. (An early childhood classroom is diverse because it has . . . .)
- Do an appraisal of what you know or don't know regarding culture and diversity. (I know that . . . . I need to learn more about . . . .)
- Check lesson plans to see if themes address diversity.
- Inspect your classroom to see if materials reflect diversity.
- Talk with other early childhood professionals about diversity practices.

About children and their families:

- Review information about families and children (culture, language, exceptionalities, and socioeconomic characteristics).
- Hold informal conversations with family members and parents to learn about their expectations from the school and from you.
- Talk with families about their traditions and special celebrations.

About the community:

- Visit the community to learn about its culture; that is, find out about languages spoken, religious groups, social rules and mores, and so on.
- Identify resources, ethnic-based organizations, and agencies serving families with diverse characteristics.

A variety of learning experiences provides for the children's diverse needs and learning styles.

Wadsworth/Cengage Learning

SNAPSH[O]T 7-1   **Never Assume You Know Everything About Your School**

One of this book's authors gave her graduate students in an early childhood education course an assignment to prepare a profile of their school and community. Students were expected to determine the 10 essential elements that define the school and the community that teachers need to consider in their planning of the multicultural curriculum. Many of the students, being practitioners, commented that they could write the 10 elements without doing a survey.

When the time came to report the findings, the majority of students (almost 90 percent) reported that there were more details about their school than they realized. Answers such as: "I can't imagine that I knew so little!" "Now I know what my class needs!" or "I have gained a totally new perspective of my class" were common reactions. The fact is that these professionals, some of whom have worked in their settings for a number of years, never grasped the essence of their school environment. So even if you think you know your classroom and school, take time to find out how much you really know.

---

as identify languages spoken by the child and family other than English. It is equally relevant to gain a thorough understanding about the presence of special needs and disabilities.

The family, school or center, classroom, and neighborhood or community are the major contexts in which young children interact and learn. Assessing the quality of these venues will help you appraise and determine the effectiveness of your program. Through informal interviews with children and adults, details about these environments can be gathered. Whenever an opportunity exists, home and community visits are another source to learn about the children's daily life realities. Getting to personally interact with the family and to be in the neighborhoods and places where children live provides valuable insights. Use of purposefully designed instruments is also a helpful way to collect data. Figure 7-4 is a sample questionnaire you may want to use to yield valuable information about the reality of the children and the program.

The partnership between schools and families is important for the healthy development of any young child. Families and teachers share the responsibility for creating optimal conditions in which the child can be nurtured and allowed to develop in appropriate ways. Often parents from cultures other than mainstream white European American have a very different perception of their role in relationship to the school. For example, Latino and Haitian parents view the teacher as the main person responsible for the child's education. They perceive themselves as nurturers and caretakers rather

FIGURE 7-4 **Learning About the Children's Learning Contexts**

(Sample Questionnaire)

A. The Community
1. What is the cultural and ethnic makeup of the community?
2. What languages are spoken?
3. What are the immediate priorities of the community?
4. What are the main community issues?
5. How do the community members feel toward the school, toward my classroom?

B. The School
1. What is the cultural and ethnic makeup of the school?
2. What is the diversity profile of the school?
3. What attitudes do teachers and staff have toward diversity?
4. Is anyone engaged in a multicultural program? What approaches are they following?
5. Are multicultural programs among the school's priorities?
6. Would the faculty, administrators, and staff support my efforts?

C. Children and Families
1. What are the families like? Socioeconomically, how are they defined?
2. What elements of diversity are reflected in these families?
3. What are some of the essential needs of families?
4. What are their religious affiliations?
5. Can I address those needs in my classroom?
6. What are the traits that, ethnically and culturally, characterize children in my classroom?
7. What diversity issues are unclear to my students? (for example, language differences, equality, interracial relations)
8. How do children see me?

D. The Classroom
1. What are the ethnic and cultural origins of the children in this classroom?
2. What opportunities do they have for dealing with diversity at the school?
3. Generally, how do children interact in this classroom?
4. Have there been any incidents because of racial or cultural differences?
5. Are there children who tend to use racial slurs or pejorative terms against others?
6. How do they respond when a person with given cultural characteristics comes into the classroom?

FIGURE 7-5 **Elements of Positive Family–School Relationships**

- Establish good communication between school and family.
- Clarify moral/ethical responsibilities and behaviors of the family and school.
- Create and communicate guidelines for participation and involvement of the family.
- Respect and accept all forms of diversity found within the family.
- Define and share procedures for transitioning children from home to school.
- Collaborate with and support families with resources.
- Provide opportunities for families to participate in children's learning and school decision making.

Source: Adapted from ACEI and OMEP, 2000.

than educators of their children. Schools, largely run by white administrators and teachers, hold different ideas about the parents' role in the education process. This lack of understanding and the confusion about the role of families from minority cultures in the education of young children has motivated organizations such as the World Organisation for Early Childhood Education [Organisation Mondiale pour L'Education Prescolaire] (OMEP) and the Association for Childhood Education International (ACEI) (see Figure 7-5), as well as the National Association for the Education of Young Children (NAEYC), to create generic guidelines for partnerships with families and schools. Analyzing the relationship between the family and the school is important in the curriculum transformation process.

Children with Special Needs

Successful learning for children with special needs happens in the context of an inclusive and supportive environment where experiences are geared to promote development. Awareness and understanding of the specific conditions and disabilities that may be present in the classroom are necessary to plan accordingly for children's needs. In collecting information about the child with special needs, consider the following:

- Has the child been screened and formally diagnosed? Does the child have an Individualized Education Plan (IEP)?
- What is the nature of the child's disabilities?
- What kinds of accommodations are required? What are the recommendations in the IEP?

A review of the children's files will not only reveal those who have special needs but will also provide details about the nature of their disabilities and the required accommodations. Based on their needs, modifications may range from lesson planning accommodations or use of special equipment and resources to the physical arrangement of the classroom. Conversations with the child's former teachers, staff members, and special education service coordinators will also offer relevant information. Interviews with parents and family members along with your own observations will provide valuable details.

Assessing Language Diversity: English Language Learners

Today, language diversity is one of the characteristics present in many classrooms. As discussed earlier, projections indicate that the number of children who are learning English as a second language will continue to increase in the coming decades. Nationally, Census statistics show that nearly 20 percent of children age 5 and older speak a language other than English (U.S. Census Bureau, 2006). Many young English language learners in Head Start and state prekindergarten programs were born in the United States, while others immigrated with their families before entering preschool.

Gathering information about the children's language diversity is essential in order to design activities that will meet their needs. There are several methods of obtaining linguistic information, which at all times must be conducted in a sensitive and respectful way. Some of these include the following:

1. *Interviews with parents and family members:* Parents and the family are a firsthand source of information on language preferences, including those spoken at home. Through both informal and formal conversations with parents and family members, we can learn about the primary language used at home.
2. *Classroom observations of linguistic interactions:* Anecdotal notes from observations of the children's language use during classroom activities yield valuable information about linguistic preference and level of proficiency. Individual conversations with children also provide relevant information on their ability to use English.
3. *Questionnaires and surveys:* a variety of informal and formal tools can be used to determine the linguistic needs of young English language learners. Many centers and schools use questionnaires to collect information on English language learners. School districts and state prekindergarten programs collect language data through the Home Language Survey. This information appears in the child's record.

Assessing the School–Family Environment

A thoughtful analysis of the data collected during the community and school assessment is critical to the reform process entailed in multicultural education. The data will form the framework for future actions, assist in bringing reality into the classroom, and help determine and explain future decisions and actions. More specifically, this information will help establish the instructional content and processes for children taking part in the multicultural program. For instance, in this chapter, you will see why our kindergarten teacher, Barbara, chose to address disabilities in her curriculum.

After you gain knowledge about the setting, it is important to look at the curriculum. Fundamental to any classroom change is clear knowledge about the way the program is organized. Teachers need to understand their programs in terms of content and instruction. A knowledgeable assessment of the curriculum will help the teacher determine,

---

LITERACY CONNECTIONS. . .   Using a Literacy-Based, Child-Centered Curriculum

Literacy provides a way to design a developmentally and culturally relevant curriculum. The children's books in this section are a sample of stories that can be used to integrate diversity into the curriculum. Titles in this section address children and adults with disabilities and developmental differences. Selections on other aspects of diversity are found in every chapter.

- Bodeen, S. (2003). *Babu's song.* New York: Lee & Low. (relative with disabilities)

- Davis, P. (2000). *Brian's bird.* Morton Grove, IL: Whitman. (visual disabilities)

- DeBear, K. (2001). *Be quiet, Marina!* New York: Starbright. (Down syndrome and cerebral palsy)

- Dwight, L. (2005). *We can do it!* Long Island, NY: Star Bright Books. (variety of disabilities)

- Glenn, S. (2003). *Keeping up with Roo.* New York: Putnam. (relatives with developmental delays)

- Heyman, A. (2003). *The bicycle dog.* New York: Dutton. (physical disabilities)

- Millman, I. (1998). *Moses goes to a concert.* New York: Frances Foster Books. (hearing disabilities)

- Munsch, R. (2003). *Zoom!* New York: Cartwheel/Scholastic. (physical disabilities)

- Plucker, S. (2005). *Me, Hayley!* Hollidaysburg, PA: Jason and Nordic Publishers. (Down syndrome)

- Schaefer, L. (2001). *Some kids use wheelchairs.* Mankato, MN: Pebble Books. (physical disabilities)

- Thompson, L. (2007). *Ballerina dreams.* New York: Feiwel and Friends. (physical disabilities, cerebral palsy)

- Tildes, P. (2006). *The garden wall.* Watertown, MA: Charlesbridge. (hearing disabilities)

conceptually, where she or he stands. Outcomes of this analysis will help determine the curriculum areas in need of change and prioritize those in need of urgent attention.

In early childhood education, the curriculum becomes those learning encounters teachers prepare for children to foster knowledge building. The knowledge to be built in multicultural teaching includes concepts about oneself and others in the context of a diverse society.

WHAT IS CURRICULUM CONTENT IN EARLY CHILDHOOD EDUCATION?

A curriculum framework is a dynamic system that should guide all aspects of a high quality program.

Division of Early Childhood (2007)

What should children learn? What should be the content? These are questions that we continuously explore. Content, according to general curriculum theory, is the body of knowledge that is taught in a specific grade level or class. It becomes *what* is selected for children to learn. Many teachers call it the "stuff" they teach. The content is considered appropriate whenever the concerns and the needs of the students and of society are addressed in ways that will provide opportunities for students to grow cognitively, psychologically, and socially (Bredekamp, 1987; Ornstein & Hunkins, 2004). Meaningful content acknowledges and incorporates the children's prior and current cultural knowledge and skills. Also, it is inclusive of the children's community and family experiences.

Factors to Consider When Choosing a Curriculum

Early childhood curriculum blends development with learning while focusing on the whole child; that is, "[t]he child is at the heart of the curriculum. All children are competent and their learning must be rooted in experiences appropriate to their developmental levels and cultures" (ACEI & OMEP, 2000). This position ensures that the physical, emotional, linguistic, cognitive, and social needs of young children are met. The curriculum provides opportunities to master knowledge and skills that are connected to valuable and real-world experiences. It is also important to allow young children to acquire positive values of both their cultural group and of the mainstream society to meet the expectations of families and communities.

Some schools may choose to adopt commercially produced learning materials. At times, these materials tend to be culturally inaccurate as well as developmentally inappropriate for young children. One way to avoid this is by applying guidelines or instruments specifically designed for curriculum selection. Our version is presented in Figure 7-6. Professional organizations such as OMEP, ACEI, and NAEYC are valuable resources for additional information regarding selection of curriculum content.

FIGURE 7-6 **Guidelines for Selecting Appropriate Curriculum Content**

Developmentally appropriate curriculum is based on stages of development and provides appropriate learning experiences intended to facilitate the physical, social, emotional, cognitive, and linguistic development of the child.

Culturally meaningful curriculum provides experiences that are respectful and inclusive of the children's cultural and social reality. Activities and materials contribute to support and validate the culture of children and their families. They are also reflective of and related to the settings and environments where children live.

Utilitarian curriculum is useful in that it provides real-world experiences relevant to the child's reality and the reality of the child's family and the community.

Cognitively challenging curriculum is at a level of complexity and sequentially organized to build upon the child's previous knowledge and skills as well as to serve the needs of the learner. It fosters knowledge building of relevant concepts.

Exploratory curriculum is organized to foster curiosity and a desire to learn through age-appropriate experiences guided by the child's interests.

Significant curriculum accurately and authentically presents valid multicultural issues that are experienced by the child and the family and are relevant to society.

Self-enhancing curriculum facilitates the development of positive self-image, personal identity, and a sense of pride in the child's cultural and social background.

LET'S TALK AND REFLECT... Knowledge About the Content as a Basis for Appropriate Planning

Darling-Hammond (2004) states that what teachers know and do makes the most difference in what children learn. Although early childhood education follows integrated curricular practices, sound knowledge of the content and teaching strategies provides direction and guides teachers in designing appropriate learning experiences.

As you reflect on these thoughts, consider the following questions:

- In what content areas are you the most knowledgeable?
- In what areas do you need to improve?
- What resources are available for you to further your knowledge?

F⊙CUS on Classroom Practices

Using a Conceptual Scheme to Create the Multicultural Content

Trying to choose the essential concepts for your **multicultural curriculum** is not a simple task. It means addressing how culture influences the myriad human behaviors and interactions (Banks, 1994). Banks recommends choosing high-level key concepts that are interdisciplinary and organized around five main areas. Considering the developmental characteristics of young children, we adapted Banks's list, selecting those most appropriate. We also added some that seemed pertinent in a young child's classroom. The result is a master list of concepts teachers can use as a tool for content selection.

Key Multicultural Concepts

I. Main Concept: Culture, ethnicity, identity

- culture
- cultural beliefs
- cultural symbols
- cultural celebrations
- ethnic groups in the United States/in my community
- cultural diversity
- cultural groups
- family and cultural identity
- role of language in cultural identity

II. Main Concept: Socialization and interaction

- child-rearing patterns
- family patterns
- values
- self-concept
- social interaction patterns

- racism
- prejudice
- discrimination

III. Main Concept: Intercultural communication and perception

- variety of languages
- communication patterns
- nonverbal communication
- symbols
- world/life view (how they see and interpret events)
- oral traditions
- literature and folklore (literary and musical)

IV. Main Concept: Power and status

- social classes
- homelessness and children
- locus of influence
- people with disabilities
- status of women, men, elders, and children

V. Main Concept: The movement of ethnic groups

- migration
- immigration
- purposes of migration and immigration
- immigrants in the community

Source: Adapted from Banks, 1991.

LET'S TALK AND REFLECT... Planning with a Developmental and Cultural Focus

According to DCAP, curriculum for children emerges from the blend of the children's needs, the teacher's knowledge, and the expectations of families and communities (Bredekamp & Copple, 2009). Considering this statement, visit classrooms and interview teachers about what they consider the most important element of planning appropriate and relevant curricular experiences. Write a commentary of your findings.

FOCUS on Classroom Practices

Adding the Appropriate Perspective About Ethnicity to the Curriculum

Educator James Banks shares some concerns about what the multicultural curriculum often presents. His remarks are particularly important for teachers who strive to create a responsive curriculum. According to Banks (2003), when planning multiethnic experiences, some educators assume that an ethnic group is monolithic and homogeneous or characterized by a single set of traits.

Nothing is further from reality than the presumption that all people from a cultural group possess identical qualities and views. Just as children from the same family have different characteristics, so do members of cultural groups.

Banks adds that another problem is that educators tend to believe that self-esteem and the academic achievement of youth from other cultures will be enhanced by teaching mostly about heroic characters and achievements of individuals of their cultural background, while demonstrating how their ethnic group has been victimized by the mainstream culture (Banks, 1991, 2003). The implications are clear. When the curriculum is built solely on the cultural past and a one-way description of a culture, despite the positive intentions of teachers, it will lack responsiveness and appropriateness.

Both of Banks's observations have relevance for the classroom teacher. Designing curriculum while presuming that all members of a group have similar needs and reactions would result in a curriculum that risks not just finding stereotypical information about these groups but encouraging it. To avoid falling into this kind of curricular trap, answer these questions:

- *Have I used more than one source to get information about the target cultural groups?*

- *Have I also considered and examined materials written by members of the cultures I am targeting?*

- *Have I included materials and activities based on assumptions or on what I believe about other cultures?*

- *Does the content offer a balanced view of the past and present realities of the target cultures?*

Curriculum Process in Early Childhood Education

The curriculum process includes the methods and procedures teachers follow to deliver their content (Ornstein & Hunkins, 2004). The process entails the strategies, techniques, and overall methods used in the classroom to convey specific content and skills. The processes the teacher selects will influence the child as a learner. As mentioned before, when selecting the process in the early childhood classroom, you must consider the child's developmental level and specific individual needs.

"The curriculum comes from the child" is a statement that reflects the nature of planning and curricular design in early childhood education. This is based on the premise that the best way to teach a child is always based on what the child needs. To facilitate this process, special guidelines have been created to help you select appropriate teaching approaches and strategies. Among those particularly helpful are Bredekamp and Copple's (2009) guidelines for appropriate curricular practices. Grounded in the DCAP concept, which introduced culture as an element for achieving equality, they provide clear directions regarding the nature of early childhood curricular activities and classroom experiences. More importantly, they uphold the need to follow the children's developmental needs, both universal and individual, to build a sound and fitting curriculum. At all times, good curricular practices should be guided by knowledge of the children's developmental and cultural strengths, needs, and individual characteristics.

Specific directions for designing curricular experiences are also found in the guidelines from the NAEYC and the NAECS/SDE (2003). They particularly define the need to ". . . implement curriculum that is thoughtfully planned, challenging, engaging, developmentally appropriate, culturally and linguistically responsive, comprehensive, and likely to promote positive outcomes for *all* young children" (emphasis added).

| STANDARDS FOR TEACHING IN DIVERSE CLASSROOMS

The document stating curricular standards for successful practice in classrooms serving children who are culturally and linguistically diverse, published by the Center for Research on Education, Diversity, and Excellence (CREDE), is an important resource. Funded by the Office of Educational Research and Improvement of the U.S. Department of Education, CREDE proposes five standards as a framework for teaching practices in programs serving children with diverse characteristics. Following the definition of pedagogy as an interactive experience between children and teachers and framed in the tenets of developmental and sociocultural theory, the CREDE standards identify specific pedagogical practices "proven successful with majority and minority at-risk students in a variety of teaching and learning settings over several decades" (Dalton, 1998). The five standards are described in Figure 7-7.

FIGURE 7-7 **Five Standards for Effective Pedagogy (CREDE)**

Standard I. Joint Productive Activity: Teacher and Students Producing Together
Facilitate learning through joint productive activity among teacher and students.

Standard II. Developing Language and Literacy across the Curriculum
Develop competence in the language and literacy of instruction across the curriculum.

Standard III. Making Meaning: Connecting School to Students' Lives
Connect teaching and curriculum with experiences and skills of students' home and community.

Standard IV. Teaching Complex Thinking
Challenge students toward cognitive complexity.

Standard V. Teaching Through Conversation
Engage students through dialogue, especially the instructional conversation.

Source: Dalton, 1998.

MAKING DECISIONS: WHAT IS BEST FOR MULTICULTURAL TEACHING?

Deciding on the best way to develop your multicultural program is not a simple task. Both standards and approaches provide guidance in determining how to organize and create experiences. Although all early childhood approaches are valid sources to develop and implement a multicultural program, some strategies are better for creating a focus on diversity. Some approaches that are considered especially appropriate are listed in this chapter (see "Focus on Classroom Practices: Recommended Curricular Approaches for Multicultural Teaching"). Taking time to consider the diverse needs of children and their families in your community; talking with experienced teachers; visiting classrooms where multicultural teaching takes place; having conversations with families of young children; reading about curriculum for young children; and most importantly, reflecting on what you read and discover will help in identifying the best way to proceed.

Moving into Multicultural Teaching: Where You Are Versus Where You Want to Be

According to a statement presented jointly by the NAEYC and the NAECS/SDE (2003), multiculturalism should be embedded in every program for young children. More specifically, it states the following:

> The curriculum embraces the reality of multiculturalism in American society by providing a balance between learning the common core of dominant culture knowl-

---

F⊙CUS
on Classroom Practices

Recommended Curricular Approaches for
Multicultural Teaching

Although multicultural experiences can be integrated into any teaching approach, some are particularly appropriate when working with young children. Remember that a DCAP orientation must prevail.

- *Antibias approach:* Developed by Louise Derman-Sparks and the A.B.C. Task Force at Pacific Oaks, this approach proposes strategies to organize experiences and classroom interactions to prevent the formation of bias. Experiences are designed to foster tolerance and fairness and to build a community in which all forms of diversity are acknowledged and valued as unique.

- *Thematic teaching:* This approach builds curricular experiences based on themes that

appeal and are meaningful to young children. This approach provides for integration of multicultural content through theme selection. Themes emerge from those chosen together with children and by the teacher.

- *Cooperative learning:* This strategy and instructional approach allows children to work together on projects and explore challenging themes. The small-group format of this approach allows teachers to integrate children with linguistically and culturally diverse characteristics with mainstream children. Assigning and rotating children's roles provides minority and exceptional children with opportunities to assume responsibility and leadership within their group.

---

edge (for example, English language, democratic values) and knowledge of minority cultures. Curriculum accommodates children who have limited English proficiency. All cultures and primary languages of children are respectfully reflected in the curriculum.

Clearly, if schools remain mainstream-oriented and unresponsive to our pluralistic context, education will fail to provide the experiences that children and society require. Early childhood educators are urged to break away from school practices that perpetuate inequities and use their power to build nurturing classrooms where children will come to appreciate and value social diversity. The development and education of a child is a responsibility of families, teachers, caregivers, and communities. Earlier in the book we discussed findings from developmental research showing that between ages 2 and 5 children begin to form their character and construct their view about the world that surrounds them. What they learn during those formative years, both positive and negative, determines the moral nature of their character for the rest of their lives. This reinforces the need to provide experiences at an early age to foment in children an appreciation and value for diversity, encouraging them to practice tolerance by recognizing differences and similarities among people. One of the most important lessons to be learned in that regard involves resisting biases. Parents and teachers need to join forces in shaping accepting attitudes and eliminating prejudice formation in young children. Position statements and materials from professional organizations (such as the NAEYC, ACEI, Southern Early Childhood Association, and Southern Poverty Law Center) about resisting biases and fostering a healthy self-esteem are sources of ideas and activities for effective curricular practices both in the classroom and beyond it.

Building a Curriculum That Promotes Respect and Appreciation for Diversity

The following are things that teachers and parents can do to teach children how to resist biases.

- Counteract biases by voicing our opposition to them.
- Give children messages that deliberately contrast stereotypes.
- Show no bias in friends, doctors, teachers, or other service providers.
- Instill the notion that a person's appearance is never a true mark of his or her character.
- Talk positively about each person's physical characteristics and cultural heritage.
- Provide opportunities for children to interact with others who are culturally, racially, and religiously different from themselves and who have different abilities.
- Listen respectfully and answer all children's questions about themselves and others.
- Teach children how to handle biases about who they are.
- Use accurate and fair images instead of stereotypes and encourage children to talk about the differences and similarities.
- Teach children that unjust things can be changed. (Adapted from the NAEYC statement titled *Teaching Young Children to Resist Bias*, 1997.)

Mirroring Our Classrooms

Many things are best understood when you observe others in action. We invite you now to come into the classroom of kindergarten teacher Barbara, whose reflections we have been following throughout each chapter. As you may recall, Barbara, who teaches in a suburban school somewhere in this country, made the decision to transform her practices and move into multicultural education. Well grounded in her belief that teaching can help eliminate prejudice and racism, Barbara decided to take action by incorporating diversity into her teaching. Before you catch up with her through her journal entries, examine your personal convictions about multiculturalism. Like Barbara, you may want to write down your beliefs and the reasons for embedding cultural diversity into early childhood programs. Save your ideas in a journal and revisit them later. You may want to see if your views remain the same.

Becoming a successful multicultural educator is important for many reasons. Two of those are, first, to ensure that your children receive the quality education they deserve, and second, to be a part of the group of early childhood multicultural teachers who are setting the pace for others. Helping you acquire the tools to become the teacher that all children need is one of the main purposes of this book.

Focusing Our Lenses on Children's Needs

As you continue your journey into teaching with a multicultural perspective, there are several steps to follow. In order to gain an overview of what happens in the classroom, begin by considering the following about the curriculum:

1. Emphasis on diversity:
   - *Does my current program reflect the diversity of my students' community?*
   - *Do I teach in ways that reflect the lives of my students, and does my teaching help them affirm their identities?*
   - *Am I providing all children with skills to deal and interact with people who are different from themselves?*
2. Attention to special needs:
   - *Is my planning inclusive and mindful of the needs of children with disabilities?*
   - *Are experiences planned to accommodate their needs while providing meaningful activities?*
3. Attention to linguistic differences:
   - *Does my planning take into consideration the linguistic needs of young English language learners (ELL)?*
   - *Are materials appropriate based on the characteristics and needs of ELL children?*

These questions will help in establishing practices that promote respect and appreciation for diversity.

Barbara's Findings: Multicultural Teaching is for All Children

In her assessment of classroom practices, Barbara found support for her idea that her classroom teaching needed a change. The most relevant action was that, as a professional, Barbara made the determination to add "multiculturalness" to her classroom teaching. *Multiculturalness*, according to Davidman and Davidman (2007), is the perspective and posture the teacher assumes and imparts through her or his classroom practices, even when teaching an all–European American class. Simply said, multiculturalness is a quality that must define classroom teaching. This point must be emphasized, because many still believe that these efforts are important only when culturally diverse children are concerned. On many occasions, we have heard students say that they have no need for a multicultural program because they do not have any multicultural children. When asked what they meant, they have responded that their class "is all white." In another instance, during a presentation at the national early childhood conferences, someone commented that she had no need for multicultural programs because all of her students were from minority groups, so "what else could I teach them since they already know everything about themselves?" Multicultural programs need to be offered to all children so each child can develop positive perspectives toward people in our country that can be used throughout life. We also hope for multiculturalness to soon become the character that permeates the teaching and learning processes in every community.

Finding Instruments to Assess the Curriculum

We already know that Barbara concluded that something had to change. However, wanting more specific directions, she decided to identify with precision the areas where help was required most. Perhaps for some teachers, the realization that a change is needed is enough to move ahead. If teachers feel confident with the information gathered in this way, they should move on. However, others may want to follow Barbara's example and take a deeper look at their practices.

Getting ready to begin a more in-depth analysis, Barbara made another comment in her journal: "Will I be able to go ahead?" You might have a similar question. This is, after all, an expected reaction, because this is the very step where people often tend to shy away from the task that lies ahead.

Having made a decision to go on, Barbara's next concern was what instrument to use to evaluate her program. She knew there were several options:

- Reviewing professional literature to find an existing assessment instrument
- Using an instrument already available at her school or school district
- Designing her own assessment

Sample Tools for Evaluating Curricular Practices

Examples of assessment tools can be found in professional literature. Their advantages include that they are readily available, they are good sources of information for educators planning to create their own instruments, and they provide helpful indicators of the areas to address when moving into multicultural teaching. Among those found in the literature, Baruth and Manning (1992, 2004) propose a seven-point questionnaire, which we have adapted for the early childhood setting.

1. *Evidence of multicultural perspectives:* Are multicultural perspectives already incorporated throughout the entire school, my classroom curriculum, and my classroom environment?

2. *Attitudes toward diversity:* Do my attitudes and those of the rest of the teachers, administrators, and staff members indicate a willingness to accept and respect cultural diversity?

3. *Instructional materials/resources:* Do classroom materials—manipulatives, books, and so on—recognize the value of cultural diversity, gender, and social class differences?

4. *Teaching strategies/activities:* Do curricular activities and methods provide children with opportunities to work and play together in a cooperative fashion?

5. *Schoolwide activities:* Do general school activities reflect cultural diversity?

6. *Parent/community views:* Do my curricular planning efforts reflect the reality (views and opinions) of families and the community?

7. *Language diversity:* Do my curricular efforts include bilingual perspectives or provide assistance for students with limited English-speaking skills (when teaching children who are bilingual or who are learning English as a second language)?

Another tool is a questionnaire based on five dimensions needed for the implementation of multicultural teaching (Banks, 1994). The five dimensions include content integration, knowledge construction, prejudice reduction, equitable pedagogy, and an empowering classroom culture and structure. Questions to help teachers develop a detailed profile of their practices address each dimension. An adaptation of the questionnaire for early childhood education is found in Figure 7-8.

Assessment Tools Used in Schools or School Districts

Attention by schools and districts to education for diversity has dramatically increased in recent years. This heightened awareness is a result of advocacy efforts by leading professional organizations, teachers, and community members given the increasing diversity within our communities. Data about the ethnic, cultural, and social characteristics of students are regularly collected. Mandated by federal legislation, information is routinely gathered about student exceptionalities and about the number of children speaking home languages other than English. How these statistics are used depends on the priorities and commitments of the various schools and school districts.

Today, programs at schools and community agencies continue to make efforts to address the needs of children with culturally diverse characteristics. These efforts might represent interests coming from the district personnel, from a group of teachers, or from administrators. Use of data-gathering instruments is common practice in most schools where checklists and surveys designed at the district level, by teachers, or by multicultural specialists are utilized (see Figure 7-9). Multicultural assessment instruments should always be closely reviewed before they are used. Before selecting a tool, check the questions, the kind of information requested, and how this is asked. Remember to be sensitive to cultural differences and present questions in a respectful manner.

Designing Your Own Multicultural Tool

The decision to create a multicultural instrument of your own may result from the uniqueness of your setting and the makeup of your students. Regardless of the reason, preparation and good planning are in order. Before designing a multicultural assessment

FIGURE 7-8 **Identifying Classroom Practices**

A. Content Integration

1. What is my curricular content? What topics do I explore with children?
2. Is diversity reflected in my classroom topics? How?
3. Are there opportunities for children to ponder similarities/differences?
4. Are materials and resources reflective of the children's/nation's diversity?
5. Are topics on diversity consistently included? How often?

B. Knowledge Construction

1. Are experiences offered for children to examine and discover likenesses/ differences?
2. Are experiences at the cognitive developmental level of the child?
3. Are the classroom arrangement and materials exposing children to diversity?
4. Are questions used to guide the child as he or she ponders reality rather than providing the answers?

C. Prejudice Reduction

1. Is the classroom (materials, books) free of cultural stereotypes?
2. When they occur, are misconceptions examined and clarified?
3. Is the teacher proactive and not "color-blind" when situations arise?
4. Are positive attitudes toward diversity modeled and encouraged?
5. Does the classroom atmosphere inspire respect and tolerance?

D. Equitable Pedagogy

1. Are all children treated equally?
2. Are all children offered a sense of success?
3. Do I show to every child that I believe in what he or she can do?
4. Do I adapt/change the curriculum for the child?
5. Do I show children that I respect and value their cultural identities?

E. An Empowering Classroom/School Culture

1. Are my children screened/assessed in a developmental fashion?
2. Is the child's cultural identity acknowledged when planning/teaching?
3. Is my teaching mindful of the community's identity?
4. Is the classroom constantly acknowledging the children's identities?

Source: Robles de Meléndez, 2004.

tool, search the literature and learn not only what the content should be, but also how to apply good principles of instrument design.

Educator Howard D. Hill believes that teachers of minority students should become effective facilitators of learning and achievement. For that to happen, he urges teachers to ask themselves four key questions that detect the skills and attitudes you

FIGURE 7-9 **Diversity Antibias Checklist**

Goals: Program and Teacher

Do the program and the teacher	Yes	No
1. Foster multiculturalism, self-worth, a sense of dignity and unity, and understand that to be different is not to be inferior?		
2. Accept the uniqueness of each child and his or her cultural background and recognize that each has something valuable to contribute?		
3. Use the child's experiences to teach other children?		
4. Develop and encourage the teacher–learner model, where the teacher and the child learn from each other?		
5. Combine the teaching of skill with the teaching of multiculturalism and recognize that they do not need to be taught separately?		
6. Understand that all children bring with them valuable bases from which learning can occur, and understand the children's backgrounds to enhance the teacher–learner model?		
7. Develop an atmosphere in the classroom that encourages cooperation, unity, and the sharing of individual experiences?		
8. Present the children with objective materials about different cultures, instead of only those materials that have been prepared through the viewpoint of the dominant group? (They should include books, posters, and similar elements.)		
9. Help the teacher become aware of his or her own prejudices and biases?		
10. Understand that learning abilities, cognitive styles, and expectations vary among cultures and that these may have a significant impact on the teaching methods and curriculum plan?		

Goals: Children

Are children encouraged to	Yes	No
1. Become aware of their own uniqueness? (This may include body features, language, culture, and background.)		
2. Become familiar with their own historical roots as well as those of the group and the community?		
3. Accept the differences of others and realize that being different does not mean that someone is inferior?		
4. Promote equality between and respect for other cultures and arrest prejudices that breed ignorance?		
5. Encourage freedom of speech and a willingness to share without intimidation, both in their own and other cultural groups?		
6. Develop a sense of responsibility and belonging to the group and understand that unity is possible within a diverse group?		

Source: Elliot, 2002.

need when working with diversity. Hill's (1989) questions remind educators to consider not only the students but also themselves as implementers of the process.

- ■ What is it that helps students learn?
- ■ What is it that teachers can do to aid their students in learning?
- ■ What teacher qualities, personal and professional, do I possess that help or hinder student learning?
- ■ What skills must teachers possess if they are to facilitate learning and achievement for minority students?

What Needs to Be Assessed: Key Points in Young Children's Programs

The first thing our kindergarten teacher, Barbara, did was analyze the nature of her existing program. Following is what she examined about her classroom.

Checking for Developmentally Appropriate Teaching   The first thing to keep in mind is that multicultural teaching and developmentally appropriate teaching are equal partners in education for diversity. Barbara, the teacher whom we have been following, is committed to teaching in a developmentally appropriate way. For Barbara, following the DCAP guidelines begins with her review of the parameters defined in Bredekamp and Copple's (2009) *Developmentally Appropriate Practices for Programs Serving Children from Birth through Age 8*, which provides sample portrayals of children's behaviors and characteristics. Reviewing professional sources is an important step because it gives teachers a chance to validate their own knowledge and practices. Such resources are also helpful when conducting an assessment of one's practices (see Barbara's findings in Figure 7-10).

Identifying "Things That Happen" in the Classroom   Analyzing the program in your classroom is easier when you think of it as all that happens in the classroom. The topics and themes the children explore and the materials they use represent the real curriculum. How these topics are presented and developed depends on the particular instructional strategies and processes employed by the individual teacher. To further analyze this, you may want to ask yourself the same question Barbara asked herself: "What do I teach and how do I teach it?" As you answer this question, three main aspects

FIGURE 7-10 **Barbara's Findings**

DCAP areas Barbara needs to work on:
- More age-appropriate literacy materials
- Increase opportunities for thinking, pondering (use more questions)
- Work on the learning stations (more areas for working independently)

Assessing the learning of young children requires using many different assessment tools.

will emerge: *the content, the process,* and *the resources.* An honest answer to each of the following questions will help you identify the nature of your classroom reality.

- *The Content:* What are the themes or topics that children work with in this classroom? What are they learning? When answering the first question regarding the topics and themes, check your lesson plans for the past month. Retrospection will tell you where your emphases have been. It will also help in identifying your learning outcomes. A way to keep track of this analysis is to use self-stick notes and jot down the diversity topics that are addressed. Also, write the dates on which they occurred to determine whether these instructional events only happened when observing holidays.

- *The Process:* How and what activities will help children learn about a theme? What things do they do? For the second question that addresses the process, write some of the activities that were used in the classroom. Try to remember how all the children responded to the experiences. Be sure to find out if, at the end of each experience, all the children came away knowing that they were successful in their own way. This will help you know if the outcomes that you established are met.

- *Resources and Materials:* What do we use when we work with a topic? Identifying the classroom materials and resources is a way of judging whether children are provided with things that either reflect their own background or that of others, or whether the materials are inappropriate or missing from the classroom. Use of ethnic items helps children clarify their perceptions about the cultures of others. When listing your resources, recall how many times you have invited people of various cultures from the community to visit your class. Ask yourself if those times included only holidays or if they only happened during the "multicultural month." Best practices tell us that for teachers to establish a bias-free environment, children need to have their parents

Curriculum planning and preparation are necessary for all early childhood professionals.

and other community members regularly involved in the classroom, not just on special occasions (Derman-Sparks & A.B.C. Task Force, 1989; Epstein et al., 2002).

Assessing the Environment: What the Child Sees   The classroom environment is another area to examine. Learning is not limited to what the teacher presents or asks the children to do. It also includes messages sent by the classroom environment. Therefore, it is necessary to detect the kinds of messages sent to the children through such media as pictures, manipulatives, and literature. Derman-Sparks (1989) believes that the environment is a powerful knowledge-building instrument. She recommends that teachers carefully analyze the environment as a first step toward change. She states: "What is in the environment also alerts children to what the teacher considers important or not important. Children are as vulnerable to omissions as they are to inaccuracies and stereotypes: What isn't [seen] can be as powerful a contributor to attitudes as what is seen."

Your analysis should begin with what you have on the walls. After all, whatever you have hanging on the walls contributes to create the atmosphere in your classroom. Take time to list the kinds of pictures and decorations in your classroom that reflect diversity. This means finding out, for example, whether the pictures reflect a balance of ethnic backgrounds and include the cultures of your children. Determine whether pictures show activities commonly engaged in by your children's parents. You also need to see whether the manipulatives and other play materials, such as dolls, reflect diversity. Check the literacy area to see whether the books address a variety of multicultural themes and languages. A detailed listing of environmental elements to check appears in Figure 7-11.

FIGURE 7-11 **Assessing Diversity in the Early Childhood Classroom**

Diversity Elements	Visuals (Pictures, Posters)	Literacy and Print Materials	Dramatic Area	Music Materials	Art Materials	Classroom Arrangement	Manipulatives and Sensorial Materials
Language • Materials are available in English and in other languages • Library includes books and other print materials in languages other than English • Children use and are encouraged to use their first languages • Signs and labels are in languages spoken by children • There is singing in other language							
Culture and ethnic groups • Materials include representation of a variety of ethnic and racial groups • Decorations and materials on display represent different cultural groups • Ethnic and culturally typical clothing is available in the dramatic area							

(continued)

FIGURE 7-11 **(continued)**

Diversity Elements	Visuals (Pictures, Posters)	Literacy and Print Materials	Dramatic Area	Music	Art Materials	Classroom Arrangement	Manipulatives and Sensorial Materials
• Materials (dolls, toys) include a variety of racial and ethnic groups • Artifacts from a variety of ethnic and cultural groups are integrated into play areas and available for children to manipulate • Listening environment includes selections representative of different cultural groups (music, rhymes)							
Exceptionalities and disabilities • Modifications are made to accommodate children with special needs (arrangement, equipment) • Materials include representation of children with disabilities							
Gender • Posters and visuals include nonstereotyped gender roles • Children's books include stories about people in nonstereotyped roles							

Faith
- Visuals and images include people from all faith groups
- Children's books include children and families from all faith groups

Age
- Pictures and visuals present positive images of people across age groups
- Visuals include images of positive intergenerational familiar situations
- Children's books include stories about successful and positive experiences of people across age groups, including children and elderly

Social class
- Images include a variety of social class groups
- Visuals portray all social groups in positive and successful roles

Reflecting on your findings and observations:
- *What messages about culture and diversity does the classroom convey?*
- *What will you change in the classroom as a result of the survey? Why?*

PUTTING THINGS TOGETHER

Verifying developmentally appropriate practices, analyzing the curriculum, and taking an inventory of the classroom environment are the three tasks that must be performed by every early childhood educator who has made a commitment to teach in a multicultural way. This information can be collected in a variety of formats. Because the findings will be for your own use, you should use the methods of collecting information you find most convenient and appropriate. What is important is to assess the program honestly and thoroughly so that the results of the inquiry present an accurate picture.

After our friend Barbara collected information about her teaching, she decided to lay out her findings. Being experienced in thematic teaching, she was very familiar with webbing, a way to graphically brainstorm and conceptualize a problem, topic, or issue. Barbara decided to use a web for her assessment. At the center of a large piece of cardboard, she drew a circle and labeled it "My classroom now." Inside the circle she wrote the diversity characteristics of her classroom. Branching out from the center were the following areas:

- Themes we learn about (content)
- Activities we do (process)
- Materials we use (process)
- What children find/see in the classroom (environment)

Using self-stick notes, she jotted down her findings. Then she placed them according to what she had found. As a working action map (see Figure 7-12), the web became a practical way to portray her classroom and her teaching.

SETTING DIRECTIONS

Like Barbara, you are invited to begin by finding out about practices in the classroom. Choose the way that will best lead you to learn about current practices and characteristics of children, families, and community. Regardless of which avenue you decide to follow, do your best to get a feel for what you actually do. This is an important step, be-

FIGURE 7-12 **Action Map**

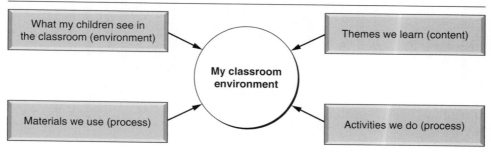

cause it builds awareness of the need for a multicultural curriculum. We will examine Barbara's findings in the next chapter.

WHAT WE HAVE LEARNED—CHAPTER SUMMARY

This chapter was about curriculum planning, a very complex process that requires knowledge, planning, organization, and commitment on the part of every early childhood educator. It is also important that each one of us be an advocate for social justice and equality on behalf of young children. There are many curriculum designs to choose from. Selecting the most appropriate one is one of the most important tasks of the early childhood educator. In addition to selecting appropriate content, you must be aware of the appropriateness of the environment and developmentally appropriate practices. Assessing the needs of your children is an important starting point in the curriculum-planning process. Many early childhood organizations provide checklists, frameworks, and other tools that are helpful in designing and selecting the curriculum for your classroom. The goal for all of us is to build a curriculum that is appropriate for the needs of all children in the classroom and promotes respect and appreciation for diversity.

THINGS TO DO . . .

1. Identify five early childhood teachers working in multicultural education. Have them examine the list of characteristics of the early childhood multicultural teacher defined in this chapter. Have them point out those characteristics they find most relevant and ask them to explain their choices. Find out what other traits they believe should be listed.

2. Visit a classroom and examine the curriculum. Identify whether it reflects integration of diversity topics. See if the topics are integrated throughout the content or if they appear only when a special event or holiday is observed.

3. A tourist approach looks at multiculturalism as a visitor does when traveling to another country—by focusing on the folklore, the exotic, and the historical aspects. Examine your curriculum and determine whether you are following a tourist-like approach. If you are, propose two alternative ways to modify your present curriculum.

4. Visit five early childhood settings and assess the environment using the guidelines presented in this chapter. Determine the areas that most frequently appear in need of change.

5. Find the ethnic and social characteristics of the community where you work. Then, determine what materials you could include in the classroom to represent them.

RECOMMENDED INTERNET RESOURCES

- National Association for Multicultural Education
  www.nameorg.org/

- "Promoting Positive Outcomes for Children with Disabilities," from the Division for Early Childhood of the Council for Exceptional Children
  www.dec-sped.org/pdf/positionpapers/Prmtg_Pos_Outcomes_Companion_Paper.pdf

■ Rethinking Schools
www.rethinkingschools.org/

YOUR STANDARDS PORTFOLIO

NAEYC Standard 1: Promoting Child Development and Learning*

Planning is essential to high-quality learning. Getting ready to create a multicultural program calls for effective planning. Good planning requires teachers to use knowledge about the content and also about children, families, and the community. Having the child as the core influence for what is planned is crucial for developing culturally responsive experiences. Complete the following activities to help you acquire experience in applying planning skills to classroom teaching.

■ The classroom environment is considered a pedagogical tool. To include appropriate elements in your classroom, learn about the ethnic and social characteristics of the community. Articulate your vision about how to design a culturally responsive environment based on the community's characteristics.

■ Planning for the child requires knowledge about his or her strengths and needs. Using the DCAP concept, describe the kind of developmental information you need to plan responsive experiences for young children.

■ Visit an inclusion classroom and interview the teacher. Inquire about the Individualized Education Plan (IEP) and how it is used in the planning process.

REFERENCES

ACEI & OMEP. (2000). Partnership with families and communities. *Global guidelines for early childhood education and care in the 21st century.* Washington, DC: Author.

Banks, J. (1991). *Teaching strategies for ethnic studies* (5th ed.). Boston: Allyn & Bacon.

Banks, J. (1994). Transforming the mainstream curriculum. *Educational Leadership, 8,* 4–8.

Banks, J. (2003). *Teaching strategies for ethnic studies* (7th ed.). Boston: Allyn & Bacon.

Baruth, L. G., & Manning, M. L. (1992). *Multicultural education of children and adolescents.* Boston: Allyn & Bacon.

Baruth, L. G., & Manning, M. L. (2004). *Multicultural education of children and adolescents* (4th ed.). Needham Heights, MA: Allyn & Bacon.

Bredekamp, S. (Ed.). (1987). *Developmentally appropriate practice in early childhood programs serving children from birth through age 8.* Washington, DC: National Association for the Education of Young Children.

* NAEYC Standard 1 correlates with INTASC Standard 7: Planning.

Bredekamp, S., & Copple, C. (2009). *Developmentally appropriate practice for programs serving young children from birth through age 8* (3rd ed.). Washington, DC: NAEYC.

Bredekamp, S., & Rosegrant, T. (Eds.). (2001). *Reaching potentials: Appropriate curriculum and assessment for young children, 1.* Washington, DC: National Association for the Education of Young Children.

Campbell, J. (1995). *Understanding John Dewey: Nature and cooperative intelligence.* Carbondale, IL: Open Count Publishing.

Dalton, S. (1998). *Pedagogy matters: Standards for effective practice.* Washington, DC: Center for Research on Education, Diversity, and Excellence (CREDE).

Darling-Hammond, L. (2004). Inequality and the right to learn: Access to qualified teachers in California's public schools. *Teachers College Record, 106*(10), 1936–1966.

Davidman, L., & Davidman, P. T. (2007). *Teaching with a multicultural perspective.* New York: Longman.

Derman-Sparks, L., & the A.B.C. Task Force. (1989). *Antibias curriculum tools for empowering young children.* Washington, DC: National Association for the Education of Young Children.

Division of Early Childhood. (2007). *Promoting positive outcomes for children with disabilities: Recommendations for curriculum, assessment, and program evaluation.* Missoula, MT: Author.

Epstein, J. L., Sanders, M. G., Simon, B. S., Salinas, K. C., Jansorn, N. R., & Van Voorhis, F. L. (2002). *School, community, and community partnerships: Your handbook for action* (2nd ed.). Thousand Oaks, CA: Corwin Press.

Hernandez, H. (2001). *Multicultural education: A teacher's guide to content and process.* New York: Merrill.

Hickman, L., & Alexander, T. (1999). *The essential Dewey (Volume 1): Pragmatism, education, democracy.* Bloomington, IN: Indiana University Press.

Hill, H. D. (1989). *Effective strategies for teaching minority students.* Bloomington, IN: National Association of Early Childhood Specialists in State Departments of Education (NAECS/SDE).

National Association for the Education of Young Children. (1997). Teaching young children to resist bias. Retrieved September 30, 2008, from http://www.naeyc.org/ece/1997/10.asp.

National Association for the Education of Young Children & National Association of Early Childhood Specialists in State Departments of Education (NAEYC & NAECS/SDE). (2003). *Guidelines for appropriate curriculum and assessment in programs serving children ages 3 through 8.* Washington, DC: NAEYC.

Nieto, S., & Bode, P. (2007). *Affirming diversity: The sociopolitical context of multicultural education.* Boston: Allyn & Bacon.

Ornstein, A., & Hunkins, F. (1993). *Curriculum: Foundations, principles, and theory.* Boston: Allyn & Bacon.

Ornstein, A., & Hunkins, F. (2004). *Curriculum: Foundations, principles, and theory* (4th ed.). Boston: Allyn & Bacon.

Robles de Meléndez, W. (2004). *Theory and practice in early childhood education* (study guide). Fort Lauderdale, FL: Nova Southeastern University.

Romo, J. J., Bradfield, P., & Serrano, R. (2004). *Reclaiming democracy: Multicultural educators' journeys toward transformative teaching.* Upper Saddle River, NY: Pearson.

U.S. Census Bureau. (2006). *American community survey 2006.* Retrieved June 20, 2008, from http://factfinder.census.gov/servlet/ACSSAFFPeople?_submenuId=people_8& _sse=on.

Wadsworth/Cengage Learning

CHAPTER 8

Preparing to Bring Ideas into Action

What is presented, as well as how it is presented, shape the curriculum and therefore, the learning of children. Curricular decisions should demonstrate an acceptance of and appreciation for children of diverse backgrounds.

Southern Early Childhood Association (n.d.)

CHAPTER OBJECTIVES

In this chapter, we will

- discuss ways to bring multicultural education into practice.
- review the planning steps for successful multicultural education.
- select multicultural approaches for the young children's classroom.
- give examples for establishing goals and objectives in multicultural programs.
- organize the early childhood multicultural curriculum following developmentally and culturally appropriate practices (DCAP).

KEY CONCEPTS

- planning
- content
- goals and objectives

FROM BARBARA'S JOURNAL

It's time to begin planning activities that are multicultural. My principal was very support-ive and responsive to my efforts and provided me with the faculty responses to last year's multicultural survey. Analyzing the results was helpful. It's always good to have some fac-tual support for our actions. She also gave me a lot of good information about the com-munity that, together with my observations, helped me to know more about the environ-ment. What I know and the information that I have show me where I want to go: I want to teach responsively. I want children to become proud of who they are and to know that it is OK to be different. Oh, and most definitely, I want them to work together with everyone in harmony. No more name-calling, no more "I won't play with you." So far, I've learned a lot about my students, their parents, the curriculum, and diversity. How to put it all into effective practice so that it benefits the children is what I need to work on. Honestly, I feel some apprehension. Will I make the right decisions? Will my teaching be what my students need? I guess I will know that only after I start making the changes. All I know is that I have to do it!

A TIME FOR IDEAS: PLANNING FOR MULTICULTURAL TEACHING

The time has come to begin one of the most exciting parts of multicultural education: the planning phase. This is when you take the most concrete and definitive steps. More than anything, this will be a challenging time. We will begin by reviewing some basic concepts of curriculum planning. Then, we will examine the planning process in the early childhood classroom context.

Creating Your Teaching Framework

As you have seen, central to multicultural education is the idea that *all* children should have access to excellent and quality learning experiences. This can only happen when the curriculum is carefully designed and planned. Like architects and engineers, early childhood teachers have blueprints (curriculum) to guide their work. The curriculum lays out the routes of knowledge you will take during the learning journey with your stu-dents. Curricular blueprints vary as much as a blueprint of a high-rise differs from one of a single-family house. However, curricular blueprints share many elements in common. For example, instructional content is organized by combining knowledge, the needs of learners, societal goals, and personal ideals into a coherent instructional plan. Designing instructional plans with a focus on diversity is a complex process that requires the use of many talents and resources, such as originality, knowledge, creativity, and funds.

Curriculum development has traditionally been delegated to school curriculum specialists and commercial experts associated with publishing firms. You probably have seen many and used some of these curricula. In the area of multicultural education, however, teachers have played a major role in the curriculum development of programs focused on diversity. This can be attributed to such factors as the relatively recent emergence of multicultural education as a curriculum component, the evolving nature of multiculturalism, the lack of commitment and resources on the part of the schools to develop special curricula, and the interests and initiatives of teachers who want to align their practices with reality. Whatever the reason, classroom teachers play an important role in developing multicultural curricula. Curriculum development provides a special opportunity for teachers to implement the wealth of their ideas and explore new ways of transforming classroom teaching. Like everything new, the task is a challenging one that requires good planning, hard work, and patience. Because of the versatile nature of multicultural programs, educators who took part in the process report that they found it necessary to spend more time planning the experiences for their students than they did when developing more traditional curricula.

Making Dreams into Reality

The inclusion of multiculturalism at all levels of education is slowly becoming a reality. The process has been facilitated by the rapid transformation of the pluralistic society of the United States. The social and cultural changes have been the major catalysts in convincing educators that appropriate preparation of students must include new ways of dealing with the present and the future society.

Many early childhood educators are committed to multicultural education. Designing effective curricula centered on the individual needs of children and their social environment is one way of fulfilling that commitment. However, the implementation of multicultural programs has been difficult for many teachers, not because it requires skills, creativity, and knowledge, but because it often lacks the other essential element: support. If teachers had the necessary encouragement and support, there would be many more quality programs that embrace diversity.

Eliminating the myth about the impossibility of implementing a multicultural curriculum is important, especially at the young

Teachers can learn from each other.

Wadsworth/Cengage Learning

children's level. Thousands of teachers throughout this country have already embraced this approach and experienced success. They recognize the crucial role multiculturalism plays in the educational process and in life in general. This book is designed to offer support to early childhood practitioners who need and want to reform their teaching. Throughout this chapter, we share more practical ideas to help you launch your program.

Planning and Organizing: The Critical Steps

How to structure "what will happen in the classroom" is a challenging experience for many educators. However, teachers need to be assured that because of their experiences in the classroom, they have the practical experience and the knowledge necessary for designing effective curricula. Additional enabling forces are the teachers' dedication to their profession and their belief in equality for all children.

Multicultural teaching reform has led many educators to assume the role of curriculum innovators. Teachers engaged in curriculum improvement are much more aware of the needs of diverse students and how to meet their needs through responsive classroom experiences (Rogers, 2004). Teachers engaged in the process of changing to multicultural teaching are doing that with exceptional creativity. It can even be said that their creativity is nurtured by their commitment to multiculturalism and their devotion to young students.

Early Childhood Teaching Prepares You for Curricular Change

The nature of the field of early childhood education prepares teachers to engage in curriculum planning. A review of DCAP reminds us that the real curriculum is constantly being redesigned as the young students in the classroom reveal their needs and interests. Good professionals recognize that developmentally effective teaching can only happen if they are able to alter instructional plans to respond to the needs of young learners. Cur-

---

| In Action . . . | "I Think I Can, I Think I Can" |

Remember *The Little Engine That Could*? Well, we want you, like the engine, to become optimistic about what you are able to do as a multicultural educator. Also, we want you to be able to transform your teaching. Complete the following two sentences:

- *I know I can become a multicultural educator because . . .*

- *I know I can build a good curriculum because . . .*

As you continue this chapter, keep these two statements in mind to remind yourself that you can do it!

riculum development tasks for traditional and multicultural instruction include writing and readjusting the content of lesson plans, trying to find manipulatives for the classroom, and searching for appropriate literature. An additional task to remember when planning to teach multiculturally is to become more aware and be perceptive of the students' social interactions in the classroom. For example, consider the comments made by 4-year-old children after they are read a story with characters with exceptionalities or from a cultural group other than theirs. Also, note whom the children play with or exclude from their activities. Observe the reactions of toddlers to the voices of people with different accents. A careful assessment and discerning analysis of how children deal with each other and how they face social issues will be a source of data revealing how your activities impact children as well as a guide for finding new directions for your curriculum. In the next sections, we will explore the specific steps for making your multicultural curriculum a reality.

Good curriculum planning should include the use of a variety of sources both familiar and new to children.

What Is Planning? Do We Need to Plan?

Planning is a critical step in the development of curriculum for young children. Effective planning contributes to the achievement of educational goals and student learning outcomes in all classrooms, including those serving children with cultural and diverse characteristics. **Planning** is the process by which you build and *organize* learning experiences. By planning, you establish the directions and purposes for activities and match them with the needs of young learners. Good planning answers four basic questions:

- ■ *Who?* Planning effective instructional strategies and classroom activities begins with knowledge about the learners. This requires the early childhood professionals to know the developmental, cultural, linguistic, and individual needs of the children they teach.

- ■ *What?* Knowledge of **content** is fundamental to successful planning. We must be fully cognizant of themes and topics and how they relate to the subject matter and

LET'S TALK AND REFLECT... Early Childhood Teachers

No person can provide you with more expert information about planning than an early childhood teacher, which is why we want you to informally interview at least three early childhood teachers. Simply ask them to share what kind of curriculum they use, how they plan their activities, whether they often change them to suit the children's needs, and how they make such changes. Share your findings with class.

learning expectations for young children. Equally important is to anchor curricular experiences in academic expectations and standards for the age groups one teaches. One of the central tenets of multicultural education is a challenging and relevant curriculum planned around what children are expected to learn.

- *Why?* Good experiences have a purpose and a reason. Relevant knowledge needs to include not only important skills and concepts but also appropriate attitudes and values. For instance, teaching fairness and respect for others is important because they are keys to successful interactions.

- *How?* Knowing what instructional methods and strategies to use is essential. Good planning is based on the developmental needs of children, including their individual needs (language, learning modalities, and special needs). Appropriate strategies also take into account appropriate materials, equipment, and classroom arrangements.

Sources for Multicultural Planning

The child is the most important source for planning multicultural activities. In the multicultural classroom, curriculum is "child-centered," designed to effectively respond to the needs of both the culturally diverse and the mainstream children. Day-to-day experiences and sound knowledge about children's development yields relevant data for building curricular experiences. Careful observations of children at play and during classroom activities, as well as while talking and listening to their comments, responses, and reactions to peers and adults, provide meaningful information about concepts and skills to be taught. Awareness about "what happens" in the child's environment—the family, classroom, school, neighborhood, and in the community—is also an important source and helps to connect experiences with their social and cultural reality.

Developmental readiness is another guide for curriculum development. Rapid physical growth as well as emotional maturity in the early years occurs in distinct stages. Best practices indicate that it is imperative for teachers to be aware of what children of a particular age group are able to learn and do as related to the various stages of development. This knowledge is critical for planning individually responsive and appropriate classroom experiences. Principles of development and readiness are so important that they provide a framework for most national and state standards that define learning outcomes for children. Guidelines for multicultural education also reflect the need for curricular activities to help children develop their enormous learning potential according to the rules of nature as well as societal and educational mandates.

LET'S TALK AND REFLECT... **Academic Standards in Early Childhood Education**

The standards movement has led to the establishment of expectations for young children's academic achievement. Florida, Texas, and California, all with highly diverse student populations, established their own standards and use them in defining learning outcomes for young children.

- Find out if your state or district has and follows standards for young learners. If not,

check the standards from any of the states mentioned here. Read and review their standards. Comment on how these can be integrated into multicultural curriculum planning.

- Talk with experienced teachers about their views on using these to develop curricular experiences for children with special needs and culturally diverse characteristics.

LITERACY CONNECTIONS... Recommended References for Curricular Planning in Early Childhood

- Bredekamp, S., & Rosegrant, T. (1995). *Reaching potentials: Appropriate curriculum and assessment for young children, 1.* Washington, DC: National Association for the Education of Young Children.

- Division for Early Childhood of the Council for Exceptional Children. (2007). *Promoting positive outcomes for children with disabilities: Recommendations for curriculum, assessment, and curriculum evaluation.* Missoula, MT: Author.

- National Association for the Education of Young Children. (2005). Screening and assessment of young English language learners. Supplement to the *NAEYC and NAECS/SDE joint position statement on early childhood curriculum, assessment, and program evaluation.* Washington, DC: NAEYC.

| DESIGNING A CHILD-CENTERED CURRICULUM

To be effective, a curriculum needs to have personal relevance, an idea espoused by John Dewey many decades ago. Dewey believed that children show involvement in things in which they find a purpose commensurate to their interest. A child uses interest as a catalyst to guide the process of knowledge construction. The dynamic interaction between the child and the home, classroom, and neighborhood environments induces the active construction of new ideas that create the child's reality (Berk, 2007; Martin & Loomis, 2006). Dewey's ideas (cited in Roopnarine & Johnson, 2005) correlate with Piagetian and Vygotskian principles (cited in Berk, 2007) of knowledge construction that form the basis of child-centered curricula. They both remind us that when experiences are personally and culturally meaningful, interest and engagement in experiences facilitates knowledge building. These principles also underlie an effective classroom curriculum intended to develop multicultural perspectives.

Teachers should aspire to build meaningful hands-on curricula for all students (Bredekamp & Rosegrant, 1995). When a curriculum is formulated on the realities of the child's world, it offers purposeful, relevant, and challenging experiences. A relevant curriculum consists of experiences that keep the child constructively engaged. For that reason, our model places special emphasis on the careful appraisal of the settings where the child interacts: the family, the neighborhood, the community, and the classroom. It also centers attention on the child and his or her needs, characteristics, and unique heritage.

Activities should be varied but always child centered.

Setting Directions: A Curriculum Design of Your Choice

When selecting a design for multicultural education, it is important to decide which approach to use (see Figure 8-1). As explained in Chapter 6, education for diversity can be delivered in a variety of ways. At this point, it is important to take time to choose the approach that really appeals to you. Remember that this new pattern for organizing your teaching does not have to be your final choice. If you find it to be unsuitable for the

FIGURE 8-1 **Synopsis of Sample Approaches for Multicultural Education Curriculum**

- Banks's four levels to integration of multicultural content (additive, contributions, transformational, and the social action approach)
- Sleeter and Grant's typology of practices
- Derman-Sparks's antibias approach
- Frances Kendall's model for early childhood multicultural education

children's needs or for your setting, feel free to try another model. After you choose an approach, you can begin designing your curriculum.

Choosing a Successful Curricular Approach

Teachers searching for an appropriate curriculum approach will encounter several suitable options. Practitioners who believe that their teaching will be enhanced by using ideas from various models are encouraged to combine them in the most effective ways. When ideas from different approaches are combined, the result is an eclectic approach. For example, Banks's additive approach can be used in conjunction with the antibias approach proposed by Derman-Sparks.

Selecting an approach compatible with your professional expertise and ideas is always important. It is also advisable to choose a less difficult model or approach in the beginning and then, as you gain confidence, progress to a more complex one.

Making Decisions

All educators experience difficulties associated with decisions regarding best practices. Many of us have also experienced the disappointment associated with something that did not work as planned. Learning how

A welcoming environment communicates to children and their families that their cultures and ethnicities are valued and respected.

In Action . . .   Choose Your Own Approach

- What curriculum development approaches have you been using in your instruction?
- How much do you know about the approaches discussed in this chapter?
- What approaches seem to be most compatible with each other?
- Which one is the approach of your choice? Why?

to design effective programs through good planning will maximize success in the classroom. Effective planning will allow teachers to do the following:

- Identify the children's needs by reviewing assessment data
- Prioritize needs based on information about children, their families, and the community
- Contextualize planning based on developmental and individual characteristics
- Set realistic expectations and establish goals and objectives
- Choose appropriate teaching strategies and materials
- Become confident to address diversity in individual ways

No teacher is exempt from planning, regardless of how experienced or how new to the teaching profession. This includes Barbara, who decided to begin planning by reviewing the findings of her assessments. You may remember that she recorded her data on a concept web. Webbing provides a holistic view of data and facilitates visual analysis. The conceptual format of the web also makes it easy for Barbara to locate the teaching areas she will target for action (see Figure 8-2). Try using an organizer or web in which information about the children you teach can be detailed. Then, analyze the information and select the key areas you consider most relevant based on your knowledge about children, their families, the curriculum expectations, and the community.

Choosing Priorities

Early in this book, we examined some of the goals of multiculturalism. Reviewing them again is particularly helpful when trying to define priorities in multicultural education. The goals defined by many multicultural educators reflect the purposes advocated today by many educators and early childhood organizations (Derman-Sparks & Ramsey, 2007; and Manning & Baruth, 2004). Promoting a sense of pride in cultural identity, helping children to acquire the skills and knowledge necessary to become successful members of a multicultural society, and building a sense of respect and tolerance about diversity describe some of the current directions and concerns for multiculturalism in the early childhood classroom. Together, these ideas can serve as an appropriate guide in establishing priorities.

FIGURE 8-2 **Holistic Panorama of a Classroom**

THE SETTING

Community
- ethnicities
- services
- social class
- agencies
- languages
- other variables

Families
- configurations
- cultures
- ethnicities
- languages
- customs
- religions
- needs and issues (disabilities, employment)

Children
- ethnicities
- languages
- cultures
- interests
- other variables
- disabilities

THE CLASSROOM

School
- faculty ethnic makeup
- programs for the exceptional
- school services

Me as a teacher
- my ethnicity
- my cultural beliefs
- my customs
- my share of other aspects of diversity

The next step after selecting your goals is to decide on which ones are more important; that is, to establish priorities. Some teachers may find this difficult because of their desire to attend to, respond to, and bring about change in everything that happens in the classroom. However, it is important to initially focus on only a few goals that will target areas meeting the special and diverse needs of the majority of the students in your class. You will see that these will bring about benefits for everyone. Before setting priorities, consider the following:

■ Cultural, ethnic, and racial diversity of the group that calls for experiences that suit the children's cultural needs and establishes the basis of acceptance and healthy social interactions

■ Specific needs of children with exceptionalities that require accommodations, including classroom arrangement and equipment

■ Social situations, such as social class differences, including family occupations, income, immigration status, and cultural characteristics, among others

■ Linguistic differences that demand attention and use of effective strategies to foster acquisition of English while preserving first languages

LITERACY CONNECTIONS...

Planning for Diverse Children

We chose the following children's books as examples of literature fulfilling the different needs children may bring to the multicultural classroom. With any of the titles you read, think about how you would address their different needs. Think also about children you already know and about how to best meet their expectations.

- Cosby, B. (1997). *The meanest thing to say*. New York: Scholastic. (primary; use of slurs)

- Cowen-Fletcher, J. (1993). *Mama zooms*. New York: Scholastic. (preschoolers–primary; parent with disabilities)

- Girnis, M. (2000). *ABC for you and me*. Morton Grove, IL: Albert Whitman & Company. (preschoolers–primary; presents the ABCs using children with Down syndrome)

- Hudson, C. (1990). *Bright eyes, brown skin*. East Orange, NJ: Just Us. (preschoolers; racial pride)

- Levine, E. (1995). *I hate English!* New York: Scholastic. (primary; experiences and feelings about learning a new language and adapting to a new culture)

- Pak, S. (2002). *A place to grow*. New York: Levine Books. (preschoolers–primary; experiences of moving)

- Ransom, J. F. (2001). *I don't want to talk about it*. New York: Magination Press. (preschoolers–primary; children of divorced families)

- Southwell, J. (2001). *Little country town*. New York: Holt. (preschoolers–primary; culture, life in rural areas)

- Thomas, P. (1999). *My family is changing*. Hauppauge, NY: Barron's Education Series. (preschoolers–primary; children of divorced families)

- Williams, V. (2001). *A chair for my mother*. New York: HarperTrophy. (preschoolers; family situations, caring for a parent with disabilities)

- Curricular needs because of low achievement in key content areas
- Local, national, or global events that impact children

Priorities Show the Way

A thorough examination of the characteristics discovered in the assessment phase will help you realize how diversity is reflected in your setting. In Barbara's case, she discovered that her classroom included a variety of diversity traits: five different ethnic groups, three different languages spoken at home, several children with exceptionalities, and a community with an increasing number of immigrant families. Those diversity features served as the foundation for Barbara to establish priorities for her program. Here are the priorities she listed for her kindergartners:

- Helping children deal positively with their own cultural identities; providing opportunities for children to become aware of other kinds of cultural identities
- Learning to live with the diversity that surrounds them
- Helping children reject unfairness

What If My Classroom Is "Monocultural"?

Many times our students have asked us about how to infuse multicultural education into their classrooms when they are mostly characterized by one ethnic group. We always remind them that multicultural education is for and encompasses all children and that no classroom is ever monocultural. The notion that diversity content is solely for children with a variety of cultural traits must be dispelled. The continuously diverse nature of society, whether local, national, or global, serves as the best justification to bring multicultural education into action. In fact, even within a single ethnic group, diversity is found. You probably noticed that Barbara's first priority had a dual objective. In the second part, Barbara refers to children becoming aware of other kinds of cultural identities. This is a very important objective because it will not limit the scope of Barbara's multicultural activities to only those cultural groups already found in the community. In fact, she is determined to offer her students a much wider view of diversity. She began her planning by observing one of the basic rules of multicultural education: consider first the ethnicities present in the class (Derman-Sparks & A.B.C. Task Force, 1989). Then, she thought about other groups children should learn about. We emphasize this point because this is where most multicultural planning fails. Effective multicultural curricular planning requires teachers to consider not only the groups the children represent but also others not present in the classroom and in the community. There are reasons to support this decision. First, with the high population mobility in our country, children have the potential of being exposed to many forms of cultural diversity. Second, the media (TV, movies, and so on), where the absence or token presence of many ethnic groups provides an unclear and sometimes distorted image about social diversity, is a powerful source of cultural interaction for children. Logically, then, these experiences also should be brought into the classroom. We recommend that early childhood educators include information about one, as a minimum, additional cultural group not present in the children's community.

Learning opportunities that expand the children's scope of understanding about others should be integral to classroom planning. True "monocultural" classrooms are very unlikely to exist in our present society when we consider the comprehensiveness of diversity (Derman-Sparks & Ramsey, 2005). Remember that diversity includes not only ethnic differences but also a wide range of other factors, such as religion and physical disabilities, that influence and determine people's behaviors and views about life. So, if your classroom happens to be characterized mostly by a single culture or diversity element, make sure to incorporate into the curriculum experiences about other groups the children would most likely interact with. Exposure to other ways and behaviors, abilities, or differences will help children in forming a more practical view about society. For instance, use of purposefully selected children's literature is an appropriate tool to introduce the young to people with disabilities or to activities from other groups. Persona dolls are another way to introduce children to other diversity aspects. In this context, a doll character helps children in learning about the experiences of individuals with other social and cultural realities. The choice of including other cultural groups or aspects in the curriculum depends on the developmental level of your students as well as on the interests of the children, needs of the school, and events in the community.

Now, ask yourself: *What are my goals in teaching with a multicultural perspective? What are my goals for the children? What will they gain?* Once you find the answers, try to identify your own priorities that will constitute the basis of your multicultural program. Write them down and use them as guides throughout your planning phase.

| FOCUS ON THE ENVIRONMENT

The first tangible changes toward multiculturalization should take place in the classroom physical environment. Because in early education the classroom environment is another teaching and learning tool, focus your attention on it first. From our classroom experiences we have learned that changes in the physical environment are a first and relevant step when moving into multicultural teaching. Rogers (2004) corroborates this and recommends making changes in the physical arrangement of the classroom before moving to the curriculum content. Change is more visible when dealing with the concrete than the abstract. Seeing visible changes will give you a more immediate sense of accomplishment that will motivate future efforts.

Taking Action: Changing the Physical Scenario

In Barbara's journal: *I just finished taking inventory of my classroom, and I can't believe what I found. I thought this was going to be the easiest part of my planning because I was sure I had plenty of materials my children could relate to. But, gosh, I'm shocked! Play materials are so generic, without any ethnic dolls at all. Actually, they all look alike. The housekeeping area barely has anything that represents what my children use at home. At least I do have nice posters with children of different ethnicities. But, the literacy corner is so poor . . . two or three books about African Americans and Hispanics and nothing on any other groups. There is so much to do!*

What gives you the first impression of any classroom? Without any doubts, what you *see* sends the initial messages used to form a frame of reference for that particular setting. This is also how children form impressions and interpret the environment. Early childhood educators (Bredekamp & Rosegrant, 1995; Derman-Sparks & the A.B.C. Task Force, 1989; Gordon, 2003; Rogers, 2004) agree that the classroom environment is an important teaching-learning component of the educational process. Unlike in

Selecting appropriate materials that foster tolerance and celebrate diversity is a skill all early childhood professionals should acquire.

other grades, the total classroom environment plays a crucial role in the development of young children. In fact, the environment is considered an essential medium for learning because every aspect of the classroom serves as a stimulus for challenging the child during the intensive knowledge construction phase that occurs during the early school years. This is why many early childhood educators spend much effort in constructing classroom environments that offer something for every child.

The physical arrangement of an early childhood classroom is very complex because there is so much to include and so much to choose from! Typically, early childhood classrooms offer a wide range of possibilities. Just look at the wealth of activities learning centers can provide the child.

All objects in the classroom have the potential of influencing the child socially, emotionally, and intellectually. Teachers must constantly examine the contents of the environment because it constantly influences the developing child. Materials including equipment, artifacts, pictures, and posters play a relevant role in setting the mood for diversity in the classroom. Consider, for instance, the soft and open spaces that invite infants and toddlers to explore objects and interact with peers and adults. Listen to the music and sounds representative of different cultural groups that are played while children are actively engaged in activities. Look at the arrangement that facilitates movement in a classroom of children with physical challenges, the inclusion of materials in Braille that supports the needs of visually challenged children, and the posters and labels that include languages other than English. These and other elements contribute to building a sense about the presence of children with diverse needs and characteristics while communicating the message that they all belong.

- What are your teaching priorities?
- How did you identify them?

In Chapter 7, we shared several ideas on how to assess the classroom. For instance, observe the interest areas first, move to the literacy resources, and then examine everything that hangs on the walls. You can facilitate your appraisal by using an observation instrument. The *Checklist for Diversity in Early Childhood Education and Care*, published by the Southern Early Childhood Association (SECA), is an excellent example. This resource is designed around three important areas: the overall image of the classroom, the materials in the interest areas, and the diversity of languages (Peck & Shores, 1994). A review of the goals for multicultural education in early childhood like those stated by Kendall can also help in determining the priorities that guide planning for young children (see Figure 8-3).

We Need To Be Practical!

Transforming the physical environment of a classroom requires time and a budget, both of which may sometimes be unavailable. Teachers are advised to proceed slowly in transforming their classrooms. Begin by generating a list of all things needed to achieve

In Action . . . **Classroom Messages**

Consider what messages your classroom environment conveys. With the eyes of a child, look for and find the ideas conveyed through your classroom environment. After your survey is over, write down what things made you feel "uncomfortable" and what made you feel "welcome," the way a child might.

FIGURE 8-3 **Kendall's Primary Goals for Multicultural Education**

1. To teach children to respect others' cultures and values as well as their own.
2. To help all children learn to function successfully in a multicultural, multiracial society.
3. To develop a positive self-concept in those children who are most affected by racism.
4. To help all children experience in positive ways both their differences as culturally diverse people and their similarities as human beings.
5. To encourage children to experience people of diverse cultures working together as unique parts of a whole community.

Source: Kendall, 1983.

FIGURE 8-4 **A Classroom Menu to Meet the Developmental Needs of Children**

Housekeeping area: kitchen area (cooking and eating utensils, make-believe food items); living room (furnished, including a phone, decorations); bedroom (including a baby area, a closet or trunk with clothes, shoes, bags, accessories)

Art area: easels for free painting; a variety of painting materials (finger paint, materials for sponge and vegetable painting, straws for blow painting, materials for leaf printing, modeling clay, and others)

Block area: blocks of different sizes, props to play with the blocks such as cars, trucks, people, animals

Drama area: different props, costumes, hats, puppets, paper to draw on and/or to make a scene

Literacy and writing areas: books, newspapers, catalogs, magazines, pictures, phone book, taped books; for writing: paper, templates, pencils, pens, crayons, and other writing materials

Water and sand tables: containers, pails, floating objects

Manipulatives: puzzles, games, beads

Music area: a variety of musical instruments such as drums, tambourines, maracas, cymbals, and others

a cultural balance in the classroom. Concentrate on removing all images that either distort or misrepresent cultures and people. Notice what is missing. Derman-Sparks (1989) asserts that what is omitted in the classroom can be as negative as what is inaccurate and stereotypical. Think about all the materials and resources that may be included in the classroom and choose to add those that will best meet the cultural and developmental needs of children. You may want to use the sample list of developmental materials typically found in preschool classrooms that appears in Figure 8-4.

Selecting one learning area to change at a time rather than trying to change them all at once is a good idea. More details about materials and guidelines on how to select activities and resources will be described in Chapter 9.

Changes Yield New Insights

Changes in the environment will result in a variety of responses from the students. Perceptive teachers will use these responses to generate additional ideas that will assist them in moving into the more complex part of the multicultural education change process: the content.

ESTABLISHING THE CONTENT

The traditional curriculum has given way to the new multicultural one as a result of the growing diversity of our society, which is mirrored in our schools. The acceptance of the multicultural curriculum is the result of not only the societal trends but also the new assumptions about teachers, students, and learning. Today's educators realize that culture as a framework for the curriculum blurs the boundaries between the lives of children, the schools, and society at large. It aids in unifying knowledge and skills with the cognitive, emotional, and psychomotor development of the whole child. Choosing content that will meet the mission of the multicultural curriculum presents a real challenge.

Setting Expectations: Goals and Objectives

Every curriculum contains a plan based on expectations and suggested ways to meet those expectations. Expectations are the reasons and the purposes of the learning the students are supposed to accomplish. In education, the reasons and purposes are also known as **goals and objectives.**

Multicultural Education Encompasses the Whole Child

The purposes of a multicultural program will depend on the established priorities. The teacher needs to keep in mind a whole-child approach when selecting curriculum priorities. A whole-child program considers the interactions between the environment and

---

FOCUS
on Classroom Practices

Getting Others to Help You Assess Your Classroom Environment

Although sometimes we fail to detect the stereotypes used and present in our classrooms, help is available:

- Question yourself: *Does everything I have in this classroom reflect my own cultural style? Are there any objects that show my acceptance of the children's cultures? If I were in a different culture, what things would make me feel accepted?* Being honest in your answers will help you discover what your classroom fails to reflect.

- Colleagues: If some teachers are already teaching multiculturally, visit their classrooms. Talk to them and observe what they have and how they arrange the environment. Ask them to share some tips. Invite

them to visit your classroom and ask them to suggest ways to improve it.

- ESOL teachers and exceptional education teachers: These professionals can also provide good ideas about how to meet diversity. They are especially capable of identifying stereotypical or culturally biased objects and materials.

- Parents and community members: If you have parents from a variety of cultures, have some of them share their impressions of your classroom. Ask them what things about their cultures they would like to see in the classroom. They can probably become sources of additional materials and cultural activities.

the child. For that reason, the targeted instructional areas must reflect what is pertinent and relevant to the children. Pertinence is achieved when the curriculum addresses points that convey meaning to the child. This is where teachers need to reconcile the developmental characteristics of the children they teach with the expected aims of the program. More specifically, this means paying special attention to the principles of child development in the physical, cognitive, and social-emotional domains.

Knowledge about developmental patterns and characteristics during the period from birth through age 8 contributes to the establishment of meaningful goals for any program and particularly for a multicultural one. For example, being cognizant of the social-emotional and cognitive characteristics of 5-year-olds will permit selection of literature materials at the correct level. Similarly, knowledge of young children's physical needs and capabilities will offer a solid basis for choosing and structuring experiences for motor skill development.

Multicultural Education Is Grounded in General Educational Goals

The goals and expectations of multicultural programs are not isolated from the goals of general education. The National Standards, also known as America 2000, establish the educational aspirations for all U.S. students.

The first standard addresses the national concern for appropriate early education. Goal 1 states that every child will begin school ready to learn. It also specifies what schools must provide and do for children. Embedded in this goal is more than just providing the child with developmental readiness for learning. "Ready to learn" also implies that children have a positive concept about themselves as individuals. This means that young children are ready to learn only after they have established identities and self-concepts that allow them to feel good about themselves. Early in life, a child's personal identity is constructed through familial relationships, interaction with peers, and relationships formed with other members of the community. This entire process is influenced by the child's culture. The process of forming a sense of identity is more complex when children enter school and encounter others whose ways are different. The new conflict that this creates can be resolved positively if children have a strong self-concept based on positive feelings about their own cultural identities.

My Goals and Objectives Are . . .

A program is established when the goals and objectives are defined. Goals are the purposes of efforts made in schools. They define in broad, long-range terms what children are to gain from the teaching-learning process. In early education, goals need to respond to the developmental characteristics of children. When trying to establish the goals for a program built around diversity, teachers must consider the developmental aspects along with the concepts to be taught. This establishes realistic and achievable purposes for the program (see Figure 8-5).

F☉CUS
on Classroom Practices

Planning for the Whole Child

Developmental teaching has a basic rule: Consideration of what the child needs is essential for creating an effective curriculum. The same rule applies to multicultural education. Planning for the whole child means considering how the child's developmental needs are met through the selected curriculum content. Here is an example of this as presented by Barbara. She used one of her own priorities, "to help children appreciate their own cultures and interact in a positive way with others," to begin identifying ways to fulfill the children's developmental needs while using multicultural content.

1. *Topic*: Discovering what makes us alike and different

2. Target areas and sample activities:

   a. Language/literacy

   - Write their names in the air. Use sandpaper letters to form their names. See who has the longest/shortest name.

   - Play "name soup" (identifying the names of our classmates). Find out how many of the classmates' names have the same first initial.

   - Have children show and tell about "What I can do best."

   - Read and discuss the story *This Is the Way We Go to School*.

   - Include books in the learning centers about children from different ethnic and cultural groups.

   b. Cognitive skills
   - Discuss the things we like to eat, play with, do, and so on. Do a Venn diagram to find out what things we have in common as a group or with a class member.

- Discuss breakfast preferences. On paper plates, have children draw and share what they usually have for breakfast. Prepare a graph to see how many children prefer the same items for breakfast.

- Explore measurement. Find out how many have the same height or weight. Discuss findings.

   c. Social skills
   - Use manner words. Learn to say greetings in different languages.

   - Work cooperatively to create a class mural titled "How Alike We Are."

   - Prepare a "This is Me" book.

   - Learn the song "We Are Alike" (following the tune "Are you sleeping?" or "Frere Jacques"):

     We're alike, we're alike. Yes, we are. Yes, we are.
     (Name of child) **can dance and jump** (substitute with those things the class found in common)
     And so do I. We're so much alike. Oh, that's nice!

   d. Art/fine motor skills

   - Explore with different art forms. Use paper plates and cutouts from magazines to create "Me Mobiles" (things children like to do).

   - Create tactile self-portraits. Use skin-color paints, fabrics, buttons, yarn (for hair), and so on.

   - Prepare brown-bag puppets about our favorite pets and improvise a skit.

FIGURE 8-5 **Wheel of Development Areas**

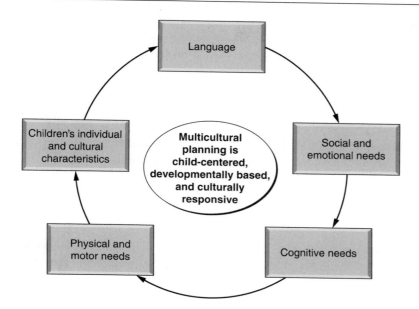

Be Realistic When Setting Expectations

Goals and objectives should be established based on realistic expectations of what the child can accomplish. This involves considerations of special elements that must underlie the teacher's approach to the children's learning process. The following are the elements to consider:

- *What is developmentally sound for the group?* Consider the age level and developmental needs of the learners. Select objectives you know they need and can meet. Your best guide comes from your own observations of children and from reviewing the outcomes of assessment activities. For instance, most 4-year-olds require experiences to strengthen oral expression and build social skills. These areas should become priorities as well as guides in your planning.

- *What is meaningful to the group?* Consider the interests and things familiar to the class. Weigh how much interest children would have if presented with experiences to further explore those topics. Observe children, talk to them, and listen to them while working at the learning centers, and you will learn what they value as important. Do webbing experiences around some topics to detect what they know and how much interest they have in those themes. Use the children's interests, not yours, as a guide for planning.

- *What is relevant knowledge versus what is trivial?* Consider what will provide valuable experiences and knowledge children can use to build upon. Stay away from what seems "nice" but does not provide opportunities for children to gain concepts or skills that contribute to meeting age-appropriate learning expectations. It is important to consider whether the content will provide opportunities for learning accurate and valid information about the children's own diversity and that of others. Consider also whether what is presented are merely "frills" that carry little value and sometimes lead to stereotypes. Sometimes content may be controversial, such as use of hurtful expressions or rejection of others because of skin color, language, or exceptionality. But bringing these concepts into the classroom provides real-life experiences that support the formation of prosocial behaviors.

- *What constitutes the children's prior knowledge?* Always consider the children's experiences. Awareness of the children's family backgrounds and personal life experiences will let you know what experiences or funds of knowledge (González, Moll, & Amanti, 2005) they bring to the classroom. Always value what they bring and use it to plan activities to either foster exploration of new concepts or to expand and refine what they already know.

- *What is culturally relevant to children?* Consider the immediate cultural world of the children. Be aware of the elements of diversity they represent. Knowing the children's families and the neighborhood environments also provides clues as to what is significant to the child. For example, if a child holds religion and a physical exceptionality as his or her distinctive diversity traits, find out how the traits are viewed by the child, the family, and his or her culture. Use this knowledge to select materials and content congruous with the realities they represent. Consider presenting the special qualities of this child to the rest of the class to help them learn about and become aware of differences.

Using Professional Guidelines and Standards

Various educational standards and guidelines establish learning expectations for school children in the United States. They provide direction and ensure that educational experiences are solidly connected to valuable learning. Because multicultural education is based on enhancing the opportunities for success of children, teachers need to link experiences with the expectations of the agencies, state, schools, and/or districts.

Every early childhood educator has the responsibility to know what standards and guidelines are to be followed in his or her workplace. Some programs, such as Head Start, have their own expectations and learning outcomes. Others adhere to generic standards such as those outlined by the NAEYC (i.e., the Early Learning Standards). Content-specific standards developed by national professional organizations are also available and provide relevant guidelines. A list of professional organizations appears in this section.

As a result of the No Child Left Behind mandate, states have developed their own academic content standards, including readiness expectations for children ages

3 and 4. It is important to become familiar with them because they affect curriculum development, classroom activities, and learning expectations for children in multicultural classrooms.

ASSESSMENT IN MULTICULTURAL CLASSROOMS

Assessment is the process by which attainment of goals, standards, and progress is measured. No planning process is complete until you select ways to assess the out-

Welcoming parents into the classroom promotes goodwill and mutual respect. It also contributes to knowing the child's and the family's characteristics.

comes. Decisions about teaching strategies, curriculum development, and, ultimately, the future of young children are based on assessment results.

Appropriate assessment for young children from birth to age 8 is multidimensional; that is, it uses an array of sources and techniques to gather information about the child. In early education, assessment is a collaborative task among teachers, parents, and other staff members. Parents and family members in particular are invaluable sources of information regarding developmental and cultural expectations and authentic perspectives of the child's needs and strengths. Because of its emphasis on improving achievement, the passing of the NCLB Act led to a focus on assessment and testing activities for young children. This has brought to light many concerns about practices deemed appropriate for young children with culturally and linguistic diverse characteristics.

Early childhood is a time of learning and discovery, and traditional paper-and-pencil assessment practices are not consonant with the nature of young children, particularly preschoolers. The use of unknown test administrators and unfamiliar settings presents problems. Additionally, research has shown that normative comparisons of young children are not good indicators of advancement and growth due to vast developmental differences and the presence of many variables in early life (Cohen & Spenciner, 2006; NAEYC & NAECS/SDE, 2003; Stipek, 2005). It is therefore important to assess the learning and progress of young culturally diverse children in familiar contexts (surroundings), with adults who are known to them, using daily learning experiences. The more "authentic" the assessment is, the better it is for the young child.

Appropriate assessment is grounded in knowledge about developmental and cultural characteristics of children (NAEYC & NAECS/SDE, 2003). At all times, assessment methods must be based on what is appropriate for the child and what meets the purpose of assessment. Use of both informal and formal sources provides a more accurate portrait of the child's challenges and strengths. In the multicultural early childhood classroom, it becomes especially important to gather information through multiple sources to best see what the child knows and at what level he or she is performing. Some of these sources are listed in Figure 8-6.

When selecting assessment activities for linguistically different children, it is essential to know whether modifications are necessary to facilitate understanding. If an interpreter is needed, arrangements should be made ahead of time. If using translated materials, have a native speaker check the translation. Translations often have unfamiliar terms with multiple connotations.

Children with exceptionalities may require certain accommodations based on their particular needs. These should be considered prior to administering any assessment. Accommodations should be discussed with the coordinator for exceptional students to ensure that the assessment is conducted in a way that is fair to the child and that the integrity of the instrument is respected.

FIGURE 8-6 **Using Multidimensional Assessment Sources**

- Observations (from teachers, parents and family members, staff members, and service personnel)
- Anecdotal observations
- Photographs and videotapes
- Informal conversations
  - With children
  - With peers
  - With parents and family members
- Home visitation (notes and observations)
- Formal interviews
  - With parents, family members, children, peers
  - With other professionals (caregivers, teachers, social workers, and others)
- Products (work samples, drawings, recordings, designs, etc.)
- Journal entries by children
- Data from checklists and inventories
- Portfolios
- Test results

Concerns About Formal Testing

Formal testing in multicultural classrooms has long been a concern for educators. In spite of well-documented opposition to the practice, formal testing of young children is widespread. One of the key issues of contention is the fact that most commercially produced tests are normed on groups from the mainstream culture, which bear little resemblance to children from diverse backgrounds. This diminishes the integrity of the instrument and sets up unfair barriers for those who are tested. Unfamiliar expressions and illustrations negatively influence the answers, resulting in inaccurate portrayals of the children's knowledge and abilities. Fair practices remind us that all children should be provided with activities with which they have the same opportunities to demonstrate what they know and are able to do.

Use of formal assessment instruments is sometimes mandated by an authority higher than the early childhood professional. If so, the early childhood professional is responsible for learning as much as possible about the tool. The instrument must be developmentally sound and of high technical quality. Reading the test manual will help you learn about the validity and reliability of the instrument. The manual will also help you determine whether the test was validated with and normed on a population similar to your children. Be sure to consult with the ESOL specialist or the coordinator for exceptional students to gain more information about a particular assessment instrument. They will be able to provide guidance in choosing and making any necessary assessment modifications.

Appropriate testing practices also require making modifications or adaptations for children with special needs or those with cultural and linguistic differences. When testing children with disabilities who belong to an ethnic group other than the mainstream culture it is important that they should are tested using their primary language. The person conducting the testing should be fluent in the child's language and knowledgeable about the child's cultural heritage (Division of Early Childhood, 2007; Dunlap, 2009). Although not always practiced or available, we, as advocates for children, must insist on it.

Authentic Assessment and Portfolios

Authentic assessment is the recommended method for evaluating the progress of young children. It evolved as a response to the controversies regarding formal and standardized testing and is the result of the increase in knowledge about young children. Defined as the process by which evidence is collected that demonstrates how and what the individual child knows, it allows you to document and see progress as it unfolds. Authentic assessment is continuous and based on real events and situations in the classroom and other learning environments. It does not employ standardized testing or the use of norms. Rather, it is a collection of work compiled by the child in response to particular skills and knowledge presented in the classroom or learning environment. One of the

LET'S TALK AND REFLECT. . . **Elements Influencing Curriculum Planning for Young Children**

A position statement from the NAEYC and the NAECS/SDE about effective early childhood curriculum highlights the elements that contribute to building a sound and child-appropriate curriculum. Specifically, it mentions the following:

Curriculum is influenced by many factors, including society's values, content standards, accountability systems, research findings, community expectations, culture and language, and individual children's characteristics. (NAEYC & NAECS/SDE, 2003)

- Reflect on the statement and share your thoughts with your colleagues or classmates.
- Interview teachers and find out their opinions about the elements identified by these organizations. Ask which ones they include in their planning.

most common authentic assessment tools is a portfolio. The framework of the portfolio is based on internal and external criteria defined by many different agents, such as early childhood professionals, a care agency, a specific school, a school district, a professional association, state standards and practices, and national standards. Sometimes the early childhood professional determines the nature of the portfolio, whereas other times, various mandates·define what will be included in this very personal portrait of a child. The portfolio is not just a file where the child's work is kept; instead, it is a purposeful document constructed collectively by the child, parents or caretakers, early childhood professional, and other significant individuals who play a role in the learning process of the child. The goal of the portfolio is to show the growth and progress of each child in comparison to himself or herself rather than to compare the child's progress to that of other children. Many different artifacts, such as anecdotal records, parent–teacher conference notes, child's work, official school records, and so on can be included in the portfolio. It is imperative that the portfolio is well organized and understandable to current and future readers, particularly the teacher of the next grade or level. Knowing where the child has been is very important in planning relevant future experiences.

| PUTTING EVERYTHING TOGETHER

We have discussed several essential elements that will help create a child-responsive multicultural program. Let us review what you have learned by listing things you can use in planning your program:

- Results from classroom assessment (children, community, environment, my current curriculum)

■ List of priorities identified from the assess-
ment data

■ Professional guidelines

It's Your Turn, It's Your Decision!

The next step is to begin drafting your goals and objectives. This phase requires independent decision making. Now, you must assume a leadership role and define the specific goals for your program. We have purposely avoided a prescription of a specific

Responses to informal activities and daily observations are valuable sources of information.

approach or even of a specific set of objectives and goals to empower teachers to design their own educational improvements. Teachers have been prevented far too long from making curricular decisions for which they are qualified and to which they are entitled. It has almost become a tradition that teachers are to follow curricula written by individuals completely unfamiliar with their classroom experiences. This practice amounts to telling teachers what to do. This has made many teachers feel trapped and limited as educators of young children (Gardner, 2001). When teachers are entrusted with the task of educational reform, the results are highly positive for both the child and the teacher. With the knowledge you have acquired, you can choose the most appropriate targets for your program. Only when teachers select and establish the program goals will children reap the benefits of a culturally responsive and pedagogically sound program. Examples and models presented in this book are intended to illustrate the process, but we do not intend them to identify "the way" to construct a multicultural program.

Selecting the Content for Multicultural Teaching

Content, in curricular terms, is the *what* included for the purposes of learning (Ornstein & Hunkins, 2003). There are many divergent opinions regarding what constitutes content in the context of early childhood education. This is partly due to the many instructional modalities associated with the field. Each early childhood instructional model has its own particular way of constructing or selecting the contents of instructional experiences (Roopnarine & Johnson, 2005). However, one thing on which most

FIGURE 8-7 **Teaching Blueprint (Planning Matrix)**

I. What kind of multicultural program do I want? Your answer will include aspects of your personal philosophy.

II. What guidelines will I follow? We suggest you review some of the ones presented earlier in this chapter.

III. What are the priorities I will target? In determining the answer to this question, you will have to define priorities similar to the following:

Priority #1 To deal positively with the children's cultural identities.

Priority #2 To live with the diversity in the school and the community.

Priority #3 To learn to reject unfairness.

IV. How can I meet my priorities? Remember that priorities become goals. (Use the charts to plot your answers to the rest of the questions.)

Goal:	Goal:

V. What are my objectives for meeting the goals? These are the specific targets from which you will later generate activities.

Objective #1	Objective #2	Objective #3

VI. Comments/changes? Remember to conduct periodical self-assessments during the planning process.

August:	October:	January:	May:

early childhood educators agree is that there is a given and basic set of ideas regarding the content children should learn. It is an accepted notion that early childhood teachers will use a variety of ways to teach that basic content.

Scholars of multiculturalism believe that instructional content is the major conduit for infusion of diversity into educational programs. The *what* the child discovers in the classroom has a decisive impact on the child's development of ideas and acquisition of knowledge. For that reason, the content needs to be worthy of learning. Earlier in this chapter, we defined the characteristics of classroom content. Among the characteristics mentioned were the need for validity, usefulness, interest, and significance. Those four traits should serve as guiding principles in selecting and establishing the content of a curriculum for diversity in the early childhood classrooms.

Infusion of Diversity as a Key Strategy

Common questions asked by teachers are "How can I change what I teach?" or "How can I prepare a new content?" Behind those questions are sometimes reluctance and a realization that the task may be difficult. The teachers using prescribed or mandated curricula are often even more hesitant about the transition to multicultural teaching. Preparing and organizing new curriculum content is not only a difficult activity, but it also requires time and experience. We, therefore, recommend content infusion as a method to facilitate that process.

Multicultural content infusion is a strategy used to incorporate the perspective of a pluralistic society into the existing curriculum. It allows teachers to continue using the existing curricula and, at the same time, incorporate new material. This also gives teachers more confidence in the transformation process. In the approach recommended by James Banks (1992, 2005) the contributions and the additive levels represent examples of content infusion. Teachers can infuse the curriculum by introducing appropriate views and ideas about diversity into the context of the curriculum. To accomplish that successfully, teachers must have a thorough knowledge of various diversity concepts.

Teachers of young children need to begin the infusion process by examining the topics and the units taught through a prescribed curriculum. A careful analysis will reveal *how* the topics can accommodate the inclusion of diversity perspectives. The process will also show *where* and *what* types of multicultural views and ideas need to be included. To begin, simply take your current planning book or curriculum guide and perform the following steps:

1. If you use an emerging curriculum (built around the interests of the child) or if you follow a teacher-made curriculum, go through your lesson plans and find the topics, or themes, you teach. List them. If you use a prescribed curriculum, check your guide and list all the topics/themes/units that you teach.

2. Review the profile of your students and look for the traits that are descriptive of cultural diversity (ethnicities, religions, languages, social class, and exceptionalities).

3. From the list of topics/themes/units, circle or highlight those that you find lend themselves best to infusion of diversity. Begin by considering how to incorporate those characteristics that are found in your classroom, and then consider those of others.

4. Next, brainstorm how you could incorporate diversity into the selected topics. Begin by asking yourself: What other views could help children expand their understanding of this topic? Write down all the ideas you think are plausible.

5. Gather all the ideas and rewrite your list of themes or units, including the additional diverse perspectives. The only way to know if your approach will work is to try it with your students. So, the next step is to implement your ideas!

6. Keep notes during the lessons on the children's reactions. This will help you assess the success of your venture and offer constructive information for revisions.

Avoiding Infusion of Trivial and Stereotypical Content

So many times, we find children involved in experiences that are purely for fun and that do little to expand their level of knowledge about human diversity. This commonly occurs when content without relevance is infused into the curriculum. The result is called *trivializing*.

The rule for avoiding trivializing is to first identify how a selected topic is consistent with the curriculum. Second, it is necessary to determine whether what is incorporated elicits any valuable learning, particularly whether it will contribute to the understanding of life in our diverse society. To prevent choosing unimportant topics for infusion, ask yourself the following:

- Is the topic presenting, elaborating, and/or expanding concepts on diversity that are commonly and currently found among the target groups?

- Does the topic fit logically into the child's learning and experiencing? Does it give a sense of real learning versus the unimportant?

- Can the topic be made to include the perspectives of how people with diverse cultural views would behave or react to it?

FIGURE 8-8 **Infusing the Perspective on Diversity**

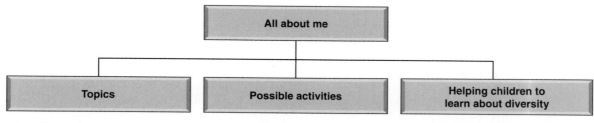

All about me

Topics	Possible activities	Helping children to learn about diversity
• I am like you but I'm different, too • Things I can do • Stories I like • Stories my friends like • Where do I come from? (community, state, country) • Things my friends and I enjoy doing • Things I do at home • Things I do in the classroom • My favorite game • Clothes I like to wear • My favorite words • Things I like to eat • My favorite song	• Visit local grocery store to pick favorite fruits, vegetables • Learn games from other countries • Invite parents to tell us about their favorite games and songs • Read stories from other countries; learn about the authors • Prepare a graph about the physical characteristics of children in the class • Learn words in other languages (greetings, names of food) • Look at the pictures of children from Haiti/India to see how they dress; compare with how we dress in the United States	• Learning about what children in other states and countries do (i.e., India, Haiti)* • Learning about the communities of other countries • Stories children like in other countries • Games from other countries • Activities children do in other countries • Clothes children use in, for example, Haiti and Venezuela • Learning basic words in other languages • Typical snacks and food in other places • Music children sing in other countries

Emphasis on what is current in those countries or cultures

- Is the topic reflective of issues that children in this classroom or people in the community commonly face?
- Does the topic offer opportunities to present other positions that expose the children to divergent views or allow the children to respond to them?
- Can the topic serve as a link to discuss emotions and feelings as perceived through the eyes of the children?
- Can the topic facilitate clarification of stereotypes and biases? How?

What Is the Next Step?

"There is still much to be done, and my next step is to check the classroom materials and the experiences that I've planned. I know there are many things I need to consider before I am finished," Barbara wrote in her journal. That will our task as well as our journey takes us to Chapter 9.

WHAT WE HAVE LEARNED—CHAPTER SUMMARY

Bringing about changes in your teaching is a process that takes time. Several steps are essential to building your multicultural curriculum. Among these, planning is one of the most important ones. Because multicultural education is a reform process, taking time to carefully lay out the expectations and overall design is critical to achieving success. Key to the process of moving into multicultural teaching that addresses the diversity and cultural reality of the classroom and of society is the fact that its goal is to promote responsive and effective learning. Planning is a process where you gather information, set goals, and establish the directions your teaching is to take. Selection of the curricular approach to follow is a personal decision. This should be guided by the knowledge about the needs of children and developmental characteristics. It is necessary to reflect on the characteristics and needs of children, as well as those of their families and community, and the education expectations for the age group in order to identify program and learning goals. Also necessary is reflection on the nature of the experiences and on the selection and integration of diversity content. Knowledge about child-appropriate academic expectations and selection of assessment practices is integral to an effective and meaningful design for multicultural curriculum. By planning with clear goals in mind and carefully selecting content and strategies, you will be able to design a meaningful curriculum for young children.

THINGS TO DO . . .

Thinking about your classroom (or future classroom), describe the approach you would choose to implement your program for diversity. Give two reasons for your selection.

- Considering all the steps involved in good classroom planning, which one would you say is the most important and why?

■ Some teachers believe they can initiate a program transformation "overnight." Do you agree or disagree? Give specific reasons for your position.

■ Using the blueprint that Barbara followed to plan her program transformation, determine whether it would facilitate the beginning of multicultural teaching in your classroom. Explain your answer.

■ Define *multicultural infusion*. Look back and see how Barbara implemented the process. Then select a theme for your curriculum and try to do the same.

RECOMMENDED INTERNET RESOURCES

■ Critical Behaviors and Strategies for Teaching Culturally Diverse Students (ERIC Digest)
www.ericdigests.org/2000-3/critical.htm

■ Position Statement on Inclusion, from the Division of Early Childhood
www.dec-sped.org/pdf/positionpapers/PositionStatement_Inclusion.pdf

■ Position Statements on Curriculum, Assessment, and Program Evaluation, from the NAEYC
http://naeyc.org/about/positions/cape.asp

YOUR STANDARDS PORTFOLIO

NAEYC Standard 3: Observing, Documenting, and Assessing to Support Young Children and Families*

Assessment is an important element of effective and responsive teaching. Take time to complete the following activities that will assist you in assessing children's learning in a multicultural classroom.

■ Visit a local school district or an early childhood center (such as Head Start or a local readiness agency). Find out about its assessment policies for children with disabilities and those with linguistic differences. Meet and interview their ESOL coordinator and find out about practices followed to ensure fair assessment.

■ Conduct interviews of experienced early childhood teachers and find out about the techniques used to assess children in their classrooms. Ask them to share comments about modifications made to meet the needs of children with special needs.

■ Plan a short assessment activity for young children with diverse cultural and linguistic characteristics. Describe the adaptations or modifications made.

* NAEYC Standard 3 correlates with INTASC Standard 8: Assessment and INTASC Standard 7: Planning.

REFERENCES

Banks, J. (1992). Reducing prejudice in children: Guidelines from research. *Social Education*, 33(2), 3–5.

Banks, J. (2005). *Cultural diversity and education: Foundations, curriculum, and teaching* (5th ed.). Boston: Allyn & Bacon.

Berk, L. (2007). *Infants and children: Prenatal to middle childhood* (6th ed.). Needham Heights, MA: Allyn & Bacon.

Bredekamp, S., & Rosegrant, T. (Eds.). (1995). *Reaching potentials: Appropriate curriculum and assessment for young children, 1.* Washington, DC: National Association for the Education of Young Children.

Cohen, L., & Spenciner, L. (2006). *Assessment of children and youth with special needs.* Needham Heights, MA: Allyn & Bacon.

Derman-Sparks, L., & the A.B.C. Task Force. (1989). *Anti-bias curriculum: Tools for empowering young children.* Washington, DC: National Association for the Education of Young Children.

Derman-Sparks, L., & Ramsey, P. (2005). What if all the children in my class are white? Anti-bias/multicultural education with white children. *YC Young Children*, 60(6), 20–27.

Derman-Sparks, L., & Ramsey, P. (2007). *A framework for culturally relevant, multicultural, and antibias education in the twenty-first century.* Retrieved May 17, 2008, from http://www.achievementseminars.com/seminar_series_2007_2008/readings/sparks_from%20a%20framework.pdf.

Division of Early Childhood. (2007). *Promoting positive outcomes for children with disabilities: Recommendations for curriculum, assessment, and Program Evaluation.* Missoula, MT: Author.

Dunlap, L. (2009). *An introduction to early childhood special education: Birth to age five.* Upper saddle River, NJ: Pearson.

Gardner, P. (2001). *Teaching and learning in multicultural classrooms.* New York: David Fulton Publishers.

González, N., Moll, L. C., & Amanti, C. (2005). *Funds of knowledge: Theorizing practice in households, communities, and classrooms.* Mahwah, NJ: L. Erlbaum Associates.

Gordon, A. M. (2003). *Beginning and beyond: Foundations in early childhood education* (6th ed.). New York: Thompson Delmar.

Kendall, F. (1983). *Diversity in the classroom: A multicultural approach to the education of young children.* New York: Teachers College Press.

Manning, L., & Baruth, L. (2004). *Multicultural education of children and adolescents* (4th edition). Boston: Allyn & Bacon

Martin, D. J., & Loomis, K. S. (2006). *Building teachers: A constructivist approach to introducing education.* New York: Wadsworth Publishers.

National Association for the Education of Young Children & National Association of Early Childhood Specialists in State Departments of Education (NAEYC & NAECS/SDE).

(2003). *Position Statement: Early childhood curriculum, assessment, and program evaluation: Building an effective accountable system for children birth through age 8.* Washington, DC: Author.

Ornstein, A. C., & Hunkins, R. (2003). *Curriculum: Foundations, principles, and theory* (4th ed.). Boston: Allyn & Bacon.

Peck, N., & Shores, E. (1994). *Checklist for diversity in early childhood education and care.* Little Rock, AR: Southern Early Childhood Association.

Rogers, R. (2004). *Planning an appropriate curriculum for under fives: A guide for students, teachers, and assistants.* New York: David Fulton Publishers.

Roopnarine, J. L., & Johnson, J. E. (2005). *Approaches to early childhood education* (4th ed.). New York: Merrill.

Southern Early Childhood Association. (n.d.). Valuing diversity for young children: A position statement of the Southern Early Childhood Association. Retrieved September 30, 2008, from http://www.southernearlychildhood.org/position_diversity.html.

Stipek, D. (2005). Early childhood education at a crossroads. *Harvard Education Letter.* Retrieved May 18, 2008, from http://www.edletter.org/current/crossroads.shtml.

CHAPTER 9

Activities and Resources for Multicultural Teaching: A World of Possibilities!

> An environment that is rich in possibilities for exploring gender, race/ethnicity, and different ableness sets the scene for practicing anti-bias [and multicultural] curriculum.
>
> *Louise Derman-Sparks (1989)*

CHAPTER OBJECTIVES

In this chapter, we will

- discuss the characteristics of a child-appropriate environment.
- establish guidelines to select developmentally appropriate multicultural materials.
- give examples of appropriate activities for multicultural teaching.

KEY CONCEPTS

- behaviors
- attitudes
- creativity
- instructional experiences
- instructional materials
- learning encounters
- awareness
- exploration
- inquiry
- utilization

FROM BARBARA'S JOURNAL

I have always believed that learning happens when children have a safe, stimulating, and inviting classroom environment. That is why it was so nice to hear a group of 4- and 5-year-olds who came to visit us talk about our classroom. One of them said that my classroom made her feel at home, and that, for me, was the best compliment. Actually, our classroom is a reflection of all the children I teach and their families. I have asked the children and the parents to contribute objects, books, and items that reflect their cultures. Their response still amazes me. They have sent so many wonderful things that are displayed in the classroom throughout the year. What a difference that has made in the mood of the children! Among the things that we have, some are donations and others are on loan and will be returned to the children's families at the end of the year. Some family members have come to tell stories, teach us songs and dances, and share so many other special things. On such occasions I make a special effort to ensure that the experiences are developmentally and culturally appropriate for the children. I will continue to do everything I can to provide for my children developmentally appropriate experiences that are relevant, engaging, creative, and stimulating. The possibilities are endless.

BUILDING A CLASSROOM FOR OUR MULTICULTURAL SOCIETY

You learned in the previous chapters that the classroom is a very important place of learning for young students. The classroom is where the microcosm of reality is encountered in forms of the new ideas, concepts, and social interactions the student experiences. The classroom environment is, therefore, a vital component of the multicultural education transformation process. In this chapter, we will discuss how to design appropriate activities and use materials and resources that will help the students learn about diversity. You will see how the ideas discussed throughout the book become classroom practices.

Remembering Classrooms

You know from many years you've spent in schools as a student that not all classrooms are alike. Some you remember by the hard seats, others by the funny windows. You remember the pictures on the walls that gave you your first glimpses of far-away parts of the world and the phrase at the top of the chalkboard that seemed to admonish you every day. Perhaps the maps and replicas of houses and ships in the social studies classroom come to mind when you try to remember one of your old classrooms. Rosales (1992), who came to the United States from Puerto Rico, recalls her impressions of the first U.S. classroom she encountered:

> My eyes were fixed on the door. It was closed and it remained closed *all the time!* I couldn't help but miss the classrooms in my island where the doors were always open, where I could always see the sky and hear the world outside. And, we had win-

dows from which we could see the mountains and hear the noises of the airplanes ready to land. This room has those high windows that don't let you see anything. Here, well, it's different. One feels like being trapped inside the room.

The classroom environment is an important teaching vehicle at the early childhood level. The classroom is not only a place where the teacher and the students meet but also a part of the teaching process as a communication medium. We need to look closely at the impressions and messages conveyed to the children through the classroom environment. What makes classrooms so powerful?

The Many Environments of a Classroom

The organized and informal activities that take place in the classroom include complex intellectual and social actions that represent a microcosm of the real world. Individuals, young and old, who find themselves in classroom settings create ideas, make discoveries, exchange views, and rehearse ways to interact in a larger social context. Changes in visions, positions, and attitudes are often among the outcomes derived from classroom activities.

Classroom activities and events can be classified into four major worlds or environments: the physical, the cognitive, the social–emotional, and the creative (Figure 9-1). These four environments need to be both developmentally based and child centered.

FIGURE 9-1 **Classroom Environments**

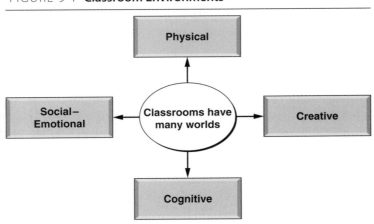

In Action . . .   **Your Classroom Memories**

- What do you remember about the classrooms of the schools you attended?
- If you are currently teaching, what does your classroom say to those who enter?

Learning about their heritage is important to young children.

The Physical Environment

The physical environment—defined by all the objects found within an identified space—is considered the most overt of the four classroom worlds. The space itself is something over which the teacher usually has little or no control because it is assigned by the center or school administrators. Adequate classroom space is frequently a problem in early childhood programs. According to the accreditation criteria from the National Association for the Education of Young Children (NAEYC), space should be allocated according to the number of children enrolled. A minimum of "35 square feet of usable space indoors per child" is required as acceptable physical space (NAEYC, 2005). NAEYC standard indicates that the physical environment must be of high quality because it affects the behavior and development of people.

The physical environment also encompasses the equipment, furniture, and teaching materials located in the classroom. The adequate and developmentally based combination of all these elements makes a good classroom for children.

Research in classroom practice shows that the classroom environment impacts the behavior, knowledge acquisition, and emotional state of the child. This has direct implications on the physical aspects of the classroom. Curtis and Carter (2003) indicate that young children's learning spaces should be inviting, warm, and colorful. Such stimulating environments contribute to the development of appropriate behaviors and attitudes as well as support the major goals of multiculturalism.

The efforts of many early childhood educators have been hindered by the disregard for the physical setting as a determining element for success of children. John Holt (cited by Ornstein & Hunkins, 2003) once pointed out the value of the physical setting as being an effective motivator of students. He also stated that if the role of the learning

A carefully designed classroom arrangement can facilitate children's interactions.

Wadsworth/Cengage Learning

setting were more seriously considered in the teaching-learning process, teachers would achieve more success.

The Cognitive Environment

A classroom is a place of continuous intellectual activity. Intellectual or cognitive activity is the process of forming and acquiring ideas and concepts. Cognition thrives in young children when they are given opportunities to experience and discover realities on their own. One of the major ways for children to grow and develop cognitively is through play. A good cognitive environment facilitates experiences that challenge and allow the children to discover and make sense of their reality. They are expected to make errors during the process. For Piaget, this stage of error making is as important as that of discovering the truth. Teachers act as facilitators and companions for the children as they work around the challenges. Questions rather than answers abound because the intention is to lead the children into self-discovery. Learning about diversity issues depends on cognitive processes where children are led to ponder experiences and examine consequences rather than be told the "accepted truths." For a child, a truth is what he or she has gathered, what the child owns. Appropriate environments invite children to explore, ponder, and construct their truths.

The Social–Emotional Environment

The social–emotional environment can be perceived by the "feeling" a child gets from being in the classroom. Social interactions in the classroom between the teacher and the students, as well as among the students themselves, can clearly convey a sense of welcome and acceptance or of something quite the opposite, such as fear and rejection. Because the early childhood years are a formative period, attention to social and

Every area of the classroom presents opportunities for children to explore and discover their culture and those of others.

Wadsworth/Cengage Learning

emotional development is fundamental. Much of the children's time is dedicated to further development of this domain. The emerging social experience of the child underlines the need for making social–emotional development a major focus of the teacher's efforts.

Behaviors are actions exhibited by individuals in response to certain situations or stimuli. **Attitudes** are the dispositions people have toward others and/or to a circumstance that guide their overt and covert behavior. The behaviors and attitudes of adults and of other children convey messages that a child can use to construct his or her own responses and ideas. Classrooms and homes are among the ideal settings for acquiring the responses and behaviors commonly related to multicultural education, such as tolerance, understanding, and acceptance of the cultural differences present in society (Figure 9-2).

The Creative Environment

Creativity can be defined as the special ability to see things in unusual or unconventional ways (Cropley, 1992). A classroom where nontraditional ideas and views are fostered among young children is an ideal setting for promoting creativity. An environment that is open and flexible serves as a vehicle for growth and development, especially if the children are encouraged to find alternative ways to approach realities. For example, children are encouraged to find solutions to situations presenting unfair treatment to others. Creativity is an important resource in multicultural education and an essential element of the classrooms where teaching about diversity is taking place.

| MAKING THE BEST USE OF TEACHING ENVIRONMENTS

For years, educators have focused attention on the intellectual content taught in schools. Little attention, however, has been paid to the setting, or the physical space, where instruction takes place. Comments about procedures, goals, and objectives abound in cur-

FIGURE 9-2 **Words Can Reveal the Emotional Atmosphere of the Classroom**

What are the messages conveyed? Which ones are culturally and developmentally appropriate?

"You can do it. Try it again!"

OR

"You never seem to do anything right. Do it again."

"Perhaps you want to ask Jeannie if you can use her tempera."

OR

"That's Jeannie's. You can't use it."

"You did work a lot today. Maybe tomorrow we can work some more on that."

OR

"Why are you so slow?"

Comments can send strong messages to a child. Think about the impressions that these comments make:

1. "...he can't do it. He doesn't know English."
2. "...they can't understand the story. In their country they do not have things like that."
3. "...oh well, she is LD, you know."
4. "It doesn't look like food to me." (referring to an ethnic snack)
5. "I learned to read already. If you don't learn, that's up to you."
6. "Here we use utensils, not our hands!"

riculum materials, but directions on how to organize the stage—that is, the classroom—are much more difficult to locate. In teaching for diversity, the role of the physical context is as important as what is discussed and shared. A teacher of young children knows that imagination and ability to conceptualize are sparked when children are surrounded by an environment that is visually and emotionally inviting. To maximize the power of the classrooms, let us examine how they can be turned into powerful instruments of education about diversity.

A CLASSROOM FOR TEACHING AND LEARNING ABOUT DIVERSITY

The multicultural classroom is a place where the teacher attempts to guide young children through the process of learning to live with diversity. This process of social transformation requires a special setting conducive to the children's dreaming, fantasizing, skill building, and socialization. Such classrooms already exist in many schools across the

United States; however, many more need to be transformed into the learning settings that children deserve and need. Although difficult to accomplish, it is not impossible. Now consider what you need to do to make your classrooms become the exciting environments where learning about diversity can take place.

In Search of the Multicultural Classroom Setting

You may remember how Barbara, the kindergarten teacher we have been following, started making changes in her teaching. Now, as she plans to begin the selection of classroom activities, she realizes that she first has to consider her setting. This is what Barbara wrote in her journal: "Nothing will ever succeed if I don't start making changes in the classroom. I realize that what I currently have in the work and play areas sends contradictory messages to the children. I want everything to be consistent with what I am trying to do. My next move: find out how I can make the classroom more culturally responsive."

Multiple Intelligences and Multicultural Education

Barbara learned that young children absorb the information transmitted by the classroom environment both directly and indirectly. These transmissions occur largely through the senses, the major learning avenues for young children. She now recognizes that the setting plays an important role in the teaching-learning process. Barbara also realizes that children have specific predispositions toward learning, what Howard Gardner calls "intelligences." Gardner contends that multiple intelligences are the capacities and abilities of humans to master skills and concepts through one of the eight intelligences: language, logical-mathematical, spatial, bodily-kinesthetic, musical, interpersonal, intrapersonal, and natural (and others as his research continues). This theory requires congruency between the classroom environment and children's learning styles. In multicultural teaching, congruency needs to be achieved among the children's learning styles, the environment, and the curriculum goals.

| WHAT WE FIND IN THE CLASSROOM

Before thinking about what to change, consider the physical components of the classroom. Essentially, three elements make up the classroom: the space and the arrangements of objects, the interest areas, and the instructional resources. Awareness about these elements will help target your change efforts (Figure 9-3).

A Flexible Space Where Objects Are Carefully Arranged

All classrooms are spaces designated for teachers and children where learning takes place. How the space is arranged is what personifies early childhood education classrooms. Equipment and furniture in young children's classrooms are selected according

FIGURE 9-3 **Multicultural Early Childhood Classroom Arrangement**

Space	Interest areas	Arrangement	Instructional resources
– Flexible, well ventilated and lighted. – Meets DCAP criteria for physical space. – Includes access to a DCAP playground.	– Includes the following: housekeeping, art, dramatic play, blocks, literacy, language, discovery, and manipulatives. – Includes rotating areas. Areas can be converted to accommodate new interests or topics. – Interest areas are periodically rotated or modified to replicate organization in other cultural groups (i.e., the dramatic area, the house-keeping area).	– Equipment is flexibly arranged and periodically modified. – Children use arrangement freely. – Display of objects and materials are child-oriented and reflect a learning target. – Needs of exceptional children are reflected in the arrangement.	– A variety of nonbiased, nonsexist, multicultural materials exists. – Resources reflect the characteristics of children, their families, and the community. – Labeling in more than one language is observed. – Pictures, posters, and other visual aids reflect diversity. – Emphasis on what is actual practice or typically current is depicted in the resources. – A balance between what is current and what is traditional is found in the materials.

to the developmental needs of the children and are multifunctional. This gives each classroom its own character. For example, tables and chairs are not just for children to work at and sit on but also to use for other purposes. A rocker in the infant room is not just a place to soothe the child but also a place where lullabies and stories are shared. In the preschool classroom, a table turned on its side can become a puppet theater, or it can serve as a workplace for arts and crafts. Because of its flexible use, teachers need to ensure that the arrangements correspond not only to the age level of the group but also to their needs. For instance, children with exceptionalities may require specific furniture or materials to accommodate their needs.

The Interest Areas

The space in early childhood classrooms is best organized and distributed into learning or interest areas. Terms such as *learning area*, *center*, or *station* refer to those spaces where activities can take place and related materials are displayed for children's use. A major portion of what the child learns occurs in learning centers.

Learning areas offer a variety of **instructional experiences.** Each learning center is usually organized around a specific developmental area or topic and is intended to promote acquisition of concepts and skills. Careful selection of age-appropriate materials, how these are displayed, and opportunities to engage in their use will influence the children's responses and learning. What to include for diversity will be described later during this chapter.

Instructional Materials

Didactic or instructional materials are the common denominator of all classrooms. **Instructional materials** include a broad category of objects ranging from commercially produced resources to teacher-made classroom materials, real objects, objects on the wall and hanging from the ceiling, the costumes in the play chest, and any item that promotes learning.

All objects that comprise the classroom environment have the potential of influencing children. Consider, for instance, the impact of a poster of community helpers in which all the professionals, such as the physician, the lawyer, and the engineer, are portrayed as European Americans, whereas the custodian and the sanitation employee are depicted as minorities. Take, for example, a classroom with children with special needs but where no images convey the idea that they are part of the group. The message sent is a subtle but an influential one for the children, who are just beginning to form ideas about the world.

GUIDELINES FOR A MULTICULTURAL CLASSROOM ENVIRONMENT

Central to effectively planning and organizing the space for multicultural teaching is answering the following question: What characteristics of the classroom make it suitable for teaching about diversity?

There are many sources of valuable ideas for creating the ideal classroom environment for teaching about diversity. Several experts in the field and professional organizations have shared their vision about an ideal multicultural classroom (Banks, 2007; Byrnes and Kiger, 1992; Davidman & Davidman, 2000; Derman-Sparks & the A.B.C. Task Force, 1989; Hernandez, 2000; Neugebauer, 1992; Nieto & Bode, 2008; Peck & Shores, 1994). Although some recommendations were not particular to early childhood classrooms, their insights provide relevant ideas (i.e., Banks, 2007; Davidman & Davidman, 2000; Hernandez, 2000; Nieto & Bode, 2008). Through this analysis, we found emphasis on seven specific areas.

- learning materials, including all manipulatives, books, toys, props, classroom decorations, and everything written
- art
- literature
- music and movement
- games and play activities

- attitudes and behavior
- activities

We will focus our attention on the first five areas. The remaining areas, *attitudes and behavior* and *activities*, will be discussed in another section of this chapter.

To better understand the multicultural classroom environment, it is important to consider the following questions about the first five elements above:

- How do they contribute to a successful multicultural education program?
- How do they meet the needs of young children?
- What should each one be like in a multicultural classroom?
- What does each one consist of?

These are the questions that we plan to answer as we "walk through" the multicultural early childhood classroom environment.

Learning Materials

Children use learning materials to experience, ponder, produce, and process ideas. Instructional materials are necessary resources that help children acquire and shape knowledge. The Piagetian approach suggests that materials are an important resource

---

In Action . . . **Powerful Images**

Try to remember the images that made an impression on you as a child and still have an impact on you today. They could have been a part of your classroom, a store display window, a neighbor's house, or a television program.

- How did you react to a powerful image when you first noticed it?
- Was anyone with you at the time, and how did that person react?
- Does that image still have the same degree of power for you today? Why?
- Does that image have the identical type of impact today? Explain.

In Action . . . **What's Your Opinion?**

In regard to the classroom aspects that were suggested as important to consider, what is your opinion?

- Do you agree with these categories? Why?
- Would you add any others? Which ones?

to provoke cognitive construction in the child. Because they incite interest and learning, careful and intentional planning is essential. As a first step, ask yourself: *Are these resources developmentally appropriate? Do they match the age and individual characteristics of the children?* Guidelines to help early childhood educators answer these questions are presented in Snapshot 9-1, in which we summarize ideas and suggestions for selecting classroom materials with a developmental focus. These suggestions offer ways to choose resources that are appropriate and cognitively challenging, a pertinent aspect in multicultural education for young children.

Good multicultural classroom materials need to be free of biases, stereotypes, and misrepresentations of cultural groups. Attention to this is especially important when selecting multicultural materials. As a practice, never rely on the title or content of a resource. Instead, take time to verify the nature of learning materials by asking the following: Do these materials present an accurate, bias-free, and stereotype-free picture of the group?

Karen Matsumoto-Grah (in Byrnes and Kiger, 1992) establishes seven guidelines for selecting materials that include all the aspects of diversity. She recommends observing to determine whether the materials do the following:

SNAPSH📷T 9-1   Using a Developmental Focus to Select Instructional Materials

Selection of learning materials is a task that requires time and where caution should be exercised. Here are some helpful tips for selecting items for the early childhood multicultural classroom:

1. Before selecting materials, keep in mind the age levels and needs of children in your classroom or care.

2. Be mindful about what is meaningful and relevant for children to learn. Make sure that materials match the content and the needs of children (special needs, linguistic differences, cultural differences).

3. Always take time to carefully examine materials or resources before they are selected. Check the instructions, if any, and identify the purpose and goals.

Verify that these connect with the curricular experiences and expected learning outcomes.

4. Consider materials that provide opportunities for all intellectual levels and that may be used to promote a variety of skills and concept learning.

5. Select materials that intrigue children and promote exploration and inquiry. For example, consider real and unconventional items that will spark the children's curiosity. Remember that interest guides learning, which becomes the foundation for knowledge.

6. Consider the physical needs of children, including those with disabilities. Choose materials that are appropriate and safe to manipulate by all children.

1. Present the contributions of groups other than European Americans; reflect a cross-cultural perspective of what women have contributed

2. Portray people, including women, without stereotypes (for instance, European Americans portrayed as professionals and minorities portrayed as poor) across socioeconomic classes and religions

3. Depict religious issues appropriately "when religion is integral to the context of the subject"

4. Give socially balanced views of famous people; that is, include outstanding people from both the privileged and working classes

5. Reflect the cultures and ethnicities of the classroom children and of their community

6. Exhibit and include the native languages present in the class (for example, if the class has children who speak Spanish and French-Creole, materials in those languages should be available)

7. Are at the developmental level of the children and offer challenges with opportunities to experience success

Both Kendall (1996) and Derman-Sparks (1989) call attention to the need for teachers to ensure that classroom resources are totally bias-free. In their opinion, during the formative years, it is of utmost importance to make the classroom a place where the child will experience and encounter human and social differences as an aspect that characterizes people. Targeting unbiased representations should be one of the first aspects to emphasize when choosing materials. This means scrutinizing what and how the content is presented in resources (see Figure 9-4).

FIGURE 9-4 **Ways to Appropriately Depict a Cultural Group**

What is presented shows
- A variety of gender roles and racial and cultural backgrounds
- A variety of occupations
- A variety of ages
- A variety of abilities (includes special-needs individuals from different backgrounds)
- A variety in time (past and present) and place (local, national, international)

How it is presented portrays
- An assortment of social contexts
- Contrasting lifestyles and configurations
- A variety of languages (those of the children must be acknowledged first, and then others as chosen by the teacher)
- An assortment of representations or symbols to depict a given event or fact
- Different social and racial groups
- An accurate portrayal of racial characteristics (pictures do not use the Caucasian facial traits to depict different races/ethnic groups)

Avoiding "Token Diversity"

Many times, classrooms exhibit what is called *token diversity* (Derman-Sparks & the A.B.C. Task Force, 1989). Tokenism happens, for instance, when there is just one doll or artifact of a given ethnic group. While it may seem a way to evidence representation, it minimizes the existence of certain cultures and groups, such as women and the elderly. Token representation reduces the importance and significance of the contributions and roles of a group (King, Chipman, & Cruz-Janzen, 1994). More importantly, a minimal inclusion of the elements of diversity will not transform your classroom into a culturally responsive setting.

Two main reasons for tokenism are the lack of awareness among teachers about the importance and the need to establish appropriate settings for diversity and the lack of time to transform the classroom environment. In examining the first reason, many new and experienced teachers throughout this country still refuse to acknowledge the importance of teaching multiculturally. Some of them still argue that in the past, children learned fine without any special materials "about the others." Others still cling to the traditional phrase: "Children don't see colors. They only see children." Research does not support either one of these positions. Allocating time to choose good, child-appropriate materials and for adapting the classroom environment is essential to effectively plan and design an environment that promotes multiculturalism.

The best way for teachers to avoid tokenism is to not display the single item, such as a doll, from a specific culture and to save it until other items are acquired. Some early childhood teachers have found that families and staff members are a good source for obtaining images that more accurately convey diversity. For example, in a migrant program, teachers took digital images of parents, family members, and staff. With the help of a computer photograph program, these were reproduced and printed as classroom posters. Another solution, as observed in some classrooms, is to use pictures along with the dolls or real objects. Teachers in a classroom of 3-year-olds visited by one of the writers, for example, selected magazine and catalog pictures of ethnic dolls, pasted them on pieces of cardboard, and laminated them. The pictures were placed among the real dolls. The children used the paper dolls in much the same way as they used the real ones because of the magic of "pretend play."

When to Keep and When to Remove Materials

You may find that some of your multicultural materials may not meet the criteria for appropriate classroom resources. Decisions to remove a given item should be based only on the character of the stereotypic or misleading information that it contains. Even materials depicting stereotypes can serve as teaching resources (Derman-Sparks & the A.B.C. Task Force, 1989). Used only by the teacher, and not available to the class, they can be kept as part of the materials.

Two things can be done before making the determination to remove any inappropriate resources from the classroom. One, incorporate the cultural elements into the existing material; and two, consider the possibility of altering or transforming the materials. Start by checking how the resource could be altered or modified (Derman-Sparks & the A.B.C. Task Force, 1989). For example, a set of manipulatives depicting people can be altered by adding figures with different ethnic characteristics. The dramatic area can be enhanced by including dresses representing different ethnicities. Artifacts common to specific cultures and a balance of gender objects can also be included. In the case of pictures and posters, collages can be prepared with pictures portraying other cultures. You can also paste pictures over those in posters or even in books (Derman-Sparks & the A.B.C. Task Force, 1989). This will visually change and broaden the resources. For the manipulatives area, puzzles reflecting different elements of diversity can be easily made by teachers or volunteers. Curtis and Carter (2003) suggest preparing flash cards and other manipulatives with pictures that depict characteristics of the various cultures represented by the children in the classroom.

Familiarity Supports Understanding of Diversity

In one instance, in a classroom for 2-year-olds, teachers enhanced their resources by simply using the pictures of the children, of the children in other classrooms, and of the members of the staff. Taped to a table and to one of the walls, the photographs offered the children a display of racial diversity associated with familiar faces. In another case, first-grade teachers began changing their classrooms by adding labels and signs in languages other than English. With the help of other teachers, they also wrote the names of the children in two languages, Spanish and Arabic. The classroom became a very popular place where children soon began to look for their names and the names of their peers. This helped them to expand their awareness of the representations in other languages. It was also a thrill for the students to understand that they could establish their identities in other cultures by writing and recognizing their names in other languages.

Art as a Source for Awareness About Diversity

The arts are humanity's expression of life itself.

Merryl Goldberg (2006)

The art center is another important place in the classroom. Art serves the purpose of offering children the opportunities to explore ways to use the materials to represent what they perceive through their senses. Art is a powerful source for learning that can also facilitate learning about diversity.

The colors of the paints are the first art objects that should be changed. Adding more browns, tans, and black induces the child to notice other color tones. Creative ways of developing these tones include using chocolate or coffee, which can be diluted to create various shades of brown. Having children work with such color tones is an appropriate way to facilitate understanding the role of melanin as the agent responsible for

---

SNAPSH⊙T 9-2   **"I'm Not That Doll!"**

A student visiting a mostly European American kindergarten classroom overheard a discussion among three girls. Two of the girls were European Americans and one was an African American. The girls were working in the dramatic area. One of the girls was holding a black doll. Everything had been going well until one of the girls called the black doll "Elissa," the name of the African American child. "That's not me. I told you. Give her another name!" said the child, clearly upset. Judging by Elissa's reaction, this was not the first time this had happened. The two girls continued calling the doll by the same name. "Oh, yes, see, it has her face. It is Elissa," said the younger one, while her friend gave an affirmative nod. This time, Elissa snatched the doll away and threw it into the trash can. At that point, the teacher intervened and took the opportunity to talk about what happened. While talking with the children, she realized that the African American doll was the only ethnic doll in the classroom.

The teacher realized what negative effect "tokenism" can have on children.

In Action . . .   **Inexpensive Multicultural Resources**

Teachers frequently ask where to find good pictures as well as other ethnic materials. We have found three good sources. Two of them provide excellent pictures and learning resources. They are the United Nations International Children's Emergency Fund (UNICEF) and the National Geographic Journal. A third source is any local ethnic store that actually carries not just exotic things but items people actually use on an everyday basis, such as cooking utensils. There are many others. Which additional sources can you recommend?

---

the different skin tones of people. A third-grade teacher created the activity described in Snapshot 9-3 to clarify that no one is truly white.

Art can help young children dispel the most damaging of myths: that people are divided by the color of their skins (Allport, 1986). Tempera paints, crayons, and markers can be selected to include more colors reflecting the range of skin tones. There are effective multicultural art materials, such as the multicultural crayons that contain many varieties of skin shades. Another very useful item is the multicultural modeling clay. Teachers can also shade play dough to produce various skin shades using powdered tempera and even cocoa powder (see Figure 9-5). Whether teacher-made or commercially produced, multicultural art supplies should be available in the classroom at all times.

SNAPSHOT 9-3   Discovering the Colors of People

The first-grade class was working on a project, "Friends Across the Border," when the teacher discovered that most of the children thought the people in the countries neighboring the United States were "not white." This incited an argument among some fair-skin Hispanics who refused to be described as "not white," arguing that their skin was as light as that of others in the class. Everything reached a climax when several members of the class agreed: "They can't be white because they speak Spanish." The teacher understood that the children were using not only race but also language to define others. She decided to do something immediately to correct the misconceptions.

The teacher proceeded to divide the class into teams of five. Then, using white play dough as well as different shades of play dough that resembled the various colors of the skin, she asked the children to match the play dough to the colors of the skin of their group members.

The results were recorded on a graph. Upon completing the survey, the teacher entered the names of the colors the children chose during the discussion. The colors ranged from peachy, rose, and dark peach to tan, burnt brown, and "kind of creamy vanilla." All names were accepted and entered. Then, the groups began to share their findings. At the end, the column that read "white" was empty, while the rest of the entries appeared in all the other categories. "What do we see in this graph?" "Where do we have most of the names? Where do we have the least names, or no names?" Without hesitation, the answers began to show the truth. Entries of colors with a variety of fancy names were entered in the graph. At the end, no entries were made for the category depicting "white." "No one is really white," said a child of very fair skin, who described himself as being "golden vanilla." "Why do they say that people are white or black? They lied to us," said one girl.

The teacher, by using self-discovery, helped the children to clarify their ways of looking at others and ensured the continuous harmony in the class.

FIGURE 9-5 **Easy-to-Make Multicultural Play Dough**

You will need the following ingredients:

   4 cups corn starch

   1 cup salt

   1 1/2 cups water

   powdered tempera (brown, red) or cocoa

   2 1/2 cups water

Mix all the ingredients. The amount of tempera or cocoa to add will depend on the skin colors you want to make. Place on medium heat for 5 minutes, until it thickens. Remove from heat. Cover the pot with a wet paper towel. When cool, knead for about 5 minutes, working on a surface covered with waxed paper. When making objects, allow them to dry before painting.

Felt, art paper, and construction paper in shades of brown and black are other important materials to include in the art center. Traditionally, only white paper has been used. However, when children are drawing pictures of themselves, family, and friends, they should find paper in shades that more accurately reflect their reality. The shades of tan and natural are more appropriate than the plain white paper. An inexpensive source is the packing paper that comes in a natural shade. Also useful are brown grocery bags. Manila folders and a roll of manila paper are additional sources of art materials.

Educator Aurelia Gómez (1999) states that crafts are one of the universal elements that define people across cultures. Crafts have the power to captivate interest and the imagination through artistic expression. Crafts are an excellent source to help us learn about ourselves and about other people. Because arts and crafts represent how individuals have learned to make art with what is present in their environments, they become a source for valuing and appreciating people's resourcefulness and creativity.

Arts and crafts activities contribute to the holistic development of the child by providing opportunities for "actively solving problems, thinking critically, becoming visually literate, making aesthetic decisions, weighing and measuring, expressing themselves, using their imaginations, communicating with peers, and developing motor skills" (Gómez, 1999). Children need to have access to the materials used in handicrafts to explore and experiment. Part of the classroom art area should include selected art forms and handicrafts from the children's own cultural groups as well as from other groups they will learn about. A sample of the materials listed in Figure 9-6 can enhance the child's perspective of other people. In parentheses, we have indicated the cultural groups that more frequently use these art materials. You may add some others. A preschool teacher shared another interesting source for materials, described in Snapshot 9-4.

The colors white and black have been ascribed with the symbolism of good and evil in Western society. Unfortunately, this concept has been extended into the racial context that children encounter very early in life. Classroom activities can be designed to disperse and correct these unfounded views. Teachers can set aside specific days when the only art items to be used are those of less frequently used colors, such as blacks and browns. This is a way of helping children overcome their socially based fear of these colors. For instance, a preschool or kindergarten class can take a field trip around their neighbor-

FIGURE 9-6 **Common Art Materials Used by Different Cultures**

- dry gourds, dry coconut shells, beans, seeds, leaves (Caribbeans, Africans, Native American groups)
- feathers, clay, colored beads, strings (Latin Americans, Native American groups)
- yarn, scraps of fabric, sequins, glitter, watercolors (Asians, Europeans, Latin Americans)
- straw, sticks, twigs, raffia (Latin Americans, Native American groups, Africans, Asians)
- sea shells, dry fish scales, coral rocks (Caribbeans, Asians)

SNAPSH◉T 9-4   Teachers Are Always Resourceful!

A first-grade teacher ran out of art paper one day. She found some brown boxes that had been discarded and had an idea. She cut the boxes into pieces of various sizes, placed them on the art table, and waited for the reactions. When children asked what they were, she said they were "special art canvases for pictures they could easily hang after they finished them." The result was a lot of "artistic canvases" the children displayed around the classroom. The experience was so successful that the teacher decided to make corrugated cardboard a permanent part of the art supplies.

---

hood to see all the things that are the various shades of brown or black. We can already anticipate a long list of items! The realization that these colors are part of our daily life is a start for children to see that there is nothing mysterious or malicious about them.

Using Artwork to Promote Diversity

The arts as an aspect of culture provide insights into various groups. For example, artwork representative of different ethnic groups is a valuable source that brings cultures

Artwork like this painting from artist Nicoll Nicoll, which provides glimpses into her family and childhood traditions, can lead children to discuss their own families.

Wadsworth/Cengage Learning

and diverse images into the classroom. It also engages the child in appreciating the artistic work of famous masterpieces and of local artists.

Artwork also offers a channel that connects children with tangible aspects of their own culture and those of peers and adults. Use of color, choice of materials, and representations all provide ways to learn more about the traditions and ideas of a group. There are many sources of artwork that can be used in the classroom. Some of these include the following:

- *Visits to local art museums:* Your local museum is one of the best sources. Contact the museum education department and find out about current and upcoming exhibits. Plan a field trip to the museum and have a guided visit. After the visit, engage children in a discussion about what they saw.

- *Posters and reproductions:* Posters of many well-known masterpieces are usually available from museums, bookstores, and teacher supply stores. Choose those that represent the work of different artists and different cultures.

- *Picture books:* Aside from the literary content, children's picture books are an excellent way to create awareness about how life events are interpreted and represented by different cultural groups. For example, Carmen Lomas Garza's *Cuadros de Familia/Family Pictures* (1990), Arthur Dorros's *Por Fin es Carnival* (1995), Demi's *One Grain of Rice* (1997), and Faith Ringgold's *Tar Beach* (1996) are among those that also introduce children to cultural artistic representations.

- *Photographs:* Photo collections are an excellent medium to expose children to the arts. Using a digital camera, create your own collection by taking pictures of artwork in the community and from local fairs.

- *Art fairs:* Local art fairs are one of the best sources for crafts typical to the community and representative of various cultures. Information on local activities can be found in newspapers, on public radio, and from community centers.

The Literacy Area

Literature is one of the most powerful sources of ideas, personal values, and wisdom. Donna Norton (1995) says that literature plays an important role in helping people learn and appreciate their cultural heritages. She further maintains its critical relevance in a multicultural society like ours:

> Carefully selected literature can illustrate the contributions and values of the many cultures and is especially critical to fostering an appreciation of the heritage of the minorities in U.S. society. A positive self-concept is not possible unless we respect others as well as ourselves; literature *can contribute considerably* [emphasis added] toward our understanding and thus our respect.

Some of the impressions, fantasies, and words many of us still cherish are from the stories, rhymes, and poems we heard or read as children. Our favorite books made us dream of unknown places and people. The benefits of literature go beyond the pleasure and enchantment they provide. Literature is a complementary developmental element for the young child. Joan Glazer (cited by Norton, 2003) has listed four ways that literature promotes good emotional development. According to Glazer, a good selection of books in the classroom can (1) help children see that other people have the same emotions and feelings they do; (2) facilitate the exploration of feelings and emotions from a variety of perspectives; (3) show different ways to deal with emotions and feelings; and (4) demonstrate that, at times, what we feel might be in conflict with our own emotions (Norton, 2003).

Literature is one of those common denominators found across cultures. You can learn about the ideas, beliefs, values, and struggles of daily life in any country around the world through literature. Because of its powerful character for cultural transmission, literature is an ideal resource for multicultural education. In the opinion of Tway (cited by Norton, 2003), "[i]n a country of multicultural heritage, children require books that reflect and illuminate that varied heritage."

The emphasis on literacy development has opened the door to more quality literature for children. With it, a profusion of ethnic literature has also emerged because of the recognition given to the absence and misrepresentation of cultural groups. Today, most classrooms have a good supply of multicultural books. Discovering what kinds of books are in the classroom is important because of the power literature has for young children. Bonnie Neugebauer (1992) recommends assessing the classroom library corner to determine (1) how the books portray the characters; (2) the types of situations they present; (3) the value, accuracy, and appropriateness of the illustrations; (4) the nature of the messages conveyed in the stories; (5) the credibility of the author and illustrator to tell the story and portray the characters; and (6) whether the stories depict the ethnic groups and the diversity of the class and community (see Figure 9-7).

Sources of good multicultural literature have significantly increased. Many book publishers have begun to include titles covering all aspects of diversity. For example, the series Big Multicultural Tales includes stories from Russia (*Little Masha* and *Misha the Bear*), Haiti (*Horse and Toad*), Kenya (*The Crocodile and the Ostrich*), and a story about the Pueblo Indians (*Coyote and the Butterflies*), among others. Several book publishers and distributors specialize in the distribution of ethnic literature. Most local libraries also include multicultural books in their children's sections. A visit to the local library will lead teachers to find a wealth of literary resources appropriate for young children.

Using Journals, Magazines, and Newspapers

Journals, magazines, and newspapers are considered part of literature that can be used to enhance the children's learning process. They are excellent sources of pictures children can view while learning about their world and the worlds of others in our society. Periodicals and newspapers in different languages should be included in the classroom literature areas. They provide unique opportunities for the children to explore the

FIGURE 9-7 **Using Literature to Develop Multicultural Awareness: Sample Planning Web**

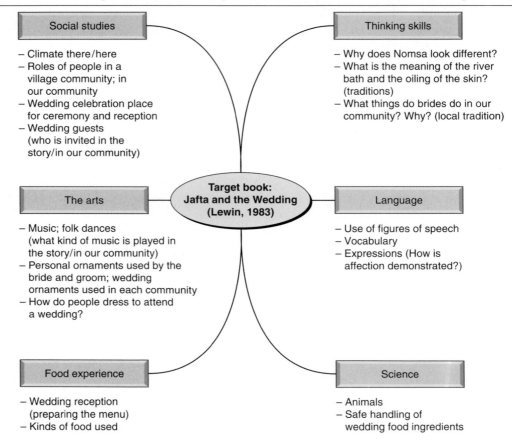

Social studies

– Climate there/here
– Roles of people in a
  village community; in
  our community
– Wedding celebration place
  for ceremony and reception
– Wedding guests
  (who is invited in the
  story/in our community)

Thinking skills

– Why does Nomsa look different?
– What is the meaning of the river
  bath and the oiling of the skin?
  (traditions)
– What things do brides do in our
  community? Why? (local tradition)

The arts

– Music; folk dances
  (what kind of music is played in
  the story/in our community)
– Personal ornaments used by the
  bride and groom; wedding
  ornaments used in each community
– How do people dress to attend
  a wedding?

**Target book:
Jafta and the Wedding
(Lewin, 1983)**

Language

– Use of figures of speech
– Vocabulary
– Expressions (How is
  affection demonstrated?)

Food experience

– Wedding reception
  (preparing the menu)
– Kinds of food used

Science

– Animals
– Safe handling of
  wedding food ingredients

Source: Robles de Meléndez & Henry, 1994.

linguistic symbols of other languages. Analyses of the various sections, such as the advertising section, found in foreign papers can turn into interesting activities for the children. Teachers can obtain international papers and journals from local bookstores, at airport newspaper stands, and, in some cases, from local ethnic stores. Other sources are the donations made by children's parents or by staff members who buy ethnic publications. Teachers are advised to examine the donated literature materials carefully to verify the appropriateness and the quality of the content.

Many journals can also be added to the book center. For example, *National Geographic* and *World* (both from the National Geographic Society); *Faces: The Magazine About People* (Cobblestone Publishing); and *Smithsonian* (from the Smithsonian Institution) make good additions to the classroom literature corner. They can be found in most public and school libraries.

LITERACY CONNECTIONS...

Ten Books with Animal Characters for Discussions About Diversity

- **Bayley, N. (1989). *Polar bear cat*. New York: Alfred A. Knopf.**
  This is a story about a cat that tries to look at the world through the eyes of a polar bear. Other books in the series are *Parrot Cat, Elephant Cat, Crab Cat,* and *Spider Cat.*

- **Best, C. (2002). *Goose's story*. New York: Farrar, Straus and Giroux.**
  This is the true story of a goose with one foot and how he managed.

- **Brett, J. (2003). *Town mouse, country mouse*. New York: G.P. Putnam Juvenile.**
  The book is very wordy but a good comparison of two distinct cultures. It is good for use with a Venn diagram.

- **Bruss, D. (2001). *Books, books, books*. New York: Arthur A. Levine Books.**
  This is a great book to begin a discussion about linguistic diversity. The animals try to get a book from the library, but the librarian doesn't understand any of their languages until the hen says "book, book, book."

- **de Beer, H. (1998). *Ahoy there, little polar bear*. Gossau, Switzerland: North-South Books.**
  This is the story of a polar bear who finds himself in a culture very far away and very different from the North Pole where he lives. Good for "place" differences as well as cultural differences.

- **Heine, H. (1994). *The most wonderful egg in the world*. New York: Atheneum.**
  Three chickens try to discover who is the most beautiful and find that they are all wonderful in different ways.

- **Jenkins, S., & Page, R. (2003). *What do you do with a tail like this?* Boston: Houghton Mifflin.**
  This is a fantastically illustrated book showing animals with different kinds of eyes, noses, tails, and other body parts. The differences allow for different abilities. The book is also very good for predictions.

- **Kirk, D. (2000). *Little Miss Spider: Sunny Patch School*. New York: Scholastic Press Callaway.**
  This is a rhyming tale of a spider who goes to school with other bugs. They all seem to be able to do something special. Finally, she discovers her specialty.

- **Lowell, S. (2000). *The three javelinas*. New York: Scholastic.**
  This book is great for comparing cultural differences between the javelinas and pigs in other *Three Little Pigs* stories.

- **Seuss, Dr. (1984). *The butter battle book*. New York: Random House.**
  Although not animals, these characters are certainly not really people either. This story is a great way to introduce prejudice and how to begin to find alternatives.

Contributed by Laurie R. Noe, EdD, early childhood education and literacy consultant.

Artistic expression is an important part of the development of young children.

Wadsworth/Cengage Learning

Selecting Authentic Multicultural Literature: Evaluation Criteria

When selecting children's multicultural books, take time to find out if the story meets the following criteria, adapted from Cullinan and Galda (2005); Kasten, Kristo, and McClure (2005); Norton (2003); and Robles de Meléndez, 2004:

- The story and characters present an accurate portrayal of a specific culture.
- The story is free of any historical distortions or stereotypes. Messages about the cultural group, including race and social class, are free of any biases.
- Characters are portrayed according to the time and setting. If set in contemporary times, characters reflect current lifestyles.
- Characters reflect a variety of physical diversities.
- Story presents people with disabilities in a positive, nonstereotypical way.
- Female and male characters are presented in a variety of roles that exemplify nonstereotypical tasks. Roles of females and males are consistent with those in their cultural groups.
- Elderly people are presented in respectful and culturally accurate ways.
- Roles and importance of families are reflective of views held by the cultural group.
- People from diverse groups are portrayed in positive and leadership roles.
- Illustrations depict the culture and people in culturally accurate ways.
- Language representative of the cultural group is used to enhance the message. Linguistic expressions of the cultural group reflect their oral traditions.
- Authors and illustrators are members of the cultural group or have firsthand knowledge about the culture.

Newspapers are an inexpensive source of rich cultural materials. They offer glimpses into the realities of other individuals and groups. A newspaper also reports on current views, attitudes, conflicts, and values of different ethnicities. Newspapers can help the child discern a variety of human characteristics through the racial and physical portrayals of people living in our communities.

We know a second-grade teacher who developed a project about people solely from newspapers. During an entire year, her students saved the pictures they thought best portrayed different people. More than 800 pictures pasted on tagboard became a permanent picture file that captivated the children's imagination throughout the year.

Pictures are an important element of any literature corner. Journals, newspapers, and magazines are good sources of provocative illustrations. Postcards are an inexpensive source of good pictures, as well. Most people who travel are tempted to bring home cards that end up not being used. They can become an excellent resource in the classroom. Robles de Meléndez (2001) recommends that professionals use their "teacher's eye" in selecting postcards when traveling. The good "eye" alerts us to the images children will enjoy and savor in their imaginations. Postcards can easily be used to make picture books that will expand the literacy resources. A world map or globe should always be close to the literature area for easy consultation. The notion of "here and there" gives appropriate opportunities to compare and contrast for the purpose of finding out what makes us so alike.

Postcards have been successfully used by many educators at all levels to teach about communities and local history. Postcards were organized into thematic areas (architecture and historical scenes; major industry scenes, agriculture, and transportation; environment and tourist sites) that provided a wealth of perspectives for children. Teachers can either file them by topic or make picture books with them. A list of themes commonly found in postcards is given in Figure 9-8.

Ways to Enhance the Literature Area

An optimal literature area can be built by using some of the resources common to all schools: the stories of children and families. Grandparents and senior volunteers are invaluable sources of information and anecdotes about traditions and lifestyles. Teachers

FIGURE 9-8 **Ways to Organize Pictures and Postcards**

Sample theme topics in postcards

- How we dress (clothing)
- Things to eat
- Flowers and trees
- Faces
- Places to visit
- People's hats
- Musical instruments
- Celebrations/festivals
- Houses and buildings
- People everywhere
- Colors and decorations
- Natural landscapes
- Fun places

FOCUS
on Classroom Practices

Cinderella, A Traditional Literature Character Connecting Cultures

Literature is one of the elements that link us in our multicultural and global community. Around the world, some story characters are common to many cultures. Such is the case of Cinderella. We selected a list of Cinderella stories to get you started in exploring more about how this character is seen through the lenses of people from other cultures. You may want to try some of the following activities. They include the key multicultural concepts for each activity.

- *Cultural heritage:* Using a map, locate the settings of the stories read. Talk about the locations and find out if anyone is familiar with the place. Identify whether any of the children or their families are natives of those countries.

- *Linguistic diversity:* Talk about the names of the Cinderella character in each of the stories. Highlight any words in other languages and have a discussion about the importance of languages. Prepare a Cinderella word chart and write down words in other languages learned from the stories.

- *Cultural patterns:* Using a Venn diagram, compare and contrast the stories (characters, name of the main character, setting, ways they are dressed, problem, and problem resolution). Have children draw their favorite scene and talk about what they liked best.

- *Gender issues:* Share with children any of the Cinderella stories with male characters (for example, *Sumorella: A Hawai'i Cinderella story* or *Joe Cinders*). Discuss how the situation applies to both boys and girls. Have children talk about and draw pictures of activities that can be performed across gender lines.

African:
- Climo, S. (1991). *The Egyptian Cinderella.* New York: HarperCollins.
- Steptoe, J. (1987). *Mufaro's beautiful daughters: An African tale.* New York: Viking Books.

Native American:
- Chenkie, B. (1999). *Naya, the Inuit Cinderella.* Green Bay, WI: Raven Tree Press.
- Pollock, P. (1996). *The turkey girl: A Zuni Cinderella story.* New York: Little, Brown.
- San Souci, R. (1994). *Sootface: An Ojibwa Cinderella story.* New York: Dell.

Appalachian:
- Compton, J. (1994). *Ashpet: An Appalachian Tale.* New York: Holiday.
- Schroeder, A., & Sneed, B. (1997). *Smoky Mountain Rose.* New York: Penguin Books.

Cajun:
- Hebert, S. (1998). *Cendrillon: A Cajun Cinderella.* New York: Pelican.

Hawaiian:
- Takayama, S. (1984). *Sumorella: A Hawai'i Cinderella story.* Honolulu, HI: Bess Press. (boy Cinderella)

Southwest and Western United States:
- Mitchell (2002). *Joe Cinders.* New York: Henry Holt. (boy Cinderella)

Caribbean:
- San Souci, R. (1998). *Cendrillon: A Caribbean Cinderella.* New York: Simon and Schuster.

Latino/Hispanic:
- DePaola, T. (2002). *Adelita: A Mexican Cinderella story.* New York: Putnam.
- Reinhart, J. (2000). *Domitila: A Cinderella tale from the Mexican tradition.* San Diego, CA: Shen.

Middle East:
- Climo, S. (1999). *The Persian Cinderella.* New York: HarperCollins.
- Hickox, R. (1998). *The golden sandal.* New York: Holiday House.

Asian:
- Climo, S. (1993). *The Korean Cinderella.* New York: HarperCollins.
- de la Paz, M. (2001). *Abadeha: The Philippine Cinderella.* San Diego, CA: Shen.
- Louie, A. (1982). *Ye-Shen: A Cinderella story from China.* New York: Philomel.

- Sierra, J. (2000). *The gift of the crocodile: A Cinderella story.* New York: Simon and Schuster. (Indonesia)

European:
- Climo, S. (2000). *The Irish Cinderland.* New York: HarperTrophy.
- Huck, C. (1989). *Princess furball.* New York: Greenwillow Books.

With thanks to Audrey Henry, EdD, professor of Reading Education, for providing the list of recommended Cinderella stories.

can have the elderly as guest "tellers" and record their stories to form a "story bank" for later enjoyment. This is also a way to save the wisdom of the past for future generations and to develop an appreciation for the elderly, a diversity group frequently overlooked. Recordings of stories special to each family are also a valuable addition to the listening center. You may want to select a theme or topic and invite parents and family members to share their favorite stories or songs typical of their cultural group. Reasonably priced and easily available, blank tapes or CDs can be sent home for families to tape their stories, which will then become part of the listening library.

Persona Dolls, Another Useful Literacy Resource

All of us have enjoyed the stories told by puppets at one time in our lives, largely because we believed they were real. That is precisely why the persona doll is another child-appropriate resource (Figure 9-9). A persona doll is a vehicle for telling stories about the lives of children and their families in a method developed by Kay Taus (cited in Derman-Sparks & the A.B.C. Task Force, 1989). According to Taus, persona dolls also bring into the classroom the lives of people who have "differences that do not exist within one classroom." Each doll acquires a "persona" from a character it represents in a story. A script accompanies the doll, which periodically visits the classroom and becomes a part of it. Because they are intended to serve as a teacher resource, persona dolls should be kept in the teacher's area. However, they can be available to children whenever they ask for them. Stories with persona dolls are created from four main sources:

1. Issues emerging from the children's lives and experiences
2. Current world and community events
3. Relevant information that the children should learn
4. Significant historical events (Derman-Sparks & the A.B.C. Task Force, 1989)

Movement and dance are young children's favorite activities.

Wadsworth/Cengage Learning

FIGURE 9-9 **Sample Persona Doll Story**

Using Persona Dolls

One way to establish a diversity-responsive classroom environment is by incorporating characters that reflect the cultural nature of your group and of the community. Teachers know that puppets, dolls, and masks are good developmental resources that spur the child's imagination. They also serve to stimulate the child to talk, revealing feelings and emotions otherwise known only to the inner self. When addressing issues of diversity, a persona doll (Derman-Sparks & the A.B.C. Task Force, 1989) helps teachers to focus on a variety of situations suitable for discussion.

But, what is a persona doll? Basically, it is any resource used to personify a given character. What makes it different is that the doll is given a specific personality that will reflect any of the variables that define the concept of diversity (i.e., ethnicity, religion, social class, gender, special needs, race). The object receives personal attributes that establish a very distinguishable identity; that is, it becomes a "person."

The goal behind each doll is to provide teachers with a resource they can use to help children face situations that are typical for people of diversity. Using the principles of storytelling, the doll is then used as the key character in teacher-made stories that are shared with the children. They can become permanent "members" of the classroom, helping children to learn how "they view" different circumstances as they arise. When dolls are placed in the housekeeping area or in the "guest visitor" corner, children can reflect and reenact their problems.

Designs of persona dolls are as varied as classrooms are. The basic rule is to frame them according to the diversity parameters characteristic of the community and children. In this way, they become a device to help teachers address issues before or as they arise. Also, they will serve to expose children to aspects of diversity that are not part of their environment. For example, in a school with a predominantly upper-middle class student population, a teacher might use the persona dolls to expose children to issues such as homelessness.

Another use would be to have children share specific problems faced by persons with special needs. Issues of race and ethnicity are equally feasible to be displayed through the "personas."

If you are planning to use the dolls, here are three key suggestions to remember:

1. Have a clear purpose for each "personality" that will enter into your classroom. Ask yourself: *"Why is _____ in our classroom? What will the children derive from or learn through _____?"*

2. Create a believable story about the character. Dolls must present daily life situations faced by people of those same characteristics. Remember, children are to construct ideas through their stories, thus, stories must be faithful to the diversity circumstance that is being personified. Avoid unreal, hard-to-believe personalities. Select situations you are familiar with that will also be at the child's level. Ask yourself: *"Is the character an example of a real person? What makes the character authentic?"*

3. Use appropriate artifacts or materials to design and prepare the persona dolls. Avoid objects that would misrepresent the character. Remember, you are dealing with very sensitive issues! Ask yourself: *"Is the characteristic an accurate portrayal? Is it realistic?"*

Stories to Enhance the Child's Perception of Social Differences

Topic:
   Learning about the contribution and role of farm workers in our society.

Goal:
   To enhance the social value of migrant workers.
   To learn about family life in a migrant worker community.

Concepts:
   • Work as a valuable activity
   • Interdependence
   • Migrant/farm worker
   • Pride in one's social world

Focus on Diversity:
   Social class; ethnicity

Materials:
   • Map of Florida; world map
   • Persona dolls
   • Pictures of flowers, live flowers and ferns

Procedure:
Using a persona doll, the teacher will introduce " Guillermo," a child whose parents are migrant farm workers.

   Guillermo came to Crescent City, Florida, two months ago. His father works in a fern farm. He likes this town because it is less warm than Homestead where they lived before. Guillermo also enjoys the new apartment where he lives with his family. Now, after losing everything they owned during the *huracán Andrés*, he finally has new clothes and, in particular, a new pair of tennis shoes that shine at night!

(continued)

FIGURE 9-9 (continued)

His father works all day long. With his little sister, he goes to school while his mother stays at home taking care of Lalito, his baby brother. In the afternoon, when he comes back home, he likes the *pupusas* that his mom prepares.

Today he feels very proud. He just learned that the ferns that his father helps to grow are highly valued in countries far away from Florida. Yesterday, when he went to the packing house, he saw how they prepared the ferns for their long trips. He saw the farm owner and a man from an airline making all the shipping arrangements. With a lot of care, every fern was carefully wrapped and placed in special boxes.

Guillermo was going to ask where they were being sent when he heard the *capataz*, his father's boss, saying, "Those ferns are going to Amsterdam." "There they are used to make all the finest bouquets," said the person from the airline. He talked about the huge flower market in Amsterdam where ferns are sold and distributed all over.

Guillermo felt proud to hear that those plants that his father grows are so important. This morning, during circle time, he told his kindergarten teacher about the ferns. And he also said that there is something else he wants to learn: where is Amsterdam?

To think and do . . .

1. If you were Guillermo's teacher, what would you do with his question?
2. What activities would you design to involve the rest of the children?
3. In what ways could you use this opportunity to enhance the child's self-esteem?
4. Think about other circumstances or stories that define the daily lives of children with diverse cultural backgrounds. Select one and describe how you can address their situations to make the rest of the class aware of the things that they all have in common.

Music and Movement Experiences

Another of the universal traits that characterize human cultures is music, along with its counterpart, movement. They are considered important because they provide avenues to becoming culturally literate. Children seem to have a natural inclination toward anything involving rhythm and body movement. They are constantly exposed to a variety of experiences in the classroom, such as listening to music, singing, performing, and movement, that contribute to their holistic development. Singing and dancing should be incorporated into many daily activities such as story time, circle time, outdoor play, and so on. Because of the appeal these activities have for the child, they also serve as an avenue of learning about themselves and about others.

Folk songs and ethnic music need to be incorporated into the regular curriculum to initiate an appreciation for these art forms. They should not be limited to whenever a given holiday approaches. Reserving music representative of different cultures and dancing for specific dates only serves to reinforce a sense of cultural remoteness of a particular group. Typical ethnic musical instruments like a *güiro* (a percussion instrument made out of a gourd) and a *quena* (Andean flute) should be included in the music and listening center. Figure 9-10 presents a list of selected musical instruments that can be added to the classroom. When integrated into the regular plan of experiences, children learn to hear and sing the music of other countries as logical expressive representations of human beings.

Music is also known for conveying emotional feelings, which children seem to emulate easily (Haines & Gerber, 1995). This affective characteristic of music offers an opportunity for learning about the similarity of feelings people express through music. An effective strategy is to organize your musical selections as well as dances according to the many emotions that originate from life events and that are shared by a group of people. Children can listen to the tone and rhythm used to describe the different feelings and emotions and form body movements to accompany their interpretations. Introducing some of the typical dances can also occur as part of the learning about things people share. For example, dances commonly performed during weddings or other festivities provide an understanding of the existing multiple views.

Music of different cultural groups is easily obtainable through most local public libraries. Many libraries even include examples of typical musical instruments as well as recordings from various cultural groups. Performers such as Ella Jenkins, Raffi, José Luis Orozco, and Hap Palmer have recorded multicultural music appropriate for young children. Most music stores now have an ethnic music section where teachers can also find adequate instrumental and vocal pieces. When making selections, remember to look first for the musical representations of those cultural groups present in your classroom, and then look for others. Integration of music into classroom experiences provides not only a source to meet the children's developmental needs but also another way to explore cultural expressions (see Figure 9-11).

Games and Play: The Medium of All Cultures

Jean Piaget defines play as a natural and inherent characteristic of individuals found across cultures. He established that children respond spontaneously to any gamelike activity. This inclination facilitates the acquisition of knowledge across cultures. Piaget's theory stresses the role of play as a common learning strategy and a central channel for knowledge formation about the world. Aside from their recreational aspects, play and games are found to keep their power throughout our lives.

FIGURE 9-10 **Suggested Ethnic Musical Instruments for the Classroom**

- Native American: drums, horns, conch shells
- Caribbean; African: guitars, maracas, güiros (gourds), percussion instruments
- Latin American: guitars, tambourines, wind instruments (for example, the Andean *quena*), xylophones (to represent the marimba), maracas
- Asian: string instruments, percussion instruments

FIGURE 9-11 **Suggested Themes to Select and Incorporate Ethnic Music into the Curriculum**

Life events
- happiness (marriage, births, successes, holidays)
- sadness (death, losses)
- solemnity (graduations, patriotic events, some cultural celebrations)

Daily life
- home and family
- nature
- motherhood/fatherhood
- children
- games

Which other ones can you name?

F CUS
on Classroom Practices

Using Music to Build Cultural Awareness

Music is a universal element of cultures that is integral to early childhood development. In the classroom, music offers a developmentally sound opportunity for building awareness about self and other cultures. From infancy to the primary age, music provides young children with opportunities to express themselves, learn about their own heritage, and discover the cultures of others. Here are some suggestions for activities that involve music:

- Recess and quiet time: Using as background music selections representative of children's cultures, provides opportunities for children to become familiar with the musical tradition of other groups. In a classroom with 3-year olds, we observed teachers interchangeably using classical music along with soft popular music representative of children's cultures. The experience served the purposes of both exposing the youngsters to other rhythms and validating the musical traditions represented in the class.

- Transitions: Multicultural chants and songs with short lyrics are ideal to signal and prepare children for activities to come. Select those with simple lyrics so that children can learn and follow. For example, in a classroom we visited, teachers used "El Coquí [Little Frog]," a lullaby from Puerto Rico as the children prepare for their naptime.

- Morning circle time: Singing songs in other languages is a good way to both help children become aware of linguistic diversity and engage them in learning words in other languages. Several teachers we visited told us that while they sang bilingual morning songs, others even included the use of sign language as they sang. One of our graduate students uses a repertoire of children's folk music to start the day's activities. She adapts the songs to the season, making it a versatile learning experience for the children.

LITERACY CONNECTIONS...

Recommended Multicultural Music Resources

Many multicultural music books provide valuable literacy learning opportunities while exploring diverse musical traditions. Some of those we have used and found especially relevant are listed here:

- Cohn, A. (1993). *From sea to shining sea: A treasury of American folklore and folk songs.* New York: Scholastic.

- Delacre, L. (2006). *Rufi and Rosi: Carnival!* New York: Scholastic.

- Fox, D. (2003). *A treasury of children's songs: Forty favorites songs to play and sing.* New York: Henry Holt.

- Goode, D. (1996). *The Diane Goode Book: A treasury of American folk tales and songs.* New York: Puffin.

- Grand-Bernier, C. (2002). *Shake it, Morena! and other folklore from Puerto Rico.* New York: Millbrook Press.

- Kantor, S. (2003). *An illustrated treasury of African American read-aloud stories.* New York: Black Dog & Leventhal Publishers.

- Orozco, J. (1999). *Diez deditos: Ten little fingers & other play rhymes and action songs from Latin America.* New York: Dutton.

- Orozco, J. (2002). *Fiestas: A year of Latin American celebrations.* New York: Dutton.

- Sullivan, K. (2005). *The best Hawaiian style Mother Goose ever!* Honolulu, HI: Hawaya.

- Yolen, J. (2000). *Sleep rhymes around the world.* Honesdale, PA: Boyds Mills Press.

Educator Frances Kendall (1996) believes play "enables children to grow out of their egocentric and ethnocentric picture of the world." Play and the games children learn offer an excellent foundation for developing and increasing the awareness about human diversity. Kendall contends that despite their differences, children around the world share the culture of childhood through play, another universal characteristic. Attributes of play make it a vital resource for teaching about diversity. Kendall (1996) contends that culture influences the meaning and interpretation of play. For some, play is seen as a solitary or interactive creative and spontaneous process. For others, play is structured and rule-driven, such as ballet or tennis lessons. In today's society, watching television and DVDs, playing video games, reading aloud, and listening to stories are all considered to be play. Two theorists, Jean Piaget and Lev Vygotsky, have dominated the research and theories about play. Piaget believed that play evolves "from practice play, to symbolic play, to play with rules. In other words play is carried out as part of the individual child's development growth. Vygotsky, on the other hand, believes that the child's primary purpose for play is not individual but social" (Kendall, 1996). Since Piaget and Vygotsky, many other experts on play have put forth their theories. No matter what model a teacher adopts, it is essential that she or he recognize that play is an important element of positive social, emotional, and physical development of all young children. Play is

- *voluntary and intrinsically motivated:* It is initiated by things that present challenges and where children find an interest.
- *symbolic and meaningful:* Children will assign meanings to their play items as they serve to bridge realities.
- *active and pleasurable:* The child's social context will determine the kind and type of activities.
- *rule-governed:* Rules established by children reflect the cultural values they know. Encountering different views is a way to learn about the ideas of others.
- *episodic:* Experiences shape the roles and purposes of play (Jalongo & Isenberg, 2008).

Observing what the child does when playing in the learning centers offers a window into the cultural ideas and values the child is acquiring. Some classroom areas are especially conducive to revealing the role culture plays in the child's interactions. For example, the block and dramatic centers serve as stages for young preschoolers to practice and apply their social and cultural ideas. Attention to what takes place there helps the teachers follow the dynamic lives of their students.

Games from the students' cultures should be the first ones to consider when teaching about diversity. Information about traditional game activities can be located in libraries and through the physical education specialists in the schools. A good way to begin is by inviting parents to share some of their favorite childhood games with the children. Learning games enjoyed by significant adults helps children to value their experiences. Fingerplays, rhymes, and songs accompany many of the ethnic and folk games, which make them a source of integrated learning. Lulu Delacre's *Arroz con leche: Popular Songs and Rhymes from Latin America* (1989) and *Rafi and Rosi: Carnival!* (2006) are examples of traditional children's folklore that are good sources for integrated learning.

LET'S TALK AND REFLECT... **Using Play to Learn About Diversity**

Play is another universal element of culture. Taking into account the role of play in child development, think about the multicultural learning opportunities that play presents in the context of the classroom.

| In Action . . . | **Play in the Classroom** |

- Visit a classroom and observe children while at play.
- Consider the types of play taking place in the classroom. Think about ways to enhance them for the purpose of multiculturalism.
- To encourage learning about others, what items would you add to the block area or to the dramatic area? Why?

PREPARING TO DESIGN ACTIVITIES FOR THE CLASSROOM— IDEAS IN ACTION

The time to bring ideas into practice has come. This is your opportunity to use and apply all the information about multicultural education as well as all the ideas presented in the previous chapters. This is the most exciting part of your journey into multicultural education. Your desire to create the best learning environment for children, your professional knowledge, and your sense of commitment to the young will guide you as you design and create your program. We have already defined the ideal multicultural classroom and taken inventory to find out what is available and needed to create an environment conducive to learning about diversity. Now let's think about appropriate activities that will transform ideas into action.

What Are Our Goals?

A primary goal of education for diversity is teaching children to be productive members of a culturally eclectic society. An appropriate classroom environment, where considerations for multiculturalism are followed, constitutes an ideal place for children to develop the appropriate social cognition. Social cognition allows the child to perceive life from the perspectives of others. Perspective taking, or the ability to see and understand one's position and the positions of others, is developed by growing up in a supportive environment (Berns, 1994). Early childhood classrooms must become such places that promote learning about diversity. The classroom activities lead children in discovering diversity as a normal part of life and, at the same time, adhere to the principles of cognitive development. In the next section, we will examine what cognitive and developmental characteristics teachers must consider as they prepare the classroom experiences. We will also examine the steps in lesson planning that will help us achieve instructional goals.

Planning for Multiple-Perspective Learning

Teaching is defined as developmentally appropriate when it provides children with *accurate* and legitimate views about our contemporary society that help build social knowledge and a *valid* assortment of interaction skills that are reflective of contemporary

society. Both are acquired and developed through the quality experiences the child encounters. But what are the attributes that characterize those activities or encounters?
What is the framework that will help the professional to organize them?

Defining the Elements of Developmentally Appropriate Learning Encounters

The whole philosophy of developmentally and culturally appropriate practice (DCAP)
is based on the belief that the child follows a process of growth and development that
defines what the child needs to learn to grow. Education for diversity is solidly founded
in this DCAP principle. Its aim is not to expose children to the pluralistic society because "it is fun" but because they need it.

An Environment for Active Learning

Piaget's research on how children learn revealed that knowledge building is a process
resulting from the dynamic interaction of the child with the environment. Piaget also
found that the child's active learning depends on the stage of the child's cognitive development. Both the concept of active learning and the existence of cognitive stages are
relevant for designing classroom activities. He defined four cognitive stages (see Figure
9-12), spanning birth to adolescence.

Active learning in children occurs when the child forms concepts about the world
from direct experiences or "hands-on" learning. Because of the need for appropriate active learning, teachers need to carefully structure the child's learning encounters (Forman and Kushner, 1987). This term refers to the child's experiences that occur in the
environment *purposefully* set and organized by the teacher. Learning encounters are
emphasized in a program based on DCAP. The classroom where the children are able
"to encounter" denotes an active involvement and obvious participation of the environment with the children. This requires that the activities be interesting to children to
promote the acquisition of meaningful knowledge.

FIGURE 9-12 **Piaget's Stages of Cognitive Development**

Sensorimotor Stage (Birth-2 years)*: Learning occurs mostly via the senses and via motor activity,
which facilitates the child's interactions with the environment.

Preoperational (2–7 years): Learning happens through the senses and via language, which gives
the child access to communicate interests and ideas and to inquire. Play is used as a means to
"play out," or represent, actions from reality.

Concrete Operations (7–11 years): Learning occurs as a result of reasoning and direct experiences. Child still requires direct experiences (hands-on).

Formal Operations (11–15+): Learning is based on reasoning of abstract ideas and suppositions
about reality.

---

* Ages do not indicate rigid age periods but rather when the particular reasoning ability is most characteristically observed.

Traits of Quality Learning Experiences

An organized environment is an integral part of multicultural education, in which the classroom prepared to facilitate experiences is based on diversity. Quality experiences should include special traits, such as the following:

- active involvement
- child participation
- age appropriateness
- cognitive appropriateness
- developmental relevance to the child
- holistic learning

A Framework for Planning: The Cycle of Teaching and Learning

The possibilities for learning encounters in a multicultural classroom are endless. Translating many opportunities into action requires a child-appropriate framework for planning. Bredekamp and Rosegrant (1992) refer to this framework as "the cycle of learning and teaching." The cycle, consisting of four major levels, represents a practical and meaningful approach for implementing what Bredekamp and Rosegrant call a "mindful curriculum." A mindful curriculum should be meaningful, integrated, and based on the realities of the classroom. This is also the most appropriate curriculum for teaching about diversity issues.

The four levels of the cycle of learning are awareness, exploration, inquiry, and utilization (Figure 9-13). Like building blocks, the experiences at each level are built upon the previous ones. This kind of planning and teaching strategy is considered to be constructivist in nature. Let us examine more closely how the circle of learning and teaching can be used to set up your classroom scenario.

The learning process described in the cycle has two distinctive levels. The first level consists of the **awareness** and **exploration** phases. At this stage, the child is presented with what is new or different. The novelty or the "intrigue" of the new experience triggers the child's interest to learn more about it.

LET'S TALK AND REFLECT... Favorite Games

- Do you remember what your favorite games were when you were a child?
- Can you name some of the songs and rhymes you used with the games?
- Which ones are still used by children today?

FIGURE 9-13 **Cycle of Learning and Teaching**

What Children Do		What Teachers Do
Awareness	Experience	Create the environment
	Acquire an interest	Provide opportunities by introducing new objects, events, people
	Recognize broad parameters	Invite interest by posing a problem or question
	Attend	Respond to child's interest or shared experience
	Perceive	Show interest, enthusiasm
Exploration	Observe	Facilitate
	Explore materials	Support and enhance exploration
	Collect information	Provide opportunities for active exploration
	Discover	Extend play
	Create	Describe child's activity
	Figure out components	Ask open-ended questions—"What else could you do?"
	Construct own understanding	Respect child's thinking and rule systems
	Apply own rules	Allow for constructive error
	Create personal meaning	
	Represent own meaning	
Inquiry	Examine	Help children refine understanding
	Investigate	Guide children, focus attention
	Propose explanations	Ask more focused questions—"What else works like this?" "What happens if . . . ?"
	Focus	
	Compare own thinking with that of others	Provide information when requested—"How do you spell . . . ?"
	Generalize	Help children make connections
	Relate to prior learning	
	Adjust to conventional rule systems	
Utilization	Use the learning in many ways; learning becomes functional	Create vehicles for application in real world
		Help children apply learning to new situations
	Represent learning in various ways	Provide meaningful situations in which to use learning
	Apply learning to new situations	
	Formulate new hypotheses and repeat cycle	

Source: Bredekamp & Rosegrant, 1992.

1. *Awareness:* The child becomes familiarized, or apprised of the existence of an idea or an issue. The following questions can be used to guide the teacher's planning in this phase:

   ■ How can the child become cognizant about this issue or idea?

   ■ In what ways can the environment be set up to engage the child's interest?

2. *Exploration:* The child begins to search for the elements that define the issue or idea that captured his or her attention. In the process, the child will process information according to his or her own experiences. The child is actively using his or her cultural knowledge to filter what is meaningful. The following questions guide the teacher's planning:

   ■ How can I facilitate and support the students' investigation?

   ■ What activities and materials can help the children in the process?

   ■ What questions should I ask the students to verify their progress and understanding?

   Level 2 is more advanced and requires careful planning. In this level, the child, who already has acquired an individual understanding and is cognizant about the issues or concept, begins to reformulate the existing knowledge. During this reformulation, children discover the views of others as well as ways to apply the acquired knowledge. This is what happens when the child enters into the **inquiry** and **utilization** phases.

1. *Inquiry:* Child begins to reexamine and compare the acquired knowledge. The child begins to consider his or her own beliefs while comparing them to the beliefs held by others. The outcome of this process is a refined view of the issue or concept where common points are ascertained. The following questions can be used to guide your planning:

   ■ What are the additional experiences that will help the child see the idea from the point of view of others?

   ■ What questions can I pose to the child that will help him or her focus on other aspects of the topic?

   ■ What other areas, information, or resources would the child need to examine?

2. *Utilization:* The child begins to bring things into a functional reality. Activities and opportunities are offered to help the child apply what has been learned. This validation of knowledge occurs as the child finds its usefulness in daily life. The following questions will help you plan this phase:

   ■ What opportunities can I create in the classroom for the child to apply or demonstrate what was learned?

   ■ What real-life situations can I use to illustrate the applicability of the knowledge learned?

   A learning cycle implies a series of events that will lead to the reinitiation of the process. After a child learns a concept, it can be applied to other contexts that lead the child to examine new ideas. In teaching about diversity, leading the child to examine

LET'S TALK AND REFLECT... Successful Planning

Early childhood professionals who want to create successful experiences for young children must engage in many planning steps. Reflection is a very important step in the planning process. You should learn to reflect on daily events in the classroom and determine the high and low points of the day and what worked and what did not. One of the ways to do that is to keep a daily journal. Find out about other ways that are also effective.

Ask experienced teachers to share their ideas about how they use reflection in their classrooms. Find out what strategies experienced teachers use to help them reflect on the day's events. Based on their comments, decide on the one that you feel best suits you.

the perspectives of others will create endless situations where the cycle of learning will be repeated over and over again. As that happens, you will see how the children's consciousness about diversity grows and becomes more concrete.

Using the Cycle of Learning: An Example

The cycle of learning is a useful planning tool. Here is an example in which a teacher decided to try the cycle of learning using a topic that she observed made the children uncomfortable. Let us see how she applied it.

Group: Kindergarten
Problem/issue: Learning that my peers' families can be different from my own

I. Awareness/What they seem to know
1. Read and discuss Taylor's story *All Kinds of Families* (Delacorte, 2005).
2. Draw our families and display them on our "classroom mural."
3. Have posters about families displayed around the classroom. Ask the children to bring pictures of their families and display them in the classroom.
4. Include family sets in the block area.

II. Exploration/Investigating
1. Make paper bag puppets of our families. Have the children present "families."
2. Prepare family trees. Make a list of terms used to describe family relationships.
3. Invite family members to the classroom to talk about their families.
4. Have persona dolls talk about their families (single parent, foster).
5. Include pictures of different families in the literacy area.
6. Find and learn lullabies or *canciones de cuna.*
7. Have a grandparent or any other relative come to sing to the students.

8. Use play dough or paints to make representations of our families. Present them during circle time.

9. Make a graph about the sizes of families and types of family members.

10. Prepare a chart about things families do. Search for pictures in old magazines. Do a Venn diagram to compare and contrast children's families.

11. Include baby and toddler items from other countries, such as India and Haiti, in the housekeeping area. Observe reactions and ask questions.

12. Talk about the roles and tasks done by family members. Make stories about what we do at home. Role-play some of those stories. Share Gary Soto's story *Too Many Tamales* (Putnam Juvenile, 1996).

III. Inquiry/Self-Investigation

1. Bring family prop boxes. Have the children examine the contents. Ask them to infer what families they represent. Draw or make with play dough the family members they think each box represents. Guide children to describe their inferences. *(Why do you think there are _____ in this family? How did you discover that?)*

2. Using art materials, make or draw families based on the characters in favorite stories. Discuss and compare them with the families of the children. Ask: *Why do you think we have families?*

3. Read stories about grandparents (such as *Song and Dance Man* by Karen Ackerman [Dragonfly, 1992]). Discuss other relatives in our families.

IV. Utilization/Applying What We Know

1. Read and discuss Sol Gordon's *All Families are Different* (Prometheus, 2000). Have children talk about what keeps families strong even when they live apart or when a parent works until late at night. Discuss how children can help parents (What can I do at home?). Role-play some of the suggestions.

2. Display pictures of families from other countries (these can be made into a book and placed in the literacy area). Add and read stories such as Ifeoma Onyefulu's *Welcome Dede! An African Naming Ceremony* (Frances Lincoln Children's, 2004).

3. Add family figures to the manipulatives in the block and manipulatives areas.

4. Make game cards showing different family configurations as well as configurations of other kinds of groups. Ask the children to identify what family configurations the cards depict.

5. Have children create their own persona doll story. Have the dolls tell the class about their families.

6. Make a collective chart about "things in common and things that make families different." Refer to it whenever needed.

7. Have the children make a picture vocabulary depicting the different family configurations. Reinforce the terminology that defines them. Keep it available as a reference.

8. Take children on a field trip to observe how many families they see. Have them take a small note pad to jot down their findings.

Sources for Planning the Content and the Experiences

Developmentally appropriate content is characterized by being child-centered and integrated (Morrison, 2006). The content in early childhood is derived from the children's interests and needs. It can also originate from what the teacher considers to be relevant for the children. The content identified by the teacher usually targets the needs and aims of families, the school, and the community in relationship to the children. Issues relevant to the community need to be targeted because children are members of and interact with the communities in which they live. Meaningful issues identified by the particular groups of which the children are members, and of the society at large, should be integrated into the instructional content as well. Content based on the interests of the child, the needs of society, and the concerns of the teacher is considered child-centered and integrated (Figure 9-14).

FIGURE 9-14 **Sources of Child-Appropriate Content for Multicultural Classrooms**

Classroom incidents that entail verbal and/or physical behaviors involving children with diverse characteristics
– On the playground
– During center time
– At recess or lunch time

Questions from children that offer developmentally appropriate teachable opportunities for the group
– Integration of multicultural content

Presence of new children or staff members with diverse characteristics

Meaningful curricular sources for integration of multicultural education

Comments from children related to diversity
– Bias language
– Racially charged terms
– Racial issues
– Gender issues
– Disabilities
– About linguistic diversity

Holidays and seasonal celebrations
– Traditional
– Local and regional

Curricular themes

Events and happenings
– Family
– Community
– National and global events

Appropriate content presents topics as parts of a whole, not in isolation. When examining a theme, the child is led to view it holistically by providing opportunities to examine the theme from all angles and never in isolation. This integrated approach facilitates valid learning that occurs when the child knows how an idea relates and applies to a general context (Figure 9-15).

This same rule applies to selecting topics for teaching about diversity.

Two things are important for teachers who are trying to define the content of the multicultural curriculum:

1. First, accurately observe the actions and interactions of children in the learning areas.

2. Second, become a proactive teacher and bring the multicultural issues into the classroom. Throw away your "color-blindness" and seek ways to prevent the behaviors and beliefs that act against diversity and equity. Discard any misleading and inaccurate views about children and consider them individuals capable of facing situations when appropriately presented.

FIGURE 9-15 **Web of Integrated Topics**

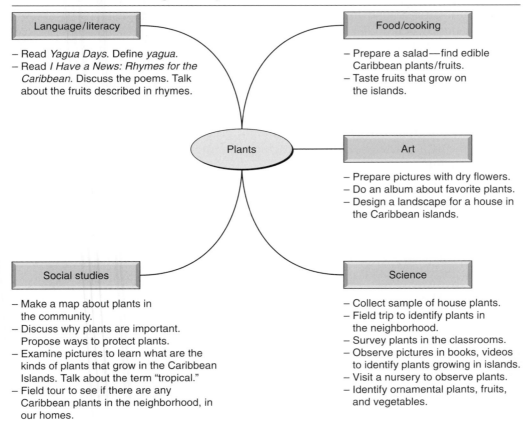

Language/literacy
- Read *Yagua Days*. Define *yagua*.
- Read *I Have a News: Rhymes for the Caribbean*. Discuss the poems. Talk about the fruits described in rhymes.

Food/cooking
- Prepare a salad—find edible Caribbean plants/fruits.
- Taste fruits that grow on the islands.

Plants

Art
- Prepare pictures with dry flowers.
- Do an album about favorite plants.
- Design a landscape for a house in the Caribbean islands.

Social studies
- Make a map about plants in the community.
- Discuss why plants are important. Propose ways to protect plants.
- Examine pictures to learn what are the kinds of plants that grow in the Caribbean Islands. Talk about the term "tropical."
- Field tour to see if there are any Caribbean plants in the neighborhood, in our homes.

Science
- Collect sample of house plants.
- Field trip to identify plants in the neighborhood.
- Survey plants in the classrooms.
- Observe pictures in books, videos to identify plants growing in islands.
- Visit a nursery to observe plants.
- Identify ornamental plants, fruits, and vegetables.

You also can define the content when you are alert to the following:

- Comments made about other children in the class because of their race, language, or disability; about other children in the school; about adults and staff members; about story or TV characters; about stories read; about pictures; and about visitors
- Use of pejorative words and terms to describe or allude to others; use of intentional name calling
- Nonverbal expressions (puzzled faces, frowns, nuances) made in a response to a person, an incident, or a story
- Open rejection or being upset about others
- Fear and distress when in front of other people (Derman-Sparks & the A.B.C. Task Force, 1989; Robles de Meléndez, 2004)

Creating Your Own Curriculum Using Thematic Teaching

Thematic teaching is a DCAP strategy that facilitates integrated teaching. Introduced by Dewey and Kilpatrick (cited in Katz & Chard, 2000) in the early part of the twentieth century, it is a popular classroom strategy. It is also an appropriate way to develop a classroom curriculum for diversity. Theme teaching is a holistic approach to a broad content area that includes many different related topics. The thematic approach is child centered and rooted in problem-based learning and inquiry. It is a discovery method that facilitates meaningful experiences for children. Developed around the topics that are of interest to children, theme studies present an opportunity to create a curriculum that addresses the reality of the classroom. The flexible nature of theme studies allows teachers to incorporate issues as they arise in the classroom. Several other characteristics define the appropriateness of theme teaching. We suggest the following guidelines for theme teaching.

1. Select a theme because of its relevance to children and their ability to assimilate it based on their developmental characteristics.
2. Emphasize development of skills and acquisition of knowledge, not the accumulation of facts.
3. Place balanced attention on both the content and the process by providing developmentally sequential ideas and skills that are similar to building blocks.
4. Encourage group work, collaboration, and social interaction that promote tolerance, compromise, and coping skills.

In Action . . .   **Formulating the Content**

What additional details should teachers observe that may serve as a basis for multicultural instructional content?

5. Instill in children responsibility for their own learning by guiding them to solutions through finding sources, examining information, and arriving at conclusions.

Many times theme-based studies take the form of projects. Also called the project approach (originally called the project method by Dewey and Kilpatrick), theme-based studies are actually active investigations. The approach also offers an opportunity to have more than one topic "investigated" at one time. Theme teaching, or project work, in early childhood education for diversity is centered on four goals: knowledge, skills, dispositions, and feelings (Katz & Chard, 2000). According to Katz and Chard, in an early childhood classroom, each of these goals indicates different types of learning.

1. *Knowledge:* describes concepts, ideas, facts, information (for example, learning correct names to designate ethnic groups or the significance of a given cultural celebration)
2. *Skills:* refers to specific discrete units of behavior, such as social skills and thinking skills (for example, acquiring the ability to participate in a group or to make friends)
3. *Dispositions:* describes the patterns or habits of mind that characterize the individual's ways of responding to experiences (for example, curiosity, desire to learn about others, desire to share with others, and unbiased responses)
4. *Feelings:* indicates the emotional or affective stances exhibited during and because of a given circumstance (for example, a positive attitude, tolerance, and acceptance of others)

Areas of study in thematic teaching originate from the children's interests. However, the teacher can also introduce topics when they are based on the children's needs identified through the teacher's observations. Topics chosen by the teacher should guide the children to recognize the universal cultural traits shared with other groups first. Emphasizing what makes us alike reduces the possibilities of children distancing themselves even further from the group. Consider, for example, a classroom where there are children of different Caribbean ethnicities who are the subject of name calling by their classmates, probably because their peers have limited exposure to members of those cultures. The teacher who observes such a confrontation is presented with an opportunity to introduce a very relevant and timely project. Possible topics that offer an initial awareness about Caribbean children could be "colors" and "decorations." Both topics depict universal concepts found in every culture that permit children to discover and establish the similarities among people. A description of the possible areas of investigation appears in Figure 9-16.

Selecting Topics for Teaching

According to some educators, it is advisable to observe the following rules when selecting topics for classroom exploration (Katz & Chard, 2000):

■ The topic is based on things of direct interest to the child. It leads to information or skills readily applicable to the child's reality. Teachers can generate the appropriate topics based on their knowledge of individuals and groups in their classrooms and based on classroom observations.

FIGURE 9-16 **Sample Concept Web**

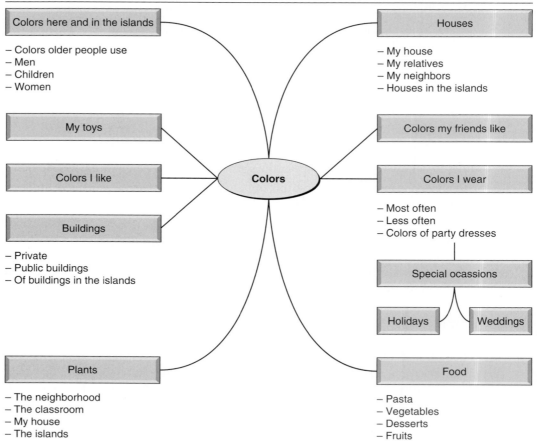

- The chosen topics are feasible to investigate and allow for the child's involvement for a minimum of one week.
- Topics should be interdisciplinary in nature. Integration into several areas should be possible.
- Children work on topics for which there are sufficient resources at the school.
- Appropriate concrete and print materials are available for the investigation of the topic.
- The investigation of a topic will provide for the acquisition and enhancement of knowledge, feelings, and dispositions.
- Opportunities for parent, family, and community collaboration are possible through the investigation.
- Outcomes will have validity and usefulness in the child's current and future life.

A group-specific curriculum framework, developed around the concept of islanders, has also been proposed by Robles de Meléndez (1999). This model provides sample ways to create experiences aimed to help children develop an appreciation and an understanding about a particular cultural group (Appendix D). Rationale for the curriculum emerged from two facts: (1) The islanders are an underrepresented minority across the curriculum that infrequently defines them in common and real-life settings, and (2) the islanders constitute a cultural entity demographically significant in the United States. Using social studies as a key organizer, Robles de Meléndez suggests a series of themes, all leading to develop an understanding about this ethnic group. Focus is on similarities, and it serves as a way of discovering and establishing the aspects that make the identity of the islanders so unique. The model for the curriculum is founded on a developmental framework in which the tenets of education for diversity were incorporated (Figure 9-17).

FIGURE 9-17 **Framework for the "Children of the Islands" Curriculum**

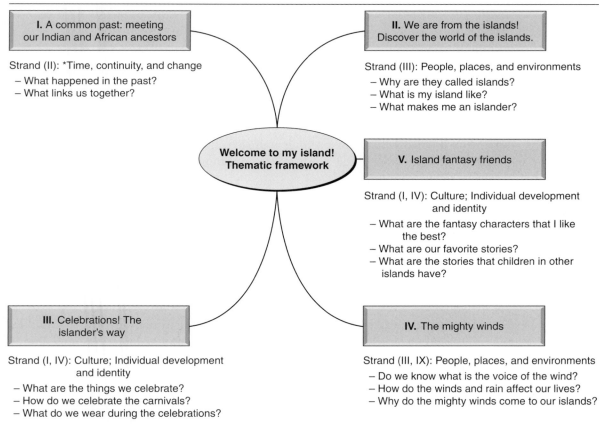

I. A common past: meeting our Indian and African ancestors

Strand (II): *Time, continuity, and change
- What happened in the past?
- What links us together?

II. We are from the islands! Discover the world of the islands.

Strand (III): People, places, and environments
- Why are they called islands?
- What is my island like?
- What makes me an islander?

Welcome to my island! Thematic framework

V. Island fantasy friends

Strand (I, IV): Culture; Individual development and identity
- What are the fantasy characters that I like the best?
- What are our favorite stories?
- What are the stories that children in other islands have?

III. Celebrations! The islander's way

Strand (I, IV): Culture; Individual development and identity
- What are the things we celebrate?
- How do we celebrate the carnivals?
- What do we wear during the celebrations?

IV. The mighty winds

Strand (III, IX): People, places, and environments
- Do we know what is the voice of the wind?
- How do the winds and rain affect our lives?
- Why do the mighty winds come to our islands?

* Indicates social studies curricular strand.

Suggestions for Culturally Appropriate Planning

Creating curricular experiences based on the ideas of diversity is a difficult task that will not be accomplished overnight. The progress for some teachers may be slow if they are required to follow a state or district curriculum. Whatever the reason for moving into multicultural change, to implement an optimum program, it is important to focus on what is culturally and developmentally valuable for all children. This belief is central and must guide the design, implementation, and modification of an effective and relevant program for the children you teach. As one begins to develop a multicultural education program, there are some points to remember that will facilitate the transition from current practices to teaching from a multicultural perspective. These points are equally helpful when following a prescribed curriculum.

Points to Consider When Planning for Culturally Appropriate Teaching

- Begin by knowing the expected learning outcomes for the age level you teach. Check and be mindful about the learning standards. Look at these as opportunities to validate the meaningfulness of planned experiences.

- Review your present content to determine what was successful and what felt comfortable.

- Go through your lesson plan book and identify the topics developed in class.

- Find in your curriculum *where* you could add or expand the children's views by including another perspective. Determine *what* other perspective you can add. Begin with only one additional perspective; then, as you gain confidence, add others.

- Adopt a flexible thematic teaching approach. It facilitates the integration of topics and views and helps guide children into examining things they like or in which they have shown an interest.

- When including a second perspective, think about the ways in which it relates to the children's own cultural experiences. Remind yourself to always center your selections first on what is connected to the lives of your students.

- Include as many concrete experiences as possible. Children need things to do, things to touch and manipulate, if they are to construct new knowledge. In dealing with views and perceptions about others, present common daily-life situations where they can see the meaningfulness and the impact of the behavior.

- Make sure the experiences offer accurate portrayals and not stereotypes. Avoid the exotic and include what defines the current lifestyles and realities. When presenting the folklore and traditional dresses or customs, clarify that they may describe what happens during a holiday or a festivity, not everyday life.

- If uncertain about a detail from a particular group, postpone the experience until you have clarified it. Remember that children see you as an authority.

■ Present perspectives in time frames that define the present first and then move into comparisons of the present with the past. Bring in ideas in terms of place (here/there) where there are elements children can relate to, such as common climate, topography, and so on. Several reference sources can help teachers select the curriculum content. Consider having copies of resource materials like Bredekamp and Copple's (2009) book on developmental practices, which includes the guide to DCAP teaching. Talk with colleagues and visit the library, where you may find relevant and helpful sources describing a variety of activities teachers can use as they launch their multicultural programs. Include multicultural literature as well as materials from professional journals such as *Childhood Education, Teaching Tolerance, Children Our Concern, Dimensions*, and *Young Children*. When using activities from manuals or books, be sure to adapt or modify them in accordance with the realities of your students.

As you get yourself ready to design and experience your curriculum, make sure that you keep good notes during your implementation. Prepare yourself to jot down the reactions and comments children make after and during the activities. These will be your sources for future adaptations and improvements.

| THE STAGE IS SET!

Barbara looked around her classroom and realized she was almost ready to begin. She also began thinking about finding ways to work with the parents and families of her students. As an experienced teacher, she knows that without parental involvement and collaboration, her program will be only partially successful. We will help Barbara achieve this goal in the next chapter.

WHAT WE HAVE LEARNED—CHAPTER SUMMARY

In this chapter, we discussed the importance of the classroom environment as well as instructional materials and learning experiences. The classroom is intended to foster the cognitive, social, and emotional development of all children. Such a place must be very special. It must be safe, inviting, and welcoming, and, at the same time, it must be a place of learning where everyone is valued and treated with equal care and respect. The early childhood classroom has to have many different learning environments, which, in a multicultural classroom, presents additional challenges. The various centers in the room must contain materials that are developmentally appropriate and accommodate children from different cultures and with various physical, emotional, and linguistic abilities. The early childhood educator is tasked with providing a wide range of rich learning materials from many different sources and ensuring that, through play and other more structured experiences, the children are afforded the best opportunities to further their development. This chapter also contains specific suggestions for activities using literature, music, and art.

THINGS TO DO . . .

1. Visit a local teacher supply store and examine its multicultural materials. Make a wish list of those you would like to have. Use the multicultural evaluation guidelines presented in this chapter to determine whether or not they are developmentally appropriate. If you find any that are not DCAP, describe what made them inappropriate.

2. Select two topics that are commonly taught in a multicultural classroom. Interview a media specialist or a librarian and find 10 resources for each topic that will help you develop two new perspectives about them.

3. Select three learning centers found in classrooms for children of the age level of your preference. Assess them and determine what needs to be added or replaced. Make a plan of the things you would incorporate to make them suitable for learning about diversity.

4. Using the wheel of diversity, visit your local library and see what books are available for each area.

5. Select an area of diversity and prepare your own persona doll story. Share it with your colleagues.

6. Visit a local ethnic store and see which of its items you could include in your learning centers. List them and describe the learning areas where you would include them.

7. Examine the sample curricular topics that appear here. Determine *what* you would incorporate and *where* in order to transform them into content for learning about diversity. Do the same with your own current curriculum.

Grade: Prekindergarten

Topics:

1. Who am I?
2. This is my family
3. My friends in the classroom
4. My favorite games
5. Special places in the community

RECOMMENDED INTERNET RESOURCES

Book awards:

- Coretta Scott King Book Award
  www.ala.org/ala/emiert/corettascottkingbookaward/corettascott.cfm
- Pura Belpre Medal
  www.ala.org/ala/alsc/awardsscholarships/literaryawds/belpremedal/belprmedal.cfm
- Sydney Taylor Book Award for Jewish children's literature
  www.jewishlibraries.org/ajlweb/awards/st_books.htm

Children's books on selected topics:

- African Americans
  http://falcon.jmu.edu/~ramseyil/mulafro.htm

- Appalachian culture
  www.carolhurst.com/subjects/appalachia.html

- Japanese Americans
  www.multiculturalchildrenslit.com/japaneseamericans.html

- Multicultural literature
  http://falcon.jmu.edu/~ramseyil/multipub.htm

- Women in history
  www.carolhurst.com/subjects/history/women.html

YOUR STANDARDS PORTFOLIO

NAEYC Standards 4a: Teaching and Learning: Connecting with Children and Families*

Positive relationships with children and their families are vital to successful classroom experiences. An emotionally positive, supportive, and sensitive atmosphere makes children and adults feel welcome and respected. In this kind of environment, learning is enhanced. Complete the following activities to demonstrate your understanding of this important standard.

- Think about the cultural and ethnic characteristics of your community. Meet with colleagues or classmates and discuss the characteristics of a classroom environment that would be culturally sensitive to both children and their families. Identify the elements that the group considers most important and describe each one in writing.

- Personal dispositions are behaviors that affect how we approach and respond to working with children and their families. Reflect on your personal dispositions and behaviors that could help you build respectful and sensitive relationships with children and their families. Write a list of those that you feel are your strongest assets. Ponder your challenges as well.

REFERENCES

Allport, G. (1986). *The nature of prejudice.* New York: Anti Defamation League of Benai.

Banks, J. (2007). *Multicultural education* (7th ed.). Newton, MA: Allyn & Bacon.

Berns, R. M. (1994). *Topical child development.* Clifton Park, NY: Thomson Delmar Learning.

* NAEYC Standard 4a correlates with INTASC Standard 5: Learning Environment.

Bredekamp, S., & Copple, C. (2009). *Developmentally appropriate practice in early childhood programs* (3rd ed.). Washington, DC: National Association for the Education of Young Children.

Bredekamp, S., & Rosegrant, T. (Eds.). (1992). *Reaching potentials: Appropriate curriculum and assessment for young children, Vol. 1.* Washington, DC: National Association for the Education of Young Children.

Byrnes, D., & Kiger, C. (Eds.). (1992). *Common bonds.* Wheaton, MD: Association for Childhood Education International.

Cropley, A. (1992). *More ways than one: Fostering creativity.* Norwood, NJ: Ablex.

Cullinan, B., & Galda, L. (2005). *Literature and the child* (6th ed.). New York: Wadsworth.

Curtis, D., & Carter, M. (2003). *Designs for living and learning environments.* Saint Paul, MN: Red Leaf Press.

Davidman, L., & Davidman, P. T. (2000). *Teaching with a multicultural perspective* (3rd ed.). Needham Heights, MA: Allyn & Bacon.

Derman-Sparks, L., & the A.B.C. Task Force (1989). *Anti-bias curriculum: Tools for empowering young children.* Washington, DC: National Association for the Education of Young Children.

Forman, G., & Kuschner, D. (1987). *The child's construction of knowledge: Piaget for teaching children.* Washington, DC: National Association for the Education of Young Children.

Goldberg, M. (2006). *Integrating the arts: An approach to teaching and learning in multicultural and multilingual settings* (3rd ed.). Boston: Allyn & Bacon.

Gómez, A. (1999). *Crafts of many cultures: Thirty authentic craft projects from around the world.* New York: Scholastic.

Haines, J. B., & Gerber, L. L. (1995). *Leading young children to music.* New York: Merrill/Macmillan.

Hernandez, H. (2000). *Multicultural education: A teacher's guide to content and process* (2nd ed.). New York: Prentice Hall.

Jalongo, M. R., & Isenberg, J. (2008). *Exploring your role: An introduction to early childhood education* (3rd ed.). Upper Saddle River, NJ: Merrill.

Kasten, W., Kristo, J. V., & McClure, A. (2005). *Living literature: Using children's literature to support reading and language arts.* Upper Saddle River, NJ: Pearson Merrill Prentice Hall.

Katz, L., & Chard, S. (2000). *Engaging children's minds: The project approach* (2nd ed.). Norwood, NJ: Ablex.

Kendall, F. (1996). *Diversity in the classroom: A multicultural approach to the education of young children* (2nd ed.). New York: Teachers College Press.

King, E. W., Chipman, M., & Cruz-Janzen, M. (1994). *Educating young children in a diverse society.* Needham Heights, MA: Allyn & Bacon.

Morrison, G. S. (2006). *Early childhood education today* (10th ed.). Englewood Cliffs, NJ: Merrill.

National Association for the Education of Young Children. (2005). NAEYC *Early childhood program standards and accreditation criteria: The mark of quality in early childhood education.* Washington, DC: NAEYC.

Neugebauer, B. (1992). *Alike and different: Exploring our humanity with children* (Rev. ed.). Washington, DC: NAEYC.

Nieto, S., & Bode, P. (2008). *Affirming diversity: The sociopolitical context of multicultural education* (5th ed.). New York: Pearson/Allyn & Bacon.

Norton, D. (1995). *Through the eyes of a child: An introduction to children's literature* (5th ed.). Englewood Cliffs, NJ: Merrill.

Norton, D. (2003). *Through the eyes of a child: An introduction to children's literature* (6th ed.). Englewood Cliffs, NJ: Merrill.

Ornstein, A. C., & Hunkins, F. (2003). *Curriculum foundations, principles, and theory* (4th ed.). Boston: Allyn & Bacon.

Peck, N., & Shores, E. (1994). *Checklist for diversity in early childhood education and care.* Little Rock, AR: Southern Early Childhood Association.

Robles de Meléndez, W. (1999). *Vocesillas de los niños de las islas: Un modelo multicultural para el nivel Pre-K–2 (Voices of the children of the islands: A multicultural model for the pre-K–2 level).* Unpublished document.

Robles de Meléndez, W. (2001). Creating the multicultural environment. Paper presented at the annual conference of the Early Childhood Association of Florida. Orlando, FL.

Robles de Meléndez, W. (December 2004). Using multicultural literature to learn about families. Paper presented at Blue Ribbon Schools Conference. Biloxi, MS.

Robles de Meléndez, W., & Henry, A. (October 1994). Using constructivism to develop literacy skills. Paper presented at Florida Reading Association Annual Conference. Orlando, FL.

Rosales, L. (1992). *Listen to the heart.* Unpublished manuscript.

CHAPTER 10

A World of Resources: Engaging Families, Friends, and the Community

> All men [individuals] know their children mean more than life.
>
> *Euripides (480–406 B.C.)*

CHAPTER OBJECTIVES

In this chapter, we will

- identify activities that involve the family and the community with the classroom.
- describe the roles of families and the community in a multicultural program.
- explain the importance of working with families and the community of early childhood students.
- identify ways in which teachers can develop family support for their multicultural programs.

KEY CONCEPTS

- involvement
- intervention
- collaborative efforts
- community resources

FROM BARBARA'S JOURNAL

I think my hard work is paying off! I feel so good about what is happening in the classroom in terms of the children's progress and their joy of learning. All the pieces of the puzzle are falling into place, and I feel so much more confident. With good planning, I have been able to enrich the curriculum with my own developmentally appropriate, creative, and relevant activities. It is a lot of work, but it's definitely worth it. One thing I would like to improve is the level of parental involvement. Many of my children's parents are from cultures other than the mainstream. Some of them have been to the classroom to see me teach and to offer help. Others seem to be shy and have kept their distance. I've also learned that many parents from different cultures perceive the teacher in different ways. In many cultures, teachers are treated with great respect and deference. I am not looking for that, but I would like to make the parents make feel welcome and aware of what we are doing in the classroom. Figuring out how we can collaborate to best help the children is important to me and to them.

| WORKING TOGETHER: THE ESSENCE OF A CHILD'S SUCCESS

The old adage "No man is an island" reminds us that we all need and depend on each other. The same is true of schools and families. Classroom practices reveal that when parents work together with their children's teachers, there are positive emotional and intellectual gains. This partnership becomes even more important in contemporary society, where family patterns and routines have drastically changed, forcing parents and children to depend more and more on the schools (Figure 10-1). Furthermore, the need for collaboration among teachers and families of young children is most critical because the parents and the family are the child's first and most influential teachers.

| CHANGING COMMUNITIES, CHANGING REALITIES

Not only have families changed as you saw in Chapter 3, but neighborhoods have also become different. Today, across the United States, neighborhoods are experiencing high population mobility, which lessens the possibilities of establishing any stable, long-lasting

FIGURE 10–1 **Family Configurations and Living Arrangements of Children**

Family Structure	Percentage of Children
Two-parent families	69%
Living with mothers only	22%
Living with fathers only	4%
Living with neither parent	4%

Source: Federal Interagency Forum on Child and Family Statistics, 2005.

relationships. Serious economic pressures have caused the deterioration of many neighborhoods, forcing their character to change (Children's Defense Fund, 2005). These events have eroded the social relationships and changed the lifestyles and practices in our neighborhoods. More impersonal and less caring, they are no longer the safe havens our children and families need. As one of the results of this transformation, schools have taken over more of the social responsibilities that parents and neighbors used to have. Thus, more and more families and children now depend on schools as one of their main sources of social support.

The transformation of the U.S. family and the neighborhood have resulted in the need for closer collaboration in the educational arena among the key players—schools, families, relatives, and the community. The purpose of this alliance is perceived as a way of solving problems of students in schools that also impact the society at large. Offering children a better and more responsive education has become a priority in the United States, because it has been recognized that without an effective education system the future of our society will remain in jeopardy. Educators recognize that one of the keys to the successful

Including parents and family members in early childhood multicultural programs ensures success. We believe that. Do you agree?

schooling experience can be found in the close collaboration between teachers and families. This is also a premise for developmentally and culturally appropriate practices (DCAP) that recommend creating classrooms where the child's needs are being met, the child's individuality as a cultural entity is respected and strengthened, and all efforts are made to enable the child to become a successful person. This kind of a DCAP environment cannot be established without the joint efforts of teachers and families. Early childhood educators need to develop a close **involvement** with families and parents to jointly build a common foundation that will brighten the children's futures. Failure to bring parents closer to their children's school causes even the best of interventions to fail (Swick, 2004). **Intervention** consists of any special efforts done to assist the child who may not be performing to his or her potential.

Evidence abounds throughout the literature regarding the impact of parent and family involvement in their children's successful performance (Barrera & Warner, 2006; Berger, 2007; Jung-Sook & Bowen, 2006). Creating the atmosphere for learning both in the classroom and at home is a necessary component of effective education. Goals 2000, which define the national standards of education, speak to such learning environments for our children. Educator Ernest Boyer (1994) eloquently explained this idea in his interpretation of what "ready to learn," addressed in Goal 1, actually means.

> HOME IS THE FIRST CLASSROOM [capitalized in the original]. Parents are the first school and most essential teacher. . . . [We] recommend that preschool PTAs be organized to give support to parents and build a bridge between home and school.

Our classrooms can become the best kind of bridge between home and school. To build it, educators need to reaffirm their commitment to children and families. The social web that teachers and families can form together will nurture the child and guide development. Not only is this necessary, but it is also the most ethical way to deliver quality and appropriate experiences for all children.

DEFINING FAMILY INVOLVEMENT

To develop relationships of mutual trust and create partnerships with the families we serve.

NAEYC Code of Ethical Conduct, Ideal 2.2 (2005)

Research in early childhood education has shown that family and parental involvement are central to successful schooling experiences (Berger, 2004; Moles, 1996). Findings from studies reveal that children exhibit higher achievement when parents are directly involved in the children's school activities (Henderson & Mapp, 2002; Pelletier & Brent, 2002). Although there is no best way to successfully engage parents and families, concerted efforts by early educators will usually make involvement possible. Examples of successful involvement abound in Head Start, which is the model program dedicated to serving families and children. The pioneer work of Ira Gordon with Head Start programs set the tone for many of today's parent and family engagement strategies. Gordon's parental model was focused on interventions directed to address the characteristics and needs of individual families. His seminal work evidenced the impact of parent participation in classroom activities on children's performance (Berger, 2004).

A Definition of Family Involvement

Family involvement consists of efforts aimed at providing parents and families with opportunities to participate in the children's classroom and school activities. A review of the literature shows that family involvement is characterized by the following beliefs and areas of service (Berger, 2004; Children's Defense Fund, 2005; Garbarino & Garbarino, 1992; Swick, 2004):

- A holistic vision of those who are the sources of influence in the lives of children
- Consideration of the entire family as the target client for services
- An inclusivist approach that considers *all* individuals (including the extended family and those without blood relationship) in the family unit as important when deciding on an intervention strategy (see Figure 10-2)

FIGURE 10–2 **Families Have a Myriad of Structures**

Cross-Cultural Configurations of Families	
Nuclear:	The unit where parents and children live together. It is the more commonly found unit in countries where life expectancy is high. Includes such configurations as
	—Biological
	—Social (cohabitation)
	—One-parent
	—Adoptive
	—In vitro
Extended:	A combination of several family members who together form an extended family. It does not imply size. It can be, for example, a grandparent and grandchild living together. Includes configurations such as
	—Three generations
	—Kinship
	—Tribal
Reorganized:	A unit that happens through marriage, remarriage, or cohabitation of persons who had children by former partners. Some of the causes are
	—Remarriage (step-parenthood)
	—Community living due to migration, exile, economics
	—Same gender

Source: United Nations, 1994.

■ A systems perspective to deal with the reality of the child and to determine all the elements the school looks into that may affect an influence

■ A realization that any attempts to plan and establish services without the whole family would prove unsuccessful

There are many benefits for children when parents and families participate in classroom activities. Such involvement influences student performance and individual development. Among the outcomes noted are successful schooling and higher retention levels (Broussard, 2003).

Planning activities to engage parents and family members begins with a good knowledge of the families. Learning about the families, who they are, and what problems and issues they face provides ways to initiate appropriate actions. This is especially important when working with families from diverse cultural backgrounds.

Overcoming Barriers to Successful Family Involvement

Working with families with diverse characteristics calls for early childhood educators to examine their views about what it means to "be involved." One's ideas about participation and involvement may reflect points of view that differ from those held by fami-

---

F⦶CUS
on Classroom Practices
|
Engaging Fathers in Early Education:
The Fatherhood Initiative

Fathers, like all family members, play a leading role in children's development. Research reveals that their participation can positively influence children's school achievement, self-esteem, and social competence. However, statistical data show a high incidence of children living without a father figure. It is estimated that 60 percent of children born during the 1990s will spend an important part of their lives growing up away from or without their fathers (U.S. Government, 2001). According to the Department of Justice, 7.3 million children under the age of 18 have an incarcerated father. In response to this situation, a national initiative was created with the goal of increasing awareness among fathers

about their role and their participation in their children's activities during the early years. Sponsored by the U.S. Department of Health and Human Services, the initiative Promoting Responsible Fatherhood is aimed at fostering responsibility and engagement of fathers in raising their children and becoming their role models. A variety of activities are delivered through community agencies and Head Start programs.

For more details about activities in your community, contact your local community action agency or Head Start program. Information can also be obtained on the Internet at http://fatherhood.hhs.gov/index .shtml.

lies. Many times family involvement efforts are challenged because of these differences. Each cultural group holds its own concepts about the role of education in the lives of their children. Some believe that education is the sole responsibility of the school and therefore rely on the teacher's knowledge and experience. Many hesitate to differ or argue with the teacher because they see him or her as an authority figure. Family members' negative personal experiences with the education system may also account for a lack of involvement. Lack of knowledge about how the education system works is yet another factor that prevents families from being involved in the education of their children. Realities of family life, such as economic pressures, illnesses, and presence of disabilities, also influence how family members may balance time and how they set priorities. Social class differences may account for contrasting ideas about participation and classroom involvement.

Relationships between the young child and family members are essential for positive development.

Beyond the factors that may hinder school involvement, it is important to consider that at home, families may provide valuable support to children by passing on stories and traditions, sharing ideas about the importance of education, helping with learning tasks, and being aware of their children's performance. All these play a leading role in the children's overall success (Epstein, Sanders, Simon, & Salina, 2002).

Collaboration, Also a Goal of Education for Diversity

Every school and home will engage in partnerships that will increase parental involvement and participation in promoting the social, emotional, and academic growth of children.
Goals 2000, Educate America Act of 1994

Education for diversity cannot exist without including and considering families as a fundamental element in the lives of children. The process of teaching and learning is enriched by bringing parents and entire families into the classroom as our partners. One of the main objectives of multicultural education is to have parents sharing with teachers the miracle of the children's learning. The proper development of any program about diversity must include the issues and needs of the families. Combining the ideas

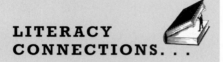

LITERACY CONNECTIONS. . .   Books About Families and Children

Stories are a special way to learn about families in your classroom and community. Sharing these with children or during a parent and family meeting can lead to a very interesting discussion that facilitates everyone learning more about families. These are some of our favorite titles:

- DiSalvo-Ryan, R. (2000). *Grandpa's corner store*. New York: HarperCollins.

- Frasier, D. (2005). *On the day you were born*. New York: Harcourt.

- Greenfield, E. (1991). *My father and I*. New York: Writers and Readers Publishing.

- Kaksa, K. (1996). *A mother for Choco*. New York: Putnam.

- Krisnawahmi, U. (2006). *Bringing Asha home*. New York: Lee & Low Books.

- McCaughrean, G. (2002). *My grandfather's clock*. New York: Clarion Books.

- Newman, L. (2000). *Heather has two mommies*. New York: Alyson Wonderland.

- Polacco, P. (2000). *The trees of the dancing goats*. New York: Aladdin.

- Ryland, C. (2005). *The relatives came*. New York: Aladdin.

- Simmons, J. (2004). *Daisy and the egg*. New York: Little, Brown.

- Smith, W. (2005). *Just the two of us*. New York: Scholastic.

- Valentine, J. (2004). *One dad, two dads, brown dad, blue dads*. New York: Alyson.

and concerns of parents and families improves the quality of the service provided to the child and increases the responsiveness of the program to the child's needs. Quality and responsiveness are vital elements that must be considered by teachers as they transform their teaching.

What Does Collaboration Mean?

Collaboration, identified by some as a current buzzword in the field of early childhood education, refers to the quest to remedy the inequalities and sparse existence of social programs and services (Couchenour & Chrisman, 2004). In schools, collaboration calls for the concerted efforts of educators, families, and communities. A kind of joint work ambition, collaboration is based on "a vision of better society" (National Commission

F⊙CUS
on Classroom Practices

Families in the Classroom

Learning about the family configurations in our classroom is an important step. The first days of school present a particularly opportune occasion to do so. For instance, as family members come to bring the children, you might want to try a more personal registration form for those very first days. Instead of just having a list where they will sign in the child, have a piece of butcher paper (size 14" × 17") or poster board and a basket with markers in different colors. As they come in, ask family members to draw their families. Having your own family drawing conspicu-

ously displayed will help to encourage family members to share theirs. Make sure each work is labeled with the child's name. The result will be a graphic depiction of the family configurations. Take time to carefully examine each one and make notes about the patterns in your classroom. Of course, display them in your classroom for children and family members to enjoy. They will draw many good discussions and will be a good starter for a thematic study you could title "This Is How We Are."

on Children, 1991). A better society, where equity exists for all individuals regardless of their characteristics, is the principle on which education for diversity is founded.

We envision a nation of strong and stable families, where every child has an equal opportunity to reach his or her full potential and where public policies and personal values give highest priority to healthy, whole children (National Commission on Children, 1991). Educators Sharon Kagan and Ann Rivera (1991) define collaboration as "those efforts that unite and empower individuals and organizations to accomplish collectively what they could not accomplish individually." Applying their definition to what multicultural educators advocate implies the need for establishing **collaborative efforts** (Figure 10-3). Multicultural programs cannot exist without the support and constant sharing with the families of the children served. Attempts to do so would be fruitless. Pretending to separate our classrooms from the families can only produce fragmented, if not isolated, views of the children's realities. When our programs are linked to the children's and families' realities, the programs acquire a sense of valid connectedness. Collaboration begins when we learn more about the wealth of ideas and potential for learning that families bring to classrooms.

Consider the Community as Your Partner, Too

Successful collaboration also includes the community. Now more than ever, public agencies and the private sector are willing to offer their support to schools. Consider them as partners and as a part of your team for multicultural education. Every community

FIGURE 10-3 **Sample Questionnaire for Family Collaboration**

Can you help us in our classroom?

Our class wants to count you among its collaborators. Please tell us in what ways you would like to participate. Just enter check marks to indicate your preferences. Any kind of collaboration is always welcome!

_____ 1. I can serve as a room parent. I am available during (please indicate weekdays and times) _____.

_____ 2. I can help prepare materials for the class.

_____ 3. I can help organize activities.

_____ 4. I can help collect materials for the students.

_____ 5. I can accompany a group during field trips.

_____ 6. I can share my knowledge about (please indicate)_____.

_____ 7. I can serve as an interpreter of _____ (indicate language).

_____ 8. I can be a member of the PTA.

_____ 9. I cannot volunteer in the classroom; however, this is what I can do at home: (for example, cutting pictures, making crafts, evaluating materials, calling other parents, typing, or recording songs and music) _____.

Collaboration among significant adults shapes the futures of young children.

F◯CUS
on Classroom Practices | Welcoming Families

Nothing makes a better start for positive relationships with families than making them feel important and welcome in the classrooms. Professionals know that showing our sincere respect for and interest in them and their children will open many doors. Here are two simple tips to make families feel welcome in your classroom, especially during the beginning of the year.

• During the first days of school, have a basket of simple treats right next to the sign-in sheet. A simple sign reading "Have a good and sweet day!/¡Que tenga un buen y muy dulce día!" could be placed next to the treats. Choose healthy treat such as fruits (grapes, apples, and bananas are especially

good), granola bars, and low-sugar hard candies. Even those family members who rush in and out will enjoy taking a sweet bite as they leave their children.

• Send welcome notes. A simple message presented in a creative and colorful manner is another way of reaffirming the desire to work together with the children's families. If some families speak languages other than English, write the message in both languages. Your school or the school district probably has resource people to help you with the translation. To make families remember your note, try rolling or attaching a sweet or lollipop to the note. They will certainly remember the detail!

In Action . . . **Community Support**

Have you considered the community agencies that could support your program? Make a list of possible groups to contact. Use the local phone directory and look for the agencies you think may be willing to help. Begin a list titled "Community Resources for My Program."

---

is the hub for a variety of agencies, civic organizations, services, and programs that can greatly contribute to what we do for families in our classroom. Whether through services, enhancement of existing resources, or community members sharing their expertise, schools can find countless resources right in their communities (Olivos, 2006). Take the time to learn about existing programs and organizations and you may find that you have a treasure trove waiting for you. You may find that resources like the two community initiatives described in Snapshot 10-1 are available in your community.

SNAPSHOT 10-1   **Supporting Families and Children Through Literacy: The *Lee y Serás* and *Read and Rise* Initiatives**

There are many examples of national initiatives sponsored by communities and corporations. Among those aimed at promoting literacy success we find *Lee y Serás* (Read and You Will Be) and *Read and Rise*. These two initiatives were developed under the sponsorship of Scholastic and in collaboration with other organizations with the goal of providing support while responding to the cultural needs of both Latino and African American families.

Lee y Serás was designed to support and enhance early literacy development for Latino families, children, and child-care teachers. The initiative began as a response of the corporate community to close the gap in reading skills development for Latino children by promoting early literacy skills. Scholastic, in collaboration with Verizon and the National Council of La Raza (NCLR), developed curricula for families and child-care providers and formed an institute for community leaders. Available in English and Spanish, each curriculum is embedded in Latino values and traditions. Free literacy workshops for families and child-care teachers are offered by NCLR affiliates, local nonprofit agencies, and school districts in communities across various states including Texas, Florida, California, Illinois, New York, Connecticut, and Georgia. Through its website, *Lee y Serás* also provides suggestions for families, child-care teachers, and communities.

Read and Rise was developed in collaboration with the National Urban League with the goal of helping African American children and their families improve literacy skills. The initiative provides a guide for parents, a monthly *Read and Rise* magazine, and reading tips available on the Internet. To this date, over a million *Read and Rise* guides have been distributed, offering families ideas and suggestions for promoting their children's reading development.

AT HOME: WHERE THE SELF BEGINS, WHERE WE BECOME

To properly appraise the important role of families and the need for their involvement, it is important to remember how critical they are in the life of the developing child. Also central is the need to understand that families bring valuable knowledge and skills, or "funds of knowledge," that can become the best resource for multicultural education. We all want to know more about the children and their families. But how much do we actually know? Comments from Barbara's journal about her class may remind us about similar questions we have posed: *Twenty-one 5-year-olds! All of them have names that mean something special to their families. I know I'll learn them quickly, but I wonder*

*if I'll be able to discover the real child be-
hind each long or short name. I wonder if
I'll be able to "read" the stories they bring to
the classroom. Their files tell me little about
them, and none of it means much until I
meet and work with their families.*

*Family routines contribute to the passage of
cultural values and heritage.*

Do you agree with Barbara? We do.
As Barbara stated, it is impossible to know
what each child brings into the classroom
from a list of unfamiliar names or a stack of
official files. It is equally hard to anticipate
the children's needs. The secret to who
they really are rests with their families.
Families are the children's primary source
of care and contact, holding firsthand and
intimate knowledge about their young.
Good multicultural early childhood educators know that and strive to work closely
with the children's families. As they join
hands with parents, they come to know
their students. They also discover new directions for their curriculum.

We are all products of our families and our home environments. In Chapter 3,
you saw how your family and relatives influence your ways and behaviors. You examined their roles in transmitting ideas and beliefs. From our families, we even learned
the gestures and nuances that characterize each of us.

When you try to "read" a child, one comes to understand that the key to decipher-
ing some of the behaviors and attitudes lies in the family. The more we know about the
values, culture, and ways of the families, the better equipped we are to provide a setting
that is responsive to the children's needs.

A Positive Approach for Our Children's Families

The early childhood professional is characterized by an open and tolerant attitude. This
facilitates success in the endeavors to build strong relationships with families. Professional early childhood educators promote positive communication and interactions
with families. As a person who believes in equity and in the rights of all families and
children, your attitudes and behaviors affirm your aspiration and desire to engage in
practices geared to meeting the needs of culturally and linguistically diverse children.
This positive attitude should also extend to the families of children in the classrooms.
We ask you to set aside your own notions of what families should be like or how they

should act. By putting aside personal biases, you will see your children's realities clearly, without blurring them with your value judgments.

Working with families of different ethnic and cultural backgrounds brings the early childhood teacher in contact with value systems not necessarily consistent with those held by the educators. We base many of our opinions on our particular value systems. Our perceptions and reactions are many times the hardest roadblock to overcome.

Because we all rely on our own values when meeting and communicating with others, it is important to realize that a difference in ideas will affect our communication and interaction with the family members of the children we teach. Sadly, a lack of awareness about the interference of our own ideas often hinders even the best-intended efforts.

To say that the solution lies in teachers becoming more aware of their attitudes is overly simplistic (Turnbull & Turnbull, 2004). Although evidence exists that attitudes are modified over time, central to successful multicultural education is the need to demonstrate our commitment to children by exhibiting a positive, nonjudgmental attitude about their families. This reaffirmation needs to be shared in visible ways such as written communications, statements posted in the classroom, daily activities, and, more importantly, through our interactions with parents and family members. Let's remember that our belief in those we work with establishes the emotional tone of any involvement efforts and that successful programs are built by people who believe in the individuals with whom they work.

Building Trust with Families

Developing and achieving a sense of trust among families and early educators is essential to a successful program. It is important to remember that families will trust us when they see that they are respected as individuals. They will also believe in teachers when they find that we are safeguarding the information about them and the children. Because early childhood teachers gather a lot of details about the families they work with, it is necessary to emphasize the need for confidentiality. This is essential to establishing a relationship of mutual trust between the family and the teacher.

There are two relevant points that underscore confidentiality. First, families are not required to give information about what happens inside the family unit; it is their choice to do so. Second, any information a family member gives to the teacher furthers the understanding of the child and the child's reality. Even the simplest detail offered by families must be used professionally and treated confidentially. Professionals need to remember that protecting data about children is among what defines ethical practices in early childhood education. Section II of the NAEYC Code of Ethical Conduct and Statement of Commitment (2005) specifically addresses responsibilities and practices with families.

FOCUS
on Classroom Practices | Surnames, Like Looks, Can Be Deceiving

Have you ever attempted to use your students' surnames to identify their families' cultural backgrounds? Or, have you tried to use them to learn who is a non-English speaker? We hope your answer is "NO" to both questions, because names can often prove deceiving. Because today we have a more open level of acceptance for social interaction, which has resulted in more frequent interethnic marriages, chances are a family surname might not necessarily reflect that a person belongs to a specific cultural or language group. Also, remember that many families might not be recent immigrants but possibly second and third generations or groups who

have historically inhabited a given region. In both cases, the child and his or her family might be proficient English language speakers. Unfortunately, there are occasions in which children have been assigned to special groups because they are presumed to be non-English proficient. So the moral here is to never assume children with names such as Perez, Takeshita, and Singh cannot speak English. (Also, do not assume that they speak the languages of the ethnicities their names suggest!) Always wait until you meet the child and the family. Decisions should always be made based on concrete evidence and never on assumptions or stereotypes.

In Action . . .   **Family Influences**

- Have you ever thought about where you learned some of the gestures and phrases you use or where you acquired the tastes you have? Try to identify one of them, and explain its origin.
- Observe the children at the housekeeping area. What adult-like behaviors do they show while role-playing at the center?

Developing a Philosophy About Families

What will be your philosophy about families? What affirmations will you share with them? Take time to outline your beliefs about the concept of family. Have them posted in a place where parents and families can see them. We will share what Barbara wrote on a chart that she posted on the classroom door and from which she made flyers to send home.

> All families are important in this classroom.
> Families are the child's richest source of nurturance.
> Families want the best for their children.
> All families and family members can help in this classroom.
> Here, we learn about children through their families.

F◯CUS
on Classroom Practices

Learning About the Families in Our Classroom

The more you know about the families in your classroom, the better prepared you will be to effectively work together. Because culture influences how we raise our families, learning about child-rearing patterns opens doors to understanding of the family's and the child's behaviors. A favorite unit in most early childhood classrooms is learning about ourselves when we were babies. An important theme because it helps children to explore the concepts of time, change, and cause and effect, it is also a source of cultural data for teachers. Three aspects in particular yield interesting details about rearing practices: food, nursery rhymes and songs, and infant toys.

1. Food: A thematic unit titled "What We Used to Eat as Babies" could offer good opportunities to explore the variety and kinds of foods considered appropriate for infants. Ask families to share what they served children during the first year of life. You may want to ask families to share what children's favorite foods were and which ones they disliked most.

2. Nursery Rhymes/Songs: A unit titled "Our Favorite Baby Songs and Rhymes" could lead to many creative experiences. For example, the opportunity to compare how babies react to music and rhymes and how the class reacts now (concept of change) presents an excellent way to explore traditions and movement.

3. Toys: One of cultures' common denominators is toys. Exploring what the class enjoyed during infancy gives children an opportunity to discover how their preferences have changed. A unit titled "Toys We Used to Like" can also provide chances to explore materials used to build toys and could introduce children to view toys in a nonsexist way.

If you work in a community of high cultural diversity, do not be surprised to find that families have more in common than you expected. Remember that not all families are recent immigrants and that social status and the level of ethnic identity also influence their behaviors.

In Action . . .   Examining Our Position About Families

- What can you say about the families in your community and in your classroom?
- What ideas are revealed through Barbara's statements about the families in her classroom?
- If you were to create statements affirming your views about families, how would they read?
- What is your viewpoint about parents and families in the classroom?

Teachers and parents have the best interests of the child at heart.

Wadsworth/Cengage Learning

Learning More About the Families in Our Classrooms

Knowledge about the families and planning for their participation have increased in importance as a result of continuous changes experienced by families in our communities. Experts in parent and family involvement agree that in order to plan effective involvement activities, it is necessary to learn about families (Berger, 2007; Coleman, 1991).

This is an ongoing process. One can never get to know everything about a family from the answers on a questionnaire or from a parent conference. Such strategies only emphasize the need to find additional ways to learn more, formally or informally. Formal sources include the following:

1. Information included in the child's file
2. Formal interviews
3. Parent questionnaires, surveys, or checklists administered by the school or district
4. Interviews with other professionals, such as a guidance counselor or social worker
5. Reports of formal home visits

Data obtained through formal sources provide necessary documentation to support program decisions and services for the child and the family. Analysis of the data provides an initial insight into the children's families, particularly in terms of the home culture. Learning about the home cultures of the children will help readdress curricular planning and guide parent involvement activities. Additional data can be collected through informal means. Actually, many relevant details can only be gathered through more informal methods. Some of those methods teachers can use are the following:

1. Meeting and talking to parents or family members as they bring their children to school

2. Holding unscheduled parent–teacher interviews

3. Establishing periodic telephone contacts

4. Doing informal interviews and surveys

5. Inviting parents and family members to share morning "coffee/tea"

6. Using a "pony-bag" (a plastic bag in which teachers periodically send a note asking about a particular detail about the family, such as things they like to eat, things they do together, and so on)

7. Using a classroom "family sharing tree" (a collection of interesting details that identify each family and that are shared on a weekly or monthly basis in the classroom)

Using Surveys and Checklists

There are many instruments teachers can develop to use in acquiring more information about the families of their students. They can create their own surveys and checklists structured to the unique needs of their families. When deciding to use a teacher-made tool, there are some rules to remember:

1. *Purpose:* To create a good instrument, first identify its purpose and goal. Knowing what information you want and need to obtain defines the questions to be asked.

2. *Missing data:* A way to begin learning about the families is to review the children's files and see what relevant data are missing. What is not included, and what you consider important, should be incorporated into your instruments. Among the information to be considered could be details such as nicknames used at home, the meaning of the child's name, the correct pronunciation of the child's name, holidays that are more important for the family, and so on.

3. *Data relevant for curricular planning:* Information that is relevant to the curriculum also needs to be included in the instrument. For example, data that will help teachers know more about the cultural ways of the family can clarify what should be emphasized in the classroom. Remember, the more you know about families, the better prepared you will be to organize your teaching.

4. *Family needs and interests:* When teachers are aware of the family's needs, issues, and interests, actions can be taken to provide the support or assistance at the classroom level. The information concerning the diversity variables that characterize particular families is most important for establishing an effective classroom curriculum. This knowledge also establishes a foundation for a sound collaboration between the school and the family.

A teacher-made instrument is not only to be used for "writing in" answers. It can also be used as a guide during a parent interview. Instruments should not be too lengthy, and they need to be clear and simple in language and format. Some samples are included in Figure 10-4.

FIGURE 10-4 **Survey of a Family**

SURVEY OF THE FAMILY—PART A
Sample Letter to the Family

Dear Parent/Family Members:

In this classroom, we believe families are an important part of the child's life. We also believe that to create a good program for your child, we need to know more about your family. For that reason, we are asking you to share some information about your family by answering this questionnaire. Answering this questionnaire is optional; however, it will help us to better know your family and your child. As we learn more about the students and families, we will discover more ways to make your child succeed in school. Please know that all information will be kept confidential and that it will be used only for planning purposes. Thanks!

Sincerely,

(classroom teacher)

Sample Questionnaire

Dear family of _____ (child's name):

Please read each question carefully and write your answer in the space provided.

1. Who are the members of your family?

2. Does your family use any language other than English? Is the child encouraged to use that language?

3. Who is the family member we should contact in case of an emergency? Please give name and relationship to the child.

4. What is your family's favorite TV program?

5. Does your family have pets?

6. What are some of the activities that your family enjoys doing together?

7. What are the holidays that your family celebrates?

8. Are there any religious or cultural traditions your family considers very important?

9. What expectations does your family have of this school/classroom?

10. We would like to know in what ways we can collaborate with you. From the list below, please check all those areas that represent areas of **interest** or **concern** for your family. If the point is of interest, write an *I*; if a concern, write a *C*.

    _____ Understanding my child

    _____ Learning more about my child's behavior

    _____ Planning activities at home for my child

    _____ Locating good materials for my child.

    _____ Learning more about my child's development

    _____ Dealing with nutrition (appropriate feeding)

(continued)

FIGURE 10-4 **(continued)**

_____ Obtaining after-school care services

_____ Dealing with health problems in the family

_____ Locating health services for the child

_____ Learning more about what the community offers for my child (for example: parks, library, and others)

_____ Obtaining information about housing, food stamps, county services

_____ Other: (please comment)

SURVEY OF THE FAMILY—PART B

Name of the child: _____ Age: _____ Gender: F _____ M _____

Directions to the teacher:

(This part is to be administered in the classroom. After a motivational experience, have the child draw his or her family. Provide crayons and/or markers.) After the child has finished, ask the following questions:

1. Can you tell me what this drawing shows?
2. Can you tell me who are the people in your drawing?
3. Are you in this drawing? Show me where.
4. What is the family doing in this drawing?
5. Can you tell me what you like most about your family?

Working with children from a variety of cultural and ethnic backgrounds underlines the need to know more about their families' cultures. This is especially important when teachers may be unfamiliar with some of the cultural groups. A good way to initiate positive interaction with family members is by showing interest in learning more about their cultures.

One helpful way to learn more about families' cultures is the questionnaire developed by Saville-Troike (1978). Teachers can use it as a guide when trying to learn more about the culture of the family. The questions provide a way to profile the cultural life of an individual and an opportunity to depict the family in a nonstereotypical way. Questions are categorized by different areas that are commonly impacted by culture. Very comprehensive in nature, the questions cover points including the life cycle, roles, religion, communication, and food and can be used selectively to obtain information from the family whenever teachers feel that a particular aspect requires more clarification (Figure 10-5).

FIGURE 10-5 **Culture Questionnaire**

Selected sections from Saville-Troike's questions about culture

■ Family
    a. Who is in the 'family'? Who among these (or others) lives in one house?
    b. What is the line of authority in the family?
    c. What are the rights and responsibilities of each family member? Do children have an obligation to work to help the family?
    d. What are the functions and obligations of the family to the larger social unit? To the school? To its individual members?
    e. How close together does the family appear to be? Is there a degree of solidarity among its members?

■ The life cycle
    a. How do they refer to or define the different stages, periods, or transitions in life? (i.e., before X was born, after the divorce, etc.)
    b. What are the attitudes, behaviors, and expectations held by the family members during different life stages?
    c. What behaviors are deemed acceptable or inappropriate for children? Are they in conflict with the expectations of the school?
    d. How is language related to the life cycle?

■ Roles
    a. What roles exist in the family or group? Who holds those roles? Do they consider education an important requirement to hold any of those roles?
    b. What knowledge or perception does the child or the family have about the roles found in their cultural group?
    c. Does the group consider the use of language as an important characteristic or social marking of roles?
    d. Do expectations about children's attainment differ according to class status? Are expectations realistic?

■ Interpersonal relationships
    a. How do people greet each other? What are the forms of address used between people? Are there differences because of status held (age, position)?
    b. What are the expectations held for interaction between girls and boys? Do these differ from what is expected in school?
    c. When and how is consideration or deference shown? What are the social courtesies expected by and from the family?
    d. What constitutes an insult or an offense? How are these expressed?
    e. Who is allowed to disagree and with whom? When are individuals allowed to disagree?

■ Communication
    a. What are the languages and language varieties used by the family? In the community? When? Who uses what? For what purposes? Are children expected to know these varieties?

(continued)

FIGURE 10-5 **(continued)**

b. Which varieties of the language are written? Is there a widespread knowledge of the written form? Does the family use it?
c. How does the family define "speaking well"? How does it relate to age, gender, social context?
d. What is the acceptable speech behavior? What roles, attitudes, and personal characteristics are commonly associated with particular ways of speaking?
e. What is the current level of functionality of the native language in the house? In the community?
f. What are the gestures or postures considered socially objectionable? What are their meanings? What meaning is ascribed to direct eye contact? To eye contact avoidance?
g. What are some of the terms or words that are socially unacceptable? Why?
h. Who is allowed to talk to whom? Under what circumstances? What topics are acceptable for discussion?

- Food
  a. What do the family members eat? How often?
  b. What foods are favorites, taboos, typical?
  c. What rules are observed during meals regarding age and sex roles within the family (order of serving, seating, appropriate verbal formulas)? What social rules are individuals expected to observe during meals? What utensils are used during meals?
  d. What social obligations are there in regard to food preparation? In regard to food giving, reciprocity, and honoring people?
  e. What medicinal uses are made of some categories of food?
  f. What rules exist regarding food handling, offering, or discarding?

- Dress and personal appearance
  a. What type of clothing is considered "typical"?
  b. What clothes are worn for special occasions? What seasonal differences are considered appropriate?
  c. How does dress differ for age, gender, and social class?
  d. What restrictions are imposed for modesty?
  e. How is beauty or attractiveness defined? What characteristics are most valued?
  f. What are the acceptable verbal compliments?
  g. What symbolic value, if any, is given to color of dress?

- Education
  a. What are the family's ideas about the purpose of education?
  b. What methods of teaching are used at home (for example, direct verbal instruction, modeling, proverbs, didactic stories)?
  c. Do teaching methods vary according to class, setting, or depending on what is taught?
  d. Is it acceptable for the child to ask questions or volunteer information?
  e. What is accepted as a positive response by teachers to students? By students to teachers?
  f. How many years are children expected to normally attend school? Does it differ by gender?

■ Work and play
   a. What range of behaviors are considered as "work" and as "play"?
   b. What kind of work is considered prestigious, and why?
   c. Do they hold any stereotypes regarding the occupations of particular groups?
   d. What is the purpose of "play"? Who is allowed to participate?

Source: Adapted from Saville-Troike, 1978.

 **SNAPSHOT** 10-2   **Families, Schools, and Communities Making a Difference in the Lives of Children**

Programs for children and their families have dramatically grown in the past decade. Let's sample a few that have made a difference in the lives of children.

- *South Dade Child Care Center, Leisure City, Florida:* Located in the southern part of Miami-Dade County, the center was built as part of the South Florida reconstruction efforts following the devastation of hurricane Andrew. With programs for young children from three months to age 4, the center is an example of cultural and ethnic diversity. With an ethnic profile that includes Latinos, African Americans, and European Americans, the commitment of the director and the teaching staff to working with children and their families is evident in every aspect of the program. Accredited by the NAEYC, the center is also distinguished by its bilingual program, developed in an effort to preserve the children's first languages while they learn English. Along with its developmental programs, it serves as a resource center for all families, with services that include GED classes and parenting training. On any day, it is not uncommon to find par-

ents sitting in the center's patio sharing ideas together with staff or participating in the classroom with their children.

- *CentroNía, Washington, DC:* Established more than 20 years ago, CentroNía (formerly known as Calvary Bilingual Multicultural Learning Center) serves a multicultural and bilingual community in the District of Columbia. The name reflects the program's commitment to serve the culturally diverse community of the area: Centro means "center" in Spanish, and Nía means "our" in Esperanto and "purpose" in Swahili. CentroNía has evolved from a child-care center to become a comprehensive family support organization offering education, parent services, and community leadership. The center is accredited by the NAEYC, and it is nationally known for its quality programs for young children and their families. CentroNía provides early childhood education programs along with professional development for caregivers. Through the Family Institute program, the center provides social services, consultation, referrals, and workshops for parents and families of children. They also house the DC Bilingual Public Charter School, the first of its kind in the area, which services children ages 3 through 5. Plans are to add grades one through five.

CentroNía's dedication to young children and their families, the community, and continuous commitment to provide quality and equitable services sets an example in the field of early childhood education.

• *The Redlands Christian Migrant Association (RCMA) Child Development Program, Florida:* Serving children in Florida, the RCMA is an organization that provides services to children of migrant and low-income families. Established in 1965 in the Redlands agricultural area in South Florida, today RCMA offers services to children and families through more than 75 centers and two charter schools.

Central to their mission is their belief that parents and families want to help and are capable of helping their children. The continued success of the program is the best acknowledgment of what families and parents can do. Having an active voice in the program's decision-making process, farm workers, individuals from various cultural groups, local community members, and committed educators participate as members of the State Board of Directors.

Saville-Troike (1978) suggests that educators use this set of questions to accomplish the following:

■ *Reflect on one's culture:* By answering some of the questions, teachers can clarify some of their own views about cultures. Through this introspection, teachers can appreciate and understand the similarities and differences found in the views held by their students and families.

■ *Serve as a guide for observations:* Because of their comprehensiveness, questions can be used to guide teachers' observations in the classroom or in any other setting. For instance, questions regarding communication can help teachers identify the appropriate and acceptable patterns in a family's or child's culture.

Recording What We Know About Families: The Family Folder

So much information can be gathered about the families of your students! Throughout the school year you will learn many interesting details that are worth saving. Usually, teachers keep this information in the child's portfolio, where it is often lost amid all the work samples and drawings. We recommend that teachers keep a separate file for family information. Like the children's portfolios, the family folder is open to families to incorporate samples of activities done or pictures and information about important family events. As an ongoing project, it serves as another way to bring families into your classroom. Confidentiality of the information kept in the folder is essential. Early childhood teachers need to guarantee families that the data saved in the folders are to be used only

---

In Action . . .   **The Family Folder**

- What other items would you include in a family folder?
- Who would be allowed to read the family folder?
- How would you ensure that the child's next teacher understands the information in the folder?
- Regarding the issue of confidentiality, what do you suggest to protect the contents of the family folder?

---

to plan and design activities for both children and their families. Information can also be kept in a large envelope within the portfolio. Information that teachers might want to save includes the following:

- Data about the family (surveys, checklists)
- Written communications from and between the family and teacher
- Photographs of home, school, and classroom activities
- Notes from telephone conferences
- Family referrals
- Samples of projects done by families

In some ways, the family folder lays the ground for the development of the individual family service plan (IFSP), a strategy used in programs serving exceptional students and now gaining popularity in early education programs. The IFSP was initially introduced as a result of the statements established in Part H of the Education of the Handicapped Act Amendments (PL 99-457). Experiences in the field have shown that programs for the culturally diverse child are significantly improved when they assume a family-centered approach, especially when the family is also included in the services offered.

THE SCHOOL NEIGHBORHOOD AND THE COMMUNITY

Planning a multicultural program cannot take place devoid of the community. The community has relevant qualities and characteristics that are just as important for the children's learning as the knowledge about the families.

According to Garbarino, Galambos, Plantz, and Kostelny (1992), the neighborhood is the child's territory, and it plays a leading role in the child's process of socialization. The neighborhood is the playground where the child is initiated into the community life (Garbarino, Galambos, Plantz, & Kostelny, 1992). What a neighborhood or a community offers to the child and to the family will affect their experiences and their abilities to cope with life. The characteristics that define a community even affect the

Responsibilities to Families According to the NAEYC Code of Ethical Conduct and Statement of Commitment

Section II: Ethical responsibilities to families

Families are of primary importance in children's development. Because the family and the early childhood practitioner have a common interest in the child's well-being, we acknowledge a primary responsibility to bring about communication, cooperation, and collaboration between the home and early childhood program in ways that enhance the child's development.

Ideals

I-2.1—To be familiar with the knowledge base related to working effectively with families and to stay informed through continuing education and training.

I-2.2—To develop relationships of mutual trust and create partnerships with the families we serve.

I-2.3—To welcome all family members and encourage them to participate in the program.

I-2.4—To listen to families, acknowledge and build upon their strengths and competencies, and learn from families as we support them in their task of nurturing children.

I-2.5—To respect the dignity and preferences of each family and to make an effort to learn about its structure, culture, language, customs, and beliefs.

I-2.6—To acknowledge families' childrearing values and their right to make decisions for their children.

I-2.7—To share information about each child's education and development with families and to help them understand and appreciate the current knowledge base of the early childhood profession.

I-2.8—To help family members enhance their understanding of their children and support the continuing development of their skills as parents.

I-2.9—To participate in building support networks for families by providing them with opportunities to interact with program staff, other families, community resources, and professional services.

Source: NAEYC, 2005.

internal life of its families. The following factors in the neighborhood directly influence the lives of the family (Garbarino, Galambos, Plantz, & Kostelny, 1992):

- neighborhood safety
- recreational facilities
- health and social services
- schools

FⓄCUS
on Classroom Practices | Sharing the Code of Ethics with Families

---

The purpose of the NAEYC Code of Ethical Behavior and Statement of Commitment is to help early childhood teachers define their work professionally. It also serves as a tool for parents to understand that what we do for children and for parents is guided by ethical beliefs. For that reason, the Code should be shared with parents and other professionals. It will help underline our commitment to work together. There are many ways to share the code. Some suggestions are listed here:

- Display it permanently on the classroom bulletin board. A good place is by the door or next to the sign-up sheet.

- Share copies during parent meetings and conferences. This is a good opportunity to discuss some of its vital points.

- Leave copies or segments as part of home visits.

- Share segments. Include a section in the classroom newsletter to bring attention to it at a specific point in time.

- Have copies available as part of the school registration/information packet.

- economic conditions
- opportunities to develop supportive relationships

Building Knowledge About the Community

The success of school programs is influenced by the level of awareness we have about the nature and the characteristics of the community. Discovering the cultures of our communities helps teachers obtain an accurate portrayal of the communities' expectations. This knowledge facilitates the planning of activities that will propel the collaboration between the school and the community. The fact that many educators commute to their workplaces and are not members of the local cultural and/or ethnic groups makes the need to learn about the community in which the families and the children live even more important.

Learning about the community can be accomplished in a variety of ways. You can begin by checking the school reports in which general data are found. You may "tour" the community with a local resident who can point out the various relevant places. Another way to learn is by going on a field visit on your own. When visiting the community, observe the following:

- Physical appearance (general impression)
- Types of residential areas (public housing, private developments)

- Available recreational areas and kinds of recreation offered (parks, playgrounds, stadiums, theaters, community centers)
- Public and private services (hospitals, libraries, churches, banks, public service agencies, transportation, police stations, fire stations, other educational institutions)
- Existence of religious institutions and types of denominations
- Types of businesses (grocery stores, craft shops, repair shops, etc.)
- Languages used in signs, advertisements, and in anything posted or on the walls
- Decorations and symbols found throughout the community
- Activities people do (what they are engaged in during your observation)

You can also gather information about the community by finding the answers to the following questions:

- What is defined as the perimeter or what are the different parts of the community?
- How do children define their community?
- How do residents describe their community?
- What social classes do the families represent?
- What specific services are available for families?
- What community agencies are found in the community?
- What issues or problems are present in the community?

Many communities have their own newsletters and newspapers, which are usually available in local stores. Reading them can give you an idea about current events and what is considered socially important. Local news publications will also tell you about community organizations, activities they sponsor, and who their leaders are.

Using What We Know About Families

There are so many different ways of engaging families in our classrooms. An analysis of information collected informally and formally by the school and teachers will provide information about the families' interests, traits, concerns, and talents. Together, these will serve as a foundation for building a strong family–teacher partnership.

All information yielded from surveys, checklists, and notes is important. There are some aspects, such as the following, that will be particularly relevant:

- *Family configurations:* What are the different family patterns (single-parent, extended, etc.)?
- *Social class:* What particular social and economic characteristics define the families of your students?
- *Expectations:* What do families expect from you? From the school?
- *Diversity:* What elements of diversity are descriptive of the families (language, exceptionalities, ethnicities, religion)?

- *Concerns/issues:* What are the problems and situations faced by parents?
- *Possible resources for the classroom:* What abilities and characteristics of the families can become a resource for the class? Include those parents who expressed a desire to help.

Information highlighted through such an analysis will help you refocus your efforts and decide on more effective ways to link families to your classroom. Knowing who our families are will also contribute to making decisions to help our activities become more sensitive and realistic for both the child and the families.

In Action . . .   **A Visit to Your Own Neighborhood**

Take time to visit your own neighborhood. Using the guidelines mentioned in this section, describe what you discovered about your own community.

FOCUS on Classroom Practices | Identifying Classroom Collaborators

The first source of classroom collaborators is found among the families themselves. Doing a simple survey early in the year will help to identify them. Here is a sample survey you can use to create one that is customized to fit your classroom needs.

1. Would you like to collaborate as a volunteer in our classroom?
   _____ Yes, I am interested in collaborating.
   _____ No, I am unable to help at this time.

2. If you answered "yes," how would you like to collaborate with our classroom? Please enter a check mark to indicate how:
   _____ I can help as a classroom volunteer. Please call me to discuss times and days.
   _____ I can prepare materials at home.
   _____ I can help by serving in the PTA.

After you get your surveys back, remember to tabulate the answers. An easy way to make good use of what you discovered is to classify answers according to the following categories:

1. In-classroom volunteers (those interested in coming to the classroom)
2. Resources (those interested in doing things from home and those who can collaborate for specific activities such as craft making, music and dancing, speaking, etc.)
3. Translators (important if you have children and families who speak languages other than English!)
4. Storytellers (essential because they add interest to literacy activities)
5. Community services/network (those who can provide information or help with community agencies)

Planning Successful Family Involvement Activities

Have you ever considered how richly talented the families in your classroom are? The more we get to know them, the more we come to appreciate their skills, knowledge, and experiences. Because each family has unique characteristics and circumstances, we cannot assume that they will all be ready to collaborate or participate in the children's education at the same level. Being mindful of the families' needs and expectations will help in planning activities that foster partnerships. The following guidelines will help us plan appropriate and culturally respectful experiences for parents and families.

- *Be mindful of the social and cultural characteristics of families.* The key to successful activities is to always respond to the needs of the participants. Keep in mind that a program that is successful in one community may not be suitable for families in your community. Use the information about the families to select the type of activities and programs you offer. Engagement occurs when activities are related to the parents' and families' realities.

- *Consider language differences.* If your classroom includes parents and families who speak languages other than English, it is important to provide translators and to have materials available in their languages. This will facilitate communication and increase their participation and involvement in the classroom.

- *Use your knowledge about families to select and present the content.* Your knowledge about the family's social and cultural characteristics is instrumental in planning successful meetings. Consider the cultural values of families and carefully select content and presentation strategies. If addressing any sensitive issues, be mindful of their cultures and present the information in culturally respectful ways.

- *Plan activities with all parents and families in mind.* Always consider what you know about the characteristics (such as educational levels and cultures), special skills, and interests of parents and families and plan events that will promote their participation. Keep in mind the importance of the extended family and plan experiences that facilitate their participation.

- *Plan activities with a purpose.* Be considerate of the parents' time and plan activities and meetings that have a clear goal and purpose. Remember that time is very precious for all, so make sure that you carefully plan any meetings and activities. Always ask yourself, what is the purpose of the meeting? What will parents and families learn or gain from the meeting?

- *Be creative and provide a variety of activities.* Use your creativity and plan different types of activities that will build interest in attending classroom events. Consider the purpose of the meeting or activity and select appropriate delivery strategies.

- *Consider the parents' schedules in planning activities.* Planning responsive activities always begins by taking into consideration the time factor. Find out from parents and families about times that are more convenient to attend. Be flexible and try schedul-

FIGURE 10-6 **Epstein's Six Types of Roles of Parent Involvement**

1. *Parenting:* Providing support to families to build a supportive home environment that promotes development and meets the needs of children
2. *Communicating:* Creating and maintaining appropriate and effective communication between the classroom and homes
3. *Volunteering:* Establishing a group of volunteers to collaborate in classroom and school activities
4. *Learning at home:* Providing information, ideas, and resources to extend and support classroom-related learning at home
5. *Decision making:* Creating opportunities for active participation of families in classroom and school decisions
6. *Collaboration with the community:* Locating, coordinating, and integrating community resources and services that support the families, children, and classroom activities

Source: Epstein, Sanders, Simon, & Salina, 2002.

ing activities at different times during the day in order to increase participation. Also, plan activities of reasonable length to avoid imposing a long time commitment.

■ *Show your appreciation.* Always take time to express your sincere appreciation for the family members' attendance and participation. Before ending the meeting or activity, sincerely show how much you value their presence. Be ready to say "thank you" to all who come. Try learning or having signs reading "thank you" in all families' languages.

Joyce Epstein's six roles of parent involvement are another relevant guidepost that promotes successful collaboration with families. Her research focuses on the various ways to promote participation and engagement of parents and family members. As you review, in Figure 10-6, the six roles that she proposes, consider those that may fit the needs and reality of families in your classroom.

COMMUNICATION: THE ROAD TO POSITIVE RELATIONSHIPS

Good communication is the key to any successful relationship. Teachers are in a position to establish the foundation for a productive and lasting relationship the very first time parents come to the school. Everything you say from the very first time you meet the families counts! What can you do to develop good communication with them? To begin, be open-minded and assume a nonjudgmental attitude regarding the family members. This will contribute to the establishment of a successful and effective multicultural program.

Communication is a process that involves sending and receiving messages. Good communication begins when the messages are not just received but actually understood by the receiver. There are many times in our schools when we fail to complete this

A multicultural classroom environment welcomes families and parents of all children.

process. For example, parents receive our notes and letters; however, they may not grasp our intentions. The chance of this happening is much greater when working with families whose ethnicities or languages differ from our own. Therefore, it is important to verify that the messages we send are received and understood by the recipients. In a study done with parents of children with disabilities, Beth Harry (1997) found that in cases of parents with different cultural backgrounds, written communication was usually received but failed to convey any messages. Harry found that miscommunication was not just restricted to what was written. She found that even during personal interviews, the school personnel failed to communicate effectively with parents. Three important points influencing communication with those with cultural differences are derived from Harry's study:

1. Language used in written communications should be explicit and free of professional jargon. Even when letters are written in the parents' native language, professional jargon should be avoided. If any such terms are used, they should be explained.

| In Action . . . | **Parent–Teacher Relationships** |

In the following quote, educator James Hymes describes how parent–teacher relationships can become positive or negative.

> Show your interest in a child, and parents are on your side. Be casual, off-handed, be cold toward the child and parents can never work closely with you. . . . To praise the child is to praise the parent. To criticize the child is to hit the parent. The two are two, but the two are one.

• Do you agree with what Hymes says? Why?

• How else could you express this relationship?

• How do your personal experiences support or deny his premise?

Source: Berger, 1995.

2. A bureaucratic tone might fail to convey the message. The tone of written communication should be personal and not intimidating. The message should indicate the school's concern and desire for success for the child and the parent.

3. Communication should not be limited to what is sent in writing. Opportunities for participation in open conversations should be encouraged. A person whom parents can trust should serve as a liaison during meetings.

Opening Doors to Collaboration with Parents and Families

Positive communication in diverse settings is built when teachers show their honest desire to help families. Your frank intent to collaborate with them and the children, accompanied by a friendly smile, opens doors to many opportunities. Those opportunities also arise when you invite the families for a closer look at your classrooms. But, how will they know they are welcome and that their help is wanted in our schools? This is where skillful communication works like magic.

Effective communication requires a combination of one- and two-way methods. One-way communication happens when parents receive letters, handbooks, memorandums, or printed materials aimed at *informing* them about the school plans. On the other hand, two-way communication occurs when schools and families *interact by sharing* views and ideas. In two-way situations, each part gains from each other's knowledge and experience (Berger, 2004). Teachers working in multicultural settings will find many opportunities to share ideas and communicate with families. Let's examine some of the strategies you can use to establish better communication.

Sharing Ideas in Writing

Perhaps one of the things that parents value most is being informed about the events and activities in their children's schools. Good and appropriate written communication is important to keep parents well apprised of what occurs in the school. It can be either periodic or incidental. Whether formal or informal, written communication sent home should be clear and simple. Newsletters, reports, and notes with curriculum information are examples of periodic communication. Forms of incidental communication include notes, letters, and flyers about special events. Here are a few points to guide your written communications:

■ Use simple and clear language. When there is a language difference, write your messages in that language, if possible. When writing in a language you do not have mastery in, ask someone fluent in the language to edit your materials. Remember, you represent the school.

■ Avoid using figurative language in communications to parents who have limited English language proficiency. Figurative language is usually culturally based and not

---

SNAPSH◎T 10-3   **What Comes First:
Compliance or Communication?**

A study done by Harry with parents of exceptional students of culturally different origins revealed that many schools often seek and achieve compliance with the law while failing to establish positive communication with parents. In her study, Harry examined the incidents and perceptions held by a group of Puerto Rican parents of children with disabilities regarding the educational system. She found that communication styles due to language differences, not the experiences and expectations between parents and schools, were found to be the leading cause of miscommunication. Although parents wanted to trust the school, the impersonal approach used by the school personnel only served to widen the distance between the groups. Harry documented various instances where use of educational jargon and the bureaucratic tone, even when written communications were in the parents' language, failed to convey the urgency or importance of the situation. In one of the cases studied, a parent realized after a year that her son had been placed in an exceptional student self-contained classroom. Although the parent had received a letter, she was unable to comprehend its meaning. When the parent visited the school, she received oversimplified information about what the school intended to do with her son. Told by a social worker that the boy was going to receive "extra help in English and math," and not that the boy was being assigned to a self-contained classroom for exceptional students, the parent accepted the school's decision. Her trust in the school made her accept the decision without knowing the implications of her child's placement. A year later, during a meeting with the teacher, the parent discovered not only what the self-contained classroom was, but also that her child was classified as emotionally disabled in accordance with PL 94-142.

Harry found that to develop an appropriate level of communication with culturally diverse parents, schools need to use a more personal tone as well as a more open-ended type of communication. Although compliance with the law is important, it should not be done at the expense of the clients, especially when they are not being properly informed.

Source: Harry, 1997.

---

easily understood by those who do not share that culture. Remember that sometimes it is difficult for a nonnative speaker to grasp the meanings of metaphors and analogies.

- Communications should be attractive and appealing to the reader. For newsletters, Berger (2004) recommends using colorful paper and clear headlines, using samples of children's work, and including practical suggestions for the families.

- Communications should have something relevant to tell. Make sure that the message is important to the reader.

- Include topics that relate to the families' cultures. Try to incorporate ideas or points that recognize the value of the cultural groups in your classroom.
- When writing notes or letters, always include something positive about the child.

Classroom News

Families enjoy receiving materials that are both informative and fun to read. A good practice that enhances a constant flow of communication is to have a classroom newsletter. Simple and not difficult to prepare, teachers can send home one-page weekly or semimonthly news briefs. Decide on an appealing name, which can be suggested by your class, and get ready to become an editor. If your students' families are linguistically diverse, having a bilingual edition is a great help. A parent can volunteer to serve as a translator if you do not have mastery of the other language. The next step is to select your content. For example, teachers can include notes about topics studied, a list of songs learned, highlights about children's accomplishments, and a schedule of upcoming events. When working with a multicultural curriculum, this kind of communication is important because it allows parents to learn and know what is happening in the classroom.

Another useful technique is regularly sending a list of suggested activities for parents to do at home with their children. This not only allows families to participate in extending the curriculum into the home, but it also provides parents with good activities to share with their children. Including a section for parents to provide feedback about the activities they like the most is a way to invite their participation.

Planning Meetings and Conversations

Nothing takes the place of personal interactions. What is shared through personal contacts carries a totally different meaning from any other kind of communication. The opportunity to share an actual moment in time with another person enhances the quality of the experience. You probably know of many instances where the impression you had about someone drastically changed after meeting the individual in person. Whether face-to-face or by telephone, personal contact should be established with families and parents. Personal interaction requires attention to such communication elements as the tone of voice, voice inflections, and body language. All convey messages that can never be transmitted by a letter or a note. Results from research done by Miller Wackman, Nunnaly, and Miller (cited in Berger, 2007) confirm that in an interpersonal communication, many more things are "said" through our gestures and movements and our tone of voice than by words alone: "Oral, verbal messages (the spoken word) account for only 7 percent of the input; vocal and tonal messages (the way in which the word is spoken) account for 38 percent; visual messages account for 55 percent." Conversations need to be carefully planned because they provide the perfect opportunities to initiate real partnerships. Effective interactions involve consideration of several factors. The first thing to understand is that the impression you leave on a parent is not solely conveyed through your words but also through the context and the manner in which they are spoken. The place and time chosen for a conversation also play an important part in creating effective communication. Working with families who have cultures and languages different from yours requires even more careful planning. Always remember that in some cases, the parents' views of education may be very different from yours. Their perceptions and knowledge about the philosophical concepts and systemic issues of education are grounded in their cultural heritage. That alone establishes how they will approach and react toward "a meeting with the teacher." Try to be sensitive to this by just considering how you would feel in a setting where your values and ideas might be distinctively dissimilar from those of the school.

When planning to talk with parents, consider the following:

- Select a pleasant environment. If the conversation takes place in the classroom, have adult seats available.

- When planning a telephone conversation, make sure the time you plan to call is convenient. Know in advance how much time you have. However, avoid long telephone conversations. A series of short, specific ones are usually more productive than very long ones.

- Whether on the telephone or in person, always treat parents with respect and courtesy. Even if your values and ideas are not in harmony with theirs, show your professionalism by respecting their ways.

- Be aware of your own body gestures and avoid any nuances that might send a distorting message. For instance, if the parent or adult dresses in a different way or wears a particular personal decoration, avoid staring at it.

- Remain focused on the conversation. Avoid looking around, which sends a message of "I'm not interested."

- When meeting the parent or family for the first time, introduce yourself in a friendly manner. Avoid giving the impression of being a "know-it-all" kind of person (Eliason & Jenkins, 2002). Show that you are a professional through your work with children and not by presenting yourself as the "power person."

- To maximize your meeting, it is important to send a note in advance describing in simple terms the purpose of the meeting. Providing a brief description is especially convenient for those families who are linguistically different because it prepares them to have a more productive conversation (Lee, 1995). Some parents have said that before coming to school, they would ask a friend or consult a dictionary for how to say given words and phrases. A note sent in advance explaining the objective of the meeting will avoid misinterpretations. For some cultures, being called by the teacher means the child has misbehaved. Some parents have reported punishing their children in advance because of what they "might have done" (Robles de Meléndez, 2006).

- Keep your conversation friendly and professional. Avoid asking very personal questions about the family. People of some cultures might find it offensive to be asked certain personal details. Accept what they are disclosing. Remember that by establishing a positive relationship, you will encourage families to continue sharing ideas.

- When meeting parents, always refer to them as "Ms. _____, Mrs. _____, or Mr. _____" and never by their first name. In many cultures, people would feel offended if called their first name by someone who is not a close friend or relative. Using a title not only shows your respect but also establishes a professional tone. If elders are present, show deference and acknowledge their presence.

- Do not address your conversation to the mother alone if her husband, or the child's father, is also present. In some cultures, such as Hispanic and Middle Eastern, males play a strong role in the family. Acknowledge their participation and input.

- Talk in a courteous, not patronizing, way. Talking slowly and clearly can be accomplished without using a patronizing tone.

- Avoid using "teacher jargon" to show your knowledge. Speak in simple and clear terms.

- Be patient. Do not rush to say a lot because you have limited time. Also, be patient with parents who are linguistically different and for whom communicating in English is difficult. Most cultural groups show a lot of patience toward English speakers when they try to communicate in other languages. Imagine yourself trying to speak in the languages of your children's families!

- When parents or relatives are not fluent in English, have an interpreter. If you use interpreters, give them a summary or a description of the purposes of the meeting. This will help them to become aware of the content and context of a conference in advance.

- If parents speak a language different from English, try to learn a few words in that language. It is always a good opener and also demonstrates that you are interested in learning more about them and their child.

- When parents are accompanied by other family members, relatives, or friends, acknowledge their presence. Find out who they are and what their relationship is to the family. Many cultural groups include relatives and some close friends among those responsible for the well-being of the child (Lynch & Hanson, 2004).

- Be a good listener. Don't monopolize the conversation. Remember that we all have very busy lives, and time is very precious to everyone. Select topics that can be feasibly discussed in the time you have.

- Show you care and want to help their children. Be positive and show your warm feelings. Always have something positive to say about the child. Share an anecdote or a sample of the child's work.

- Try to end your conversations with a positive outlook.

Using Modern Technology to Enhance Collaboration

Because technology is an important part of our world, we need to consider using it as part of our communication system. Best practices in early childhood education today recognize the role and need for technology as a means to improve and maintain communication between families and classrooms. What technology early childhood educators use depends upon the resources available in the school.

Telephone answering machines are among today's commonly used effective technology-based communication tools. Many people rely on voice mail to keep them informed and organized. Answering machines enable teachers to establish information lines parents can access at any time. Details about activities, descriptions of the classroom events, or things children need to bring to school can be recorded in advance (Eliason & Jenkins, 2002). Families may also appreciate voice mail suggestions for possible activities during weekends and holidays. Having information in the languages spoken by the students' families is an excellent way to link them to the classroom.

In many places, schools operate a homework hotline. Parents can easily access daily assignments that have been taped by teachers. Some schools also have bilingual specialists available for consultations during specific evening hours. Often, these specialists are parents and community members who donate their time. This service helps parents clarify their children's homework, which benefits the child. Children whose parents work evening hours can call to verify and check on the next day's assignments.

If available, include e-mail among your communication tools. Many schools now have messages offered regularly to parents through e-mail. This opens another channel of interaction particularly suitable for working family members with full schedules.

The Internet has opened doors to a wealth of information for parents and families. Access to the Internet has also contributed to fostering communication with parents and families. One of the most popular methods is through school websites, which provide information to parents and the community. Accessible at any time of the day, a website makes it possible for working parents and family members to learn about school activities. By offering resources and information in languages other than English, web pages

---

LET'S TALK AND REFLECT... **Fostering Communication Using Technology**

Attending a meeting or conference is, at times, a challenge to many parents and family members because of their work schedules. Conversations with parents have revealed that many wanting to attend are unable to due to conflicts with their schedules and also because of transportation obstacles.

Think about the ways you could use technology to help parents participate in a meeting and to keep them informed about their children's progress and success.

may also facilitate dissemination of school events and program news to families from diverse linguistic groups.

| IDEAS FOR PLANNING ACTIVITIES WITH FAMILIES

What you know about the families and children in your classroom will help you plan a wide variety of activities. The innumerable differences families exhibit become your best source of ideas for learning experiences. Families can literally energize the whole school program.

Curriculum Activities

Consider first how families can enhance the curriculum. Examine your projected curriculum experiences and identify those areas where families can help with demonstrations, telling stories, teaching a song or a dance, bringing specific resources, or serving as speakers. For instance, parents and family members can help by demonstrating how to use a given ethnic instrument or how to wear a typical piece of clothing. Make a list of the instances where their collaboration is needed. If told in advance, families are usually willing to share their knowledge and their resources. Notes can be sent home asking for help with specific topics children will study. An example of this kind of note appears in Figure 10-7.

Keeping a file of resources that parents have and are willing to share is a convenient way to know what is available to support your curriculum. Include the parents as resources as well by creating a "special resources" file of materials and information shared by parents. To facilitate identification, include a note about those areas of diversity the families represent (i.e., cultures or exceptionalities). Even if you no longer teach their child, parents can always be contacted to share their knowledge with your current class. They will feel flattered to serve as your "special resources."

Parents and families are also valuable resources when planning the curriculum. Their participation is one of those required components of developmentally appropriate teaching. Considering them partners while developing units and experiences can bring in fresh and relevant ideas. Parents and family members can provide valuable suggestions when trying to determine how to address a topic from a variety of perspectives. They can also be considered a source of support and affirmation for your activities.

Support and Social Activities

Activities can provide opportunities for parents and families to interact with the school and with other families. This way they can learn more about other families and build their sense of identification with the school. The list of possible activities can be as long as your creativity allows. Here are some suggestions.

1. *Family of the month/week:* Prepare a display presenting the special characteristics and uniquenesses of families. All families have something special and particular that you

FIGURE 10-7 **Notes (Bilingual) Can Be Sent to Parents to Ask for Their Participation in the Classroom**

Can you help us? Our class needs your help!

Soon our class will be studying _____. Can you share some of your ideas? We know that sharing what you know will benefit our students. Please let us know how you can help by completing the included form.

Thanks!

The family of (child's name)_____can:

_____ bring the following: _____

_____ demonstrate a dance or a song.

_____ talk about my experiences.

_____ describe some of the traditions.

_____ other: _____

(Spanish Translation)

¿Nos puede ayudar? ¡Nuestro salón necesita su colaboración!

Estimada familia:

Muy pronto estaremos estudiando _____ . Es posible que ustedes sepan mucho sobre este tema. Sabemos que al compartir algo de lo que ustedes saben nuestros niños aprenderán mucho más. Contamos con su ayuda. Si puede colaborar, déjenoslo saber completando el volante que incluímos.

¡Gracias!

La familia de (nombre del estudiante) _____ puede:

_____ traer lo siguiente: _____

_____ demostrar un baile o enseñarles una canción.

_____ hablar sobre nuestras experiencias.

_____ leer algún cuento sobre el tema.

_____ describir algunas de las tradiciones y costumbres.

_____ demostrar como preparar algún plato típico.

_____ Otros: _____

can highlight. You can either use a bulletin board or the classroom door to exhibit your display. Make sure it is located in a prominent place.

2. *Families' get-together:* Times can be arranged to have families come to the classroom to be together and to get to know each other (Berger, 2007). The traditional potluck meal is a good idea when parents are able to come in during evenings or on a Saturday. Parents can bring something to share with others. Ask them to write the names of their dishes so that everyone can remember them. Early morning coffee can be organized for families who work. Midday or afternoon refreshments and cookies are other activities for those whose schedules are more flexible.

3. *The classroom mural family album:* A mural album of activities carried out by families and their children can be prepared and displayed in the classroom. Things to include are important events, celebrations, and participation in classroom activities. Parents can share pictures, and children can make drawings of the special times spent with their families.

4. *Classroom "experts":* Identify those areas where families are definite experts. For example, a family can become your expert for craft making or for learning typical dances. Recognition of their qualities affirms their importance.

5. *Family/parent networks:* With the collaboration of families in your classroom, you can organize a support network. Families new to the neighborhood or those with limited English language skills can benefit from the support that other parents may offer. A list with names and telephone numbers of the support persons can be made available to those in need (Berger, 2007).

6. *Storytellers' club:* Invite families and family members to share their stories. They can also read stories from their cultural groups. A pool of volunteer storytellers can add variety to your classroom activities while reinforcing to parents that their collaboration is wanted.

7. *Special multicultural events committee:* Families are the best source of ideas about what and how to celebrate cultural events. Invite families from different cultural backgrounds to form a committee. Together they will advise how to appropriately celebrate special dates.

8. *Meetings:* Good topics that are of interest to the families are always attractive. Periodic meetings can bring families together to discuss and share ideas while learning about other views.

9. *Welcome committee:* Parents from different cultural groups can form a "welcome" group for other parents. They can prepare handouts with key places in the community, recreational services, and other important information that a newcomer always appreciates. This is a particularly effective resource for families who have recently immigrated and may need resources to cope with their new reality.

10. *Educational packets:* With the help of the teacher, a group of volunteers can prepare home-learning materials. Parents and volunteers can duplicate materials to be sent home and prepare calendars of activities. With the guidance of the teacher, parents can locate resources in the school library or even develop their own set of references.

11. *Special projects:* All classrooms have special projects for which parents and community volunteers are essential resources. Call on the parents whenever you and your class plan to begin a project. They are the best resources to ensure that experiential activities are designed to define the realistic and not the idealized ways of cultures.

Counting on the Community as a Resource

There is a wealth of resources in every community. Communities are important sources of materials, information, and support for early childhood programs. Agencies, sites, organizations, businesses, and, especially, people all represent resources. You may want to create an inventory of your community to help you learn more about its exciting resources. For example, find out if your community includes any of the following:

- public library
- local civic organizations
- public agencies
- community center
- programs and activities for children and their families
- art activities sponsored by community or civic groups
- type of businesses
- local newspaper
- public places (parks, museums, sports complex)

Using **community resources** facilitates establishing collaborative experiences and promotes partnerships. It also creates appreciation of the community's heritage and diversity. This is especially relevant for families and for children. By being involved with the community, children will not only develop a greater understanding of multiculturalism but will also experience their community as a major influence in their lives. This is known as social action-based teaching.

Opportunities for social action-based teaching are created through an active link with the community. Community leaders can help with suggestions of possible experiences appropriate for young children. For example, taking action to clean the

The dream of a multicultural classroom is a reality that we can all make happen in our schools.

Wadsworth/Cengage Learning

yard of an elderly person, working in the garden of a person with a disability, preparing crafts to give as welcome gifts to children moving into the neighborhood, or painting a park fence are some of the activities that provide concrete ways to demonstrate that we care about others in our diverse community.

Establishing contacts with community-based organizations is a way to gain access to unlimited ideas and experiences for your classroom. A note or a call to learn what services are offered will open the door to a world of resources right in your community.

| WHAT LIES AHEAD?

Working with the families of children in your classroom is an experience that offers endless possibilities. Linking families and schools to work and respect each other is a way to gain equity for all, an important goal of multicultural education. If our classroom doors are truly open, the futures of children will be brighter. Building positive relationships with parents and families takes time. So, be patient and work toward productive relations with your partners in educating the children in your classroom.

| BEFORE WE END, A WORD TO THE READER

Caminante, no hay camino. Se hace camino al andar. [Traveler, there is no road. You blaze it as you go.]

Antonio Machado (1875–1939)

We could not conclude this work without saying to our readers: "Congratulations on your determination to explore how to create multicultural classrooms for young children!" Now that you are familiar with the basic knowledge about multiculturalism and have the working tools for teaching about diversity, the rest of the challenge lies ahead. This is your opportunity to become a change-agent for educational reform on behalf of young children. You can now put into practice your own ideas regarding diversity and education. This is, in fact, your best opportunity to demonstrate your personal and professional commitment to equality for young children.

Multicultural early childhood teaching is still unfolding. Although there are examples and ideas that tell us how it should be done, additional efforts are still required to give this teaching its definitive shape. The challenge sometimes seems insurmountable. However, the beliefs that brought you here and your determination to provide an empowering environment for young children will let you conquer the obstacles. We have faith in your ability to create culturally empowering classrooms for all our children. We know you will succeed because early childhood teachers are people who have the courage to dare because they believe in children. That's why we believe in you.

Never doubt that a small group of thoughtful, committed people can change the world. Indeed, it's the only thing that ever has.

Margaret Mead (1901–1978)

WHAT WE HAVE LEARNED—CHAPTER SUMMARY

The last chapter emphasizes the importance of collaborating with parents and the community in helping young children. Parental involvement in a diverse classroom is very special. It presents unique challenges that teachers must overcome. One of the most important things teachers must learn is how to work with adults from different cultures. This requires effort, tolerance, and sensitivity. Parents must be made to be allies in the process of positive development of the children. It is also important to meet the parents and other significant family members halfway. A comprehensive collaboration also includes the community and its resources. Teachers need to step out of the classroom to learn about the nature of the child's community and what it has to offer. Again, this means stepping out of the teacher's comfort zone and being proactive in exploring resources that will benefit the child. Profiling the community where the children live is essential in creating partnerships and collaborative efforts. There are also many professional organizations and publications that offer creative and innovative ideas about how to help the child and facilitate positive development. It is highly recommended that educators become members of professional organizations and keep up with the latest literature and research in the field of multicultural education for young children.

THINGS TO DO . . .

1. What do you think are some of the main problems faced by families today? Write a brief paper about what you believe are the most urgent issues.

2. We all have a notion of what a family is. How does your own concept differ from your students' views of families?

3. We learn about others when we interact. Create a five item questionnaire and interview two families from different social and ethnic backgrounds. Ask them about their views concerning children. Compare their responses and find how similar and different they are.

4. We all have different perspectives of appropriate family/parent involvement in schools. Ask five of your colleagues about their views. Then ask five parents and compare their responses.

5. Many communities and schools have successfully involved families in their programs. Locate information about parent and family involvement activities in your community.

6. Every classroom is different. Based on the nature of your own school and classroom, prepare a list of 10 possible ways to involve the families. Share the list with a colleague.

RECOMMENDED INTERNET RESOURCES

- The Comer School Development Program for parent involvement, from the Yale Child Study Center
  www.med.yale.edu/comer/

- "Communicating with Families," from the U.S. Department of Health and Human Services
  http://eclkc.ohs.acf.hhs.gov/hslc/Family%20and%20Community%20Partnerships/Family%20Partnerships/Communicating%20with%20Families

- The National Network of Partnership Schools' Center on School, Family, and Community Partnerships
  www.csos.jhu.edu/p2000/center.htm

- Promoting Responsible Fatherhood, from the U.S. Department of Health and Human Services
  http://fatherhood.hhs.gov/Research/index.shtml

YOUR STANDARDS PORTFOLIO

NAEYC Standard 2: Building Family and Community Relationships*

Learning more about families is essential for building successful collaborations with the early childhood classroom. The following activities will help you in developing skills and knowledge for working with families of young children.

- Prepare a visual definition representing the diversity of families. Follow the diversity elements present in your own community and classroom.

- Create an inventory of agencies in your community that provide services to families and their children. Identify whether staff is available to communicate with families in their native languages. Check to see if materials are provided in languages other than English.

- Visit the library and locate at least three journal articles about child-rearing practices across cultures. Read and summarize the contents, highlighting the aspects in common and those that are different.

- Continue to work on your journal of reflections.

ORGANIZATIONS AND ADVOCATES FOR PARENTS AND FAMILIES

Many national groups are working for the cause of children and families. You might want to contact them for information and services. Addresses of selected groups are included here:

American Home Economics Association
2010 Massachusetts Avenue, NW
Washington, DC 20036-1028

Center on Families, Communities, Schools, and Children's Learning
605 Commonwealth Avenue
Boston, Massachusetts 02215

* NAEYC Standard 2 correlates with INTASC Standard 10: School–Community Involvement.

Child Welfare League of America
2345 Crystal Drive
Suite 250
Arlington, Virginia 22202

The Children's Defense Fund
25 E Street, NW
Washington, DC 20001

Family Resource Coalition
230 North Michigan Avenue
Chicago, Illinois 60601

Easter Seals (Programs and services for individuals with disabilities)
230 West Monroe Street
Suite 1800
Chicago, Illinois 60606

National Council of La Raza
Raul Yzaguirre Building
1126 16th Street, NW
Washington, DC 20036

National Black Child Development Institute
1313 L Street, NW
Suite 110
Washington, DC 20005

National Coalition of Hispanic Health and Human Services Organizations
1501 16th Street, NW
Washington, DC 20036

National Congress of Parents and Teachers (the National PTA)
541 N Fairbanks Court
Suite 1300
Chicago, Illinois 60611

National Families in Action
2957 Clairmont Road, NE
Suite 150
Atlanta, Georgia 30329

National Head Start Association
1651 Prince Street
Alexandria, VA 22314

REFERENCES

Barrera, J., & Warner, L. (2006). Involving families in school events. *Kappa Delta PI Record, 42*(2), 72–75.

Berger, E. (1995). *Parents as partners in education: Families and schools working together.* Englewood Cliffs, NJ: Merrill.

Berger, E. (2004). *Parents as partners in education: Families and schools working together* (6th ed.). Englewood Cliffs, NJ: Merrill.

Berger, E. (2007). *Parents as partners in education: Families and schools working together* (7th ed.). Englewood Cliffs, NJ: Prentice Hall.

Boyer, E. (1994). *Ready to learn: A mandate for the nation.* Princeton, NJ: The Carnegie Foundation for the Advancement of Teaching.

Broussard, C. A. (2003). Facilitating home-school partnerships for multiethnic families: School social workers collaborating for success. *Children & Schools, 25*(4), 211–222.

Children's Defense Fund. (2005). *The state of America's children.* Washington, DC: Author.

Coleman, J. (1991). *Planning for parent participation in schools for young children.* Bloomington, IL: ERIC Digest.

Couchenour, D., & Chrisman, K. (2004). *Families, schools, and communities: Together for young children.* Clifton Park, NY: Thomson Delmar Learning.

Eliason, C., & Jenkins, L. (2002). *A practical guide to early childhood education curriculum* (7th ed.). New York: Merrill.

Epstein, J. L., Sanders, M. G., Simon B. S., & Salina, K. C. (2002). *School, family, and community partnerships: Your handbook for action* (2nd ed.). Thousand Oaks, CA: Corwin.

Federal Interagency Forum on Child and Family Statistics. (2005). *America's children: Key national indicators of well-being.* Retrieved September 15, 2008, from http://www .childstats.gov/pdf/ac2005/ac_05.pdf.

Garbarino, J., Galambos, N., Plantz, M., & Kostelny, K. (1992). The territory of childhood. In J. Garbarino, *Children and families in the social environment* (2nd ed., pp. 202–228). New York: Aldine de Gruyter.

Garbarino, J., & Garbarino, A. (1992). In conclusion: The issue is human quality. In J. Garbarino, *Children and families and the social environment* (2nd ed., pp. 304–327). New York: Aldine de Gruyter.

Harry, B. (1997). *Cultural diversity, families, and the special education system: Communication and empowerment.* New York: Teachers College Press.

Henderson, A. T., & Mapp, K. L. (2002). *A new wave of evidence: The impact of school, family, and community connections on student achievement.* Austin, Texas: National Center for Family and Community Connections with Schools.

Jung-Sook, L., & Bowen, N. (2006). Parent involvement, cultural capital, and the achievement gap among elementary school children. *American Educational Research Journal, 43*(2), 93–204, 205, 209–218.

Kagan, S., & Rivera, A. (1991). Collaboration in early care and education: What can and should we expect? *Young Children, 47*(1), 51–56.

Lee, F. (1995). Asian parents as partners. *Young Children 50*(3), 4–9.

Lynch, E. W., & Hanson, M. J. (2004). *Developing cross-cultural competence: A guide for working with young children and their families* (3rd ed.). Baltimore, MD: Paul Brooks.

Moles, O. (Ed.). (1996). *Reaching all families: Creating family friendly schools* (Publication No. OAS 96-6005). Washington, DC: Office of Educational Research and Improvement.

National Association for the Education of Young Children. (2005). *Code of ethical conduct and statement of commitment* (Revised April 2005). Retrieved September 15, 2008, from http://www.naeyc.org/about/positions/PSETH05.asp.

National Commission on Children. (1991). *Beyond rhetoric: A new American agenda for children and families. Final Report of the National Commission on Children.* Washington, DC: Author.

Olivos, E. M. (2006). *The power of parents: A critical perspective of bicultural parent involvement in public schools.* New York: Peter Lang Publishing.

Pelletier, J., & Brent, J. (2002). Parent participation in children's school readiness: The effects of parental self-efficacy, cultural diversity, and teacher strategies. *International Journal of Early Childhood, 34*(1), 45–60.

Robles de Meléndez, W. (September 2006). Working with families. Paper presented at the Annual Conference of the Early Childhood Association of Florida. Orlando, FL.

Saville-Troike, M. (1978). *Guide to Culture in the Classroom.* Arlington, VA: National Clearinghouse for Bilingual Education.

Swick, K. (2004). *Empowering parents, families, schools, and communities during the early childhood years.* Champagne, IL: Stipes Publishing.

Turnbull, A., & Turnbull, H. R. (2004). *Exceptional lives: Special education in today's schools* (4th ed.). New York: Prentice Hall.

United Nations. (1994). Changing family structure. *1994 International Year of the Family.* New York: U. N. Department of Public Information.

U.S. Government. (2001). *A blueprint for new beginnings.* Washington, DC: U.S. Government Printing Office.

APPENDIX A

Recommended List of Selected Multicultural Children's Books

| ETHNIC DIVERSITY

African

Chamberlain, M. (2006). *Mama Panya's pancakes: A village tale from Kenya*. Cambridge, MA: Barefoot Books.

Cleveland, R. (2006). *The clever monkey: A folktale from West Africa*. New York: August House.

Cunnane, K. (2006). *For you are a Kenyan child*. New York: Atheneum.

Diakite, P. (2006). *I lost my tooth in Africa*. New York: Scholastic.

Edmonds, L., & Wilson, A. (2004). *An African princess*. Cambridge, MA: Candlewick Press.

Johnson, T., & Jenkins, L. (2003). *A Kenya Christmas*. New York: Holiday House.

Krebs, L. (2004). *We all went on safari: A counting journey through Tanzania*. Cambridge, MA: Barefoot Books.

McBriar, P., & Lohstoeter, L. (2001). *Beatrice's goat*. New York: Atheneum.

McDermott, G. (1996). *Zomo the rabbit. A trickster tale from West Africa*. New York: Voyager.

Mendela, N. (2007). *Nelson Mendela's favorite African folktales*. Johannesburg, South Africa: W. W. Nelson.

Uche, G. (2006). *African folktales: Exotic stories form Africa for children around the world*. Bloomington, IN: Authorshouse.

African American

Barnwell, Y., & Saint James, S. (2005). *No mirror in my Nana's house*. New York: Voyager.

Hubell, P., & Tate, D. (2003). *Black all around!* New York: Lee & Low Books.

Katz, K. (2003). *My first Kwanzaa*. New York: Henry Holt.

Sanders, S. R. (2001). *A place called freedom*. New York: Aladdin.

Smith, P., & Boyd, A. (2003). *Janna and the kings*. New York: Lee & Low Books.

Alaska Natives

Bania, M. (2004). *Kumac'a fish: A tale from the Far North*. Anchorage, AK: Alaska Northwest Books.

Dabcovich, L. (1999). *Polar bear son: An Inuit tale*. New York: Sagebrush.

Damjan, M. (2002). *Atuk: A story*. Zurich, Switzerland: Nord-Sud Verlag.

Devine, M. (2002). *Carry me Mama*. New York: Stoddart Kids.

Edwardson, D. D. (2003). *Whale snow*. Watertown, MA: Charlesbridge Publishing.

George, J. C. (2001). *Nutik and Amroq play ball*. New York: Harper Collins.

George, J. C. (2001). *Nutik, the wolf pup*. New York: Harper Collins.

Harden, P. (2003). *Snow bear*. New York: Dutton Juvenile.

Rogers, J. (1999). *King island Christmas*. Reno, NV: Sagebrush.

Sis, P. (Illustrator). (2001). *A small tall tale from the far North*. New York: Farrar, Straus and Giroux.

Sloat, T. (Illustrator), & Huffman, B. (2004). *Berry magic*. Anchorage, AK: Alaska Northwest Books.

Chinese Americans

Bins, T. B. (2002). *Chinese Americans*. New York: Heinemann Library.

Bridges, S. Y. (2002). *Ruby's wish*. San Francisco: Chronicle Books.

Bunting, E. (2001). *Jin Woo*. New York: Clarion Books.

Chan, A. (2004). *Awakening the dragon*. Portland, OR: Tundra Books.

Cheng, A. (2003). *Grandfather counts*. New York: Lee & Low Books.

Katz, K. (2005). *My first Chinese new year*. New York: Henry Holt.

Louie, A. L., & Young, E. (1996). *Yeh-Shen: A Cinderella story from China*. New York: Putnam.

Thong, R. (2001). *Red is a dragon: A book of colors*. San Francisco: Chronicle Books.

Thomas, E. (2004). *The red blanket*. New York: Scholastic.

Filipino Americans

Aruego, J. (1993). *Rocakbye crocodile: A folktale from the Philippines*. New York: HarperTrophy.

Ferreol, Y. (2006). *Haluhalo espesyal*. Quezon City, Phillipines: Adarna House.

Robles, A. D. (2003). *Lakas and the Manilatown fish/Se lakas at ang isdang Manilatown*. Thousand Oaks, CA: Children's Book Press.

Romulo, L. E., & de Leon, J. (2000). *Filipino children's favorite stories*. Hong Kong, China: Periplus Editions.

Indian and Pakistani Americans

Arnet, R. (2003). *Finders keepers*. New York: Atman Press.

Babeaux, M. B. (2002). *Anklet for a princess*. New York: Shen's Books.

Cleveland, R. (2006). *The drum: Folktale from India*. New York: August House.

Das, P. (2004). *I is for India*. New York: Frances Lincoln.

Heydlauff, L. (2005). *Going to school in India*. Watertown, MA: Charlesbridge Publishing.

Hosell, K. P. (2004). *Pakistani Americans*. New York: Heineman Library.

Jeyaveeran, R. (2004). *The road to Mumbai*. New York: Houghton Mifflin.

Krishaswami, U., & Sitaraman, S. (2003). *Chachajis's cup*. Thousand Oaks, CA: Children's Book Press.

Novesky, A., & Wedman, B. K. (2004). *Elephant prince: The story of Ganesh*. San Francisco: Mandala Publishing.

Smith, J. (2003). *Lily's garden of India*. New York: Gingham Dog Press.

Yamate, S., & Tohanika, J. (1992). *Ashok by any other name*. Chicago: Polychrome Publishing.

Zucker, J. (2004) *Lighting the lamp*. New York: Barron's Educational Series.

Japanese Americans

Brown, T. (2000). *Konnichiwa: I am a Japanese-American girl*. New York: Owl Publishing.

Coerr, E. (2002). *Sadako and the thousand paper cranes*. New York: Putnam's Sons.

Falwell, C. (2003). *Butterflies for Kiri*. New York: Lee and Low Books.

Fisher, T., & Hirst, M. (1999). *Japan (food and festivals)*. New York: Raintree.

Iwamura, K., & Carle, E. (2003). *Where are you going? To see my friend*. New York: Orchard Books.

Lee, M. (2002). *Nim and the war effort*. New York: Farrar, Straus and Giroux.

Myers, T. J. (2004). *Basho and the river stones.* New York: Marshall Cavendish, Children's Books.

Parker, L. K. (2003). *Why Japanese immigrants came to America.* New York: PowerKids Press.

Tran, T., & Phong, A. (2003). *Going home, coming home.* Thousand Oaks, CA: Children's Book Press.

Uchida, Y. (2004). *Journey to Topaz: A story of the Japanese-American evacuation.* New York: Heyday Books.

Korean Americans

Pak, S. (2001). *Dear Juno.* New York: Puffin Books.

Park, F., Park, G., & Choi, Y. (2002). *Goodbye, 382 Shin Dang Dong.* New York: National Geographic.

Park, L. S. (2004). *The firekeeper's son.* New York: Clarion Books.

Recorvits, H., & Swiatkowska, G. (2005). *My name is Yoon.* New York: Farrar, Straus and Giroux.

Thai Americans

Hosell, K. P. (2004). *Thai Americans.* New York: Heinemann Library.

Vietnamese Americans and Hmong

Cha, D. (1999). *Dia's story cloth.* New York: Sagebrush.

Cleveland, R. (2007). *How the tiger got his stripes.* New York: August House.

Garland, S. (2002). *My father's boat.* New York: Scholastic Books.

Lin, G. (2003). *Dim sum for everyone.* New York: Dragonfly Books.

McKay, L., Lee, D., & Lee, K. (2000). *Journey home.* New York: Lee & Low Books.

Shea Deitz, P., Weill, C., Trang N., Viet-Dinh, P., Trang, N., & Pham, V. I. (2003). *Ten mice for Tet!* San Francisco: Chronicle Books.

Caribbean

Dell'Oro, S. P. (2001). *Haiti (Countries of the World).* Mankato, MN: Bridgestone Books.

Dorros, A., & Kleven, E. (1995). *Isla.* New York: Dutton Books.

Gershator, P., & Meade, H. (2005). *Rata-pata-scata-fata: A Caribbean story.* New York: Starbright Books.

Goddard, A., & Wen, G. (2000). *Mama, across the sea.* New York: Henry Holt.

Gottlieb, D. (1996). *Where Jamaica go?* New York: Orchard Books.

Patten, H., & Clemenson. J. (1999). *Clever Anansi and boastful bullfrog: A Caribbean tale.* New York: Starbright Books.

San Souci, R., & Pinkney, B. (2002). *Cendrillon: A Caribbean Cinderella.* New York: Simon and Schuster.

Hispanic Americans

Bernard Gonzales, D. (2004). *My pal, Victor/ Mi amigo, Victor (Bilingual).* Green Bay, WI: Raven Tree Press.

Calir, D. (2001). *Carlos, light the farolito.* New York: Clarion Books.

Dorros, A. (1997). *Abuela.* New York: Puffin.

Filipe, J. (2001). *Calling the doves/El canto de las palomas (Bilingual).* Thousand Oaks, CA: Children's Book Press.

Garza Lomas, C. (1989). *Family pictures/ Cuadros de familia.* Thousand Oaks, CA: Children's Book Press.

Geslin, C. (2004). *Elena's serenade.* New York: Atheneum Anne Schwartz Books.

Montes, M. (2003). *A crazy mixed-up Spanglish day.* New York: Scholastic.

San Souci, R. D. (2000). *Little gold star: A Spanish American Cinderella story.* New York: HarperCollins.

Soto, G. (1998). *The old man and his door.* New York: Putnam.

Jewish Americans

Lasky, K. (1997). *Marvin of the Great North Woods.* New York: Harcourt Brace.

Manushkin, F. (2007). *Latkes and applesauce: A Hanukkah story.* New York: Scholastic.

Newman, L. (2007). *Runaway dreidel!* New York: Macmillan.

Polacco, P. (1994). *Mrs. Katz and Tush.* New York: Dragonfly.

Polacco, P. (2001). *The Keeping Quilt.* New York: Aladdin.

Middle Eastern and Arabic

Cleveland, R. (2006). *The magic apple: A folktale from the Middle East.* New York: August House.

Climo, S. (2001). *The Persian Cinderella.* New York: Harper.

Hickox, R., & Hillenbrand, W. (1999). *The golden sandal: A Middle Eastern Cinderella story.* New York: Holiday House.

Kyuchukov, H. (2004). *My name was Hussein.* Boston: Boyd Mills Press.

Lepon, S. (1988). *The ten plagues of Egypt.* New York: Judaica Printing.

Madonna. (2004). *The adventures of Abdi.* East Rutherford, NJ: Penguin Books.

Matz Sidhom, C., & Farnsworth, B. (2002). *The stars in my Geddoh's sky.* Chicago: Albert Whitman.

Musch, R. (1999). *From far away.* New York: Sagebrush.

Zucker, J. (2004). *Fasting and dates: A Ramadan and eid-ul Fitr.* New York: Barron's Educational Series.

Native Americans

Boucharad, D., & Sapp, A. (2003). *The song within my heart.* New York: Raincoast Books.

Boyden, L. (2003). *The blue roses.* New York: Lee & Low Books.

Bruchac, J., & Locker, T. (1999). *Between Earth and sky: Legends of Native American sacred places.* New York: Voyager Books.

Bruchac, J., & Voytech, A. (1998). *The first strawberries: A Cherokee story.* New York: Puffin Books.

Cohlene, T., & Reasoner, C. (2004). *Little firefly.* New York: Scholastic Books.

Lavarde, A., & Dwyer, M. (2000). *Three little Alaskan pigs.* Seattle, WA: Sasquatch Books.

Martin, R., & Shannon, D. (1998). *The rough-face girl.* New York: Putnam.

Oughton, J. (2004). *How the stars fell out of the sky: A Navajo legend.* New York: Houghton Mifflin.

Thompson, L., & Savage, S. (2004). *A polar bear night.* New York: Scholastic.

Wakim Dennis, Y., Hirschfelder, A. B., & Ajmera, M. (2003). *Children of Native America.* Watertown, MA: Charlesbridge Press.

| GAY AND LESBIAN

Considine, T. K. (2005). *Emma and Meesha my boy: A two mom story.* Twomomsbooks.com.

Newman, Leslea. (2000). *Heather has two mommies.* New York: Alyson Books.

Parr, T. (2003). *The family book.* New York: Little, Brown Young Readers.

Skutch, R. (1997). *Who's in a family?* New York: Tricycle Press.

Valentine, J. (2004). *One dad, two dads, brown dad, blue dad.* New York: Prometheus.

| SPECIAL NEEDS

Janover, C. (2004). *Josh: A boy with dyslexia.* Burlington, VT: Waterfront Books.

Lears, L. (2003). *Ian's walk: A story about autism.* Chicago: Albert Whitman.

Lesley, H., & Thomas, P. (2002). *Don't call me special: A first look at disability.* New York: Barron's Juveniles.

London, J. (1992). *A lion who had asthma.* Chicago: Albert Whitman.

Pirner White, C. (1991). *Even little kids get diabetes.* Chicago: Albert Whitman.

Shriver, M. (2001). *What's wrong with Timmy?* New York: Little, Brown.

Whitehouse Peterson, J. (1999). *I have a sister, my sister is deaf.* New York: HarperCollins.

GENDER

Brown, J. (1996). *Flat Stanley.* New York: HarperCollins.

Lovell, P. (2001). *Stand tall, Molly Lou Melon.* New York: G. P. Putnam's Sons.

AGE/INTERGENERATIONAL

Ackerman, K. (2003). *Song and dance man.* New York: Knopf Books for Young Readers.

Bowen, A. (2004). *When you visit grandma and grandpa.* Minneapolis, MN: Carolhoda Books.

Exley, R. (2000). *Grandmas and Grandpas: You lovable old things (3rd ed.).* Watford, United Kingdom: Helen Exley Giftbooks.

Hamanaka, S. (2003). *Grandparents' song.* New York: Harper Collins.

Katz, K. (2003). *Daddy and me.* New York: Little Simon & Schuster.

Lord, J. (2005). *Here comes grandma!* New York: Henry Holt.

Numeroff, L. (2004). *What aunts do best/What uncles do best.* New York: Simon & Shuster.

Palacco, P. (1998). *The bee tree.* New York: Putnam Juvenile.

Palacco, P. (1998). *Chicken Sunday.* New York: Putnam Juvenile.

Palacco, P. (2001). *The keeping quilt.* New York: Aladdin Paperbacks.

Palacco, P. (1998). *Thunder cake.* New York: Putnam Juvenile.

Zeifert, H. (2000). *Grandmas are for giving tickles.* New York: Puffin.

Zeifert, H. (2000). *Grandpas are for finding worms.* New York: Puffin.

GENERAL MULTICULTURAL THEMES

Adolf, A. (2004). *Black is brown is tan* (Reprint ed.). New York: Amistad.

Ajmera, M., Ivanko, J., & Rogers, F. (2004). *Be my neighbor.* Watertown, MA: Charlesbridge Publishing.

Jordan, S. (2004). *Celebrate the human race.* New York: Sara Jordan Publishing.

Kuklin, S. (2003). *How my family lives in America.* New York: Sagebrush.

Lester, J. (2005). *Let's talk about race.* New York: Amistad.

Parr, T. (2004). *It's OK to be different.* New York: Little, Brown Young Readers.

Scillian, D. (2003). *P is for passport: A world alphabet.* Detroit, MI: Thompson Gale.

Tabor, N. (2001). *We are a rainbow.* San Francisco: Sagebrush.

Weber, R. (2004). *Understanding differences.* New York: Compass Point Books.

Zurakowski, M. (2004). *Evening meals around the world.* New York: Picture Window Books.

APPENDIX B

Organizations That Support Multiculturalism and Diversity

National Association for Bilingual Education (NABE)
1220 L Street, NW
Suite 605
Washington, DC 20005
202-898-1829
Fax: 202-789-2866
E-mail: NABE
Website: www.@nabe.org
A professional association founded in 1975, NABE addresses the educational needs of language-minority students. It hosts an annual conference and publishes the Language Learner and the Bilingual Research Journal.

National Association for the Education of Young Children
1313 L Street, NW
Suite 500
Washington, DC 20005-4101
202-232-8777; 1-800-424-2460
E-mail: naeyc@naeyc.org
Website: www.naeyc.org
NAEYC is a professional organization serving the early childhood community. It provides resources and advocacy materials for teachers, families, and community members.

National Association for Multicultural Education (NAME)
733 15th Street, NW
Suite 4
Washington, DC 20005

202-628-NAME
Fax: 202-628-6264
E-mail: nameorg@erols.com
NAME advocates multicultural education and educational equity. The organization provides resources including lesson plans, goals and objectives, and bibliographies.

National Clearinghouse for English Language Acquisition (NCELA)
The George Washington University Graduate School of Education and Human Development
2121 K Street, NW
Suite 260
Washington, DC 20037
202-467-0867; 800-321-6223
Fax: 202-467-4283; 800-531-9347
Website: www.ncela.gwu.edu
NCELA provides information and resources about second-language acquisition and educational services and programs available in the United States and offers special resources for teachers and parents.

Teaching Tolerance
400 Washington Ave
Montgomery, AL 36104
334-956-8200
Fax: 334-956-8488
Website: http://splcenter.org
A publication of the Southern Poverty Law Center, Teaching Tolerance is a semiannual magazine mailed at no charge that pro-

vides classroom strategies and curriculum ideas for teachers that focus on diversity and tolerance. The project has also developed a number of teaching resources, including videos and curriculum guides, on the civil rights movement and intolerance in U.S. history.

U.S. Committee for UNICEF
Education Department
333 East 38th Street
New York, NY 10016
E-mail: webmaster@unicefusa.org
This center publishes a wealth of information concerning world development, including books, audiovisual materials, lesson plans, and other resources with an international

perspective. Most resources are available for the price of postage, and videos are provided on loan for free.

World of Difference Institute
Anti-Defamation League
1100 Connecticut Avenue, NW
No. 1020
Washington, DC 20036
An educational agency, the World of Difference Institute concentrates on professional development and curriculum with an antiracism focus. They sponsor an award program for outstanding teachers who exemplified goals of equity and social justice.

APPENDIX C

Developing Multicultural Awareness: Sample Activities

WORKSHOP ACTIVITY: A YEAR TO CELEBRATE TO CULTURAL DIVERSITY

Background

Have you ever thought about the many festivities that are probably taking place around the world? Probably now at some point on our planet a group of people are celebrating their culture. You and your students can join in their celebration if you decide to adopt the transformational curricular approach (Banks & Banks, 1993).[1] In multicultural education, a transformational approach (T-approach) for curriculum development implies a significant change in the structure and nature of the content area. A thorough revision of the scope, goals, and materials of a program is done to have students experience the concepts and topics from the point of view of different cultural groups (Hernández, 2000).[2] The result is a realistic, more current curriculum that will empower children with an honest vision of the essence of the society they live in.

Suggestions for Action

Concerted efforts must be taken by schools to follow the transformational approach. However, early childhood educators can initiate this approach by examining the holidays that are observed by the school. Holiday activities are fundamentally ways to manifest cultural values and ideas. Because of the very nature of celebrations, they serve to motivate and interest children. They also open the door to a more culturally responsive curriculum. During this workshop session, you will apply some of the principles of the T-approach using the holidays the main focus.

---

[1] Banks, J., & Banks, C. (2006). *Multicultural education: Issues and perspectives* (6th ed.). Needham Heights, MA: Allyn & Bacon.
[2] Hernandez, H. (2000). *Multicultural education: A teacher's guide to content and process* (2nd ed.). New York: Prentice Hall.

Into Action . . .

1. Begin by listing the cultures present in your classroom. Include also those found in the school and community. Keep this list handy to help you balance the focus of activities.

   My classroom has the following ethnicities/cultures: _____

   _____

   _____

2. Review the list of official/observed school holidays. Check whether they reflect the ethnic makeup of your children and of the community.

   The following are the official holidays observed at my school: _____

   _____

   _____

3. Now, ask people from different cultures what their main holidays are. Also, check in the encyclopedia or ask the librarian. Select those that represent activities of cultural groups in your class. Add any not listed above.

   Holidays Chosen:

   Holidays Added:

4. Enter the cultural festivities into your calendar. Select a month of your choice and design a plan to incorporate these celebrations as part of that month's activities.

LET'S COOK, LET'S THINK! A DCAP EXPERIENCE IN DIVERSITY FOR AGES 4–6: THE MANY WAYS OF . . . PASTA![3]

Introduction

Who isn't attracted by food? Almost no one, which is why cooking and food experiences are an excellent resource in the classroom. Besides allowing the obvious integration of academic areas, cooking can become a tool for multicultural education. In this example, you will use pasta to guide children in discovering how one object can hold a variety of forms and yet maintain the same identity.

Goal: To help children see that people can have a variety of characteristics while being all the same

Concepts: differences, similarities, people

---

[3] Adapted from an idea in the unit "Apples, Apples" in King, E. W., Chipman, M., and Cruz-Janzen, M. (1994). *Educating Young Children in a Diverse Society.* Boston: Allyn & Bacon.

Developmental areas targeted:

1. Cognitive—observing, predicting, comparing, evaluating
2. Language—describing, acquiring vocabulary, listening
3. Motor—pouring, stirring, sorting
4. Social—working in groups, waiting for turn, sharing utensils

Academic areas: Social studies, math, health

Materials:

- Different types of pasta (macaroni, ziti, lasagna, linguini, rotini, etc.); if possible, select those with different colors
- Paper plates
- Pot (to boil pasta)
- Sauce or sour cream (to prepare salad)

Suggested activities:

1. Have children sit in a circle. Place all the pasta in a box or any other container and have children guess what it is. Use some of these clues to guide them:

   - *What I have here are different sizes, shapes, and colors.*
   - *Although they can be placed in groups according to their shapes and sizes, they all belong to one group.*
   - *You can find them dressed differently.*
   - *They can have many purposes.*
   - *They are all made of the same things.*

   After they have guessed/attempted to guess, have one child open the box and show it to the class. Review the clues and discuss each idea with the group. Clarify any of the concepts presented through the clues.

2. Give each child a paper plate and pass around the pasta. Have each child take a handful. Invite children to observe and feel the pasta. Have them talk about it. Discuss how the types of pasta can be similar (texture, materials they are made of) and different (shapes, sizes, color).

3. Have children discuss how the types of pasta are used and say which ones they have tried.

4. Discuss the names assigned to pasta. Have labels to identify the different types. Introduce the relationship to people who, like pasta, also have different names. Have children select the ones they like best. Emphasize resemblance with people (there are some people we prefer to be with).

5. Establish the relationship between the pasta and people. Use the different characteristics they listed (color, size, shape, names) to define how people whom we find in the community may, like pasta, look different, and still be wonderful to be with.

6. Cook the pasta. Have children observe how it looks after cooking. Give each child a piece to smell, touch, and taste. Highlight once again the concept of people (still the same despite the changes).

7. Mix the pasta with sauce or sour cream and have the class enjoy it. Have a great diversity pasta snack!

Extensions:

■ Place uncooked pasta in the art center for children to make art designs.

■ Have some pasta boxes in the housekeeping area.

■ Paste pasta samples on cardboard and place them in the writing corner. (Who knows what children will have to say about it!)

■ Use the Language Experience Approach (LEA) by making a poster about the "pasta family." Ask children to describe and discuss what they did.

APPENDIX D

Island Stick Puppets

Ages: 4–6
Goal: To introduce children to common island animals (such as in the Caribbean and Bahamas)
Skills:
- To observe for details
- To compare objects based on similarities
- To work cooperatively with peers

Areas: Social Studies, Science, Art, Literacy

Suggested Activities:

1. *Whole group activities:* Have children discuss the things they think are found on a Caribbean island. Observe pictures and posters about the region. Using a map of Central America or the Antilles, locate the island Caribbean region. With a wax pencil, draw a circle around it. Have children copy some of the names of the islands. If possible, invite a person from a Caribbean island to share information about their island-country with the class.

2. *Small group activities:* Divide children into cooperative groups. Then, using a piece of ribbon or other material, have children measure to find out which islands are farther from and closer to where they live. Start planning an imaginary trip to any other of the islands. Have children investigate the animal and plant life they would find.

   Discuss with each group their findings. Guide children to make stick puppets to represent any of the animals they found. Children can write their own story and use the puppets to represent it. Have children dramatize their puppet story.

3. Involving parents: Ask parents to help children find what Caribbean foods are available at the grocery store. Have them select one item to taste and report to the class how they liked it.

APPENDIX E

Planning for Cultural Diversity: Developing a Class Profile

Responsive and developmentally appropriate planning and teaching requires having a good knowledge about the children you teach. Teachers can prepare a class profile based on the elements of diversity. The following form could be used for creating your class profile:

CLASS PROFILE

Grade Level _____ Date: _____

Ages _____ Class size _____

Area: Urban _____ Suburban _____ Rural _____ How many girls? _____ Boys? _____

Social class structure	Ethnicities present	Main religious affiliations	Languages other than English

Family configurations present in my class	Exceptionalities present in my class	Comments, points to remember

Summary/highlights:

GLOSSARY

A

antibias—an instructional approach to early childhood curriculum that centers on principles of equality and equity and strives to change existing social inequalities.

approach—a set of instructional guidelines that defines an overall method used to attain a specific purpose.

attitudes—dispositions people have toward others and/or circumstances that guide their overt and covert behaviors.

awareness—cognizance as the child becomes familiar and/or apprises the existence of an idea, concept, issue or physical objects.

B

behaviors—actions exhibited by individuals in response to certain situations or stimuli.

bias—any attitude, belief, or feeling that results in and helps to justify unfair treatment of an individual because of his or her identity.

C

checklist—an assessment instrument, usually consisting of "go" or "no go" choices used in an educational setting to collect factual data objectively observed in the classroom about student behaviors, physical arrangements, use of materials and activities, and student achievement, among others.

child development—process of biological, cognitive, and socioemotional changes common to all children that occurs from conception to adolescence. Culture is one of the elements influencing the developmental process.

civil rights movement (1954–1968)—organized political and social actions undertaken by African Americans to reform social practices and erase legal racial discrimination. The movement led to the Civil Rights Act of 1964, which recognized the civil rights of all American citizens and officially ended legal racial segregation in the United States. Dr. Martin Luther King, Jr., was the most prominent leader of the movement.

classroom environment—the overall result of the arrangement and disposition of materials and equipment within a given learning setting. Designed to promote the physical, cognitive, and social–emotional development of young learners, the classroom environment is the sum of all the parts that comprises a teaching/learning setting. It includes the space, the social and emotional atmosphere, the cognitive opportunities, and the creative opportunities.

collaborative efforts—actions and initiatives done by a variety of individuals or groups working together toward a common goal.

community resources—services, organizations, individuals, and so on that facilitate establishing collaborative experiences and promote partnerships. They also create appreciation of the community's heritage and diversity. This is especially relevant for families and children.

content—the topics, concepts, and themes selected for children to experience in the classroom.

creativity—a special ability to see things in unusual or unconventional ways.

cultural contributions—culturally rooted deeds, events, or actions that either made lasting changes and/or dramatically affected the culture.

cultural diversity—contrasts, variations, or divergences from the ways of the mainstream or majority culture that, either singly or interactively, exert influence on an individual's behavior.

cultural identity—numerous cultural elements of a group that influence a person's individuality and identity.

cultural pluralism—a social state based on the premise that all newcomers have a right to maintain their languages and cultures while combining with others to form a new society reflective of differences.

cultural schemas—information that defines how to behave in a particular culture. Information in schemes represents the way the particular cultural group interprets reality.

cultural values—common beliefs in essential principles of life rooted in a specific culture.

culture—the way of life of a social group, including all of its materials and nonmaterial products that are transmitted from one generation to the next.

curriculum—practically all "that happens" at school that lays out the paths of knowledge teachers and young children will take during the learning journey.

D

development—process of continuous change observed over time and experienced by all human beings.

developmental milestones—significant events children will exhibit at different periods of life. They describe typical characteristics of a child at a certain time during childhood, such as the onset of talking, walking, and reading.

developmentally and culturally appropriate practice (DCAP)—a concept that defines quality in early childhood practices based on cultural and developmental elements.

diversity—a social concept and a frame of reference that acknowledges and celebrates a variety of characteristics such as culture, language, religion, ethnicity, nationality, social class, exceptionality, gender, age, and sexual orientation, among others.

E

early childhood curriculum—the formal and informal experiences through which young children are empowered to continue the process of knowledge acquisition and development.

early intervention—programs and services provided to young children (birth to age 5) with at-risk characteristics and their families and which are aimed at enhancing and promoting their developmental potential.

eclectic—a combination of two or more ideas or approaches to produce a new vision, solve a problem, achieve a goal, or define a position.

educational equity—establishing the same educational resources and opportunities for all children, despite their diverse characteristics.

English language learners (ELL)—individuals who are learning English as a second language.

equality—when all individuals in a society are provided with equal access to the same opportunities and resources.

equity—fair and impartial opportunities, including access to education and services, for all children and their families.

ethnic group—a social unit that shares a common culture and history.

exploration—the unstructured process of learning filled with random experiences and directed by the child.

F

family—a basic unit of society in traditional and nontraditional configurations responsible for the welfare and the raising of the child.

family configurations—the variety of combinations of individuals found in a family unit.

family involvement—activities and programs planned for the purpose of establishing effective ways to encourage the participation of all the family members involved in the education and appropriate development of the child.

family rituals—practices depicting rites and ceremonies performed by families across cultures with the intent to signify and mark a particular event.

family structure—the composition and associated roles of family members.

first language—refers to the language that is first learned by an individual; also called *home language.*

G

goal—a statement that defines the intent and aspirations of a program or of an activity.

goals and objectives—the reasons and purposes of the education and development of the young child.

I

immigrants—individuals from a country or a nation who settle in another country for various reasons, such as political differences, economic need, or family needs.

inquiry—a process of examination and appraisal whereby the child begins to consider his or her own beliefs while comparing them to the beliefs of others.

instructional experiences—activities developed around goals and specific objectives usually organized around a specific developmental area or topic and intended to promote acquisition of concepts and skills.

instructional materials—broad categories of objects ranging from commercially produced resources to teacher-made classroom materials, real objects, objects on the walls and hanging from the ceiling, the costumes in the play chest, and any items that promote learning.

intervention—any special efforts done to assist the child who may not be performing to his or her potential.

involvement—collaborative participation of families, parents, the community, and the school in the development and education of the child

L

learning encounter—activity especially designed to lead the child into the active self-discovery of a given set of ideas, skills, or knowledge.

M

material culture—those overt or tangible aspects that are easily observed in a culture. They include ways of decoration, what people eat, manners, and what they wear.

migrants—individuals who relocate to a different geographical region of one country or cross borders of other countries on a regular basis for a specific reason. For example, farm workers move seasonally from one state to another to pick oranges.

model—a conceptual framework of sequential stages and processes designed to meet a specific purpose or to complete a process.

multicultural content—the "what" of children's experience, which is defined by its significance, validity, interest, and usefulness.

multicultural early childhood educator—a teacher with a professional commitment to offer children from birth through 8 years of age specially designed developmental experiences where both the child's immediate multicultural realities and those of the nation are considered and valued.

multicultural education—a process of comprehensive and basic education for all students. It challenges racism and other forms of discrimination in schools and society and accepts and affirms the pluralism (ethnic, racial, linguistic, religious, economic, gender, and exceptionalities) that students, their communities, and teacher represent.

multicultural ethnic group—a newly identified group in Census 2000 whose members claim to belong to more than one cultural, ethnic, or racial group.

multicultural literature—the collection of literature depicting ethnic groups and other elements of diversity.

multicultural society—a society such as the United States where groups of many different ethnicities and extractions have come together to form a culturally diverse, pluralistic nation.

multiculturalism—a philosophical position and movement that assumes that the gender, ethnic, racial, and cultural diversity of a pluralistic society should be reflected in all the institutionalized structures of educational institutions, including the staff, the norms and values, the curriculum, and the student body.

multiple perspectives learning—the process of discovering reality through more than one point of view.

N

needs assessment—an evaluation process used to determine the needs of a group or of an individual and where the results are used to develop culturally and developmentally appropriate activities and programs.

non-European Americans—a broad category that includes all those who are not, or whose ancestors were not originally, from any part of Europe.

nonmaterial culture—represents those things not overtly seen but discovered through interaction with people of a specific culture. Nonmaterial aspects include ideas, values, ethics, beliefs, and behaviors.

nontraditional family—a family with a configuration different from the heterosexual two-parent model.

O

objective—a statement that establishes the specific purposes for an activity or exercise. It describes the nature and the level of knowledge the student will derive from the experience.

P

planning—the process through which actions are taken and decisions are made to accomplish a chosen goal and the way the directions and procedures for implementation are selected and organized.

prejudice—a social perspective and an attitude of negative nature not supported by facts or evidence and based on ideas and stereotypes about individuals and/or groups.

process—ways and procedures used by teachers to deliver the curriculum content.

R

race—the physical characteristics of a large group of people with somewhat similar genetic history.

racial awareness—process of becoming cognizant of own racial characteristics and those of others. It emerges in early life and progresses accordingly with experiences. It is influenced by interactions in the environment and with adults.

S

socialization—the process through which individuals learn the accepted patterns of behavior and interactions in the context of the society to which they belong. During the process, adults pass on to the young the group's social concepts that will mold them in consonance with their patterns.

stereotype—an oversimplified generalization about a particular group, race, or sex, which usually carries derogatory implication.

survey—an oral or written assessment instrument designed to get specific answers from a designated constituency. Similar to a questionnaire, a survey usually consists of a list of open- or close-ended statements designed to elicit information about targeted points or issues.

T

traditional family—typically represented by a heterosexual two-parent family.

tolerance—an attitude of open-mindedness and understanding of diverse individuals and groups that promotes socially acceptable interactions.

U

utilization—activities and opportunities offered to help the child apply what has been learned.

INDEX